Enterprise Architecture

Good Practices

Guide

How to Manage the Enterprise Architecture Practice

Enterprise Architecture

Good Practices

Guide

How to Manage the Enterprise Architecture Practice

Jaap Schekkerman

2008

The Institute For Enterprise Architecture Developments intended not to use any copyrighted material for this publication or, if not possible, to indicate the copyright or source of the respective object. The Institute For Enterprise Architecture Developments has thoroughly checked all the references however could not trace out in all situations the original copyright owner; however it is never our intention to infringe anyone's copyrights. All Trade Marks, Service Marks and registered trademarks / service marks mentioned in this publication are the property of their respective organizations. The copyright for any material created by the author is reserved.

To learn more about the described topics, its authors, speaking engagements, or research requests, visit the official homepage of the *Institute For Enterprise Architecture Developments* at http://www.enterprise-architecture.info.

Cover Art, layout by EACS; Editorial writing by Jaap Schekkerman.

Order this book online at www.trafford.com/07-2553
or email orders@trafford.com

Most Trafford titles are also available at major online book retailers.

Note for Librarians: A cataloguing record for this book is available from Library and Archives Canada at www.collectionscanada.ca/amicus/index-e.html

Printed in Victoria, BC, Canada.

ISBN: 978-1-4251-5687-9

We at Trafford believe that it is the responsibility of us all, as both individuals and corporations, to make choices that are environmentally and socially sound. You, in turn, are supporting this responsible conduct each time you purchase a Trafford book, or make use of our publishing services. To find out how you are helping, please visit www.trafford.com/responsiblepublishing.html

Our mission is to efficiently provide the world's finest, most comprehensive book publishing service, enabling every author to experience success. To find out how to publish your book, your way, and have it available worldwide, visit us online at www.trafford.com/10510

 www.trafford.com

North America & international
toll-free: 1 888 232 4444 (USA & Canada)
phone: 250 383 6864 ♦ fax: 250 383 6804 ♦ email: info@trafford.com

The United Kingdom & Europe
phone: +44 (0)1865 722 113 ♦ local rate: 0845 230 9601
facsimile: +44 (0)1865 722 868 ♦ email: info.uk@trafford.com

10 9 8 7 6 5 4 3 2

Disclaimer

While the Institute For Enterprise Architecture Developments (IFEAD) has made every effort to present accurate and reliable information in this guide, IFEAD does not endorse, approve, or certify such information, nor does it guarantee the accuracy, completeness, efficacy, and timeliness or correct sequencing of such information. Use of such information is voluntary, and reliance on it should only be undertaken after an independent review of its accuracy, completeness, efficacy, and timeliness. Reference herein to any specific commercial product, process, or service by trade name, trademark, service mark, manufacturer, or otherwise does not constitute or imply endorsement, recommendation, or favouring by IFEAD.

IFEAD (including its partners and affiliates) assumes no responsibility for consequences resulting from the use of the information herein, or from use of the information obtained from any source referenced herein, or in any respect for the content of such information, including (but not limited to) errors or omissions, the accuracy or reasonableness of factual or scientific assumptions, studies or conclusions, the defamatory nature of statements, ownership of copyright or other intellectual property rights, and the violation of property, privacy, or personal rights of others. IFEAD is not responsible for, and expressly disclaims all liability for, damages of any kind arising out of use, reference to, or reliance on such information. No guarantees or warranties, including (but not limited to) any express or implied warranties of merchantability or fitness for a particular use or purpose, are made by IFEAD with respect to such information.

The Institute For Enterprise Architecture Developments (IFEAD) shall retain ownership of all inventions, whether or not patentable, original works of authorship (whether written or visual), developments, improvements or trade secrets developed by or licensed to IFEAD or developed by third parties on IFEAD's behalf, either prior to or outside of this IPR statement, including but not limited to methodologies, analysis/architectural frameworks, leading practices, specifications, materials and tools ("IFEAD Independent Materials") and all IPR therein. Organizations may use the IFEAD Independent Materials provided to Organizations by IFEAD only in furtherance of this IPR statement or with IFEAD's prior written consent. "IPR" means intellectual property rights, including patents, trademarks, design rights, copyrights, database rights, trade secrets and all rights of an equivalent nature anywhere in the world.

The Institute For Enterprise Architecture Developments (IFEAD) is using an open publication policy. Organizations can use IFEAD's materials for their own purposes with a reference notice to IFEAD's copyrights. Organizations that want to use IFEAD's materials for commercial purposes can achieve a license from IFEAD.

Preface

Enterprise Architecture is a complete expression of the enterprise; a master plan which *"acts as a collaboration force"* between aspects of business planning such as goals, visions, strategies and governance principles; aspects of business operations such as business terms, organisation structures, processes and data; aspects of automation such as information systems and databases; and the enabling technological infrastructure of the business such as computers, operating systems and networks.

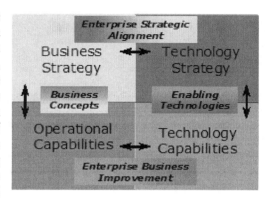

In a modern enterprise, a rigorously defined enterprise architecture approach is necessary to be able to capture a vision of the *"entire organisation"* in all its dimensions and complexity.

Enterprise Architecture (EA) is a Program (EAP) supported by processes, methods, tools and frameworks, which are able to coordinate the many facets that make up the fundamental essence of an enterprise at a holistic way.

An Enterprise Architecture establishes the organization-wide roadmap to achieve an organization's mission through optimal performance of its core business processes within an efficient information technology (IT) environment. Simply stated, Enterprise Architectures are "zoning or city plans" for systematically and completely defining an organization's current (baseline) or desired (future) environment and the transformation path between. Enterprise Architectures are essential for corporate governance, change management and portfolio management as well as for sourcing situations where (parts) of the business and or IT are co located at a third party. This is accomplished in a coherent set of landscapes of business & IT, expressed in business elements (e.g., vision & strategy, business functions / activities, information flows, and systems environments) and technical elements (e.g., software, hardware, communications, networks), and includes a transition plan from the current environment to the future environment.

If defined, maintained, and implemented effectively, these zoning- city plans assist in optimizing the interdependencies and interrelationships among the business operations of the enterprise and the underlying IT that support these operations. It has shown that without a complete and enforced EA (Strategic) Business Units of the enterprise run the risk of buying and building systems that are duplicative, incompatible, and unnecessarily costly to maintain and interface.

For EA's to be useful and provide business value, their development, maintenance, and implementation should be managed effectively. This Enterprise Architecture Good Practices Guide is intended to assist in defining, maintaining, and implementing EA's by providing a creative but disciplined and rigorous approach to effective EA management.

The Need for this EA Good Practices Guide

While EA frameworks and models provide valuable guidance on the content of enterprise architectures, there is literally no guidance how to successfully manage the process of creating, changing, and using Enterprise Architecture. This guidance is crucially important. Without it, it is highly unlikely that an organization can successfully produce a complete and enforceable EA for optimizing its business value and mission performance of its systems. For example, effective development of a complete EA needs a corporate commitment with senior management sponsorship. Enterprise Architecture development should be managed as a formal program by an Enterprise Architecture Department that is held accountable for success.

Since that EA facilitates change based upon the changing business environment of the organization, the enterprise architect is the organization's primary change agent.

Effective implementation requires establishment of business and system compliance with the enterprise architecture, as well as continuous assessment and enforcement of compliance. Waiver of these requirements may occur only after careful, thorough, and documented business case analysis. Without these commitments, responsibilities, and tools, the risk is great that business changes or new systems will not meet organizations business needs, will be incompatible, will perform poorly, and will cost more to develop, integrate, and maintain than is warranted.

Background

The content of this Enterprise Architecture Good Practices Guide is based on the set of EA guides that the Institute For Enterprise Architecture Developments has developed over the past years. Several contributions from practitioners are added to these popular guides based on their experiences with these guides. Contributions to the EA community from the US CIO Counsel as well as the US Architecture Working Group are approved over the past years, refined based on good practices and included in this guide. New EA applications are also added to this guide as well as example results from several EA programs.

We will thank all the researchers and practitioners for their contributions and we hope with this guide to set a complete standard to manage the Enterprise Architecture Practice.

Content

Figures

Tables

1   Introduction

1.1   *Purpose*

The purpose of this guide is to provide guidance to organization's in initiating, developing, using, and maintaining their enterprise architecture (EA) practice. This guide offers a set of Enterprise Architecture Good Practices that have proven their benefits to organizations and that addresses an end-to-end process to initiate, implement, and sustain an EA program, and describes the necessary roles and associated responsibilities for a successful EA program.

Enterprise Architecture is a complete expression of the enterprise; a master plan which *"acts as a collaboration force"* between aspects of business planning such as goals, visions, strategies and governance principles; aspects of business operations such as business terms, organization structures, processes and data; aspects of automation such as information systems and databases; and the enabling technological infrastructure of the business such as computers, operating systems and networks.

1.2   *Scope*

This guide focuses on EA maturity, processes, results, frameworks, methods, tools, and roles and responsibilities. While this guide addresses the enterprise life cycle, it describes in detail how the EA programs and processes relate to solution architecture, enterprise program management, and budget planning and investment processes.

The breadth and depth of information presented here should be tailored to your own organization. Some detailed explanations and examples are presented in the appendices, and references to supplementary material are included in the text or bibliography. Feel free to individualize these examples as needed.

1.3   *Audience*

This guide is intended primarily for organization enterprise architects tasked with the generation and institutionalization of EA's as well as management of EA departments, CIO's and students. This document provides guidance to organizations that currently do not have EA's and those that can benefit from improvements in their EA methods for development and maintenance. For organizations without an EA, this document provides useful guidance to the organization Head and the Chief Information Officer (CIO) for educating and obtaining key stakeholder commitment in establishing an effective EA.

Although the guide specifically addresses the roles and responsibilities of major players in the enterprise architecture development process, it is also a handbook for anyone who needs to know more about the EA process. Regardless of your role or responsibility — if you are involved in the enterprise life cycle, this guide is for you.

1.4   Guide Overview

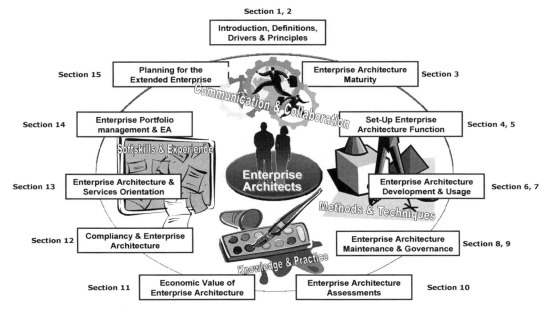

Figure 1. EA Domain Section Overview

1.5   Guide Sections

This guide is organized as follows:

Section 1:	**Introduction**	Defines the purpose, scope, audience, and organization, of the guide.
Section 2:	**Definitions, Drivers, and Principles**	Presents the context for the EA process, i.e., principles and legislative drivers, and defines the architecture development, implementation, and maintenance process.
Section 3:	**Determine Enterprise Architecture Maturity**	Describes and defines EA maturity models to determine the EA maturity of organizations as baseline for setting up the EA program
Section 4:	**Set-Up an Enterprise Architecture Program**	Defines EA program procedural steps to initiate the program, typical EA organization, and results of the EA.
Section 5:	**Define an Enterprise Architecture Process and Approach**	Defines a process for creating an enterprise architecture.
Section 6:	**Develop the Enterprise Architecture**	Provides the procedural steps for developing current and future architectures and a transformation plan.
Section 7:	**Use the Enterprise Architecture**	Demonstrates how the EA process interacts with Budget planning and investment control and with the Systems Life Cycle.

Appendix G:	**Enterprise Architecture Tool Selection Guidelines**	Guidelines in the selection of EA Tools. Questionnaire to tune to organizations own purpose as selection tool for EA support.
Appendix H:	**EA Quality of Services**	Description of the EA Space Ufo method to define the required Quality of Services in EA.
Appendix I:	**TOGAF ADM**	Description of the TOGAF ADM process.
Appendix J:	**Example of Enterprise Architecture results**	Provides a list of EA sample results from real life EA programs.
Appendix L:	**EA Modelling**	Explanation about the Archimate EA modelling language.
Appendix M:	**Other EA books in this series**	Other EA Books in this Series: How to survive in the jungle of EA frameworks & The Economic Benefits of EA.

Table 1. EA Sections Overview

1.6   *How to Use this Guide*

This guide is a "how-to" manage the EA practice manual for enterprise architects and stakeholders in the initiation, development, use, maintenance, governance and positioning of EA's.

Several real life examples as well as methods & techniques are described in such a way that the reader will find guidance in "how-to-do".

To find answers to your specific needs or questions, please consult the following table for frequently asked questions.   These and many other questions are answered throughout this guide.

	Question	**Section**
1.	**Why to set up an EA practice?**	2.0
2.	**What are the primary benefits of using an EA?**	2.0
3.	**What are the legislative drivers and mandates for using an EA?**	2.0
4.	**What is the Enterprise Life Cycle?**	2.0
5.	**Why to define the EA maturity?**	3.0
6.	**How to define the EA maturity?**	3.0
7.	**How to initiate an EA Program?**	4.0
8.	**How to get buy-in from Top Management?**	4.0
9.	**How to establish management structures?**	4.0
10.	**How to define the appropriate EA Program activities?**	4.0
11.	**How to define the intended goals & objectives?**	5.0
12.	**How to define the scope of EA programs?**	5.0

48.	**Where to learn more about the background of the E2AF?**	5.0 and Appendix F
49.	**Where to find guidelines for EA Tool selection?**	5.0 and Appendix G
50.	**How to define the EA Quality of Services / Space Ufo Method?**	Appendix H
51.	**Where to find more info about TOGAF ADM?**	5.0 and Appendix I
52.	**What do enterprise architectural results look like?**	5.0 and Appendix J
53.	**What about EA Modelling languages?**	Appendix K
54.	**Are there more EA books in this series?**	Appendix L

Table 2. EA Questions

2　Definitions, Drivers and Principles

2.1　*Enterprise Architecture Defined*

EA terminology carries many variations within each organization and in the vast array of literature. Therefore, IFEAD have settled on one consistent set of definitions for key terms used within this guide.

Appendix B contains a listing of additional terms, their definitions.

> **Key Definition**
>
> **Enterprise Architecture**—*'Enterprise Architecture is about understanding all of the different elements that go to make up the enterprise and how those elements inter-relate'*
> So EA is a strategic information asset base, which defines the mission, the information necessary to perform the mission, the technologies necessary to perform the mission, and the transformational processes for implementing new technologies in response to the changing mission needs. An enterprise architecture includes a baseline enterprise architecture, target enterprise architecture, and a transition plan.

2.2　*The Uses and Benefits of Enterprise Architecture*

An effective Enterprise Architecture approach and accompanying framework, tools and methodology produces Enterprise Architectures that:

- o Create and maintain a common vision of the future shared by both the business and IT, driving continuous business/IT alignment
- o Create a holistic, end-to-end future-state enterprise architecture process that accurately reflects the business strategy of the enterprise
- o Build agility by lowering the "complexity barrier," an inhibitor of change
- o Increase the flexibility of the enterprise in linking with external partners
- o Develop a proactive organization capable of meeting customer demands,

> **Key Definitions**
>
> **Architecture**—the structure of components, their interrelationships, and the principles and guidelines governing their design and evolution over time.
>
> **Enterprise**— A good definition of "enterprise" in this context is any collection of organisations that has a common set of goals/principles and/or single bottom line. In that sense, an enterprise can be a whole corporation, a division of a corporation, a government organisation, a single department, or a network of geographically distant organisations linked together by common objectives.
>
> **Elements**— A good definition of "elements" in this context are all the elements that enclose the areas of People, Processes, Business and Technology. In that sense, examples of elements are: strategies, business drivers, principles, stakeholders, units, locations, budgets, domains, functions, processes, services, information, communications, applications, systems, infrastructure, etc.
>
> **Baseline enterprise architecture**—the set of resultss that portray the existing enterprise, the current business practices, and technical infrastructure. Commonly referred to as the "As-Is" enterprise architecture.
>
> **Target enterprise architecture**—the set of resultss that portray the future or end-state enterprise, generally captured in the organization's strategic thinking and plans. Commonly referred to as the "To-Be" enterprise architecture.
>
> **Transition Plan**—a document that defines the strategy for changing the eneterprise from the current baseline to the target. It schedules multiple, concurrent, interdependent activities, and incremental builds that will evolve the enterprise.
>
> **Enterprise Architecture Results**—the graphics,

outpacing the competition, and driving innovation
- o Reduce risk and prepare the enterprise for rapid, unplanned change
- o Avoid the pitfalls of business-unit IT functions operating at odds with one another
- o Institute a program of progressive technology refinement
- o Create, unify, and integrate business processes across the enterprise
- o Unlock the power of information, unifying information silos that hinder corporate initiatives such as customer relationship management and e-business
- o Eliminate duplicate and overlapping technologies, decreasing support costs
- o Reduce solution delivery time and development costs by maximizing reuse of technology, information, and business applications

To accomplish this, an Enterprise Architecture approach must be:

Holistic in Scope: It must address all aspects of the Extended Enterprise and directly associated with business technology alignment: business structure, business activities, business processes, information flows, information-systems, and infrastructure, standards, policies. The notion of "Extended Enterprising" is growing in importance, and extends stakeholder status to include external value net members.   Most enterprise architecture efforts are too inwardly focused, and do not include the customers and key business partners. This results in miss-aligned enterprise architectures, and lost opportunities to gain competitive advantage and government effectiveness. The "Extended Enterprising" focus directly supports Business 2 Business initiatives, E-Government and cross-community initiatives critical to global trading and communication today.

Collaboration Based: The effort must include representatives from all key stakeholders and value net members into the EA program: business domains, senior management, business partners, and customers. This is critical to obtaining "buy-in," ongoing support and business / partner, customer alignment and collaboration.

Alignment Driven: It must address the need to directly align 'extended' business and technology drivers in a way that is comprehensible and transparent to all key stakeholders, with a continued process of tracing enterprise architecture initiatives to the business strategy.

Value Driven: It must provide mechanisms to define business cases that help ensure and demonstrate the business value of enterprise architecture solutions.

Dynamic Environments: It must include analytical methods that support the development of enterprise architectures that are flexible and dynamic to changing business drivers, new opportunities or roadblocks, and enterprise architectures that provide transformation options that mitigate risks and are flexible and dynamic to budget and other organizational constraints.

Normative Results: It must provide the ability to define solution sets that can be measured, validated and mapped to real world solutions.

Non-Prescriptive: It must not presume an implementation approach. That is out of the scope of the enterprise architecture program.

The primary purpose of an EA is to *inform, guide,* and *constrain* the decisions for the enterprise, especially those related to Business - IT investments. The true challenge of the enterprise architecture function is to maintain the enterprise architecture as a primary authoritative resource for enterprise Business & Technology planning.

> *An Enterprise Architecture* relates organisational mission, goals, and objectives to business tasks, activities and relations and to the technology or IT infrastructure required to execute them.
>
> *A Solution Architecture* relates requirements and the external world to system / solution structures, including both hardware and software, so that the effectiveness of a system design concept can be communicated.
>
> *A Software Architecture* relates requirements, fixed system hardware, and infrastructure (i.e., COTS or GOTS) to software structures in order to demonstrate software effectiveness.

This goal is not met via enforced policy, but by the positioning, value and utility of the information provided by the EA.

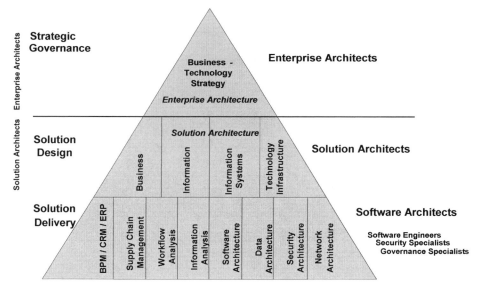

Figure 2. EA Domain Positioning

Therefore it has to be clear the positioning of EA in relationship to the Solution Architecture domain. There are common aspects among all these architecture types. They are models that convey structures as the fulfilment of some purpose or need, and they facilitate reasoning and communication about properties of the entities modelled.

2.3   *Enterprise Architecture Principles, Rules, Guidelines & Standards*

Principles establish the basis for a set of rules and behaviours for an organization, however there are differences in use and behaviour between standards, rules, guidelines and principles.

Key definitions

Standards

In the international community we can identify several types of standards. Standards set by an international standardisation organisation; de-facto standards adopted as a standard by the users of the techniques or products (mostly known as a supplier standard) and standards set by an organisation themselves. A standard is an agreement on how things should be done, or, in other words, *a rule (or a set of rules) on which an agreement exists.*

These agreements can reach from a project scale (using a certain layout for the documentation of the project) to an inter-company or even international scale (like the famous IEEE, ISO-OSI standards). The use of standards enhances the ease with which interfaces (couplings) can be made. They allow computers to communicate, for example. Standards, in other words, enhance the connectivity. Another benefit of standards is that once a standard has been issued, and is supported widely, this will lead to economies of scale, decreasing prices and possibly enhancing the general quality of implementation.

Rules

In general, a rule is a prescription on how something has to be done. The aforementioned discussion suggests that a rule (in the narrow sense of the word) would be a prescription that has to be followed, but on which no agreement exists. Speaking of "in the narrow sense" doesn't clarify discussions. We think it will be clearer to speak of *prescriptions* for the broader sense of the word rule, and *rule* for the narrower sense.

Guidelines

Guidelines are less strict than rules or standards. The idea behind a guideline is, that it should be followed, because in many cases it will guide to (a route to) a good solution. Creativity or craftsmanship of the user of the guideline may lead him to deviate from it. A guideline can thus be simply formulated as being a *rule of thumb.*

Principles

Principles are definitely on a higher level of abstraction than the aforementioned prescriptions. A principle expresses an idea, a message (culture / behaviour) or value that comes from corporate vision, strategies, and business drivers, experience or from knowledge of a subject.

In dictionaries (e.g. Webster), the word principle has a few meanings. The first one mentioned is that of a *comprehensive and fundamental law, doctrine or assumption.* An important word in this definition is "fundamental"; other things (rules, prescriptions, and sometimes (-mathematical) laws) follow from principles. Another important element in this definition is the word "assumption"; apart from the fact that a principle can be an assumption the most fundamental parts of sciences often have to rely on assumptions.

There are principles that govern the business and organization, EA process and principles that govern the implementation of the enterprise architecture. Principles for the EA process affect development, maintenance, and use of the EA. Principles for EA implementation establish the first tenets and related decision-making guidance for the solution enterprise architecture domain.

The Chief Enterprise Architect, in conjunction with the CIO and CEO and select organization business managers, defines the enterprise architectural principles that map to the organization's Business & IT vision and strategic plans.

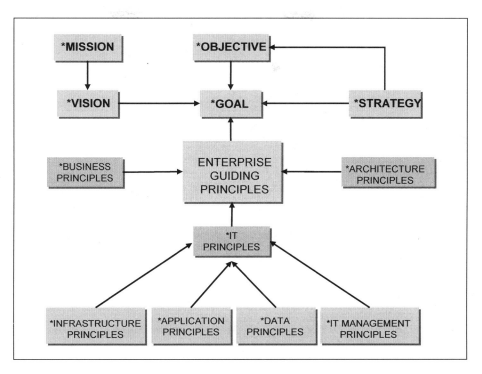

Figure 3. Enterprise Guiding Principles

As shown in Figure 3, enterprise guiding principles should represent fundamental requirements and practices believed to be good for the organization.   These principles should be refined to meet organization business needs.

It should be possible to map specific actions, such as EA development, IT portfolio management, and Project selection, to the enterprise guiding principles. Deliberate and explicit standards-oriented policies and guidelines for the EA development and implementation are generated in compliance with the principles. Each and every item of Enterprise Portfolio Management is supported by the actions necessitated by the enterprise guiding principles. Investment related and budgetary actions are governed by the implications within the principles.

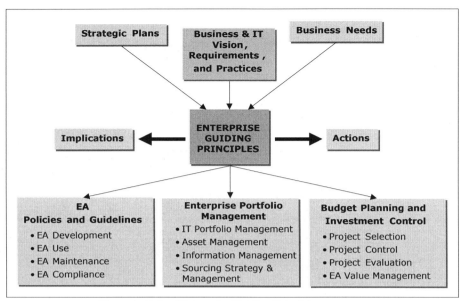

Figure 4. Role of Enterprise Guiding Principles

Appendix D provides sample EA guiding principles for considering as a starting point, as well as the rationale for and the impact of implementing each principle. Each organization should apply, add to, or modify these sample principles. Formulating these supporting statements should be an essential part of an organization's effort to define its principles.

2.4   *The Enterprise Life Cycle*

The enterprise life cycle is the dynamic, iterative process of changing the enterprise over time by incorporating new business processes, new technology, new capabilities, as well as maintenance and disposition of existing elements of the enterprise.

Although the EA implementation and development processes are the primary topic of this guide, it cannot be discussed without consideration of other closely related processes. These include the solution architecture and enterprise program management aspects that aid in the implementation of an EA, and the Budget Planning and Transformation processes that selects, controls, and evaluates investments and changes over time.

Overlying these processes are human capital management and information security management. When these processes work together effectively, the enterprise can effectively manage Technology as a strategic resource and business process enabler. When these processes are properly synchronized, systems migrate efficiently from legacy technology environments through evolutionary and incremental developments, and the organization is able to demonstrate its return on investment. Figure 5 illustrates the interaction of the dynamic and interactive cycles as they would occur over time.

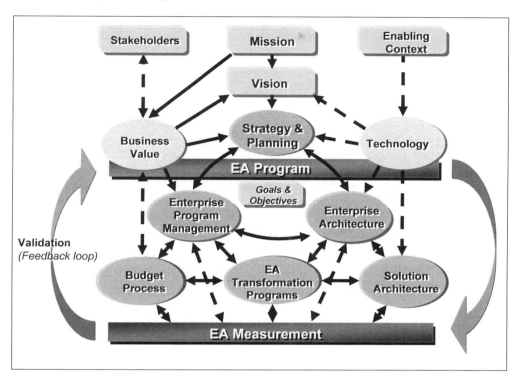

Figure 5. The Enterprise Life Cycle

2.5   *The Enterprise Architecture Program (EAP)*

As a prerequisite to the development of every enterprise architecture, enterprises should establish the need to develop an EA and formulate a strategy that includes the definition of a vision, objectives, and principles. Figure 6 shows a representation of the EA implementation program. Executive buy-in and support should be established and an enterprise architectural team created within the organization. The team defines an EA approach and program tailored to organization needs. The enterprise architecture team implements the program to build both the current and future EA's. The enterprise architecture team also generates a transformation plan for the transformation of business practices and associated systems and applications, predicated upon a detailed gap analysis. The enterprise architecture is employed in the investment/budgeting activity and solution architecture and enterprise program management processes via prioritized, incremental programs and projects and the insertion of emerging new technologies. Lastly, the enterprise architectures are maintained through a continuous modification to reflect the current baseline of the enterprise and future business practices, organizational goals, visions, technology, and infrastructure.

The picture below represents the implementation steps of the Enterprise Architecture Program (EAP); this is an enhanced version of the earlier published US FEAF EA Process cycle, based on best practices.

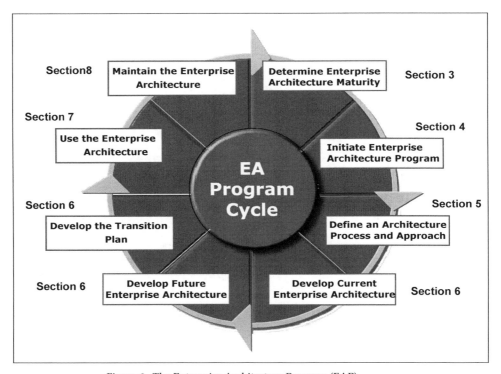

Figure 6. The Enterprise Architecture Program (EAP)

The following sections will explain in detail the different steps to implement the Enterprise Architecture function.

3   Determine Enterprise Architecture Maturity

Enterprise Architecture Maturity Models provides a path for enterprise architecture and procedural improvements within an organization. As the enterprise architecture matures, predictability, process controls and effectiveness also increase. Development of the enterprise architecture is critical because it provides the rules and definition necessary for the integration of information and services at the operation level across organizational boundaries.

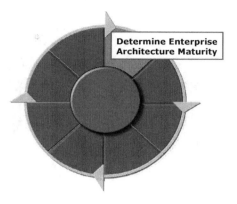

Enterprise architecture includes business tasks and activities and representations, and supportive technology components. At its fullest maturity, enterprise architecture becomes an extended-enterprise concept and prescribes the technologies for extended-enterprise businesses and provides the conditions and structures for allowing information to flow from organization to organization, just as radio waves flows through the radio and electricity flows through the wiring of a building.

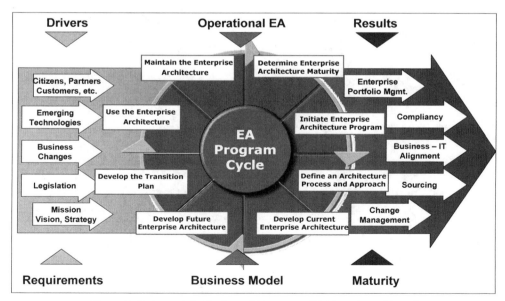

Figure 7. Drivers of the Business & Impact on EA Maturity and Results

However the quality and maturity of the results delivered by the EA team is strongly related and depended of the EA maturity of the team and the organization.

3.1   *How to Plan the EA Maturity Growth*

In addition to the EA process, the models, definitions, principles, and other artefacts that make up the EA, it is important to assess the EA Program and the other aspects of how the EA is being utilized within the organization. Most EA maturity models are identifying a 5 phases approach to identify the EA maturity level of an organization. The (Extended) Enterprise Architecture Maturity Growth Plan shows these steps for future improvements.

Figure 8. The Extended Enterprise Architecture Maturity Growth Plan

3.1.1   Business Value of Enhancing EA Maturity

The best way for an EA Program to deliver a meaningful impact on the business/mission of the organization is to enhance the EA Program's maturity level. To raise the maturity level, the EA Program must develop close collaboration with organization's business partners, efficiently leverage the IT portfolio for focused results based on organization mission, and adopt best practices and prevailing compliancy guidance. Neither of these EA maturity frameworks today would have been developed if there were not at least a very prominent relationship between the EA and EA Program maturity and the resultant impacts to the business/mission functions. The relationship may be somewhat delayed in that the impacts of an increase in EA maturity are generally delayed by one or more budget cycles after the improvements in the maturity level are achieved, but that is not unreasonable give the amount of work that may be required to achieve greater maturity.

Again, the issue of metrics is important. It is important to try to determine in advance areas that EA is intended to impact in order to establish the criterion for measuring the relationships of increased maturity on programs and business initiatives.

3.1.2   Need for Consistent and Complementary Maturity Models

Multiple Enterprise Architecture maturity models that overlap and do not consistently measure the goodness, the impact, and the completeness of Enterprise Architectures can be confusing and very frustrating to the management of organizations and departments that are trying to use them to improve Enterprise Architecture maturity. IFEAD's E2A Maturity Model could be tuned to ensure it is consistent and complementary, if not mutually exclusive in the measured assessments.

3.2   *Public Enterprise Architecture Maturity Models*

3.2.1   USA - GAO – EAMMF[1]

To contribute to the evolution and maturity of the enterprise architecture discipline, the USA GAO published its *Enterprise Architecture Management Maturity Framework* (EAMMF). This framework provides a common benchmarking tool for planning and measuring enterprise architecture efforts. EAMMF is made up of five stages of maturity, each of which includes an associated set of elements along with all the elements of the previous stages. In addition to the maturity stages, each core element is associated with attributes that are critical to the successful performance of any management function.

Stage 1: Creating EA Awareness
At Stage 1, either an organization does not have plans to develop and use an enterprise architecture, or it has plans that do not demonstrate an awareness of the value of having and using an enterprise architecture. While Stage 1 organizations may have initiated some EA activity, these agencies' efforts are ad hoc and unstructured, lack institutional leadership and direction, and do not provide the management foundation necessary for successful EA development as defined in Stage 2.

---

[1] *GAO-03-584G Enterprise Architecture Management; A Framework for Assessing and Improving Enterprise Architecture Management (Version 1.1), 2003 http://www.gao.gov/new.items/d03584g.pdf*

	Stage 1: Creating EA awareness	Stage 2: Building the EA management foundation	Stage 3: Developing EA products	Stage 4: Completing EA products	Stage 5: Leveraging the EA to manage change
Attribute 1: Demonstrates commitment		Adequate resources exist. Committee or group representing the enterprise is responsible for directing, overseeing, or approving EA.	Written and approved organization policy exists for EA development.	Written and approved organization policy exists for EA maintenance.	Written and approved organization policy exists for IT investment compliance with EA.
Attribute 2: Provides capability to meet commitment		Program office responsible for EA development and maintenance exists. Chief architect exists. EA is being developed using a framework, methodology, and automated tool.	EA products are under configuration management.	EA products and management processes undergo independent verification and validation.	Process exists to formally manage EA change. EA is integral component of IT investment management process.
Attribute 3: Demonstrates satisfaction of commitment		EA plans call for describing both the "as-is" and the "to-be" environments of the enterprise, as well as a sequencing plan for transitioning from the "as-is" to the "to-be." EA plans call for describing both the "as-is" and the "to-be" environments in terms of business, performance, information/data, application/service, and technology. EA plans call for business, performance, information/data, application/service, and technology descriptions to address security.	EA products describe or will describe both the "as-is" and the "to-be" environments of the enterprise, as well as a sequencing plan for transitioning from the "as-is" to the "to-be." Both the "as-is" and the "to-be" environments are described or will be described in terms of business, performance, information/data, application/service, and technology. Business, performance, information/data, application/service, and technology descriptions address or will address security.	EA products describe both the "as-is" and the "to-be" environments of the enterprise, as well as a sequencing plan for transitioning from the "as-is" to the "to-be." Both the "as-is" and the "to-be" environments are described in terms of business, performance, information/data, application/service, and technology. Business, performance, information/data, application/service, and technology descriptions address security. Organization CIO has approved current version of EA. Committee or group representing the enterprise or the investment review board has approved current version of EA.	EA products are periodically updated. IT investments comply with EA. Organization head has approved current version of EA.
Attribute 4: Verifies satisfaction of commitment		EA plans call for developing metrics for measuring EA progress, quality, compliance, and return on investment.	Progress against EA plans is measured and reported.	Quality of EA products is measured and reported.	Return on EA investment is measured and reported. Compliance with EA is measured and reported.

maturation →

Source: GAO.

Figure 9. The USA GAO - EAMMF

Stage 2: Building the EA Management Foundation

An organization at Stage 2 recognizes that the EA is a corporate asset by vesting accountability for it in an executive body that represents the entire enterprise. At this stage, an organization assigns EA management roles and responsibilities and establishes plans for developing EA results and for measuring program progress and quality; it also commits the resources necessary for developing an enterprise architecture—people, processes, and tools. Specifically, a Stage 2 organization has designated a chief architect and established and staffed a program office responsible for EA development and maintenance. Further, it has established a committee or group that has responsibility for EA governance (i.e., directing, overseeing, and approving enterprise architecture development and maintenance).

This committee or group is often called a steering committee, and its membership includes both business and IT representatives (i.e., the committee has enterprise wide representation). At Stage 2, the organization either has plans for developing or has started developing at least some EA results, and it has developed an enterprise wide awareness of the value of EA and its intended use in managing its IT investments. The organization has also selected a framework and a methodology that will be the basis for developing the EA results and has selected a tool for automating these activities.

Stage 3: Developing the EA

An organization at Stage 3 focuses on developing enterprise architecture results according to the selected framework, methodology, tool, and established management plans. Roles and responsibilities assigned in the previous stage are in place, and resources are being applied to develop actual EA results. Here, the scope of the enterprise architecture has been defined to encompass the entire enterprise, whether organization-based or function-based. Although the results may not be complete, they are intended to describe the organization in business, performance, information/data, service/application, and technology terms (including security explicitly in each), as provided for in the framework, methodology, tool, and management plans. Further, the results are to describe the current ("as-is") and future ("to-be") states and the plan for transitioning from the current to the future state (the sequencing plan). As the results are developed and evolve, they are subject to configuration management. Further, through the established EA management foundation, the organization is tracking and measuring its progress against plans, identifying and addressing variances, as appropriate, and then reporting on its progress.

Stage 4: Completing the EA

An organization at Stage 4 has completed its EA results, meaning that the results have been approved by the EA steering committee (established in Stage 2) or an investment review board, and by the CIO. The completed results collectively describe the enterprise in terms of business, performance, information/data, service/application, and technology for both its current and future operating states, and the results include a transformation plan for sequencing from the current to the future state. Further, an independent agent has assessed the quality (i.e., completeness and accuracy) of the EA results. Additionally, evolution of the approved results is governed by a written EA maintenance policy approved by the head of the organization.

Stage 5: Leveraging the EA to Manage Change

An organization at Stage 5 has secured senior leadership approval of the EA results and a written institutional policy stating that IT investments must comply with the enterprise architecture, unless granted an explicit compliance waiver. Further, decision-makers are using the enterprise architecture to identify and address ongoing and proposed IT investments that are conflicting, overlapping, not strategically linked, or redundant. Thus, Stage 5 entities are able to avoid unwarranted overlap across investments and ensure maximum systems interoperability, which in turn ensures the selection and funding of IT investments with manageable risks and returns. Also at Stage 5, the organization tracks and measures EA benefits or return on investment, and adjustments are continuously made to both the EA management process and the EA results.

Critical Success Attributes

Associated with the maturity stages described above are characteristics or attributes that are critical to the successful performance of any management function. These critical success attributes are (1) showing a commitment to perform the function; (2) putting in place the capability (people, processes, and technology) needed to perform the function; (3) demonstrating, via production and results, that the function has been performed; and (4) verifying, via quantitative and qualitative measurement, that the function was satisfactorily performed. Collectively, these attributes form the basis by which an organization can institutionalize management of any given function or program, like EA management.

3.2.2   USA - OMB EAAF Overview[2]

The USA - OMB EA Assessment Framework (EAAF) was created to take a look at how the EA's at organizations are being utilized and are impacting the deployment of e-Government solutions and technologies to support citizen centric services. More so than the USA GAO EAMMF the self-assessment allows for some flexibility in the interpretation of the evaluation criteria. This is both a plus and a minus. It encourages the organizations to read between the lines in their assessments and allows some degree of inflation of the results.

Overall, if the criteria are tightly applied to the letter of the intent, it is actually more difficult to achieve the higher maturity levels using the OMB Framework than using GAO's. The plus is that it generally reinforces the progress made with higher average scores that don't penalize the agency's maturity a whole level if a single criterion is not achieved. The OMB EA self assessment was designed to help each agency assess the capability of its EA Program and that it compliments the GAO EAMMF which assesses EA Program capacity.

The OMB EA Assessment Framework (EAAF) looks at the following two capability facets of an Agency's EA Program:

o Maturity of the Agencies EA, including the work product development and the capability of the Agency's EA Program to provide specific investment recommendations as a part of the CPIC process;

o Integration of the Agency's EA with the FEA, including the reflection of the reference models and good EA principles and the potentials for inter-Governmental collaboration on information technology solutions.

The OMB assessment framework primarily seeks to identify the extent to which the agency **has developed an EA** that supports agency program performance by influencing IT planning and investment decisions, rather than on the structure and results within and agency's EA Program as is the case with the GAO EAMMF.

---

[2] *USA Office of Management & Budget (OMB)*

The EAAF contains four capability areas: Change, Integration, Convergence, and Business Alignment. There are several sub-areas within in each of the capability areas, and each is rated on its level of achievement. The levels are assessed at values of zero to five, where zero is "no evidence provided" and five is "IT planning is optimized through the EA."

3.2.3   IFEAD - Extended Enterprise Architecture Maturity Model (E2AMM) [3]

The table on the next page provides IFEAD's Extended Enterprise Architecture Maturity Model v2.0, describing the maturity levels of implementation of an Enterprise Architecture Program, including the extended environment.

The cells in the E2AMM are describing in short the level of maturity related to the maturity phases as well as the related topics.

At first, use the E2AMM to define your baseline EA maturity level then you know where you are. Based on that point, then define the topics for growth in EA maturity and organize your self in such a way that you can achieve the next level in a certain timeframe.

3.3   *Emphasis on Benefits at Each Level and Each Aspect*

It is also important to track the achievement of benefits at each successive maturity level. In particular, as the maturity levels increase, using either framework, the returns and the impacts should be clearer and increasingly easy to articulate. If the benefits derived from increasing levels of maturity seem to level off or cause a higher cost/benefit ratio, then careful review of the EA Program may be in order. There are some organizations where the level of EA maturity may not need ever to reach a stable level 5 or the incremental cost of doing so is not justified in terms of potential impacts or results. It is not a given that every organization should continue to strive to achieve the highest levels on either framework, especially if it is only for the sake of having achieved it.

Again, it must be emphasized that, in general, the higher the maturity level, especially for very large enterprises with large IT investment budgets, the greater the potential for benefits.

---

[3] *E2AMM* SM = *Service Mark of the Institute For Enterprise Architecture Developments. For more info about the E2AMM visit the website http://www.enterprise-architecture.info*

E2AMM	Level 0: No Extended Enterprise Architecture	Level 1: Initial	Level 2 Under Development	Level 3: Defined	Level 4: Managed	Level 5: Optimized
Business &Technology Strategy Alignment	No awareness of aligning business strategies, business drivers & principles and IT strategies, drivers & principles.	Initial alignment of business strategies, business drivers & principles and IT strategies, drivers & principles.	First activities to align business strategies, drivers & principles and IT strategies, drivers & principles.	Formal alignment of business strategy, drivers, principles and functional / non-functional requirements and IT strategies, drivers, principles and functional / non-functional requirements.	Frequently reconsideration of business strategy, drivers, principles & functional / non-functional requirements and IT strategies, drivers, principles and functional / non-functional requirements.	Business –Technology cost / benefits validation metrics for end-to-end value chain examination. [E2-Grid]
Extended Enterprise Involvement	No involvement of Extended parties; No collaboration agreements.	Incidental involvement of Extended parties.	Awareness of collaboration with extended parties. First initiatives to involve extended parties in the E2A program	Extended parties involved in E2A program. Definition of collaboration levels and information exchange standards	Extended Enterprise management & governance structure in place.	Measurement structure in place to manage Extended Enterprise environment.
Executive-Management Involvement	E2A is not for us. We do not need to be involved. We know how to do our job. Don't tell me about.	What is Extended Enterprise Architecture about? I have heard something about E2A	Little awareness by management of Extended Enterprise Architecture possibilities. Spread skepticism to adopt Extended Enterprise Architecture.	Executive management aware of Extended Enterprise Architecture benefits. Executive management supports pro-active Extended Enterprise Architectural program.	Executive management evaluates periodic the Extended Enterprise Architecture program and results.	Executive management participating in the E2A optimization process.
Business Units Involvement	Extended Enterprise Architecture is not recognized by any business unit.	Some Business Units support the Extended Enterprise Architecture program and will deliver some added value to the Business – IT alignment process	Identification that it is hard to maintain too many different business processes and supporting technologies in n dynamic business world.	Identification that an Extended Enterprise Architecture program can reduce complexity and can enhance business flexibility. Adaptive Business – IT alignment is the answer to business dynamics.	Enterprise wide business units are actively involved in the Extended Enterprise Architecture program.	Extended Enterprise Architecture is established in all business units and part of their decision making process.
Extended Enterprise Architecture Program Office	E2A program does not exist.	First cut of E2A program in place. E2A architects identified.	E2A program being actively defined. E2A program office established.	E2A program established. E2A program office actively working together with business and IT units in defining E2A value.	Extended Enterprise Architecture program office is involved in the line of business and the Enterprise budget process.	Continuously measurement of E2A program activities and results. E2A measurement, process of the overall Enterprise improvement activities.
Extended Enterprise Architecture Developments	No Extended Enterprise Architecture recognition.	Some Extended Enterprise Architecture activities are started. Recognition about focusing on business value and IT standards + cost reduction activities. Ad hoc alignment of Business and IT.	Extended Enterprise Architecture program is set up. Business and IT strategy and standards are developed and linked. EA framework and methodology are chosen but not yet widely spread.	Extended Enterprise Architecture program established. Business & IT principles, drivers and strategies are defined and communicated. Extended Enterprise Architecture and Solution Architecture areas are defined and aligned.	Extended Enterprise Architecture program managed by E2A steering committee. Reference models are rolled out and accepted by business units. E2A program office involved in the definition of new projects. Extended Enterprise Architecture reflects current and future state.	Extended Enterprise Architecture program office manages projects portfolio landscape and aligns continuously the overall activities and initiatives.
Extended Enterprise Architecture Results	None.	E2A results are documented in a single way. No access to the results for others.	E2A results are shared with others. Most results are documented using traditional office tools. Access to the results is limited. Sharing of information in a traditional way. Modeling and visualization techniques are developed.	Extended Enterprise Architecture results are updated frequently. Standards, modeling methods and visualization techniques are used. E2A repository is set-up.	Extended Enterprise Architecture results are controlled and managed regularly. Business units are using the E2A results in their planning business. E2A results are accessible in an electronic way for all participants.	E2A results are mandatory used in the Enterprise wide strategic planning and governance activities. Continuous improvement of strategic planning and decision making cycle based on E2A results.
Strategic Governance	Strategic Governance in not in place.	Strategic Governance is in place and the first activities are set up to link the E2A program and Strategic Governance.	E2A results are part of the Strategic Governance process. The Enterprise Program management office and the Extended Enterprise Architecture office are working together on an incident base.	Strategic decision making and governance are based on the E2A results. The E2A program office is involved in the formal governance processes.	Formalized strategic governance of all business & IT investments based on E2A results.	Value measurement techniques are adopted to continuously measure the business and IT value of investments based on the E2A results and in line with the governance strategy.
Enterprise Program Management	Enterprise Program management not recognized.	Project management upgraded to program management. Recognition of the added value of Enterprise Program management. Program management executed almost in isolation.	Enterprise Program management and Extended Enterprise Architecture linked together. Enterprise Program management office responsible for the transformation part, Extended Enterprise Architecture office responsible for the Content part.	Enterprise Program management office and Extended Enterprise Architecture office, officially working together. Program management approach and E2A program aligned. Accountability en responsibility of activities defined.	Project and program initiatives under auspices of the Enterprise Program management office with participation of the Extended Enterprise Architecture office. Procedures, standards and methods are aligned.	Enterprise Program Management Office and Extended Enterprise Architecture Office are participating in the enterprise strategic planning process. Measurement techniques are in place to determine the added value to the business of all initiatives.
Holistic Extended Enterprise Architecture	Awareness of aligning business and technology not present.	Awareness of aligning business and technology present. First initiatives set up to align business and technology activities, based on the Enterprise its mission, vision strategies and business drivers.	Activities are set up to continuously align business and technology initiatives. Alignment of business and information modeling methods with the technology modeling methods.	Extended Enterprise Architecture framework is used to define the business IT alignment areas. Results of business and IT modeling methods are stored in a repository. Traceability of business and IT alignment.	Every project or program initiative is measured against the added value to the business and the cost of investments. The current and future state Extended Enterprise Architectures are used as a management tool to plan transformation initiatives. Business and Technology are operating on the same level of maturity.	The holistic E2A approach is part of the organizations culture. Business initiatives are continuously reflected to the technology impact and IT possibilities are driving new business activities.
Enterprise Budget & Procurement Strategy	Separated Business & IT budget & procurement strategy.	Almost no awareness about aligning and managing the Enterprise business & IT budget and procurement strategies.	First awareness about the alignment and management of the Enterprise business & IT budget and procurement processes.	The extended Enterprise Architecture office is participating in the enterprise budget and procurement strategy. Request for information or proposals are defined in co-operation with the enterprise architecture office.	The future state Extended Enterprise Architecture acts as a blueprint for investments, is formalized and part of the enterprise budget process.	All investment plans and initiatives are related to the Extended Enterprise Architecture results, the budgets and procurement strategy.

Figure 10. The Extended Enterprise Architecture Maturity Model (E2AMM)

4   Initiate an Enterprise Architecture Program

The Enterprise Architecture is a corporate asset that should be managed as a formal program. Successful execution of the EA process is an organization-wide endeavour requiring management, allocation of resources, continuity, and coordination. Organization business line executives should work closely with the organization enterprise architecture team to produce a description of the organization's operations, a vision of the future, and an investment and technology strategy for accomplishing defined goals.

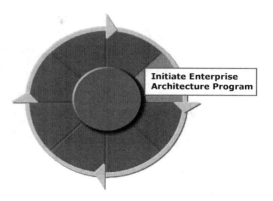

Experience shows that obtaining the needed cooperation among organization executives is not an easy task. Creating an EA program calls for sustained leadership and strong commitment. This degree of sponsorship and commitment needs the buy-in of the organization Head, leadership by the CIO & CEO and senior management an the early designation of an experienced Chief Enterprise Architect (CEA).

4.1   Obtain Executive Buy-in and Support

Gaining executive commitment to any new initiative requires the development of a strong business case and a communications approach to effectively convey that business case. Since the concept of an EA is not intuitively understood outside the IT organization, a marketing strategy should be created to communicate the strategic and tactical value for EA development to the organization management, other senior executives, and (strategic) business units.

4.1.1   Ensure Organization Management Buy-in and Support

Without buy-in from the organization top management (CEO), the CIO will find it hard to maintain the necessary sponsorship desired to fund and implement improved businesses, systems and processes. The CIO takes the lead to provide understanding and gain the organization's head's buy-in. This can be accomplished by:

o   Leveraging success stories from other organization and private sector organizations as well as the experience and knowledge of EA experts
o   Using examples to demonstrate how an EA can provide a blueprint and roadmap for desired changes or improvements in mission performance and accountability

o   Emphasizing the legislative requirements for developing, maintaining, and implementing an EA.

Once the CIO is assured the organization heads understand the need for an EA, it is important to secure the organization head's commitment to pursue the enterprise architecture effort. The CIO accomplishes this by mobilizing the CEO's appreciation into the expression of clear, organization-wide support. This will establish a mandate to business and CIO to support the effort by allocating the needed time and resources. Experience demonstrates that the CIO's authority alone is insufficient to make the endeavour a success. A clear mandate from the CEO is a prerequisite to success.

4.1.2   Issue an Executive Enterprise Architecture Policy

The CIO, in collaboration with the organization head, develops a policy based on the organization's Enterprise Architecture principles that governs the development, implementation, and maintenance of the EA. The EA policy should be approved by the CEO and, at a minimum, should include:

o   Description of the purpose and value of an EA
o   Description of the relationship of the EA to the strategic vision and plans
o   Description of the relationship of the EA to Budget planning, enterprise engineering and program management
o   Translation of business strategies into EA goals, objectives, and strategies
o   Commitment to develop, implement, and maintain an EA
o   Identification of EA compliance as one criterion for new and ongoing investments
o   Overview of an enforcement policy
o   Security practices to include certification and accreditation
o   Appointment of the Chief Enterprise Architect (CEA) and establishment of an EA core team
o   Establishment of the EA Steering Committee (EASC).

4.1.3   Obtain Support from Senior Executives and Business Units

Commitment and participation of the organization's senior executive and business teams are vitally important. The CIO should initiate a marketing program to emphasize the value of the enterprise architecture and the CEO's support and commitment. The senior executive team and its organizational units are both stakeholders and users of the enterprise architecture. Therefore, the CEA invests time and effort in familiarizing the staff with what an EA is and how it can help achieve organizational goals and commitments. Even though the target audience varies among (S)BU's, the audience should include members of the MT's of the (S)BU's.

The primary goal of educating the (S)BU's and organization senior executives is to obtain their concurrence and commitment to having their organizations as active participants in the EA process. Participation can involve the executives (or their designees) in attending planning sessions, committing resources (people and funding) for specific tasks, or becoming a champion or spokesperson for the effort. Maintaining the participation and support of key executives is crucial to sustaining a successful effort.

The Chief Enterprise Architect should create a plan to obtain the support of the enterprise business units. It is recommended that the business units establish an "inner circle" of domain owners and subject matter experts (SMEs). This leadership group should consist of business unit managers who "own" specific lines of business. This leadership group should be able to understand and communicate enterprise goals and objectives, and to think creatively, with consideration of budgets and other constraints. This group of managers is responsible for ensuring that the business layers of the enterprise architecture are properly documented, and that the transformation plan makes sense from the perspective of the business strategy, considering both automated and non-automated processes.

Once the EA policy has been disseminated, the CEO / CIO and Chief Enterprise Architect should organize and conduct a program kickoff meeting to explain the EA goals, objectives, processes, results, and interrelationships with activities of the systems development life cycle, Budget planning and investment process, and other related activities. The goal of the program kickoff meeting is to promote buy-in by program participants at middle and lower levels of the organization. After several of the first EA results are developed and analyzed, the results and analysis should be disseminated throughout the organization to demonstrate the value of these early results and achieve maximum exposure for the benefits of the EA development effort.

4.2   *Establish Management Structure and Control*

Figure 11 illustrates a professional EA program organization to manage, control, and monitor EA activity and progress. The organization shows the desired functional roles, interrelationships, and lines of communication. The organization structure should facilitate and advance the performance of EA roles and responsibilities. Roles, such as Quality Assurance (QA), Configuration Management (CM), Risk Management (RM), Security, and Evaluation are customary IT support roles. These roles are expanded to explicitly include EA-related responsibilities.

EA roles should be evaluated based on the size of the organization, the complexity of the business and enterprise architecture, and other factors to effectively determine the correlation of roles assigned to personnel. An individual may be responsible for one specific role. In smaller organizations, an individual may be assigned several roles and responsibilities.

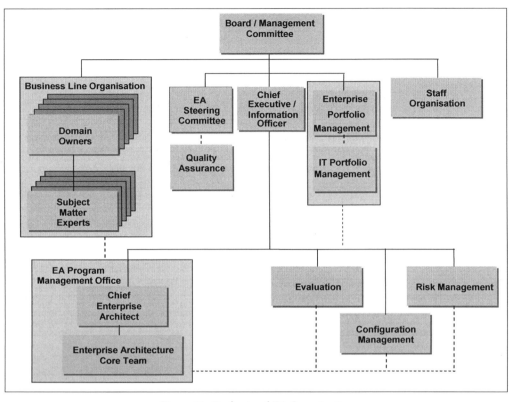

Figure 11. Professional EA Organization

4.2.1   Establish (Extended) Enterprise Portfolio Management (E(2)PM)

(Extended) Enterprise Portfolio Management (E(2)PM) is an integrated strategic investment planning, portfolio risk analysis and operating system for scheduling, settlement and risk management that facilitates tight alignment of strategic objectives with operational actions, covering business and technology. E(2)PM works by enabling separate organizational entities to use a common enterprise information management platform, common enterprise analytical methodologies and a common enterprise strategic business framework for optimal business & technology decisions, ensuring successful execution on the corporate enterprise strategy.

Figure 12. E(2)PM, IT Portfolio Managment & EA

The foundation for E(2)PM is layered down in the results of EA processes & Programs.

See Section 13 for more information about Enterprise Portfolio Management.

4.2.2   Establish IT Portfolio Management (ITPM)

The drive to react faster to business change puts increasing pressure in IT organizations. IT Portfolio Management tackles these issues head on, allowing you to:

o   Reduce costs by eliminating IT initiatives that are duplicated, off-strategy, or poorly performing;

o   Optimize resource utilization through collaborative planning, improved prioritization, and continuous performance measurement; and

o   Achieve — and demonstrate — greater ROI by objective investment selection a better balance of risk and reward, and enhanced IT governance.

4.2.3   Establish an EA Steering Committee (EASC)

The organization HEAD / CEO establishes an EA Steering Committee to direct, oversee, and approve the EA and EA program. The EASC is responsible for approving the initial EA, approving significant changes to the EA, and approving the EA Program Plan.

The EASC should be formally chartered, with a designated chair or co-chairs, and empowered to ensure organization-wide strategic direction, oversight, and decision-making authority for the EA in close cooperation with the executives responsible for Enterprise Portfolio Management. The EASC charter should authorize the chair or co-chairs to appoint the membership. By charter, the EASC membership should consist of active participants that represent and include all major organization business and technology areas as presented in the EPM figure. To perform effectively as a decision-making body, it is crucial that the EASC members are senior leaders, with the authority to commit resources and make and enforce decisions within their respective organizations.

4.2.4   Appoint Chief Enterprise Architect

The Chief Enterprise Architect is responsible for leading the development of the EA work results and support environment. The Chief Enterprise Architect serves as the technology and business leader for the development organization, ensuring the integrity of the enterprise architectural development processes and the content of the EA results. The Chief Enterprise Architect should be friend and liaison to the business line units and ensure that business unit processes are emphasized in the EA. Likewise, the Chief Enterprise Architect is responsible for ensuring that the EA provides the best possible information and guidance to IT projects and stakeholders, and that systems development efforts are properly aligned with business unit requirements.

In the role of EA Program Manager, the Chief Enterprise Architect has management responsibility for the EA program, with the authority, responsibility, and accountability for the overall enterprise architectural effort. The EA Program Manager is responsible for the planning, staffing, and the ultimate success of the program, including acquisition of sustaining funding, negotiating schedules, timely and accurate delivery of the EA results, and the establishment of an appropriate support environment that ensures proper application of these assets.

The core competencies of the Chief Enterprise Architect include expertise in strategic and technical planning, policy development, Budget planning and investment control, change management, systems engineering and architectural design, business process reengineering, and large-scale program management. In addition, the Chief Enterprise Architect becomes completely conversant with the organization's business and IT environments. As the primary technical leader of this effort, the Chief Enterprise Architect should be a good communicator who can bridge the cultural differences that often exist between the business and systems organizations, and facilitate interaction and cooperation between these two cultures.

4.2.5   Establish an Enterprise Architecture Office (EAO)

The EA effort should be treated as a formal program with full sponsorship through the organization's Budget Planning, investment and budgeting process. An EA Office should manage, monitor, and control the development and maintenance of the EA. The EAO staff includes experienced architects. The EAO identifies and performs cost analyses of alternative approaches for developing the EA, and manages in-house or outside contractor EA development work. The EAO is also charged with determining needed resources and securing funding and resource commitments.

A primary goal of the EAO and the EASC is to ensure success of the EA program. Each phase of the program (i.e., EA development, use, and maintenance) is subject to the investment and budgeting policies and procedures.

4.2.5.1 Appoint Key Personnel

The CEA should make the EA an explicit responsibility for those individuals designated as the organization's Evaluators, EA Program Risk Manager, and Configuration Manager. The Risk Manager identifies, monitors, controls, and mitigates EA program risks in light of environmental factors (e.g., external business constraints, and technical constraints). The Configuration Manager assumes responsibility for configuration management of the EA results in the same way that configuration management is imposed on any other engineering baseline.

The CEA should establish an independent QA organization to perform evaluation of the EA. This team should report to the EASC and ensure all established program and project standards and processes are met. Potential sources for review include external reference groups, impartial or uninvolved external entities, or by hiring a neutral third party specializing in assessments or validations.

4.2.5.2 *Establish Enterprise Architecture Core Team*

At the same time the organization HEAD / CEO and CIO achieve business line ownership of the effort, a core team of business line experts, EA experts, IT experts and technologists should be assigned to develop the desired process and procedures used throughout the development effort. Participants should have an understanding of the current business and technical environment and the strategic business objectives envisioned in the EA. The team includes the Chief Enterprise Architect; senior business, process, systems, data, infrastructure and security systems architects. This team should be well grounded in the existing environment and prepared to document and develop the EA that will support evolving business needs.

The EA core team is responsible for all activities involving the development, implementation, maintenance, and management of the enterprise architecture. This includes:

o   Developing EA processes, procedures, and standards (amongst which the administrative organization)
o   Developing current and future enterprise architectures
o   Developing and maintaining an EA repository (aided by an EA software tool)
o   Performing quality assurance, risk management, and configuration management
o   Guiding systems development and acquisition efforts
o   Defining EA performance measures.

Table 3 provides a listing of functional roles and the associated responsibilities assigned to EA core team members. Some of these roles and responsibilities may be shared, doubled up, or contracted out.

Role	Responsibilities
Chief Enterprise Architect	Leads the EAO, organizes and manages the EA core team; directs development of the current and future enterprise architecture.
Senior Enterprise Architecture Consultant	Provides enterprise architecture strategy and planning consultation to the Chief Enterprise Architect.
Business/Process Architect	Analyzes and documents business processes, scenarios, and information flow. Sets guidelines for processes. Advices on efficiency and efficacy of processes.
Information Architect	Analyzes and documents business information (logical and physical) and associated relationships.
Applications Architect	Analyzes and documents systems, internal and external interfaces, control, and data flow.
Infrastructure Architect	Analyzes and documents system environments, including network communications, nodes, operating systems, applications, application servers, web and portal servers, and middleware.

Role	Responsibilities
Security Systems Architect	Oversees, coordinates, and documents IT security aspects of the EA, including design, operations, encryption, vulnerability, access, and the use of authentication processes.
Technical Writer	Ensures that policies, guidebooks, and other documentation within the EA repository are clear, concise, usable, and conform to configuration management standards.
Quality Assurance	Ensures that all established program and project standards, processes, and practices are met.
Risk Management	Identifies, monitors, and controls risks in light of environmental factors and constraints.
Configuration Control	Assures that all changes are identified, tracked, monitored, and appropriately documented.

Table 3. EAO Roles and Responsibilities

4.3   *Enterprise Architecture Program Activities and Results*

4.3.1   Develop an Enterprise Architecture Marketing Strategy and Communications Plan

The purpose of the marketing strategy and communications plan is (1) to keep senior executives and business units continually informed and (2) to disseminate EA information to management teams. The CEO / CIO's staff, in cooperation with the Chief Architect and support staff, defines a marketing and communications plan consisting of (a) constituencies, (b) level of detail, (c) means of communication, (d) participant feedback, (e) schedule for marketing efforts, and (f) method of evaluating progress and buy-in. It is the CEO / CIO's role to interpret the organization's vision and to recognize innovative ideas (e.g., the creation of digital services) that can become key drivers within the EA strategy and plan. If resources permit, the Chief Enterprise Architect should use one or all of the following tools to communicate with the community of interest: seminars and forums, web pages, electronic surveys, and e-mail list-services.

One of the recommended means for marketing the EA is a primer to inform organization business executives and stakeholders of the EA strategy and plan. The primer can be used to express the organization head's vision for the enterprise and the role of EA in accomplishing that vision—for example, creating the integrated foundation for online government or streamlining business processes and technology.

The primer should describe the tenets of the EA and its many benefits as an agent of change in achieving organizational goals (e.g., integrating business services and initiatives) or as a critical resource to evaluate options for change as business and technology needs evolve. The primer should clearly describe the roles and responsibilities of the senior executives and their organizational units in developing, implementing, and maintaining the EA. It is important that the primer include customized sections that relate directly to specific business line audiences.

The primer should demonstrate the benefits of an EA for the organization's stakeholders. This is particularly important since many of the stakeholders may be needed to provide skilled resources, support, and time to the effort. Once completed, the primer should be widely distributed throughout the enterprise and made available on the organization's web site. It should be briefed to all personnel impacted by the introduction of the EA. Introductory materials drawn from the primer should be incorporated into local and organization-wide training programs.

4.3.2   Develop an EA Program Management Plan

A formal plan is desired for sound program management. The EAO creates an EA program management plan (EAPMP) that includes a roadmap to accomplish the goals set by the EAG and implementation plans to achieve those goals. The plan should include goals for the Chief Enterprise Architect in setting organization-wide architectural objectives. These goals should help the enterprise architecture core team establish and maintain lower-level architectures that comply with the EA.

The PMP delineates plans and a set of actions to develop, use, and maintain the EA, including EA management, control, and oversight. To facilitate the tracking of cost, schedule, and performance data, oversight and control procedures should be developed, documented, and implemented within the PMP. The PMP should also include:

o   Requirements for the EA Program Manager to identify all funding requirements, spending timelines/schedules, and links to performance measures
o   A Work Breakdown Structure (WBS) detailing the tasks and subtasks necessary to acquire, develop, and maintain the enterprise architecture
o   Resource estimates for funding, staffing, training, workspace requirements, and equipment needs
o   Roadmap for the initiation of project plans
o   Requirements for performing quality assurance, risk management, configuration management, and security management
o   Requirements for the establishment and maintenance of an EA information repository.

4.3.3   Initiate Development of the Enterprise Architecture

Once the EAO is in place and the EAPMP is produced, the first of the enterprise architecture projects is launched. Begin implementing and using the EAPMP by initiating the first project - development of the EA. There are several peripheral activities associated with the start of this development. The head's initial project will:

- o Establish EA development processes and management practices
- o Train EA project participants
- o Build current EA results
- o Build future EA results (as possible)
- o Create the transformation plan
- o Select a method to develop and document the EA
- o Select a modelling language for Business & IT visualizations
- o Select a tool for EA repository
- o Populate the EA repository

Sections 6 and 7 provide discussions on the details of the development of the EA.

5   Define an Enterprise Architecture Process and Approach

The next step in the EA process is establishing an EA process and approach. The EA will be used as a tool to facilitate and manage change within the organization. The goals, scope and nature of the organization and the changes to be made will dictate the goals, scope and nature of the enterprise architecture to be developed. While the EA is

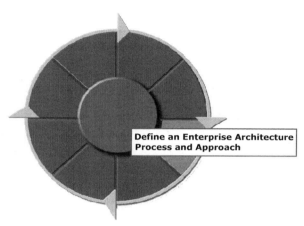

Define an Enterprise Architecture Process and Approach

an excellent tool to manage large and complex environments, the depth and detail of the EA needs to be tailored to the individual enterprise. Figure 13 illustrates how the depth and detail in the EA varies not only with the size and complexity of the enterprise, but also the many types of risks associated with change. Regardless, the scope of the Enterprise Architecture for the strategic planner and business owner views (as defined by the enterprise architecture framework selected) needs to encompass the entire enterprise. The

Goals:

- Build a baseline enterprise architecture that represents reality

- Build a future enterprise architecture that represents the business vision and IT strategies

- Develop a transformation plan that describes an incremental strategy for transitioning the baseline to the future

- Publish an approved EA and transformation plan that are accessible

organization will understand the relationships and dependencies among its lines-of-business and thus position itself to make informed decisions how to approach defining EA depth and detail for these lines-of-business.

The first activity in this process is to determine the intended use (goals) of the enterprise architecture. It drives the rest of the EA development process. The subsequent activities describe how to scope, characterize, select EA results, build, and use the EA. Before actually developing the EA, the organization needs to evaluate and select an enterprise architectural framework as guidance. This section describes several candidate frameworks currently used within the EA community. The selection of an EA framework is contingent on the purpose of the EA and the results to be developed. Additionally, a toolset or repository for the EA development and use should be employed. The chosen EA tool should be commensurate with the results to be generated.

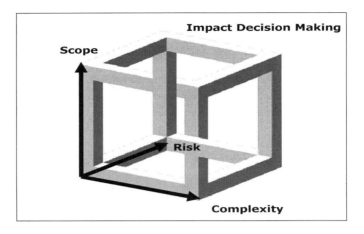

Figure 13. Scope and Complexity of the Enterprise Architecture

5.1   *Define the Intended Use (Goals) of the Enterprise Architecture*

Enterprise Architectures should be built with a specific purpose in mind. Primarily it is used to support decision-making of management on topics of e.g. business transformation, information systems acquisition, system-of-systems migration or integration, user training, interoperability evaluation, or any other intent. The purpose of the enterprise architecture is closely tied to the decision-making of Strategic and Medium Term Action Plan(s) of the enterprise like enterprise portfolio management, legislation such as IFRS, Basel II, SOX and Privacy legislations. Before an enterprise architect begins to describe an enterprise architecture, the organization determines the changes the enterprise architecture is intended to facilitate, the issue(s) the enterprise architecture is intended to explore, the questions the enterprise architecture is expected to help answer, and the interests and perspectives of the audience and users. One important practical consideration is determining the types of analyses that will be performed; i.e., knowing that the enterprise architecture may be used in some cases as input to the solution architecture domain, specific models or simulations can affect what to include and how to structure the results.

The purpose of the EA may, and likely will, evolve over time to meet new requirements. The Chief Enterprise Architect should ensure that any such EA evolution does, in fact, meet the newly determined requirements. This will increase the efficiency of the enterprise architecture development and create greater balance in the resulting enterprise architecture.

5.2   *Define the Scope of the Enterprise Architecture*

It is critically important that EA development be approached in a top-down, incremental manner, consistent with the hierarchical enterprise architectural views that are the building blocks of proven EA frameworks, including the ones discussed later in this guide. In doing so, it is equally important that the scope of the higher level business views of the EA span the entire enterprise or organization.   By developing this enterprise-wide understanding of business processes and rules, and information needs, flows, and locations, the organization will be positioned to make good decisions about whether the enterprise, and thus the EA, can be appropriately compartmentalized. Without doing so, scoping decisions about the EA run the risk of promoting "stove-piped" operations and systems environments, and ultimately sub-optimizing enterprise performance and accountability. Other considerations relevant to defining the scope of the EA include, but are not limited to:

o   Relevance of activities, functions, organizations, timeframes, etc.
o   Enterprise scope (extended, intra- and inter-organization domains)
o   Operational scenarios, situations, and geographical areas to be considered
o   Projected economic benefits
o   Projected business and technical risk areas
o   Projected availability and capabilities of specific technologies during the target timeframe (applies to future enterprise architecture only).

Defining the scope leads the planners to project management factors that will contribute to these determinations, including the resources available for building the enterprise architecture as well as the resources and level of expertise available for analysis and design tasks.

5.3   *Determine the Complexity and depth of the Enterprise Architecture*

Care should be taken to judge the appropriate level of detail to be captured based on the intended use and scope of the EA and executive decisions to be made using the EA. It is important that a consistent and equal level of depth be completed in each view and perspective. If pertinent characteristics are omitted, the enterprise architecture may not be useful. If unnecessary characteristics are included, the enterprise architecture effort may prove infeasible given the time and resources available, or the enterprise architecture may be confusing and/or cluttered with details that are superfluous. EA characteristics are influenced by the focus: whether primarily capturing the current vs. the future and vice-versa. It is equally important to predict the future uses of the enterprise architecture so that, within resource limitations, the enterprise architecture can be structured to accommodate future tailoring, extension, or reuse. The depth and detail, related to the complexity of the EA needs to be sufficient for its purpose.

5.4   *Role and Benefits of an Enterprise Architecture Framework*

An Enterprise Architecture framework provides a generic problem space and a common vocabulary within which individuals can cooperate to solve a specific problem. EA Frameworks are not necessarily comprehensive, but they can be leveraged to provide at least a starter set of the issues and concerns that must be addressed in enterprise architecture development.

For many organizations and technical professionals, enterprise architecture has traditionally meant an incomprehensible diagram or two that has been around since the beginning of the project and cannot be changed because "too much depends on it," nor can it be questioned too closely because its meaning is not really clear. What depends on it, and how was that decided?

The answers to those and many other related questions are too often lost in the push to meet schedules or market demands. Frameworks can provide guidance on a broader notion of enterprise architecture than just what can be conveyed in block diagrams. Frameworks generally adopt similar definitions of enterprise architecture but vary in their focus, scope, and intent.

Most are developed with particular domains (e.g., mission-critical defence applications or IT for large organizations) in mind. Some frameworks focus mainly on the kinds of information (e.g., types of models or data) required documenting an enterprise architecture. Others are more strategically oriented, providing guidance on organizing evolution from current to future enterprise architectures. Some frameworks also include reference catalogues of standard technology parts from which to build compliant systems.

5.5   *Evaluate and Select an EA Framework*[4]

As each organization embarks on this stage of the enterprise architecture process, it must also select an appropriate enterprise architectural framework. A

> **Framework** – a logical structure for classifying and organizing complex information.

number of well-established EA frameworks are successfully used throughout industry and the governmental sector. An Enterprise Architecture framework is a communication model for developing an Enterprise Architecture (EA). It is not an enterprise architecture per se. Rather; it presents a set of models, principles, services, approaches, standards, design concepts, components, visualizations and configurations that guide the development of specific aspect enterprise architectures.

For more information about selecting EA frameworks and descriptions of 15 well known EA frameworks, read the book "How to survive in the jungle of Enterprise Architecture Frameworks".

5.5.1   Creating an Enterprise Architecture Framework or...

Creating a framework for an enterprise may be as simple as tweaking an existing framework or as complicated as inventing your own. In most cases, you will not have to start completely from scratch.

Even if you decide to adapt an existing framework, you still have a fair amount of work. You will need to customize it to suit your organizational culture and vocabulary, for example. You will also need to put the framework through several dry runs, which will inevitably generate some lessons learned.

---

[4] *Book "How to survive in the jungle of Enterprise Architecture Frameworks", Author, J. Schekkerman; Publisher Trafford, Canada; ISBN 141201607-X*

Be prepared to spend some time refining and adding more details to the new framework because you will not get it right the first time.

o   A first step in creating the framework is to carefully evaluate and understand your enterprise business environment.
o   Second, you have to define the goals and objectives of the framework to serve.
o   Third, you have to check which existing framework fits best to your enterprise business environment and goals & objectives.
o   Fourth, you have to customize the existing framework to your needs and define the appropriate modelling techniques.
o   Fifth, you have to check your new framework through several dry runs.
o   Sixth, you have to define your lessons learned and refine the framework and the accompanied processes.

You cannot possibly decide on the framework structure without these steps. For example, most major governmental organizations are large and highly decentralized with rapidly changing business requirements. Thus, it has to be able to develop enterprise applications consistently and in keeping with the pace of its enterprise business mission.

Guidance by experienced Enterprise Architecture Framework designers / architects can speed up the development of your own framework and can prevent you from making common mistakes.

5.5.2   Choosing an Enterprise Architecture framework

Although there are several frameworks from which to choose and they are directed at different communities, they share many objectives and approaches.

There is value in understanding more than one framework if they add to your set of concepts and problem-solving approaches. If one framework has most of the things you need, but lacks something, identify the gaps, which you can then possibly fill by borrowing from another framework.
This book delivers you an overview of the most popular Enterprise Architecture Frameworks, their history and characteristics helping the reader in choosing the appropriate one.

The primary concerns in choosing a framework are the **stakeholders** and the **domain**.

One of the fundamental uses of enterprise architecture descriptions is to **communicate** with all stakeholders.

Enterprise Architectural views must provide information that stakeholders need in a way that they can assimilate and use. Different kinds of visualizations address different specific stakeholder concerns.

Fundamentally, the problem with Enterprise Architecture is

'Communication'

5.5.3   Examples of common used Enterprise Architecture frameworks

Four (and commonly accepted) enterprise architectural frameworks are used as candidate frameworks and for descriptive purposes within this EA guide. These contain essential and supporting results, and promote development of enterprise architectures that are complete, understandable, and integratable.   The organizations that developed these frameworks continue to tailor them to ensure parallel precepts, principles, and methodologies. Possible frameworks are:

o   US Federal Enterprise Architecture Framework (FEAF), developed by the USA federal government;

o   US Department of Defence Architecture Framework (DoDAF), developed by the USA Ministry of Defence;

o   Extended Enterprise Architecture Framework (E2AF), developed by the Institute For Enterprise Architecture Developments, the Netherlands.

o   Zachman EA Framework, developed by John Zachman.

The use of an EA framework ensures uniformity and standardization when migrating and integrating business and IT. The selected framework will depend on the intended use, scope, and characteristics of the enterprise architecture to be developed. Table 4 lists major factors to consider.

Areas	Factors
Policy	o Regulatory and legislative direction o Organization policy o Compatibility need with another organization or joint policy
Extended Environment	o Extended context for the enterprise—e.g., being part of a "Value Network" o External drivers – e.g., Customer groups, Partners, Int. Law & Legislations
Enterprise	o Experience with a particular framework o Mandates and drivers—e.g., emphasis on business versus infrastructure or operational versus technical issues (countervailing power)
EA results	o Priorities, intended uses and desired level of detail—e.g., large scale modernization versus stable business & IT environment o Resource and schedule constraints on modelling efforts o Availability of existing enterprise architecture results

Table 4. Framework Selection Criteria

Frameworks include concepts that drive the types of enterprise architecture results being created. The results, both graphical and textual, capture the information prescribed by the framework. Equivalent results may be substituted if the new results have similar or more extensive attributes than the original results. This is often done when specific methods (e.g. object-oriented analysis and design) lend themselves to particular modelling techniques.

Using the Zachman EA framework, DoDAF, FEAF or the E2AF framework should substantially reduce the development

Method – a prescribed way of approaching a particular problem.

process and will shorten the time to get an EA in place and put an organization on a path for success. The following sections provide a brief description of the FEAF, and E2AF frameworks.

5.5.4   Federal Enterprise Architecture Framework, USA [5]

In September 1999, the Federal CEA Council published the *Federal Enterprise Architecture Framework, Version 1.1* for developing an EA within any organization or for a system that transcends multiple inter-organization boundaries. It builds on common business practices and designs those cross-organizational boundaries. The FEAF provides an enduring standard for developing and documenting enterprise architecture descriptions of high-priority areas. It provides guidance in describing enterprise architectures for multi-organizational functional segments of the Federal Government. These Federal architectural reference models collectively constitute the Federal EA.

Version 2.2 of the FEA reference model is published in July 2007 and consists of a set of interrelated "reference models" designed to facilitate cross-agency analysis and the identification of duplicative investments, gaps and opportunities for collaboration within and across organizations. Collectively, the reference models comprise a framework for describing important elements of the FEA in a common and consistent way.

Through the use of this common framework and vocabulary, IT portfolios can be better managed and leveraged across the federal government.

As shown in Figure 14, the FEAF consists of five FEA reference models:
   o   Performance Reference Model (PRM)
   o   Business Reference Model (BRM)
   o   Service Component Reference Model (SRM)
   o   Technical Reference Model (TRM)
   o   Data Reference Model (DRM)

---

[5] *FEA Consolidated Reference Model Document Version 2.2 July 2007; http://www.whitehouse.gov*

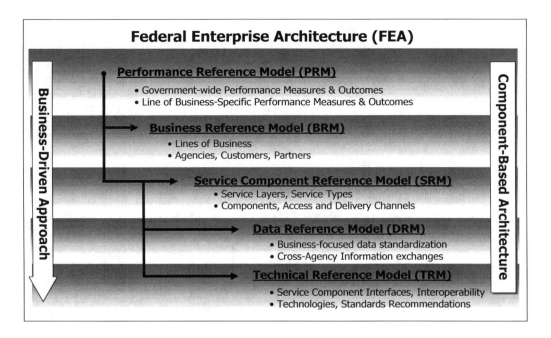

Figure 14. Structure of the FEAF Components

Performance Reference Model (PRM)

The PRM is a framework for performance measurement providing common output measurements throughout the federal government. It allows organizations to better manage the business of government at a strategic level, by providing a means for using an agency's EA to measure the success of IT investments and their impact on strategic outcomes. The PRM accomplishes these goals by establishing a common language by which agency EA's can describe the outputs and measures used to achieve program and business objectives. The model articulates the linkage between internal business components and the achievement of business and customer-centric outputs. Most importantly, it facilitates resource-allocation decisions based on comparative determinations of which programs and organizations are more efficient and effective. The PRM focuses on three main objectives:

o Help produce enhanced performance information to improve strategic and daily decision making

o Improve the alignment and better articulate the contribution of inputs to outputs, thereby creating a clear "line of sight" to desired results

o Identify performance improvement opportunities that span traditional organizational structures and boundaries

Business Reference Model (BRM)

The BRM provides a framework facilitating a functional (rather than organizational) view of the federal government's lines of business (LoBs), including its internal operations and its services for citizens, independent of the organizations, bureaus and offices performing them. The BRM describes the federal government around common business areas instead of through a stove piped, agency-by-agency view. It thus promotes agency collaboration and serves as the underlying foundation for the FEA and E-Gov strategies.

Service Component Reference Model (SRM)

The SRM is a business-driven, functional framework classifying Service Components according to how they support business and performance objectives. It serves to identify and classify horizontal and vertical Service Components supporting federal organizations and their IT investments and assets. The model aids in recommending service capabilities to support the reuse of business components and services across the federal government. IT investments can be service providers or consumers. Service providers allow consumers to reuse their business and technical capabilities.

Data Reference Model (DRM)

The DRM is a flexible and standards-based framework to enable information sharing and reuse across the federal government via the standard description and discovery of common data and the promotion of uniform data management practices.

Technical Reference Model (TRM)

The TRM is a component-driven, technical framework categorizing the standards and technologies to support and enable the delivery of Service Components and capabilities. It also unifies existing agency TRM's and E-Gov guidance by providing a foundation to advance the reuse and standardization of technology and Service Components from a government-wide perspective. Aligning agency capital investments to the TRM leverages a common, standardized vocabulary, allowing interagency discovery, collaboration, and interoperability. Agencies and the federal government will benefit from economies of scale by identifying and reusing the best solutions and technologies to support their business functions, mission, and future enterprise architecture.

5.5.5   Extended Enterprise Architecture Framework (E2AF), IFEAD [6]

The Extended Enterprise Architecture (E2A) Framework is developed by the Institute For Enterprise Architecture Developments in 2002 and is based on ideas and influences of other frameworks as well as real life experience in using several frameworks. The influences of the Zachman framework, EAP (Enterprise Architecture Planning), IAF (Integrated Architecture Framework) and the Federal Enterprise Architecture Framework can be found in this framework. The framework is the results of several years experience in using enterprise architecture frameworks.

See for a more detailed explanation about the Extended Enterprise Architecture Framework, **Appendix F.**

---

[6] *Extended Enterprise Architecture Framework(E2AF)sm; Institute For Enterprise Architecture Developments; http://www.enterprise-architecture.info*

5.5.5.1 *Purpose of the E2AF; The Extended Enterprise business model*

In a world populated by value creating and value exchanging entities, often the decision will come down to owning one of three fundamental value propositions. You will either be able to own the customer, own the content that the customer seeks to acquire, or own the infrastructure that allows the content to be produced or the value to be exchanged. Each has a different business model. Each exploits a unique core competence. Each employs a different means of generating economic returns. However, in the connected economy, attempting to own all of them simultaneously will increasingly become a game of diminishing returns. When the network allows competitors to fill the gaps in their offerings at no additional cost, owning all of these competencies only increases risk without necessarily increasing returns.

As the factors that make up the economic environment change under the influence of the Internet, we can begin to anticipate how and where they will alter the cohesion and boundaries of the entities that make up the extended enterprise. We can estimate which industries and business models will likely become threatened and which will likely survive. In the process, we can redefine the way in which our organizations will participate and continue to create value for customers and shareholders alike. In the technology, we choose the possibilities that fit best to this collaborative environment.

The extended enterprise architecture framework (E2AF) reflects the latest developments in the area of extended enterprise architectures and supports collaboration and communication with all (extended) stakeholders involved. *See **Section 15** for more information about planning for the Extended Enterprise.*

5.5.5.2 *Scope*

Within the decade, we will see highly intelligent enterprises come to dominate their space. As noted, they will capitalize on the technology to withstand shocks and to maximize fit with the environment. They will utilize their adaptiveness to shape and execute real-time strategic options. Make no mistake - these will not be simply "learning organizations" - but instead action-based entities that attack open space, defend instinctively, and anticipate possibilities. For organizations that do not upgrade their capabilities to competitively adaptive levels, difficulties will multiply rapidly.

Costs will appear out of control vis-à-vis the best-evolving players and historical knowledge of customers will quickly decay in value. In defence, the smarter of these players will elect to outsource large pieces of their core businesses to superior firms and then recombine the pieces imaginatively to suit specific opportunities - thus creating a modular or plug-and-play capability that is both strong and flexible and that extends their original boundaries.

The Extended Enterprise Architecture Framework is dealing with the processes and activities of the extended Enterprise beyond its original boundaries, defining a collaborative environment for all entities involved in a collaborative process.

5.5.5.3 *Principles*

Extended Enterprise Architecture is not a panacea for all problems in the world of business and information & communication technology in and outside the enterprise. It serves its own specific objectives and has to be used when appropriate. Extended Enterprise Architecture is driving enterprises to its boundaries.

The major principles of an E2A program, supported by the E2A framework are:

- o Create and maintain a common vision of the future shared by both the business and IT, driving continuous business/IT alignment
- o Create a holistic, end-to-end future-state enterprise architecture process that accurately reflects the business strategy of the enterprise
- o Build agility by lowering the "complexity barrier," an inhibitor of change
- o Increase the flexibility of the enterprise in linking with external partners
- o Develop a proactive organization capable of meeting customer demands, outpacing the competition, and driving innovation
- o Reduce risk and prepare the enterprise for rapid, unplanned change
- o Avoid the pitfalls of business-unit IT functions operating at odds with one another
- o Institute a program of progressive technology refinement
- o Create, unify, and integrate business processes across the enterprise
- o Unlock the power of information, unifying information silos that hinder corporate initiatives such as customer relationship management and e-business
- o Eliminate duplicate and overlapping technologies, decreasing support costs
- o Reduce solution delivery time and development costs by maximizing reuse of technology, information, and business applications

To accomplish this, the Extended Enterprise Architecture approach must be:

- o **Holistic in Scope:** It must address all aspects of the Extended Enterprise and directly associated with business technology alignment: business structure, Business activities, business processes, information flows, information-systems, and infrastructure, standards, policies. The notion of "Extended Enterprising" is growing in importance, and extends stakeholder status to include external value net members.   Most enterprise architecture efforts are too inwardly focused, and do not include the customer and key business partners.   This results in miss-aligned enterprise architectures, and lost opportunities to gain competitive advantage and government effectiveness. The "Extended Enterprising" focus directly supports Business 2 Business initiatives, E-Business and cross- community initiatives critical to global banking and communication today.

- o **Collaboration Based:** The effort must include representatives from all key stakeholders and value net members into the EA program: Business Domains, Senior Management, Business Partners, and customers.   This is critical to obtaining "buy-in," ongoing support and business / partner, customer alignment and collaboration.

o **Alignment Driven:** It must address the need to directly align 'extended' business and technology drivers in a way that is comprehensible and transparent to all key stakeholders, with a continued process of tracing enterprise architecture initiatives to the business strategy.

o **Value Driven:** It must provide mechanisms to define business cases that help ensure and demonstrate the business value of enterprise architecture solutions.

o **Dynamic Environments:** It must include analytical methods that support the development of extended enterprise architectures that are flexible and dynamic to changing business drivers, new opportunities or roadblocks, and enterprise architectures that provide transformation options that mitigate risks and are flexible and dynamic to budget and other organizational constraints.

o **Normative Results:** It must provide the ability to define solution sets that can be measured, validated and mapped to real world solutions.

o **Non-Prescriptive:** It must not presume an implementation approach. That is out of the scope of the Enterprise Architecture program.

5.5.5.4 *Structure*

The E2A Framework is a clear concept with powerful implications. By understanding any particular aspect of an organization at any point in its evolution, enterprise architects construct a tool that can be very useful in making decisions about changes or extensions.
The framework contains 4 rows and 6 columns yielding 24 unique cells or aspect levels.

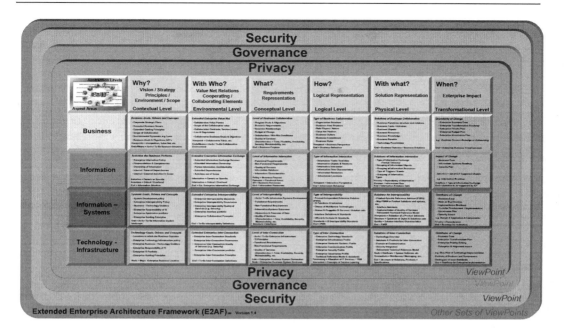

Figure 15. Extended Enterprise Architecture Framework (E2AF)

5.5.5.5 *Separation of Concerns*

'Separation of concerns' allow us to deal with conflict of interest between these concerns. We distinguish six main levels of concern within extended enterprise architecture studies often called levels of abstraction:

- o **The Contextual level,** describing the extended context of the organization and the scope of the Enterprise Architecture study. **Why**; Describes the motivations of the enterprise. This reveals organizations mission, vision and scope and the business & technology drivers.

- o **The Environmental level,** describing the formal extended business relations and the related information flows. **With Who**; Represents the business & technology relationships within the extended enterprise. The type of collaboration. The design of the extended enterprise organization has to do with the value proposition in the net and the structure of governance within the extended enterprise.

- o **The Conceptual level,** addressing the Requirements. **What**; Describes the goals and objectives and the requirements of organizations entities involved in each aspect area of the enterprise.

- o **The Logical level,** addressing the ideal logical solutions. **How**; Shows the logical solutions within each aspect area.

o *The Physical level*, addressing the physical solution of results & techniques. **With What**; Shows physical solutions in each aspect area, including business & communication changes, supporting software results and tools, hardware & communication results.

o *The Transformational level*, describing the impact for the organization of the proposed solutions. **When**; Represents the transformation roadmap, dependencies within aspect areas, supported by business cases.

5.5.5.6 Decomposition of the Enterprise

The 4 rows represent the different aspect areas of the Enterprise:

o **Business or Organization**; starting point and expressing all business elements and structures in scope.
o **Information**; extracted from the business an explicit expression of information needs, flows and relations is necessary to identify the functions that can be automated.
o **Information - Systems**; the automated support of specific functions.
o **Technology - Infrastructure**; the supporting technology environment for the information systems.

All these aspect areas have to be related to each other in such a way that a coherent set of relations can be identified. Integration of these aspect areas is a necessity for an Enterprise Architectural design.

5.5.5.7 Enterprise Architectural Viewpoints

Besides the aspect areas of Enterprise Architecture, specific views can be created, based on specific viewpoints or themes. Examples of viewpoints are 'Security', 'Governance' and 'Compliance'. The impact of viewpoints should be incorporated in the extended enterprise architecture results at all levels.

5.5.5.8 EA results

The E2A approach can deliver several results depending on the scope and the goals and objectives of the Enterprise Architecture approach. Visualizing results to communicate and share with all stakeholders is one of the key results of the E2A approach, where the E2A framework serves as a guide for all stakeholders involved.

5.5.5.9 Guidance

Extracted from the E2A framework an Extended Enterprise Architecture approach can be defined to deal with the goals & objectives of the organization. Most of the prescriptive guidance is given through publications and supporting services.

5.5.5.10 Compliance

The Extended Enterprise Architecture Framework is a standard, written by an Enterprise Architecture professional institute. The E2A framework can be used to deal with several compliance rules of different organizations (DNB, SEC, AFM, Basel II, ...) See **Section 12** for more information about EA & Compliance.

5.6   Analyze Stakeholders and Define Viewpoint sets

An enterprise stakeholder analysis is a technique you can use to identify and assess the importance of key people, groups of people, or institutions that may significantly influence the success of your activities or your organization.

5.6.1   Identify your Enterprise Stakeholders

The first step in the enterprise stakeholder analysis is to brainstorm who the enterprise stakeholders are. As part of this, think of all the groups of people who are affected by the organization, who have influence or power over it, or have an interest in its successful or unsuccessful conclusions.

The table below shows some of the groups of people who might be stakeholders of your Enterprise:

Management	Shareholders	Government
Senior executives	Alliance partners	Trades associations
Co-workers	Suppliers	The press
Employee groups	Lenders	Interest groups
Customers	Analysts	The public
Prospective customers	Future recruits	The community

Figure 16. Stakeholder Groups

Remember that although enterprise stakeholders may be both organizations and groups of representing people, ultimately you must communicate with individuals. Make sure that you identify the correct individual enterprise stakeholders within a stakeholder organization.

5.6.2   Prioritize Your Enterprise Stakeholders

You may now have a long list of groups of people and organizations that are influencing the enterprise. Some of these may have the power either to block or advance. Some may be interested in what you are doing, others may not care.
Map out your stakeholder groups using the Power /

Interest Grid shown in the next figure and classify them by their power over the enterprise and by their interest in the enterprise. For example, management is likely to have high power and influence over the enterprise and high interest. Analysts may have high interest, but are unlikely to have power over it.

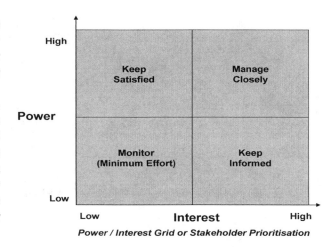

Power / Interest Grid or Stakeholder Prioritisation

Figure 17. Power / Interest Grid

Someone's position on the grid shows you the actions you have to take with them:

- o **High power, interested groups of people:** these are the groups of people you must fully engage and make the greatest efforts to satisfy. Their viewpoints must been considered with a high importance.
- o **High power, less interested groups of people:** put enough work in with these groups of people to keep them satisfied, but not so much that they become bored with your message. Their viewpoints play a role but don't focus too much at them.
- o **Low power, interested groups of people:** keep these groups of people adequately informed, and talk to them to ensure that no major issues are arising. Their viewpoints can play an important role but balance them against the high power interested groups of people.
- o **Low power, less interested groups of people:** again, monitor these groups of people, but do not bore them with excessive communication.

5.6.3   Understanding your key Enterprise Stakeholders

Now the enterprise architects need to know more about the key enterprise stakeholder groups. You need to know how they are likely to feel about and react to the enterprise architecture activities and results. You also need to know how best to engage them in your (extended) enterprise architecture program and how best to communicate with them.

Key questions that can help the enterprise architecture group to understand enterprise stakeholders are:

- o   What financial or emotional interest do they have in the outcome of the enterprise architecture program? Is it positive or negative?
- o   What motivates them most of all?

- o What information do they want from you?
- o How do they want to receive information from you? What is the best way of communicating your message to them?
- o What is their current opinion about the enterprise architecture activities? Is it based on good information?
- o Who influences their opinions generally, and who influences their opinion of the enterprise architecture group? Do some of these influencers therefore become important stakeholders in their own right?
- o If they are not likely to be positive, what will win them around to support the enterprise architecture activities?
- o If you don't think you will be able to win them around, how will you manage their opposition?
- o Who else might be influenced by their opinions? Do these groups of people become stakeholders in their own right?

A very good way of answering these questions is to talk to your enterprise stakeholder group's representatives directly - people are often quite open about their views, and asking people's opinions is often the first step in building a successful relationship with them.

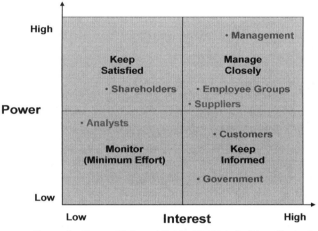

Example: Power / Interest Grid with Stakeholders Marked

Figure 18. Power / Interest Grid with stakeholders

You can summarize the understanding you have gained on the enterprise stakeholder map, so that you can easily see which enterprise stakeholders are expected to be blockers or critics, and which enterprise stakeholders are likely to be advocates and supporters of the enterprise architecture program. A good way of doing this is by colour coding: showing advocates and supporters in green, blockers and critics in red, and others who are neutral in orange.

5.6.4   Weighting Extended Enterprise Stakeholders Viewpoints

After identifying the power and interests of extended enterprise stakeholders, their corresponding sets of viewpoints has to be weighted against two dimensions.

- o Priority in terms of contributing to the goals and objectives of the enterprise.
- o Dependency in terms of how difficult is it to fulfil the needs of this group of enterprise stakeholders.

Enterprise Stakeholder Management (ESM) is the process by which you identify your key enterprise stakeholders and win their support. Enterprise stakeholder analysis is the first stage of this, where you identify and start to understand your most important extended enterprise stakeholders and their set of viewpoints.

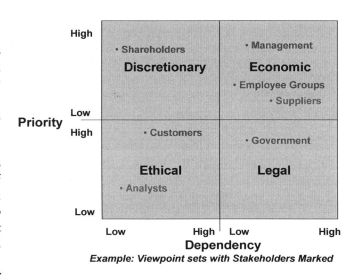

Example: Viewpoint sets with Stakeholders Marked

Figure 19. Power / Interest Grid grouped with viewpoint sets

The next step is to prioritize them by power and interest, and to plot this on a Power / Interest grid. The final stage is to get an understanding of what motivates your stakeholders, what is their set of viewpoints and how you need to win them around.

5.7   *Identify your Extended Enterprise Architecture Viewpoint Sets*

Extended Enterprise Architecture Views are representations of the overall enterprise architecture that are meaningful to **all** stakeholders in and outside the organization. The enterprise architect chooses and develops a set of views that will enable the enterprise architecture to be communicated to, and understood by, **all the stakeholders**, and enable them to verify that the Enterprise Architecture will address the generic concerns.

Extended Enterprise Architecture Viewpoint Sets are themes of viewpoints that can be determined based on different ways to look at the enterprise and its environment. From literature and best practices the following Extended Enterprise Architecture Viewpoint sets are generic and common for all extended enterprise architecture programs and activities and represents stakeholders' responsibilities. See **Appendix E** for more information about Views & Viewpoints.

5.7.1   Stakeholders responsibilities and their sets of viewpoints

Despite the variety of stakeholder groups and their demands in Enterprises, stakeholders' responsibilities can be classified into four broad sets of extended enterprise architecture viewpoints: **Economic**, **Legal**, **Ethical**, and **Discretionary** responsibilities. Strategic governance can therefore be defined as the extent to which organizations meet the responsibilities imposed by their various enterprise stakeholders.

5.7.2   Economic set of viewpoints

As social economic elements, organizations are expected to generate and sustain profitability, offer goods and services that are both desired and desirable in society and of a good quality, and reward employees and other elements that help create success. To satisfy these expectations, organizations develop strategies to keep abreast of changing customer / citizen needs, to compensate employees and investors fairly, and to continually improve and innovates the effectiveness and efficiency of organizational processes. A long-term perspective is essential when establishing these strategies: A responsible organization must continue to earn profits from its ongoing activities in order to benefit its stakeholders. Examples of economic viewpoints are: Benefits, Costs, Quality, Innovation, etc.

5.7.3   Legal set of viewpoints

Regardless of their economic achievements, organizations must abide by established laws and regulations in order to be good citizens. Even so the privacy legislations have to be respected. The identification of legal issues and implementation of compliancy requirements are the best approach to preventing violations and costly litigation. Accounting and control mechanism have to be in place according to the rules and legislations. Examples of legal viewpoints are: Law & Regulations, Privacy, Accounting & Assessment, etc.

5.7.4   Ethical set of viewpoints

The establishment of strict ethical standards in the workplace may also be an excellent way to prevent legal violations by creating a focus on integrity in management style. In addition, an organization guided by strong ethical values may also be better able to satisfy ethical responsibilities, the third type of responsibility imposed by enterprise stakeholders. Incorporating ethical standards and handling in the corporate culture will create respectful organizations where the corporate governance structure is reflecting these ethics and where people are involved in identifying legal violations, corporate risks and security vulnerabilities. Examples of Ethical viewpoints are: Culture, Strategy, risks, etc.

5.7.5   Discretionary set of viewpoints

In addition to meeting economic, legal, and ethical responsibilities, organizations are also expected to display a genuine concern for the general welfare of all constituencies. Companies must balance the costs of these discretionary activities against the costs of manufacturing and marketing their products or services in a responsible manner. Example of Discretionary viewpoints is: stakeholder groups individual perspectives or specific enterprise stakeholder themes, etc.

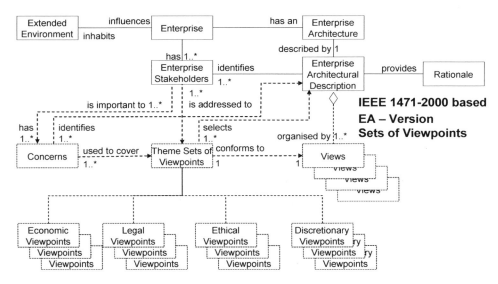

Figure 20. IEEE 1471-2000 EA Version with sets of viewpoints

5.8   *Define your EA Process Principles*

5.8.1   EA Process Principles in General

The following enterprise architecture process principles derive from best practices throughout a lot of complex enterprise architecture assignments.

They are identified as a starting point in the enterprise architecture process. Each individual organization, with unique needs and requirements, should first consider these, then modify, add to, or replace this list as appropriate to its purposes.

5.8.1.1 *Enterprise Architectures must be appropriately scoped, planned, and defined based on the intended use of the enterprise architecture.*

Rationale: The enterprise architecture development effort needs direction and guidance to meet expectations for specific uses of the enterprise architecture end results. Detailed models may not be needed for high-level decision-making; similarly, simple, descriptive enterprise architectures may not provide enough information to support engineering choices.

Implications: The enterprise architecture must be generated with a specific purpose and for a specific audience to ensure it meets the expectations of its intended stakeholders.

5.8.1.2 *Enterprise Architectures must be compliant with the law as expressed in legislative mandates, executive orders, Governmental regulations, and other Governmental guidelines.*

Rationale: Organizations must abide by laws, policies, and regulations. However, this does not preclude business process improvements that lead to changes in policies and regulations.

Implications: Organizations should be aware of laws, regulations, and external policies regarding the development of enterprise architectures and the collection, retention, management, and security of data. Changes in the law and changes in may drive changes in architectural processes or applications.

5.8.1.3 *Enterprise Architectures facilitate change.*

Rationale: In the rapidly changing Business & IT environment, organizations need tools to manage and control their business and technical growth and change. As the technical development life cycle shortens, with new technologies replacing older systems every 18 months, organizations require overarching enterprise architecture to capture their systems design and operating environment. Even so dynamics in business had to be supported by an enterprise architecture.

Implications: Systems developers and the enterprise architects should ensure the coordination between technology investments and business practices. Enterprise architectures must be used in the evaluation function of the Budget Planning and Investment Control process.

5.8.1.4 *Enterprise architectures must reflect the Business strategic plans.*

Rationale: The future enterprise architecture has maximum value when it is most closely aligned with the organization's strategic plans and other corporate-level direction, concepts, and planning.

Implications: The future enterprise architecture must be developed in concert with strategic planners as well as the operational staff. As the strategic plan changes, so do the future environment and the future enterprise architecture.

5.8.1.5 *Enterprise Architectures continuously change and require transformation.*

Rationale: The organization is constantly evolving towards its future. As today's enterprise architecture transformation to the future enterprise architecture, the future becomes the organization's baseline enterprise architecture at some point in the future. The baseline enterprise architecture continuously moves and transformations toward the to-be enterprise architecture as a continuous change of the as situation.

Implications: The to-be enterprise architecture is a rolling set of results, continually portraying the out-year environment. As a component of strategic planning and change management, the to-be architecture captures the future environment including all business requirements and systems transformations. The transformation plan is the organization's roadmap to systems migration.

5.8.1.6 *Future enterprise architectures should project no more than 1 to 3 years into the future.*

Rationale: Technology life cycles currently are in the neighbourhood of 6 - 12 months, and new IT products appear on the market every 12 - 18 months. Acquisition practices must be aligning to these rapid changes, which mean that an organization's future information needs and technical infrastructure requirements are changing just as rapidly. Consequently, no one can accurately predict what business practices will prevail 5 to 10 years into the future and what type of IT capabilities and resources will be available.

Implications: To-be enterprise architectures will need to be revised and updated regularly. The transformation plan, illustrating intermediate points in time, may become more valuable than the future enterprise architectures.

5.8.1.7 *Enterprise Architectures provide standardized business descriptions and common operating environments (COEs).*

Rationale: Commonality improves interoperability, cost avoidance, and convergence. For example, the integration of enterprise architectural Activity Models and Operational Transformation Diagrams (on the business side) and the Technical Reference Model and technology forecasts (on the technical side) helps establish a COE within the organization's logical and physical infrastructures.

Implications: The systems architect and the enterprise architect must ensure the coordination between technology investments and business practices. A COE grounded on standard business practices yields improved information structures.

5.8.1.8 *Enterprise Architecture results are only as good as the information collected from subject matter experts and domain owners.*

Rationale: The enterprise architect is not vested with the organizational information. It is incumbent upon the enterprise architect to collect the needed enterprise architectural information from the members of the organization who possess the knowledge of the business processes and associated information. These subject matter experts tend to be process owners, operational staff, field representatives, systems developers, software designers, users, etc. The domain owners are the responsible managers of specific business areas.

Implications: The development of the enterprise architecture can be a slow process, dependent on the enterprise architect's access to subject matter experts and domain owners. The validity of the enterprise architecture can be limited by the accuracy of the collected information. Development of the enterprise architecture is an iterative process of information gathering and interviewing to obtain verification and validity checks of the architectural results.

5.8.1.9 Enterprise Architectures minimize the burden of information collection, streamline information storage, and enhance information access.

Rationale: Information, as a corporate asset, is key to an organization's mission, vision, goals, objectives and daily work routine. The more efficiently an organization gathers information, stores and retrieves that information, and uses the information, the more productive the organization. Information is power.

Implications: Business processes are best improved by streamlining the flow and use of data and information. The development of enterprise architectural Node Connectivity Descriptions, Information Exchange Matrices, and other information models will aid in the design of improved data management systems.

5.8.1.10 To-be enterprise architectures should be used to control the growth of technical diversity.

Rationale: The rapid adoption of new and innovative IT products can easily lead to introducing a diverse set of IT products that may not always be fully compatible within the existing enterprise infrastructure. This necessitates the selection and implementation of proven market technologies.

Implications: The to-be enterprise architecture must be used in conjunction with the organization's investment review process and technology insertion plans. Relying on the enterprise architecture as an integral component of Business & IT decision-making helps control the introduction of incompatible solutions.

5.9 Define or Select your EA Process

There are several generic EA process approaches available today that will help the Enterprise Architect in defining the appropriate process steps to achieve the defined goals. Most common in this area are the EA process cycle from IFEAD and the Architecture Development Method (ADM)[7] from TOGAF.

5.9.1 Enterprise Architecture Process - IFEAD

IFEAD is using now for several years a process model that combines the different aspect areas as addressed in for example the Extended Enterprise Architecture Framework with a process model that describes the major EA process steps you will find in every EA trajectory.

---

[7] *ADM and TOGAF are trademarks / service marks from the Open Group. http://www.opengroup.org*

5.9.1.1 Standard EA Process Phases.

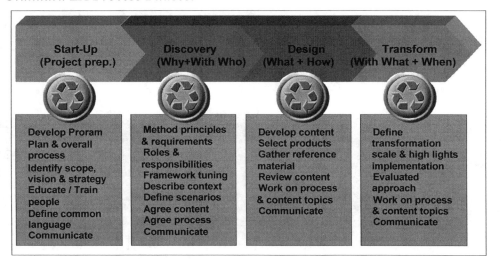

Figure 21. Standard Enterprise Architecture Process Phases

o   A four phase generic process model starting in the first phase with organizing your EA work stream like a normal program / project.

o   The second phase is called the discovery phase, where the enterprise architects together with the critical stakeholders discover the real goal and objectives to achieve. Even so in this phase the principles, rules, guidelines and standards as well as the requirements have to be identified. In this phase questions have to be answered dealing with: **Why** do we want an Enterprise Architecture, so the definition of goals and objectives. Another question in this phase is the **With Who** question. Who are the (extended) parties / partners / stakeholders that have to be involved in the EA process and what their influence is. (formal as well as informal)

o   The third phase is called the design phase where we have to answer the questions of: **What** do we really have / want and **How** could we achieve that. The What questions is also the question about the requirements and quality of services. The How question is dealing with logical descriptions or visualizations that represent possible logical scenarios.

o   The fourth phase has to deal with the transformation steps from a current situation to a future. Questions in this phase are **With What** kind of solutions do we achieve our goals and **When** (timeframe) do we achieve these goals or intermediate steps in the direction of these goals.

The Why, With-Who, What, How, With-What and When questions are strongly related to the Enterprise Architecture areas addressed in most of the EA frameworks. So EA process steps and EA content topics strongly relate.

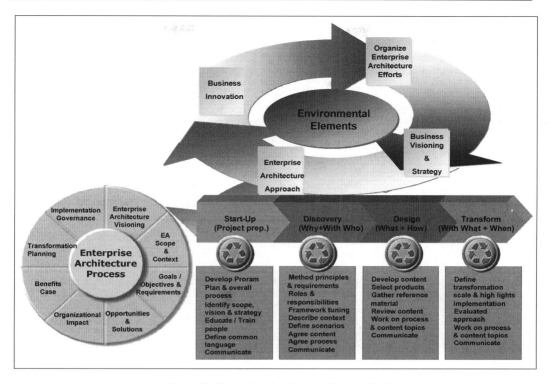

Figure 22. Enterprise Architecture Process Environment

5.9.1.2 *Enterprise Architecture Process Model*

This standard EA process approach can be more refined in addressing the individual EA Process steps that the enterprise architect will help in achieving its goals.

The detailed steps in the Enterprise Architecture process are addressing the following topics:

1. **Enterprise Architecture Visioning:** Related to the Business Mission, Vision and Strategy the External Environment, Business Drivers, Guiding Principles are identified.
2. **EA Scope & Context:** What is the precisely defined scope and context of an EA program / project? Scope creep is one of the fail factors during EA trajectories. A clear definition of the scope will help the enterprise architects in managing their trajectories on time and within the defined budget. Be aware of scoop creep.
3. **EA Goals / Objectives & Requirements:** What are the goals and objectives to achieve by starting an EA trajectory? I have seen several discussions with enterprise architects about the EA activities as well as the EA results or deliverables in organizations without knowing the business goals & objectives. I asked them then, what are your business goals & objectives to achieve with this EA trajectory? Very often the business goals & objectives

are unclear or even unknown, therefore it is very important that up-front the business goals & objectives are shared and mandated by the critical stakeholders, so that all key people involved in the EA process are familiar with the business goals & objectives. Never start an EA program / project / trajectory without a clear understanding of the business goals & objectives. Other important elements are the requirements. The functional as well as the non-functional requirements (Quality of Services) have to be identified or defined. A good practice to identify the Quality of Services is defined in the Space Ufo method developed under auspicious of the European Union. (System Product Advanced Certification and Evaluation - User Focus). IFEAD has adopted the ideas and principles of the Space Ufo method and transformed that method for use in the Enterprise Architecture Domain, called the EA Space Ufo method. Core element of the EA Space Ufo method is the ISO 9126[8] standard for Quality of Services. See **Appendix H** for more information about the EA Space Ufo Method.

4. **Opportunities & Solutions:** In this step we identify opportunities and solutions based on scenarios derived from the different EA results of the description of the current and or the prescription of the future EA and the transformation steps to move from the current to the future situation. Most of the time the description of the current situation is based on an inventory of the current business situation as well of the current information technology situation based on documents, interviews, etc. and the mapping to each other. You need to realize that your EA results have to support decision making of management so the level of detail of your descriptions is only relevant in that context. With that in mind as well as your goals & objectives, the enterprise architects have to define with kind of models / results / visualizations do we have to create to support the business goals & objectives? So define up-front the different type of models / visualizations / documents as well as the different viewpoints relevant for the key stakeholders. Your EA results for the future situation have to be in line with the organizations future mission, vision and strategy as well as their future ambitions, etc. Most of the time the future EA is focused on the business drivers, the guiding principles as well the EA concepts to adopt.

5. **Organizational impact:** Based on the Business strategy, IT strategy and the Governance strategy, different scenarios / concepts can be identified that contribute to the future situation. Working out these scenarios/ concepts will show the organizational impact and risks for each of these scenarios/ concepts and will help in choosing the most preferred / appropriate scenario.

6. **Benefits / Business Case:** The most preferred / appropriate scenario will be worked out in terms of a benefits or business case. It is important to have a benefits / business case template that will help in addressing all of the relevant financial and or quality elements that are in scope of the preferred scenario. Your CFO or financial controller can help you in defining an excepted business case template. Not only the investment costs but also the

---

[8] *NEN-ISO/IEC 9126-1:2001 * System engineering - Product Quality Model: (functionality, reliability, usability, efficiency, maintainability, portability)*

operations costs have to be part of the business case. Even so costs of own personnel have to be part of the business case. Added value for the organization have to be defined in clear (measurable) terms so that no discussion will take place about the outcome of the business case. When the business case is adopted / accepted by the management (CEO, CFO or CIO) the transformation planning can start.

7. **Transformation Planning:** Based on the current EA results, the future preferred EA scenario and the supporting business case a transformation planning can be defined in line with the organizations ambition. Transformation steps can be defined; timeframes can be setup as well as a resource / capability planning to move forward. For each transformation step a financial / budget model as well as a resource / capability model has to be setup to guarantee continuity in the transformation plan. This transformation plan is a change plan for organization and IT. Depending on the organizational / IT impact changes will be implemented separately or concurrent.

8. **Implementation Governance structure:** It is very important to set up de right implementation organization in such a way that in line with the transformation planning, changes can be implemented. So you need to define your implementation governance organization with all the critical stakeholders involved. A combined business and IT implementation organization need to be set up with a steering or management committee, implementation teams, a responsible enterprise program manager, the enterprise architects involved in a controlling role, etc.

5.9.1.3 *Using the EA Spiral Approach within the EA Process*

The starting point for the EA spiral approach is in the middle of the spiral, adapting the idea of *"Think Big but Start Small"* so the cycles of the spiral are continuous learning curves for the enterprise architects and the stakeholders, it combines the benefits of the incremental and evolutionary approaches on a spiral way.

So start your first iteration with a limited scope and limit goals & objectives, learn from your first steps in approaching the EA process.

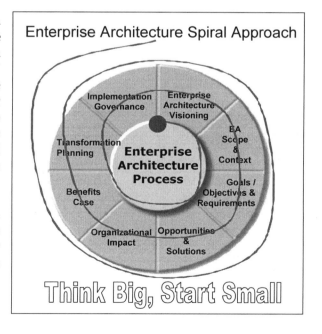

Figure 23. EA Spiral Approach & Process

The EA spiral approach addresses all steps of the enterprise architecture process & results after the first process cycle. Evaluate after the first iteration your EA process and results, get buy-in from the key stakeholders and enhance the project scope, EA process & results for the second and third, etc. iteration.

But even from start, Think Big but Start Small. So have all the elements of the whole Enterprise in mind when starting, but focus on a limited scope, process and result so that the enterprise architects can learn from their experience.

5.9.2   TOGAF Architecture Development Method[9]

TOGAF Architecture Development Method *[ADM]*, which explains how to derive an organisation-specific enterprise architecture that addresses business requirements. The ADM provides:
- o   A reliable, proven way of developing the architecture;
- o   Architecture views, which enable the architect to communicate concepts;
- o   Linkages to practical case studies;
- o   Guidelines on tools for architecture development.

The Enterprise Architecture Continuum, which is a taxonomy for all the architecture assets, both within the enterprise and in the IT industry at large, that the enterprise may consider when developing architectures. At relevant places throughout the TOGAF ADM, there are reminders to consider which architecture assets from the Enterprise Continuum might be appropriate for reuse. TOGAF provides two reference models that may be the start of an organisation's Enterprise Continuum:

The TOGAF Foundation Architecture, an architecture of generic services and functions that provides a foundation on which specific architectures and architectural building blocks can be built. This Foundation Architecture in turn includes:
- o   TOGAF Technical Reference Model [TRM], which provides a model and taxonomy of generic platform services;
- o   TOGAF Standards Information Base [SIB], which is a database of open industry standards that can be used to define the particular services and other components of an enterprise-specific architecture;
- o   The Integrated Information Infrastructure Reference Model, which is based on the TOGAF Foundation Architecture and is meant to help design architectures that enable and support the vision of "Boundaryless Information Flow."

TOGAF Resource Base, which is a set of resources including guidelines, templates, and background information to help the architect in the use of the ADM.

---

[9] ©*Copyrights ADM & TOGAF, The Open Group; source: TOGAF version 8.x Enterprise Edition; http://www.opengroup.org/architecture/togaf/*

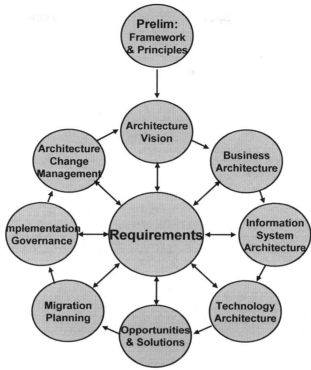

Figure 24. TOGAF – Architecture Development Method

The ADM is iterative, over the whole process, between phases, and within phases. For each iteration of the ADM, a fresh decision must be made as to:

1. Breadth of coverage of the enterprise to be defined;
2. Level of detail to be defined;
3. Extent of the time horizon aimed at, including the number and extent of any intermediate time horizons
4. Architectural assets to be leveraged in the organisation's Enterprise Continuum, including:
   o Assets created in previous iterations of the ADM cycle within the enterprise
   o Assets available elsewhere in the industry (e.g., other frameworks, systems models, or vertical industry models)

These decisions need to be made on the basis of a practical assessment of resource and competence availability and the value that can realistically be expected to accrue to the enterprise from the chosen scope of the architecture work.

As a generic method, the ADM is developed to be used by enterprises in a wide variety of different geographies and applied in different vertical sectors/industry types. As such, it may be, but does not necessarily have to be, tailored to specific needs.

*For more information about **TOGAF ADM see Appendix I.***

5.10   *Define or Select the Appropriate EA Results*

Essential results are those required for all enterprise architectures, while supporting results *may* be necessary to fulfil specific informational needs.   Only those supporting results that portray the desired characteristics should be created.   The required results should help formulate the selection of a framework and associated toolset.

It is essential that the Chief Enterprise Architect guide the development of the EA views and landscapes **to meet the needs of the Business & IT**, especially in the desired level of detail needed in the EA results. If the content is at too high level of abstraction, it may not be sufficiently useful to guide decision-making. If the content is too detailed, it may be difficult to oversee the impact and the risks.

> **Essential results** — the graphics, models, and/or narratives that every enterprise architecture description must include, to support the scope and characteristics of the EA.
>
> **Supporting results** — the graphics, models, and /or narratives that may be needed to further elaborate on essential products or to address particular domain or scope extensions (e.g. outsourcing or transformation considerations).

5.10.1   **Select EA Results that Represent the Business & IT of the Enterprise**

As the first step in identifying and creating the business definition, the Chief Enterprise Architect determines which results can be used to provide an integrated view of the organization core business.   These include functional, informational, and organizational models.
Depending on the scope, principles and goals & objectives to achieve during an EA trajectory, different EA results or deliverables can be the output of this EA trajectory.

> **Model** — representations of reality: the business, information, activities, relationships, and constraints.

5.10.2   **EA Results / Deliverables List (non limitative)**

To help organizations in defining their EA results a non limitative list of results or deliverables is developed based on the experiences within IFEAD, the US Department of Defence and the usage of the E2AF, DoDAF & FEAF.

These experiences and deliverables are the basis for this set of deliverables even so experiences and practices outside the Government & Defence world have enhanced this list with additional deliverables.

Use this list as a set of reference deliverables and select and enhance this list to your own situation depending on the goals and objectives to achieve.
Define and select your own modelling technique to visualise the models and diagrams to meet your stakeholder's demands.

Table 5. List of possible EA results

EA Results / Deliverables	Results	Description
Overview and Summary Information	EA-1	Description, purpose, scope, time frame and mission; optional external graphic
Mission & Vision Statements	EA-2	Description of the organizations mission and vision
Information Dictionary	EA-3	Enterprise Architecture Description Document (EAD), Report / Repository
Enterprise Architecture Principle Overview	EA-4	Overall table representing the weighted EA principles guiding the EA activities
Enterprise Architecture sets of Viewpoints	EA-5	Definition and description of relevant sets of viewpoints
Business Activity – Information Exchange Diagram	EA-6	Diagram representing Business processes and related information exchange items
Business Activity / Information Exchange – Systems Mapping	EA-7	Diagram representing Business processes / related information exchange items and related information systems
Information Systems –Mappings & Views	EA-8	Diagram representing the Information Systems and related Relational Database usage & positioning
Information Systems – Technical Infrastructure Mapping	EA-9	Diagram representing the Information Systems and related Technical Infrastructure
High-Level Business Concept Graphic	BA-1	Identified in repository as an External Graphic. Viewable in EA tool and incorporated in EA reports.
Business Node Connectivity Description	BA-2	Geographic diagram for Business Connections displaying the Business Nodes decomposition with Business Information exchanged and the Exchange Characteristics connecting internal and external nodes.
Organization Relationships Chart	BA-3	Hierarchy Diagram showing governance and coordination relationships of the Organization
Business Process & Activity Models	BA-4	Archimate, UML, BPMN, EFFBD, FFBD or IDEF0 representing behaviour models including control, input/output, sequencing and decomposition of Business Activities and relations. (processes)

Business Activity Sequence and Timing Descriptions	BA-5	Complete business activity model as Archimate, BPMN or IDEF0 including all relations. Optional output includes rules, a captured timeline file or an external event trace file.
Business Information Exchange Matrix	IA-1	A summary or full information exchange matrix listing Business Information exchanged and the Exchange Characteristics
Business Information Exchange Diagram	IA-2	A summary or full information exchange diagram listing Business Information exchanged and the Exchange Characteristics
Logical Information / Data Model	IA-3	Business Information characterization table
Information Systems Interface Description	ISA-1	Physical Diagram showing systems interface descriptions and standards; (external file that augments the system interface choice)
Information Systems Communications Description	ISA-2	Physical Diagram for communication components descriptions or an external file that augments the components
Information Systems Functionality Description	ISA-3	BPMN, EFFBD, FFBD, N2 or IDEF0 representing behaviour models including control, input/output, sequencing and decomposition of Functions
Business Activity to Systems Function Traceability Matrix	ISA-4	Matrix tracing between the Business Activities and Functions with an option to show the Component performing each Function.
Information System Evolution Description	ISA-5	An External File (text or graphic).
Information System Technology Forecast	ISA-6	Table containing technology forecast information for Components and their associated Interfaces, Links, Functions and Items.
Information System Activity Sequence and Timing Descriptions	ISA-7	Complete functional model as UML or EFFBDs diagrams. Optional output includes rules, a captured timeline file or an external event trace file.
Information Systems Physical Data Schema	ISA-8	Item characterization table / diagram and/or an External File.

| Technical Standards Profile | TA-1 | Table listing Standards governing the Components and their associated Interfaces, Links, Functions, and Items.) |
| Technical Reference Model (TRM) | TA-2 | Diagram showing Technical Services Categories governing the Components and their associated Interfaces, Links, Functions, and Items.) |

Figure 25. Example EA Deliverables List

The business definition should be created in the current and future enterprise architectures and the transformation plan. In the current enterprise architecture, it represents the current state of business operations and information exchange within and across the enterprise. In the transformation plan, it represents business changes and maps to planned systems and business improvements. In the future enterprise architecture, it represents planned business operations as expressed in business strategies and visions.

EA results created to support business content are often extended to represent the solution space. Thus, many of the models could be reused, extended, and referenced in order to define the technical architecture. The purpose of the technical architecture is to ensure that a conforming system satisfies a specific set of business needs and requirements. It provides the technical systems implementation guidelines. **Appendix J** will give examples of most of the listed results.

5.11   *Select an EA Toolset*

To increase the usefulness of any enterprise architecture, it is important to maintain the EA within an interactive architectural tool. Fortunately, there are many automated enterprise architecture tools available on the market today. The choice of tool should be predicated upon the organization's needs based on the size and complexity of its enterprise architecture.

The focus of enterprise architecture efforts is now shifting to become more holistic, thereby necessitating the use of comprehensive modelling tools to analyze and optimize the portfolio of business strategies, organizational structures, business processes / tasks and activities, information flows, applications, and technology infrastructure. Important to adoption of an enterprise architectural approach is the availability of tools to support the development, storage, presentation and enhancement of enterprise architecture representations. As with enterprise architecture methodologies, enterprise architecture tools to support the architectural development process are still emerging. High value is derived from consolidating this portfolio of business artefacts into a single repository in a standardized manner to support enterprise analysis and optimization.

5.11.1   Good Practice in EA Landscape Visualisations

However most management and decision making people like it to see visualisations that are in line with the image and culture of the company. Therefore more artistic visualisations in multi layer techniques are most of the time more efficient then the repository based drawings. These kinds of visualisations are mostly appreciated by CxO's and top management. Appendix G is explaining a way to create these artistic visualisations with Visio & PowerPoint. The counter side of these kinds of visualisations is that there is no control for consistency and related data is stored in separate documents. However for decision-making purposes this is most of the time not a problem.

So decide up front what you want to achieve with selecting an EA toolset and what you expect from the tool, then you can decide which kind of toolset fits the best in your situation. The EA Tool Review Framework will help you in this process.

5.11.2   EA Tools Review Framework©

To consistently review enterprise architecture tools a review framework is defined. The review framework consists of two dimensions: the basic functionality of the tool, and the utility of the tool to different professionals.

When reviewing an EA tool's basic functionality, the reviewer has to describe how well the tool performed the different functions needed for the enterprise architecture development activity. The tools basic functionality was examined in the following areas:

- o   Methodologies and Models;
- o   Model Development Interface;
- o   Tool Automation;
- o   Extendibility and Customization;
- o   Analysis and Manipulation;
- o   Repository;
- o   Deployment Architecture;
- o   Costs and Vendor Support.

The second dimension, the tool's utility to different professionals, captures the fitness for purpose of the tool, and describes how useful the tool would be to particular professionals. The types of professionals considered were:

- o   Enterprise Architects;
- o   Strategic Planners;
- o   Enterprise Program Managers.

See Appendix G for IFEAD's Enterprise Architecture Tool Selection Guide.

© *See IFEAD's, Enterprise Architecture Tool Selection Guidelines in Appendix D. or visit the website: http://www.enterprise-architecture.info*

5.11.3 Candidate Tool Requirements Checklist

First and foremost, objectives for acquiring and using a comprehensive modelling tool must be articulated and agreed to by all stakeholders. Since this tool is to support enterprise architecture, enterprise-level objectives must be included. Once that is accomplished, the objectives must be translated into requirements for both vendor presence and performance. Also, architectural principles both high-level conceptual and domain-level detailed must be included as screening criteria. Principles can either be converted into requirements or left as-is, requiring vendors to demonstrate their support of such principles.

The functional requirements of a tool must be understood prior to embarking on a selection. Only the functionality that is currently required of the tool or that which will be realistically necessary in the future should be selected.

There are toolsets available from leading vendors that can provide alignment with the chosen framework and recommended results. Tool criteria should be determined based on the intended use of the enterprise architecture, scope, levels of integration desired, and other factors. Appendix G lists candidate topics to aid in the selection of tools. The list can be tailored to a specific set of requirements for tool selection. One tool will probably not meet all requirements. Therefore, a tool suite or combination of tools will be needed. The work results should be maintained in several different types of media such as hardcopy documentation (briefings and reports), electronic files on CD-ROM, HTML documents on the web, and other EA Computer Aided Software Engineering (CASE) tools and development tools that provide a relational database management system.

Tool standardization is a recommended best practice. It proves cost-effective when determining enterprise architecture quality and alignment with the EA policy from an acquisition cost perspective and for consistent interoperability of models.

6   Develop the Enterprise Architecture

The next step is to develop the enterprise architecture results based on the purpose of the enterprise architecture and the chosen EA framework. This consists of the essential results, supporting results (if needed), and individually defined results (e.g., briefing charts, interview notes) driven by enterprise architecture specific needs and processes. To facilitate integration with other enterprise architectures, it is crucial to include all depictions of relationships with applicable external components, that is, entities outside the organization.

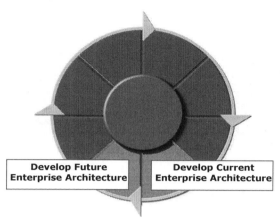

Develop Future Enterprise Architecture

Develop Current Enterprise Architecture

It may be useful, resources permitting, to conduct some proof-of-principle analysis at various stages of enterprise architecture development. For example, one could conduct trial runs of the EA development process using carefully selected subsets of the areas to be analyzed. The enterprise architecture core team should ensure that the results are consistent and properly interrelated. If the results are not applied and populated uniformly, the Chief Architect and enterprise architecture core team will be unable to compare or contrast the results or perform thorough analyses. Regardless of the scope and complexity of the views to be developed, the enterprise architecture core team should apply a consistent approach to developing the current and future enterprise architectures. The selected approach should include (1) a discovery and data collection phase, (2) design and preliminary result generation phase, (3) review and revision phases, and (4) publication and delivery of the enterprise architecture results to an appropriate repository. Figure 26 shows a typical process for developing the EA results. Each of these activities is described in more detail in the following subsections.

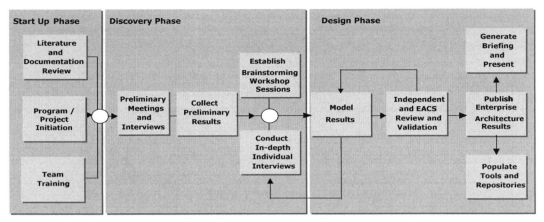

Figure 26. Approach for EA Development

6.1   Collect Information

The first step in the build approach is to identify and collect existing results that describe the enterprise as it exists today and as it is intended to look and operate in the future.   Discovery and data collection is the crucial, initial effort involving review of documentation, staging of training sessions, and interviewing SME's and domain owners.

> **Repository** — an information system used to store and access architectural information, relationships among the information elements, and work results.

All appropriate collected information and results should be placed in a centralized electronic EA repository. In the case of the current enterprise architecture, sample results to be collected include:

- o   Current organization model
- o   Current business processes & activities
- o   Current business functions and information flows
- o   Data models
- o   External interface descriptions
- o   Existing application and systems documentation
- o   Technical designs, specifications, and equipment inventories
- o   …..etc.

In the case of the future enterprise architecture, sample results to be collected include:

- o   Proposed organization model
- o   Proposed business processes and information flow models
- o   Strategic plans
- o   Value chain model
- o   Modernization plans
- o   Requirements documents
- o   ……….etc.

Many of these results may not exist or may not accurately represent the current baseline or proposed target environments. If documentation is missing, the enterprise architecture core team should develop a strategy to create the needed documentation or decide whether to make the investment. In this case, the interviewers will have to rely on business or system SME's concerning the purpose and scope of the activity and the expectations for their participation. After collecting a sufficient amount of this data, work can begin on creating the EA results and populating the EA repository.

Ideally, preliminary, draft enterprise architectural results can be generated at this time without in-depth SME involvement. With the development of strawman results, the enterprise architects can then conduct a series of stakeholder brainstorming sessions and in-depth SME interviews to solidify the results. The Chief Enterprise Architect should review and validate the proposed interview list and ensure SME participation via communications with the domain owners. The marketing and buy-in process described in Section 4 should have set the stage for this participation.

It may be useful to record these interviews for future reference. Always follow up to ensure that interview information is interpreted correctly. Once the initial interviews are completed, the enterprise architecture core team extracts information from the interviews and then refines the existing results within the EA repository.

6.2   *Create EA Results and Populate EA Repository*

Some results may be created during the first iteration of the EA development process while others may be created during later iterations depending on the framework, process, and chosen methods. In addition, depending on whether the current or the future is being created, various factors will affect the approach taken, the focus of the results, and the order in which results are generated. These key differentiators are described in Table 6.

	Current Enterprise Architecture	**Future Enterprise Architecture**
Process	Process applies the chosen framework and accompanied approach	Process applies the same framework as for Current
	Process relies extensively on existing documentation, e.g., process and procedure manuals	Documentation may not exist or is likely to be inconsistent, e.g., various vision and planning documents.
	Generation of results will begin in Business & IT organization, and eventually extend to business SME's for validation of results.	Generation of results begins with heavy participation by SME's from business units
	Reverse engineering is likely. Process needs verification that requirement and design documentation reflects reality.	Emphasis is organizations ambition, vision & strategy, building on new or enhanced business processes / activities and technological possibilities.
	Available information is standardized and normalized as a foundation for change.	Material originally produced for different time frames, e.g., 1-year plans, 5-year plans, strategic plans, is integrated to a single vision.
Results	Models are based on reality	Models are based on assumptions, plans, and recognized needs, political environment, future technology.
	Results describe the entire current enterprise at a consistent, high level. Additional analysis, detail based on priority areas, e.g., known problems areas	Results describe a vision for the entire enterprise. Additional analysis, detail based on priority areas, e.g., anticipated modernization.
	Describes all significant manual and automated operations	Explicitly includes legacy, with upgrades if they are planned, or there is an implicit decommission of what exists in the Current. Also includes planned transformational components.
	Consistency, completeness, correctness can be validated.	Consistency, completeness can be validated.
	Results are available and controlled in a repository.	Results are available, linked to the Current Enterprise architecture, and controlled in the same repository as the Current enterprise architecture.

Table 6. Current and Future Enterprise Architecture Differentiators

The information contained in the EA is usually expressed as a collection of interdependent results. The volume of information, as well as the presentation style of that information is often too great for a user to quickly comprehend. Also, users often focus on their particular area of concern and can easily overlook critical dependencies that their processes or assets may have on other processes and organizations in the enterprise. Therefore, providing electronic links among the interdependent information can highlight the interdependencies and greatly improve the understandability of the information. Change control is also significantly streamlined—by establishing the links among information at its origin, impact analysis is facilitated and change proposals can be evaluated more readily. Most organizations will document and distribute its EA's in the form of web sites and CD-ROMs, thus-easing readability, access, and distribution.

The process of getting the enterprise from where it is today to where it wants to be in the future needs formal thought and that focuses on optimizing enterprise-wide performance and accountability. This thought process is documented with the organization's strategic plan. This document defines the mission and long-range objectives of the organization and relates to plans for business reengineering and systems modernization. Together these results should drive the top-down sequence of EA product development.

6.2.1   Essentials in Creating the Current Enterprise Architecture

In building the EA, a logical first step is describing the current or "as is" state. This is an important step because it enables future progress to be measured against a baseline. It has been said that if you don't know where you are it's hard to know if you are on the way to where you are going. Establishing a set of enterprise architectural results that describe and document the current state of the enterprise from business functions to technology infrastructure sets the stage for establishing a plan for moving towards and measuring progress against a future enterprise architecture.

The scope of the current analysis and the resultant documentation is critical. The larger the enterprise, the higher the commitment and cost for a comprehensive, explicit, fully detailed and extremely accurate current analysis. For larger Business Units, there are methods and techniques, as well as models, which facilitate a sampling approach to yield currents that are useful and less costly.

6.2.2   Essentials in Creating the Future Enterprise Architecture

The future enterprise architecture should define a vision of future business operations and supporting technology. A long-term blueprint is absolutely necessary. A key consideration is the determination of the date of the target, how far into the future is the projected target. Realization of an organization's mission and vision statements needs:

o   A focus on business areas or information needs with the greatest potential payoff for the enterprise
o   Development of conceptual models and tools to enable decision makers and staff to better recognize, understand, and discuss information requirements
o   An enterprise-wide understanding of the "big picture" and the need for shared information
o   A recognition of information as a strategic resource that should be managed using enterprise architectures as tools
o   Periodic assessments of the enterprise's progress towards its future environment
o   Alignment with the enterprise's strategic plan.

The future enterprise architecture describes the desired capability and structure of the enterprise business activities, processes, information needs, and IT infrastructure at some point in the future. Therefore, the future enterprise architecture is often referred to as the "To-Be" or "Target" enterprise architecture. The future enterprise architecture may include alternatives, options, and unknowns — this is acceptable. The EA process is iterative — unknowns are filled in over time.

A future enterprise architecture almost always represents enhancements to an existing current enterprise architecture that will be necessary to adding new functionality to support new business operations as well as providing enhanced support for existing business operations. The future enterprise architecture must be fiscally and technologically achievable while being grounded in the business needs of the organization. The realities of rapid technological changes necessitate flexibility and capacity for change in the future enterprise architectures: they should project no more than 3 to 5 years into the future.

Just as the current enterprise architecture captures the existing business practices, functionality, and information flows, the future enterprise architecture reflects what the organization needs to evolve its information resources. The future enterprise architecture provides answers to these basic questions:

- o   What are the strategic business objectives of the organization?
- o   What is our place in the extended value net?
- o   What information is needed to support the business?
- o   What applications are needed to provide information?
- o   What technology is needed to support the applications?

The answers to these questions are grounded in the organization's information requirements, and in- turn, the information needs are predicated upon the organization's business practices, functionality, and operations. As business roles change, information content and information flow also change.

> **Technology Forecast** — a detailed description of emerging technologies and technology standards relevant to the systems and business processes covered in the organization's EA.
>
> **Standards Profile** — documents technology standards, protocols, and definitions.

Technology forecasts and information standards profiling can identify the necessary IT to support these changing business processes. These forecasts and standards profiles are necessary prerequisites to developing the future enterprise architecture.

The development of a picture of the organization's future business processes and information needs is central to successful future enterprise architecture development. This business view consists of a set of architectural results derived from the organization's strategic plans, business process reengineering results, Budget investment plans, and other planning documentation.

The future enterprise architecture should:

- o   Reflect the EA core team's judgment about the future uses and characteristics of information within the (extended) enterprise
- o   Reflect the organization's business requirements review for focusing on the opportunities to automate aspects of work and/or the access to information needed to perform work

- o   Incorporate technology forecasts
- o   Specify the needed level of interoperability needed between the data sources and the users of the data
- o   Identify the IT needed to support the enterprise's technical objective
- o   Reflect budgetary, legislation and territorial concerns.

6.2.3   Review, Validate, and Refine Results

Enterprise Architecture results are presented for both internal and Subject Matter Experts (SME) review. After an extensive internal review by the EA core team, the SME and domain owners assess the EA results for accuracy and completeness. This occurs at several points in the process. Prior to SME interviews, senior members of the core enterprise architecture team perform a "quick look" review. This review sets the stage for the interviewing process. It helps the interviewers formulate a template to focus the interview sessions. The next review occurs after the team has updated and expanded on the first set of results. There may be additional interview/review cycles before moving on to the SME review.

At the SME review, the review participants (i.e., Chief Enterprise Architect, enterprise architecture core team, QA, Risk Manager, SME's, OC, domain owners) determine EA result accuracy and completeness. The Risk Manager can provide an early assessment of business, technical, cost, or schedule risks. The results should then be revised as necessary and presented to the TRC and EAG for validation and final approval. Upon approval, the final enterprise architecture (results and models) can be published, briefings and documentation delivered, and the appropriate databases or enterprise architecture tools updated.

See Appendix J for more information about EA categories of results and deliverables.

6.3   *Develop the Transformation Plan*

The changes needed to transform from the current state of the enterprise to the goals and conditions expressed by the future enterprise architecture cannot be achieved in a single quantum step. Evolving the enterprise from its baseline to the future enterprise architecture needs multiple concurrent interdependent activities and incremental builds. The best way to understand and control this complex evolutionary process is by developing and maintaining a systems migration roadmap or transformation plan. The

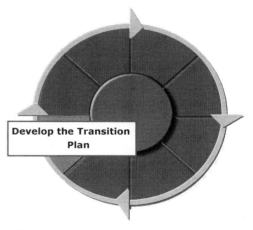

Develop the Transition Plan

transformation plan should provide a step-by-step process for moving from the current enterprise architecture to the future enterprise architecture. To simplify the base line enterprise architecture an application consolidation process should be started up.

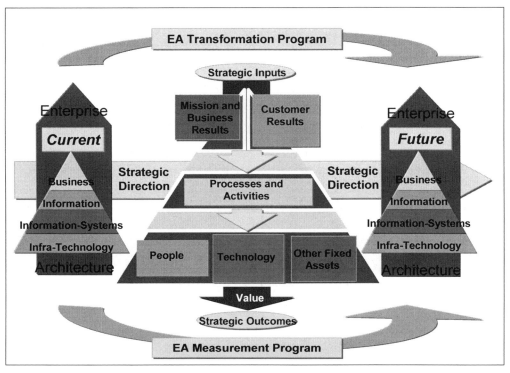

Figure 27. EA Transformation Program

The transformation plan may be supported by a set of enterprise architecture results, similar to the current and future enterprise architecture results, generated for several intermediate points in time between the current and future environments. The succession from one point in time to the next, and on to the target timeframe, establishes a migration sequence.

Because the transformation plan represents the current environment, as well as the development programs that are both planned and under way, it becomes a primary tool for program management and investment decisions. To remain current and to support continued coordinated improvements across the enterprise, the transformation plan should be maintained and updated as time and circumstances dictate.

In addition to specific development requirements for the new components in the future enterprise architecture, development of the transformation plan should consider a wide variety of inputs, including:

o   Sustainment of operations during transformation
o   Existing technical assets and contractual
o   Development programs currently underway
o   Anticipated management and organizational

- o Business goals and operational priorities (including legislation and executive directives)
- o Budget priorities and constraints.

6.3.1 Identify Gaps

The first step in transformation planning is gap analysis—identifying the differences between the current and future enterprise architectures in all related enterprise architecture results. Critical differences are those that affect the successful accomplishment of the enterprise's mission. Consequently, the gap analysis also develops the user requirements, determines political and technical constraints, and assesses migration risks and feasibility.

Through gap analysis, the enterprise architecture core team can determine the components that need to be changed to achieve the desired end-state. The gap between current and future enterprise architectures is overcome by a series of incremental builds that lead to the future environment. The size of the increments is based upon the overall time between the current and future, dependencies among developmental programs and components, critical path analysis for highly dependent activities, business-driven priorities (e.g., legislative mandates and executive directives), limitations in human capital capacity to manage the incremental projects and builds, expected return-on-investment from projects and builds, and risks. Overall, the gap analysis assesses the state of the legacy systems, technology maturity, acquisition opportunities, and fiscal reality of the transformation.

6.3.2 Implement an EA Measurement Program[10]

Key to the success of defining and implementing an EA transformation program is the implementation of a concurrent EA measurement program to really measure the progress and transformation steps in line with the goals and objectives to achieve in a certain timeframe. Measuring and controlling the transformation program will help the organization in decision-making about new transformation steps as well as about the success of the earlier transformation steps.
See Section 11 for more information about setting up an EA Measurement Program.

6.3.3 Define and Differentiate Business, Processes, Legacy, Migration, and New Systems

Business change, legacy, migration, and new systems make up the technical components for the transformation to the future environment. New or changed business activities and to be supported systems are part of the future enterprise environment. Legacy systems and their applications are those in current operation and usually are phased out during the deployment of the future enterprise architecture. Migration systems and applications may be in current operation, but certainly will be in operation when the transformation begins and for some time into the future. Therefore, they may not be specifically represented in the future

---

[10] *For more information about EA Measurement read also the book: 'The Economic Benefits of Enterprise Architecture' Publisher Trafford, Canada; ISBN 141206729-4*

enterprise architecture.   Migration systems also include systems, databases, interfaces, or other components that may be introduced and temporarily used to sustain operations between the current systems (and incremental phase) and the establishment of future enterprise architecture components.   New systems and applications are those that are being acquired, are under development, or are being deployed.   They are expected to be operational as part of the future environment.

The key to prioritizing activities and projects is the transformation of the change in business, termination of systems, the phasing out of functionality, and the timing of systems deployment, technology insertion, and the addition of new functionality into the enterprise.   The enterprise architecture core team considers dual operation of legacy systems alongside the initial start-up of new systems and account for this potential in the transformation plan.   The uninterrupted flow and management of data, its use by both the legacy and new systems, and its creation and distribution should be outlined in the transformation plan.   The migration should be managed and pursued incrementally so that the impact of unforeseen events, (e.g., technical problems, fiscal delays, etc.) on the efficient operation of the enterprise will be minimized.

Decisions about sequenced investments need to be driven by high-level analyses about respective costs, benefits, and risks, as well as sequential technical and functional dependencies.
A major section of the transformation plan is the system evolution or migration analysis captured in a set of systems migration tables, diagrams, or charts.   Figure 28 illustrates a notional migration chart.   This type of chart helps illustrate how systems and applications are expected to evolve between the current and future enterprise architectures.   Generally, a system evolves in one of five ways:

1.   Current Processes continue in operation (processes 4,5)
2.   Current systems continue in operation (System 1,4)
3.   Existing process functionality is absorbed by another processes (process 4,5 into process A, B)
4.   Legacy system transformations to migration and evolves into a new system (System 2,3 into System A, B)
5.   Current system is planned for further evolution (System 1, 4 into System A, B)
6.   A new system developed during transformation that becomes the permanent final system (System C)
7.   A merger of legacy functionality and migration systems (system 2 into System A and then absorbed into System B).

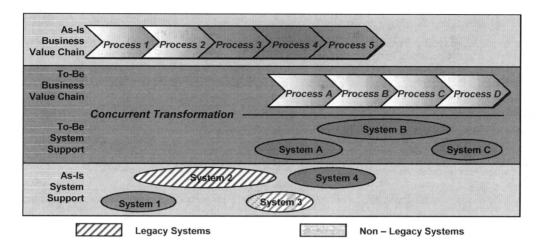

Figure 28. Business & Systems Transformation Chart

A sequenced insertion of functionality and a detailed deployment plan for IT systems is developed based upon operational priorities, risk management, and return on investment.

In case of mergers and takeovers a migration plan is crucial. PD plays an important role from a project portfolio management point of view.

6.3.4   Planning the Transformation

The rate of modernization, that is migration to the future enterprise architecture, needs to be planned in convenient, manageable increments to accommodate the organization's capacity to handle change. Understanding the level of effort is necessary to allocate and manage the work according to a scheduled migration with milestones. This will depend on proposed information systems development or acquisition, priorities, and the availability of resources, such as budget, people, and time constraints.

The implementation of changed business processes might be expressed as program initiatives with one or more projects. A review of the collection of gaps between the current and future enterprise architectures determines which enhancements, modifications, and replacements are needed. Dependency analysis determines the alternatives available for sequential and concurrent activities, and helps determine what should be accomplished in which increment or iteration of projects. Projects would then be defined to implement each of the initiatives (or sets thereof). Each project represents a logical division of work that is easier to describe and manage from the overall effort and would be assigned to an individual project manager with clear responsibility for its success.

The next step in the development of the migration path focuses on dependency analysis and consideration for the desired level of effort for each of the projects. The interdependency of systems within the organization and the dependencies among projects and initiatives is the primary driving force in determining the sequence for implementing solutions. Estimating the effort and duration for each initiative provides additional information to the dependency analysis that supports critical path analysis. After considering options offered by tradeoffs from critical vs. non-critical changes, prioritizing key enhancements to meet key management priorities (such as legislative mandates, external legislation or executive directives), and providing for sufficient leeway to reduce schedule risk, a draft sequence plan for the portfolio of projects can be created.

Final refinement of the transformation plan involves review and refinement to meet the short-term needs and potentially volatile priorities of the business units within the financial constraints of the enterprise. The following are some key issues to consider when refining the strategy:

- o   What is the potential for commitment of funds for the initial phases of the migration?
- o   What is the potential for the commitment of funds for the entire transformation to the future enterprise architecture?
- o   How soon will the business units see the initial benefits (i.e., operational enhancements or return on investment) from the plan?
- o   Does the transformation plan provide incremental improvements to system users to help sustain commitment and support to the program?
- o   What risks are inherent in the current transformation plan? How will they be mitigated?
- o   What alternatives are currently available if funding or resources are delayed?

The modification, enhancement, or development of information may include applications, data integration, and interfaces, as well as systems platform acquisition, staffing, training (or retraining), and systems deployment. Because almost all systems development implies the control and transfer of funds, systems development should be coordinated and integrated with financial management. In addition, interrelationships and interdependencies — whether architectural, organizational, and external — need to be accounted for in the transformation plan.

6.4   *Approve, Publish, and Disseminate the EA Results*

Upon verification and validation of the enterprise architectural results, the organization's management should approve the overall enterprise architecture. This step includes the approval by the EASC, the CEO, CIO, the Chief Enterprise Architect, and Directors and Managing Directors.

The organization executives, managers, and architects should have read access to the information in the EA. -By distributing the information in electronic Read-Only format, executives and managers can use the information directly while the controlled baseline is maintained. Executives and managers should use the information for more than just reference purposes — incorporating it into communications, briefings, and directives. Application architects use the information to analyze artefacts against their own reality and identifying opportunities for improvements. Enterprise architects use the information to apply "what-if" analysis against the baseline. In addition, Read-Only format versions of the EA limit the number of staff able to make changes and modifications to the results, easing the burden of change management on the enterprise as a whole.

The EA documents extensive information about the organization. Careful consideration must be made to the distribution of that information. Although it is possible that an EA may not have any confidential information, the aggregation of the information may comprise a security risk. In the wrong hands, the compilation of enterprise information in the EA could create a vulnerability to the organization by providing sufficient information for infiltration and disruption. Some of the information could be considered as exchange rate sensitive information. Some of the information (or combinations thereof) may need to be controlled and accessed on a "need-to-know" basis (e.g., network models, critical performance factors, system interfaces, etc.). The enterprise architecture core team considers what classes of EA users will need what information: contractors, management, and organization staff typically focus on particular areas of the enterprise, and thus may only need particular subsets of the EA. An EA that includes a comprehensive view of the details of the organization systems and infrastructure could be organized in levels of detail and distributed in a tiered format corresponding to security clearances and the need to know.

Enterprise Architecting is an ongoing, iterative process requiring regular modification and maintenance. Whenever the EA changes, it is imperative to update the enterprise architecture models.

A detailed discussion of enterprise architecture maintenance is presented in Section 8.

7   Use the Enterprise Architecture

Using the EA to implement new projects provides a positive impact on the enterprise. If the EA is not successfully used, the entire development effort to this point is for naught. In this section, the emphasis shifts to integrating use of the EA across multiple activities and organizational groups. Success depends on active management, proactive enterprise architects, and receptive project personnel. It also depends on integrating the EA process with other enterprise life cycle 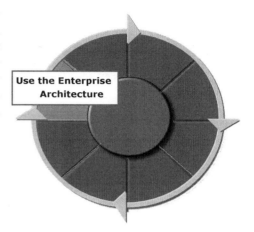 processes, particularly the enterprise program management and the investment process. Establishing the EA captures the state of the enterprise and the plan for its future—literally a snapshot of the enterprise and its plans for improvement. For the EA to provide the strategic information asset base as intended, it should become a crucial tool for decision support and communication in the mainstream of daily business operations. Accepting and applying this asset in the organization's operational paradigm is a technical and cultural challenge.

The EA is managed as a program that facilitates systematic organization change by continuously aligning technology investments and projects with organization mission needs. The EA is updated continuously to reflect changes in operational, and investment priorities that may arise due to legislation, budget constraints, or other business drivers. It is a primary tool for baseline control of complex, interdependent enterprise decisions and communication of those decisions to organization stakeholders. The transformation plan provides a strong guide for organization's decision-makers to use as they consider proposed projects. If a project is not represented in the transformation plan, it should either be denied funding, since it is not aligned with the organization strategy as embodied in the EA, or it should be granted a waiver if it is a legitimate deviation driven by valid changes in the organization's environment which have not yet been reflected in the EA. It should be noted that it is crucial that the EA represent the current organization strategies and imperatives as closely as possible, since any lag in the EA may constrain the organization's ability to effectively execute its mission until a waiver is issued or the EA is adapted. In cases where a waiver is granted, the cause of the waiver should be examined and appropriate changes to the EA considered if the cause represents a valid and ongoing gap in the EA.

7.1   *Align the EA Program with the Budgeting Processes*

Investment management and systems development/acquisition are closely linked with the EA processes.[11] The organization should only make investments that move the organization toward the future enterprise architecture and these investment decisions should comply with the transformation plan. The EA, investment, and budget processes are integrated to best suit the organization, culture, and internal management practices. Certain basic relationships exist between these functions and they have a common focus: the effective and efficient management of IT investments. The dialogue across Budget Planning and EA processes is continuous, cooperative, and facilitated by organization commitment to an integrated process.

Each organization designs its own investment process for structuring budget formulation and execution to ensure that investments consistently support strategic goals. All IT projects should align with the organization's mission and support the business needs while minimizing risks and maximizing returns throughout the investment's life cycle. The future enterprise architecture and the transformation plan provide information for the different phases of the investment process. In the Select Phase, the organization determines if the proposed investment meets business decision criteria. To assess the business alignment of the proposed investment, decision makers use, for example, the business case, acquisition plan, and the project plan to determine whether the proposed investment aligns with the transformation plan and future enterprise architecture. In the Control Phase, decision makers monitor business and technical compliance as demonstrated in, for example, the updated business case, system architecture, systems design, and test program. In addition, the investment should be monitored to ensure continuing alignment with the organization's strategic and business, which may shift over time. In the Evaluate Phase, the decision makers perform a final assessment to determine technical and strategic compliance with the EA. The results, including findings of noncompliance, should influence strategic planning for new business and IT projects, which could then lead to changes in the EA.

7.1.1   Train Personnel

It is the responsibility of organization executive management to institutionalize the control structures for the EA process as well as for the organization investment and budget processes. For each decision-making body, all members should be trained, as appropriate, in the EA, the EA process, and the relationship of the EA to the investment process. Specific training, at various levels of detail, should be tailored to the enterprise architecture role of the personnel.

Anyone who might bring forward a proposal to the management in the form of project proposals—such as business unit managers and project managers—should understand the requirement for EA assessments. To adequately evaluate an investment proposal, the EASC needs specific information. Individuals creating

---

[11] *As discussed as the beginning of this guide, these processes are also linked with information security management processes and human capital management and compliancy processes. Linkages with these processes, however, are not explicitly addressed in this guide.*

the investment proposals should be trained, as appropriate, in the criteria and submission requirements. Appropriate training will prepare the staff to assess the compliance and correct any deficiencies that exist prior to submission.

7.1.2   Establish Enforcement Processes and Procedures

The processes and procedures that enforce the application of EA guidance and those that ensure its consistency with the "reality" of the enterprise are critical components in EA institutionalization. The EA processes and procedures implement the Executive EA Policy. The Enforcement Policy defines the standards and process for determining the compliance of systems or projects with the EA and procedures for resolving the issues of non-compliance. A project's technical and schedule compliance is typically assessed in terms of how it conforms to the content, intent, and direction set by the EA.

The processes and procedures should answer the following questions:

o   How and when will projects submit project plans to be reviewed for EA compliance?
o   Who will be responsible for compliance assessment and/or justification of waivers?
o   How will compliance and non-compliance be documented and reported?
o   How will outstanding issues of non-compliance be resolved and/or waivers be processed and approved?
o   Who will be responsible for processing, authorizing, and reassessing waivers?
o   What will be the content and format of waiver submissions?
o   If a waiver is granted, how will projects achieve compliance in the future?
o   What are the ramifications if a non-compliant project is not granted a waiver (e.g., funding and/or deployment restrictions)?

The processes and procedures should, of necessity, allow exceptions. In many cases, existing systems in the operations and maintenance phase should be granted exceptions or waivers from the technical standards and constraints of the EA. Alignment of some legacy systems with new standards could be unreasonably costly and introduce additional risk to the business users. Also, it is likely that certain initiatives and innovations, such as investigative efforts and proofs-of-concept, will not comply with the EA[12].

7.1.2.1 Define Compliance Criteria and Consequences

Requirements for EA assessments include criteria for compliance, waivers, and corresponding submission requirements. In the event of a non-compliant proposal a request for waiver should be prepared and formally submitted to the Technology Review Committee (TRC). The waiver provides analytical and

---

[12] *After a non-compliant investigative or innovative effort is commenced and appropriately controlled during its execution, it may become a candidate project for consideration by the EASC and TRC. Such a project might well offer proposed changes to the EA.*

defendable justification of design changes, budget deviations, and impacts. The waiver request includes identification of the operational, economic, and productivity impacts of any waiver.

The TRC approves waivers according to the organization's enforcement process. Each waiver that is approved presents an opportunity for feedback on the EA and the EA process. For example, the need for a waiver may indicate that the future enterprise architecture, the transformation analysis, and/or the transformation plan are too constraining or too rigidly defined. In addition, rapidly evolving requirements may necessitate revisiting existing plans outside the normal EA process, since or waivers may indicate that the defined future environment does not reflect organizations needs. Also the need for reworking proposals may indicate problems in training for compliance.

The investment process should respect the integrity of the transformation plan while considering the strategic and tactical value of all proposals that pass through investment checkpoints. Project critical success factors continue to be met. This double check on project proposals assures that all funded projects meet the conditions necessary for success. These conditions include, but are not limited to:

- o   Consistency with the EA
- o   Satisfaction of project baseline cost, schedule, capability, and business value commitments
- o   Compliance with organization-published investment management policies and guidance
- o   Explicit support by executive management.

7.1.2.2 Set Up an EA Validation Process

Since the EA is a major management tool for monitoring and guiding change within the organization, the important outcome is to schedule reviews to ensure that planned investments stay on schedule, within budget, and achieve defined goals. In addition, these reviews provide the opportunity for the EA team to communicate changes in the future enterprise architecture and transformation plan to the organization as a whole as well as to the specific projects that will be affected. Deviations from compliance may be addressed by implementing changes to the project or by a waiver request.

*See **Section 10** for more information about EA Assessments.*

7.2   Execute the Transformation Plan

Progress toward the future enterprise architecture is accomplished through EA transformation plans and projects. New and follow-on projects are (1) initiated and selected, (2) executed and controlled, and (3) completed and evaluated. The following sections show the information flow for each of these three investment phases with emphasis on how the EA supports the whole process.

7.2.1   Initiate New and Follow-on Projects

Sponsors propose projects under different circumstances:

- o   New projects are identified and sponsored based on the domain owner's interpretation of the transformation plan. A project to fill the gap may result in business process reengineering, IT development, and/or change to the infrastructure.
- o   Planned follow-on projects are anticipated, but still need review and an assessment of the completion of dependencies on previous projects. Furthermore projects are on the agenda of the MT's of the initiating (S)BU's.
- o   A need for an architectural improvement is identified, e.g., to incorporate a new standard or technology identified by the future enterprise architecture, gap and transformation analysis, and the transformation plan.
- o   A sponsor may initiate a project based on a business or technical need that is not identified in the transformation plan. In this case, a waiver needs to be approved and the EA team should respond by considering modifications to the EA. This is only possible based upon a formal waiver and approval process including the EASC and other executive-level panels.

Figure 29 depicts the entry point when a project is initiated. It serves as a guide through the cycle of proposal preparation, aligning the proposed project with the EA, and making the decision to fund the effort. The information flow ensures that requirements are being addressed and that a proposed implementation meets matches expectations and requirements.

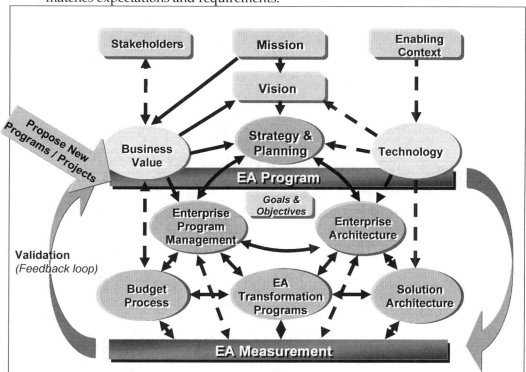

Figure 29. Define New and Follow-on Programs/Projects

ⅶ.2.1.1 Prepare Project Proposal

The sponsor of a project prepares a proposal in accordance with predefined organization requirements. The proposal presents the business case for the project and defines a business solution using information from the EA as well as other sources. Business requirements, IT needs, and technology updates all feed the definition of the effort being planned. Domain owners and program or project leaders prepare the proposal by:

o   Mapping objectives to requirements and relationships between high-level requirements to the business objectives
o   Documenting a high-level business case
o   Providing a cost study
o   Defining a business case solution and determining the level of impact introduced into the IT environment
o   Ensuring reasonableness of risk, time, and cost
o   Ensuring that technical and business implications to the organization are addressed.

The Domain Owners, (S)BU managers (project owners) and program or project leaders should comply with the enterprise architecture project reporting requirements and will provide answers to compliance criteria in the proposal documentation. For selection, they will show that the investment supports the organization mission, that the investment meets the business criteria, and that it is consistent with the future enterprise architecture and transformation plan. If an investment deviated from the transformation plan, the reasoning for the deviation should be documented.

The Chief Enterprise Architect and the architecture team can advise program/project leaders on business case/solution development. They contribute to the development of investment proposals and work to facilitate progress through the business case. They have a specific interest in ensuring that projects identified in the transformation plan are funded, and may actually introduce such projects. For other projects, they will support project leaders in initiating and developing proposals.

ⅶ.2.1.2 Align the Project to the EA

The Chief Enterprise Architect and the enterprise architecture group perform proposal assessments. Table 7 describes the types of assessments that occur as projects are subjected to periodic, iterative EA reviews. In the initial phase of defining and selecting a project, the emphasis is on the business alignment, business case solution, transformation plan, and to a limited degree, technical compliance. As the system concept matures, business and technical compliance are equally addressed.

Type of EA Reviews	Review Purpose/Goal
Business alignment	Determine if the proposed project aligns with the organization strategic plans, goals, and objectives. The goal of the review is to ensure that the expected business outcomes of the project are aligned to concept and high-level project requirements.
Business case solution	Examine the proposed solution, at a high level, to determine the impact introduced into the organization's IT environment. The goal of the review is to ensure that the proposed solution supports both the business and technical architecture.
Transformation plan	Determine whether the proposed investment is consistent with the sequence and priorities in the plan. The goal of the review is to ensure progress toward the future enterprise architecture.
Technical compliance	Determine whether the enterprise architecture of the proposed solution complies with the enterprise standards, the various enterprise architecture levels, and methodologies. The goal of this review is to ensure technical compliance of IT projects.

Table 7. EA Review Goals

Upon assessing the project's alignment to the EA, the architects may make recommendations and provide support to bring non-compliant proposals into compliance. In cases where a waiver had been requested, the architects may respond with an independent assessment of operational, economic, and productivity impacts of the waiver. They report on the conclusions to the OC, ORC and project owners/initiators.

See Section 10 for more information about EA Assessments.

7.2.1.3 Make Investment Decisions (Budget Process)

The CxO's and (S)BU MT's are responsible for the evaluation of new proposals and for oversight of ongoing investments. Among other criteria, investment decisions are based on determinations that the proposed projects submitted by the business managers are aligned with organization strategic plans, goals, and objectives. The business proposal and the results of the enterprise architecture assessments, including waivers, are reviewed by the investment decision makers. The same conditions and consequences pertain to follow-on projects and incremental funding.

In certain circumstances, it may be necessary to approve a proposal that does not conform to the future enterprise architecture and/or the transformation plan. The conditions under which a waiver is granted and the operational, economic, and productivity impacts of the waiver (the business case) are considered in the investment decision. Under most circumstances, any proposal that is not compliant or otherwise does not qualify should be denied a waiver. Non-compliant initiatives may be approved for research, concept development, prototyping, and other purposes. These efforts may challenge assumptions currently accepted in the EA and may lead to breakthroughs that could significantly improve the EA. Nevertheless, the conditions under which a project may proceed should be unambiguous and clearly stated in the EA policy and should be documented in the (final) investment decision. Once the project has been acted on, there may be recommended changes to the EA or the requirement for additional detail to enhance the EA. The funding decision will have an impact on the transformation plan and potentially the future enterprise architecture and transformation analysis.

7.2.2 Execute the Projects

Once funding is received, the project can be initiated. Figure 30 depicts the information flow as the project cycles through the EA program and budget processes. A project will pass through this cycle multiple times. There are continuous interactions between the enterprise program implementers and the enterprise architecture, with more formal reviews at prescribed milestones.

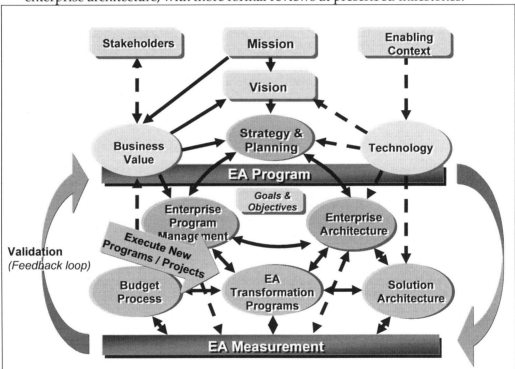

Figure 30. Execute Programs/Projects

7.2.2.1 Manage and Perform (EA) Program Development

Program/Project leaders use the EA as guidance and constraints on systems architecture and systems design. The enterprise program management goal is to ensure that the proposed solution supports the EA. The project's requirements, solutions and/or software architecture, design, and test program are developed using concepts, constraints, and recommendations from the EA. Systems migration strategies may be found in the transformation plan.

The Chief Enterprise Architect and the enterprise architecture office contribute to programs as consulting enterprise architects. Their role in the requirements and discovery phases is to provide guidance to the business unit and its project teams on business & IT related issues and emerging trends in the industry. They make recommendations for relevant parts of the EA—e.g., business, information, data, application, infrastructure, security, and standards.

Initial requirements, solutions and/or software architecture, and design rely heavily on existing artefacts from the EA. As the program progresses, results are produced that enhance and expand the level of detail in the EA. These results, generated according to the requirements, are contributed and incorporated into the EA repository.

7.2.2.2 *Evolve EA with Program / Project*

It is the responsibility of the Chief Enterprise Architect and the enterprise architecture core team, with direction from the EASC, to maintain EA alignment with the organization as it evolves. Throughout a project's development / acquisition phase, the requirement is to maintain the alignment of the evolving solution with the future enterprise architecture and transformation plan. The enterprise architecture team reviews the business and technical solution throughout the life cycle and assures compliance with the EA. In incremental reviews, assessments are performed to determine whether the project's results and documentation (the functional analysis, general design, and detailed design) comply with the EA results that have been approved through previous review processes. The projects provide additional information as progress is realized. The goal is to maintain alignment of the project with the EA throughout development to avoid construction of systems that do not meet the organization's needs.

In addition to solutions architecture and design specifics that flesh out the EA at the lower levels of detail, the projects provide new ideas to the EA for changes to the future enterprise architecture and transformation increments. The EA should be reviewed regularly and synchronized with the enterprise life cycle and investment decisions. The Chief Enterprise Architect and the enterprise architecture team incorporate this feedback into the EA maintenance process.

See Section 8 for more detailed discussion on EA maintenance.

7.2.2.3 *Assess Progress (EA Measurement)*

The Budget Process assures that the investment is being managed within the planned cost, schedule, and design and that the investment will operate effectively within the technical infrastructure. Systems development and acquisition is inherently risky. Managers and enterprise architects provide information according to the reporting requirements for enterprise architecture assessments, and this information is used as the basis for decisions about continued funding, imposition of development constrains, and possible redirection of technical efforts. This control is imposed to manage and mitigate risk. Investment decisions rely on analysis of progress reports, compliance assessments, and deviations and waivers to arrive at implications on cost, schedule, and performance.

*See **Section 11** about setting up EA Measurement.*

7.2.3   Complete the Program / Project

Most programs / projects are interdependent on other development projects. Many are followed by additional increments of capability or by additional operations and maintenance efforts.   Almost all are integrated with other initiatives when they become operational. When the project is complete, there is a final assessment of impacts on the organization, the EA, enterprise operations, future systems, and consequently, future investment and funding decisions. Figure 31 depicts the information flow upon completion of a program or project.

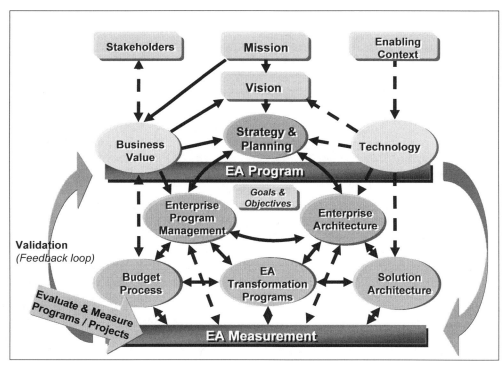

Figure 31. Evaluate & Measure Programs/Projects

7.2.3.1 Deliver Results

At the end of a program or project, system and updated business processes have been integrated into the environment. An Operations and Maintenance support is defined, training is provided, and a complete set of documentation is communicated to the operations and maintenance staff. Material is provided for the EA repository with the delivered results, to the level of detail appropriate to depict the new current enterprise architecture. A support and deployment strategy is activated for parallel or turnkey operations. There is a transformation from the development / acquisition environment and management to operations environment and management. At this time opportunities for the reuse of work results from this project to other projects should be considered.

See **Appendix J** *for more detailed information about possible EA results.*

7.2.3.2 Assess the Enterprise Architecture

The EASC performs an ongoing assessment of the EA. There is much to be learned by evaluating the extent to which a project has complied with the transformation plan, based upon the future enterprise architecture. The experience and lessons learned contribute to the ongoing robustness of the EA processes.

The final assessment of the project with respect to the Enterprise Architecture involves review of the original business case, the implementation of the business and technical solutions, the transformation plan, and final disposition of waivers. The result of the final assessment is the updating of the current enterprise architecture with changes implemented in business processes, IT products, deployment, technology, and operations. The transformation plan, future enterprise architecture, and gap/transformation analyses are also updated to show completion of the program/project. Waivers will either be permanent or may be accompanied by plans for future work. Other results can influence future priorities and dependencies in the transformation plan. These results provide lessons learned for process improvement and form the basis of business cases for other new programs or projects.

The EASC and Enterprise Program management assess program/project results for impact to the EA and the organization's business processes. The Budget Process Evaluate Phase shows that the investment meets the planned performance goals and identifies any reasons for updating the EA. After considering the results of impact to the EA, the conditions that may have necessitated a waiver may prove sufficiently pervasive to justify altering the EA to accommodate future investment proposals with similar requirements.

See **Section 10** *for more information about EA Assessment.*

7.3   *Other Uses of the EA*

The EA provides guidance and source information for change managers, program managers, requirements analysts, designers, engineers, and test planners to reference and build upon material executing their responsibilities. The following are examples of uses of the EA outside the normal project cycle:

- o   Even if an organization or (S)BU is not involved in a major IT upgrade, the EA is a resource for managing inventory, routine maintenance, and queries. Analysis of the current enterprise architecture can identify opportunities for consolidating network services, floating or site software licenses, and economies of scale for equipment and services.

- o   The organization can use the EA as a training aid, drawing on its graphics and descriptive material for instruction in the business of the organization or in the technology that is in use or planned.

- o   Investigative initiatives and proofs-of-concepts should be performed using the EA as a reference. The criteria for EA compliance should be considered, but not mandated, in such efforts. Non-enforcement allows pursuit of innovations that could change the EA, but alignment and impacts of enterprise architecture deviations should be included with the results of the experiments.

- o   (S)BU's may fund small, low risk projects outside of the Budget Planning process. Program/project managers should still rely on the EA for guidance for the business solution, enterprise architectures, requirements, and design of their effort. Compliance with the EA will facilitate integration into the enterprise, and the current enterprise architecture should be kept current with their results.

- o   Operations and Maintenance projects rely on the current enterprise architecture for context. The O&M priorities and decisions may be influenced by the transformation plan and future enterprise architectures. For example, a planner may conclude that soon-to-be-retired IT systems are more economical with minimal operations & management support.

8   Maintain the Enterprise Architecture

8.1   *Enterprise Architecture Maintenance*

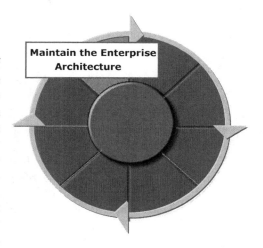

The EA is, by definition, a set of models that collectively describe the enterprise and its future. Its value to the business operations is more than just IT investment decision management. The EA is the primary tool to reduce the response time for impact assessment, trade-off analysis, strategic plan redirection, and tactical reaction. Consequently, the EA must remain current and reflect the reality of the organizations enterprise. In turn, the EA needs regular upkeep and maintenance—a process as important as its original development.

Maintaining the EA should be accomplished within the enforcement structure and configuration control mechanisms of the organization. EA maintenance is the responsibility of the CEA, Chief Enterprise Architect, and the EAO. Using a system of oversight processes and independent verification, the enterprise architecture core team periodically assesses and aligns the EA to the ever-changing business practices, funding profiles, and technology insertion. The EA should remain aligned to the organization's modernization projects and vice versa. The management controls to accomplish EA maintenance are the same ones established to initiate the program and to develop the EA.

8.2   *Maintain the Enterprise Architecture as the Enterprise Evolves*

If the EA is not kept current, it will quickly become "shelf ware"—yet another well-intentioned plan for improving the organization. Perhaps even more damaging, if the EA fails to embody the organization's most current strategy it may limit the organization's ability to meet its goals and achieve its mission. The EA necessitates a specific organizational and process structure that will ensure the currency of EA content over time. The EA should reflect the impact of ongoing changes in organization's business function and technology, and in turn, support Budget planning and investment management in keeping up with those changes. Consequently, each component of the EA, current enterprise architecture, future enterprise architecture, transformation plan, and all the results that constitute them, need to be maintained and kept accurate and current.

8.2.1   Reassess the Enterprise Architecture Periodically

Periodically, it is necessary to revisit the vision that carried the organization to this point and to re-energize that vision within the organization. Continually, typically in conjunction with the CPIC, the EA should be reviewed to ensure that:

- o The current or baseline enterprise architecture accurately reflects the current status of the IT infrastructure
- o The future enterprise architecture accurately reflects the business vision of the enterprise and appropriate technology advances that have occurred since the last release
- o The transformation plan reflects the prevailing priorities of the enterprise and resources that will be realistically available.

The assessment should generate an update to the EA and corresponding changes in dependent projects. The baseline should continue to reflect actions taken to implement the transformation plan and actions otherwise taken to upgrade the legacy environment as the organization modernizes. The EA assessment and update should be managed and scheduled to in turn update the organization strategic plan and process for selecting system investments.

8.2.2   Manage Results to Reflect Reality

An organization is a business entity that remains responsive to business drivers (including new legislation and executive directives), emerging technologies, and opportunities for improvement. The EA reflects the evolution of the organization, and should continuously reflect the current state (current enterprise architecture), the desired state (future enterprise architecture), and the long- and short-term strategies for managing the change (the transformation plan). Figure 32 illustrates the type of continuous changes that should be illustrated by the EA. At no time will a specific future enterprise architecture ever be achieved, with each iterative update of the EA, all three components shown in the figure and the timeline are recast. The future enterprise architecture is a vision of the future that evolves in advance of it being achieved.

Phases

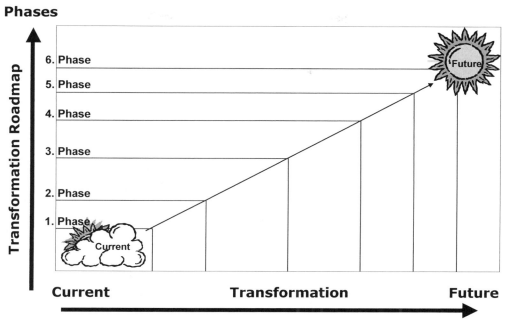

Figure 32. Enterprise Architecture Transformation

8.2.2.1 *Ensure Business Direction and Processes Reflect Operations*

A critical responsibility for the EA program is to monitor the changes in the business operations that affect the organization, the business processes, and the strategic direction of the business. Changes in business processes that were initiated by process improvement, organizational change, or mandate, may be reflected in the business artefacts of the current enterprise architecture. Business unit management and their SME's should report changes in their (S)BU's and initiatives to the Chief Enterprise Architect and enterprise architecture core team. Correspondingly, the Chief Enterprise Architect ensures that the enterprise architecture core team is gaining sufficient insight into the evolution of the operations. Plans and expectations may change as priorities shift over time — these may need to be reflected in modifications to the future enterprise architecture. Priority shifts and the realities of budget constraints may need to be reflected in the transformation plan. Thus, EA maintenance will be both reactive and proactive. In that role an EAO presence at executive management and (S)BU MT's level is vital.

8.2.2.2 *Ensure Current Enterprise Architecture Reflects Systems Life Cycle*

Despite the best operational management and systems maintenance planning, the current enterprise architecture and infrastructure may need unanticipated changes. As each new system is deployed and each legacy system reaches a maintenance milestone (e.g., renewal of maintenance contracts and a software release calendar), the baseline for the current enterprise architecture changes. In addition, system patches should be introduced frequently or system design changes implemented to respond to high-priority requests. These changes should be reflected in the current enterprise architecture artefacts.

8.2.2.3 *Evaluate Legacy System Maintenance Requirements against the Transformation Plan*

As the current enterprise architecture evolves to reflect the reality of the legacy systems, new information may emerge that will change the maintenance plans and subsequent organizational and systems transformation. For example, system vendors may unexpectedly cease supporting critical components of organization's infrastructure. Alternative actions should be weighed and decisions made regarding replacing the components, paying for additional specialized contractor support, or changing the strategy for phasing in other components in the future enterprise architecture. The total cost of ownership of the system versus alternative systems, as well as outsourcing, may need to be considered. All of these considerations, alternatives, and decisions may dramatically alter the transformation plan.

8.2.2.4 *Maintain the Transformation Plan as an Aligned Program Plan*

The development of the transformation plan is linked to the acquisition and enterprise engineering processes. The enterprise architect works in partnership with managers who understand the evolving business objectives as well as the individual program management offices that oversee the acquisition and development of new IT systems. The transformation plan should be maintained, reviewed and validated, and approved to continually reflect the organization's mission and vision just as any result in the enterprise architecture package and plan. The transformation plan delineates the IT management scheme for systems insertion in support of the organization's long-term business strategies.

8.3   *Continue to Consider Proposals for EA Modifications*

While the enforcement process helps to ensure that the EA guidance is followed, it is unreasonable to assume that new business priorities and technologies, funding issues, or project challenges will not require modification to the plans, baselines, and results incorporated in the EA. Emerging technologies continue to necessitate changes to the enterprise. Many of the considerations for changes to the EA are the same considerations that needed to be addressed during its development. Also, the architectural principles need to be continuously addressed.

Proposals for modifying the enterprise architecture should address the following questions among others, and the architectural Principles:

o   How does the proposed modification support the organization in exploiting IT to increase the effectiveness of its organizational components?

- o How does it impact information sharing and interoperability among organizational components?
- o What are the security implications? For example, will the modifications need certification of enhanced systems?
- o Does the proposed modification use proven technologies to satisfy requirements and deliver IT services? Are these technologies and related standards in the industry mainstream, thereby reducing the risk of premature obsolescence?
- o Does the acceptance of this proposal position other standards or products for obsolescence? If so, identify them.
- o What is the impact on the organization and the sub-organization's if the proposal is not accepted? What is the result of the cost-benefit analysis?
- o What external organizations or systems will be affected? What action will they have to take?
- o What is the estimated overall programmatic cost of the proposed changes including changes to the EA and/or redirection of dependent projects?
- o What alternatives have been considered and why were they not recommended?
- o What testing, and by whom, should be completed for implementations that will result from acceptance of the proposal?
- o What is the recommendation of the enterprise change control board?

Proposals requesting modifications to the EA need to explicitly address these issues. The proposal should be presented to and reviewed by the TRC (for review by architectural and SME's) and passed to the EAG with a recommendation. In cases where the EASC cannot reach a consensus, a working group may be tasked to investigate and propose recommended actions.

*See **Appendix D** for more information about Guiding Principle*

8.4   *Continuously Control and Oversee the Enterprise Architecture Program*

The purpose of EA control and oversight is to ensure that the EA development, implementation, and maintenance practices defined in this practical guide and the related EA guidance referenced in this guide (e.g., EA frameworks) are being followed, and to remedy any situations or circumstances where they are not and action is warranted. Control and oversight is a continuous, ongoing function performed throughout the EA life cycle process.

Effective control and oversight is a key to ensuring EA program success. Through it, information is gathered for accountable decision makers to permit awareness of whether effective EA development, implementation, and maintenance activities are being performed and EA program goals are being met on schedule and within budgets. To do so, the EAG and the Chief Enterprise Architect should be vigilant in measuring and validating that the EA process and product standards defined and referenced in this guide are being performed. To do less, diminishes the probability of program success.

8.4.1   Ensure Necessary EA Program Management Controls Are in Place and Functioning

In **section 4** of this guide, accountability for the EA program was assigned to the EASC, and the Chief Enterprise Architect. Also, throughout this guide, EA process and product standards or controls that should be used to produce a complete, well-defined, and useful EA have either been defined or referenced. (For example, the guide specified the need for a Program Management Plan to detail what will be done, when, and at what cost, as well as the need to establish management support functions, such as configuration management, risk management, quality assurance, change control, etc. Also, the guide references EA frameworks and tools that help define the content of the EA.)

Knowing the extent to which these controls are being implemented on a continuous basis is crucial to keeping the program on track. To do this, the EASC, CEO / CIO and the Chief Enterprise Architect will respectively seek reports (oral and written, routine and ad hoc, formal and informal) and conduct first hand reviews to obtain the appropriate level of visibility into what is occurring on the program vis-à-vis what is expected. It is the responsibility of these accountable entities to define what information they need, when and how often they need it, what the form and content of the information should be, whether it should independently validated or not, etc. Through such information, the EASC, the CIO and the Chief Enterprise Architect can position themselves to know whether established program management controls are in place and functioning.

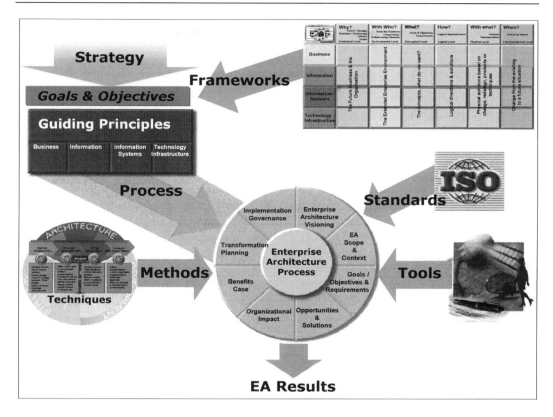

Figure 33. EA Program & Process Overview

8.4.2   Identify Where EA Program Expectations Are Not Being Met

Through their respective reports and review activities, the EAG and the Chief Enterprise Architecture will be able to identify what, if any, EA program expectations are not being met. For example, if risk management has been effectively implemented, program risk lists should be regularly generated that assign a risk level based on impact and probability, define risk mitigation strategies, report on progress in implementing these strategies, and whether the progress being made is successfully addressing the risk item. Also, periodic configuration audits should be conducted to ensure that EA configuration items are being defined, controlled, and reported. The EASC and Chief Enterprise Architect can also rely on independent reviews by the quality assurance function or a verification and validation agent to advise them of deviations from expectations. Whether these deviations be Program Management Plan related such as omission of work tasks, delays in the completion of work tasks, or additional costs to complete work tasks, or whether they be management function related such as not following change control procedures, not adhering to the selected EA framework, or not engaging SME's and domain owners within business and technical areas.

8.4.3   Take Appropriate Actions to Address Deviations

The management should take quick and decisive actions to correct problems in light of established priorities. Examples of actions include infusion of additional resources (people, tools, or money), establishment of contingency plans, and redefinition EA purpose and scope, introduction of missing or strengthening of existing control mechanisms, and increased oversight.

Any changes to the plans, projects, and/or enterprise architecture content to address deviations should be captured in an appropriate documentation trail (request for changes), and should be justified on the basis of costs, benefits, and risks. Changes should be processed through established change control processes and change board authority. The change documentation should characterize the problem, solution, and alternatives chosen and rejected in light of established priorities.

8.4.4   Ensure Continuous Improvement

Figure 34 is adapted from a traditional representation of the key success factors of Total Quality Management (TQM). This figure represents the same key success factors for enterprise architecting:

- o   The EA process should be a key support element of the operations of the enterprise, and should assist the operations function in performance of its customer-focused mission.
- o   Successful enterprise architecting is not simply a function of the IT organization, but needs the total enterprise participation.
- o   Effective enterprise architecting needs "societal networking," that is, internal and external communication and sharing of lessons learned.

The optimum EA process is not a single, one-time event, but is continuous and thus offers the opportunity for continuous improvement. This necessitates ongoing control with monitoring, reassessment, and refinement. As the discipline of enterprise architecting enters the mainstream of the operations of the enterprise, lessons can be learned from processes that worked and those that did not work, and from external organizations.

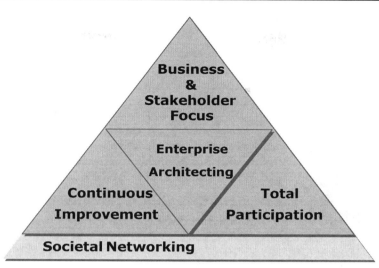

Figure 34. Key Success Factors

Total participation makes continuous improvement everyone's responsibility. The EA's central role in enterprise evolution provides an excellent opportunity to solicit feedback. Lessons learned should be collected from the operational business owners, EA teams, project development teams, and investment management teams. Once the current EA has been developed, the enterprise architecture team should take stock of the lessons learned and communicate them to their colleagues and participating senior management in order to utilize them in improving the process or the EA itself. In addition, feedback and lessons learned should be sought from other Financial Institutions (benchmarks), professional organizations and universities (e.g. Institute for Enterprise Architecture Developments and Carnegie Mellon University), commercial corporations, practioners and consultants.

9 Governance Models for Enterprise Architecture [13]

Enterprise Architecture is becoming more and more important for organizations in terms of e.g. cost-reduction, efficiency, business/IT alignment, standardization and management of complexity. Successfully implementing and working with EA requires good governance of EA. This chapter describes Enterprise Architecture from a governance viewpoint and addresses different types of EA governance, setting up the EA organization, the stakeholders involved and their roles, tasks, responsibilities, authorizations and commitment to Enterprise Architecture.

The main conclusions and conditions for setting up successful EA Governance are:
- o Setting up and organizing the EA organization within the organization's internal governance structure;
- o Pre-conditions, rules, principles, guidelines and standards;
- o Set up the EA Organization and identify stakeholders;
- o Assigning roles, responsibilities and authorizations to EA stakeholders on different organizational levels;
- o Commitment and support to Enterprise Architecture both on top-level as on operational level is necessary.
- o Best practices and practical tips for EA governance and setting up the EA organization

This section aims to provide different types of EA governance and some best practices and recommendations for successfully implementing an EA organization.

The main focus is on Enterprise Architecture and specifically on Enterprise Architecture Governance. Different types of governance models are addressed, and adopting and fitting EA governance within the internal organization's governance mode. Setting up the EA organization and its stakeholders on different organizational levels is mentioned as well.

9.1 *Positioning of Enterprise Governance*

Enterprise Architecture is a complete expression of the enterprise: a master plan which *"acts as a collaboration force"* between aspects of business planning (e.g. goals, visions, strategies and governance principles), business operations (e.g. business terms, organization structures, processes and data), automation (e.g. information systems and databases) and the enabling infrastructure of the business (computers, operation systems and networks). In a large modern enterprise an Enterprise Architecture Framework is used to capture a vision of the "entire organization". Successfully implementing, developing and management of

---

[13] *This section is a refinement of an earlier publication about EA Governance from Tom Coenen and Jaap Schekkerman.*

an organization's Enterprise Architecture isn't simple. It requires good Enterprise Architecture Governance.

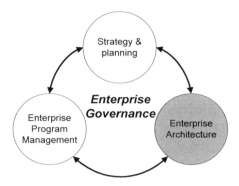

Figure 35. Enterprise Governance Positioning

As shown in figure 35, EA relates to Strategy & Planning and Enterprise Program Management. Enterprise Governance is necessary to achieve organizational goals and objectives and affects Strategy & Planning, Enterprise Architecture and Enterprise Program Management. Therefore Enterprise Governance is positioned in de middle of figure 35. In this section the focus is mainly on Enterprise Governance from an Enterprise Architectural viewpoint: Enterprise Architecture Governance.

The next sub sections concern the relation of EA to Enterprise Governance, Strategy & Planning and Enterprise Program Management.

9.1.1 Positioning of EA in relation to Strategy & Planning and Enterprise Program Management

Strategy & Planning
Enterprise Architecture is the linking pin between the 'as-is situation' (current enterprise architecture and infrastructure) and 'to-be situation' (strategy) and serves as a guideline in the enterprise architecture transformation process. Enterprise architecture prescribes the degrees of freedom and functions as a guideline: is the supply of information and corresponding infrastructure able to facilitate the organization's strategy (to-be situation)?

Enterprise Program Management
Phasing the steps in time to transform form the 'as-is' to the 'to-be situation' links Strategy & Planning to Enterprise Program Management. Programs and projects that contribute to the transformation from 'as-is' to 'to-be' are being planned and initiated to aid to organizational goals and objectives. Enterprise Architecture guarantees the planned changes of these transformations. These transformations may imply new and additional EA principles, guidelines and standards.

The role of Enterprise Governance

Executing an organization's strategy and achieving organizational goals and objectives phased in time – within the defined set of principles, guidelines and standards of the Enterprise Architecture — requires good governance. Enterprise Governance is necessary to realize goals and objectives within the context of Strategy & Planning, Enterprise Program Management and Enterprise Architecture.

9.1.2   Concepts of Enterprise Governance

The concept of governance is mostly described by 'executing certain controls and operations'. Bemelmans (1994) addresses governance as 'planning, executing and controlling purposive activities' (p.33). In this broad context governance can be seen as a continuous decision making process. Decisions are being made of what to do *(plan)*, how to do that *(execution)* and in what way actions and activities can be tested and evaluated *(control)*.

Specifications and definitions of governance are widely available in literature. In this chapter we use the definition as formulated by Wagter (2001). Wagter emphasizes that governance mainly concerns responsibilities, coordination, control and maintenance of processes:

> *'The set of organizational and procedural measures that aim to*
> *coordinate all activities of an organization in a way in which they optimally*
> *support the organization's business goals'*

Business governance and *IT governance* are part of *Enterprise Governance*, which covers and deals with all of an organization's governance.

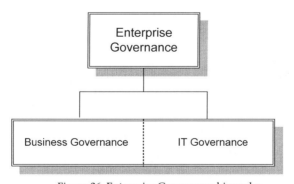

Figure 36. Enterprise Governance hierarchy

- o   Business governance: is aimed on strategy and value-creation with an organization's available resources.
- o   IT governance: IT-governance is about rules, assumptions and preconditions for IT and IT management. IT management is aimed at execution and

decision making while taking these rules, assumptions and preconditions into account. Some aspects that concern IT governance are:

- Perception of an organization's IT
- Governance and organization of IT
- IT responsibilities and authorizations
- IT strategy
- Principles, guidelines and standards

From an Enterprise Architecture viewpoint and increasing effective Business/IT alignment the dividing line between Business Governance and IT Governance is fading, as shown in figure 36.

In literature three different types of governance modes can be distinguished and are described: *centralized*, *decentralized* and *federal mode* governance. The next paragraphs concern these three governance modes.

9.2   *Understanding Different Enterprise Architecture Governance Models*

In the context of Enterprise Governance and from an Enterprise Architecture viewpoint, in this section we focus on Enterprise Architecture Governance.

Enterprise Architecture Governance concerns setting up the whole EA organization, including stakeholders, roles, tasks and responsibilities in line with the organization. EA Governance is about:

o   Setting up and organizing the EA organization within the organization's internal governance structure;
o   Preconditions, rules, principles, guidelines and standards;
o   Identifying EA stakeholders;
o   Assigning roles, responsibilities and authorizations to EA stakeholders;
o   Commitment and support to Enterprise Architecture.

The three different types of governance – centralized, decentralized and federal mode governance are being described from an Enterprise Architecture viewpoint and context in the next sections. The examples provided in the next paragraphs are from Dutch organizations in the public sector.

Besides setting up EA within an organization's governance mode both identifying stakeholders and commitment and stakeholders' roles, tasks, responsibilities and authorizations are key to successfully implementing Enterprise Architecture. Best practices for stakeholder, responsibilities, roles and tasks are provided in the next paragraphs.

9.2.1   Centralized EA governance

The centralized EA governance organization is known for its central Enterprise Architecture and strict organization-wide principles, guidelines and standards. Business units of an organization have to comply with the central formulated principles, guidelines and standards in their operation and supporting IT-services. No distinction is being made between business units (specific information systems and infrastructure) and maximum standardization in processes, information systems and infrastructure is being aimed for.

EXAMPLE OF A CENTRALISED EA GOVERNANCE ORGANISATION

The Ministry for Housing, Regional Development and the Environment in The Netherlands is an example of a centralized EA governance organization. Ministry-wide Enterprise Architecture, principles, guidelines and standards are set up by IT management and staff. Both the different directorates responsible for e.g. housing policy of the ministry (business units) and the supporting processes and infrastructure have to comply with this Enterprise Architecture and accompanying rules and guidelines in operation and supporting IT-services.

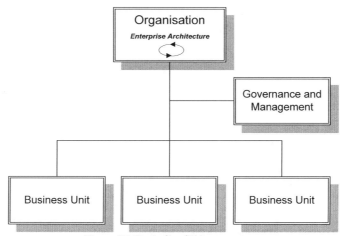

Figure 37. Centralized EA governance

The main distinctive characteristics of centralized EA governance are:
- o   Uniform organization-wide processes, data, information systems en IT-infrastructure
- o   Overall Enterprise Architecture and uniform organization-wide principles, guidelines and standardization exist
- o   Maximizing standardization
- o   Minimal deviation of enterprise architecture principles, guidelines and standards allowed
- o   Efficient centralized decision making

9.2.2   Decentralized EA governance

The decentralized EA governance organization is known for its decentralized Enterprise Architecture and business unit specific principles, guidelines and standards and freedom in decision making. Business units of an organization have to comply with decentralized business unit specific formulated principles, guidelines and standards in their operation and supporting IT-services. Maximum freedom in decision making and (IT) support for business unit specific processes, information systems and infrastructure are being aimed for.

EXAMPLE OF A DECENTRALISED EA GOVERNANCE ORGANISATION

In The Netherlands the police force used to be a decentralized EA governance organization. The different police forces in The Netherlands operated as separate business units with regard to Enterprise Architecture, principles, guidelines, standards and (IT) decision making. Specific police force (business unit) Enterprise Architecture, principles, guidelines and standards are set up by IT management and staff of that specific force.

Possible issues may demonstrate in such a decentralized EA organization concerning for example interoperability. Because of the diversity and freedom in data types, information systems and infrastructure, integration and the exchange of information and data between different police forces may be hindered. Nowadays, in The Netherlands the police forces are transforming towards a more centralized EA organization.

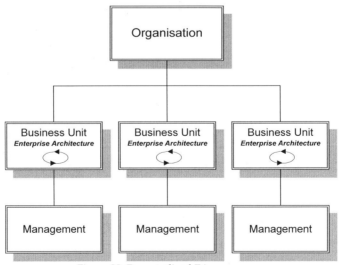

Figure 38. Decentralized EA governance

The main distinctive characteristics of decentralized EA governance are:
  o   An overall Enterprise Architecture and set of uniform organization-wide principles, guidelines and standards does not exist
  o   Business unit specific processes, data, information systems en IT-infrastructure

o Business unit specific principles, guidelines and standards
o Decentralized decision making per business unit

9.2.3 Federated EA governance

The federal mode EA governance organization is known for its central Enterprise Architecture and organization-wide principles, guidelines and standards, combined with business unit specific EA, principles, guidelines and standards. Business units of an organization operate within the central principles and guidelines, and fill in specific needs and IT-services with business unit specific principles, guidelines and standards. In this context we speak of freedom in restraint: business unit specific decision making and EA in context of organization-wide EA and rules. Distinction is being made between the central organization and business units (both organization-wide and specific information systems and infrastructure) and maximum flexibility in processes, information systems and infrastructure is being aimed for.

EXAMPLE OF A FEDERAL MODE EA GOVERNANCE ORGANISATION

The Ministry of Defence in The Netherlands is a federal mode EA governance organization. Ministry-wide Enterprise Architecture, principles, guidelines and standards exist for ministry-wide products, services and processes. For sub-sections of the ministry (business units) with specific needs and requirements business unit Enterprise Architecture, principles, guidelines and standards exist. For example the land forces have different needs and requirements on IT-services than the air force or navy. In the federal mode governance organization these specific needs can be fulfilled.

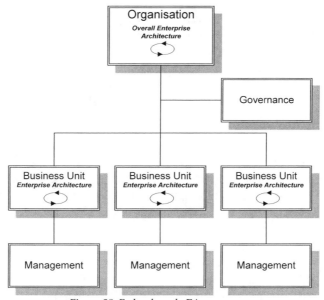

Figure 39. Federal mode EA governance

The main distinctive characteristics of federal mode EA governance are:
- o Combination of both maximizing standardization and specific processes, data, information systems and IT-infrastructure
- o Freedom in restraint
- o Increased complexity in decision making
- o Overall Enterprise Architecture and management for organization-wide processes, data, information systems and IT-infrastructure exists
- o Business unit specific Architecture and management for business unit specific processes, data, information systems and IT-infrastructure exists

9.3   *Creating EA Stakeholders Commitment*

The key to successfully implementing Enterprise Architecture within an organization's governance structure is to identify EA stakeholders and commitment to Enterprise Architecture. This paragraph provides best practices for successful stakeholder and commitment to Enterprise Architecture.

9.3.1   Successful stakeholdering for Enterprise Architecture Programs & Governance

Successful stakeholdering is critical for successful EA Programs & Governance. It is also critical for the smooth operations of a team, any cooperative relationship or a partnership venture.

Successful stakeholder techniques require political sensitivity. If you don't already have those skills, they can be developed by working with people to gain consensus until you learn what works and what doesn't.

Executives and other key individuals have a business interest in an EA program or EA initiative. Stakeholders include anyone whose business operations may change because of the EA program or initiative.

Other stakeholders may be suppliers to — or customers of — the directly affected business organization. They may be affected as they change what they provide or receive in the form of products and services.

Open communication should be maintained between Stakeholders and the Executive Sponsor, EA Steering Committee and the Chief Enterprise Architect. Stakeholders should raise issues, contribute ideas and anticipate the need for operational changes resulting from transformation plans or implementation new systems and work in coordination with the transformation plan to effect those changes.

9.3.2   Key elements of a successful stakeholder process

- o Communicate and involve stakeholders earlier rather than later. Most people hate surprises.

- o Identify the appropriate group of stakeholders who are representative of all areas.
- o Have the right representative(s) at the right place at the right time.
- o Determine who is responsible for what and how people will be held accountable.
- o Create a "Communication Template" identifying:
  - Each type of stakeholder group (e.g., steering committee, business managers, executives, department line staff, all employees, [specific groups of people], etc.)
  - What role they play in communications (e.g., must approve, have input, receive information, etc.)
- o Send the communication template to the entire stakeholder group before finalizing it.
- o Send a detailed agenda and supporting information to stakeholders before meetings where changes will be proposed (e.g., What is the change? Why do we need to make it? What are the options? Why is this the timeline? Etc.)
- o For each key milestone, identify what needs to happen, when, where, why, who and how.
- o Communicate deadlines and due dates with enough time for people to respond.
- o Set a time for response (i.e. "we see no impact to our area") so people know what is expected.
- o Follow-up on promised actions and let all stakeholders know what happened.
- o Keep detailed meeting minutes and distribute to all stakeholders.
- o Keep program documents in a central place where all stakeholders can access them and let stakeholders know where that is. In corporate environments, electronic documents should be stored on a shared network drive if possible or published via an Intranet.

9.3.3 Identifying Groups of stakeholders

In any EA Program, there tend to be 3 groups of stakeholders:

1. Those who are always out in front, who like to be first, who like to experiment or who like to be on the leading/bleeding edge of anything.
2. Those who wait for the first group to work out the kinks, and then they are ready and willing to move forward.
3. Those who will resist any change, complain about how everything is being done too fast and those who need more time to adjust to changes.

In identifying stakeholders and there interests, it is critical to identify those people who will be in the 3rd group and assign someone to work with them very early in the program. That way, they have more time to adjust. If this is not done, they can easily sabotage a program by not being ready when their help is needed.

It is also important to identify people who fit into the first group. These people can become the "Champions" or the "Ambassadors", the people who are playing a key role in communication and getting buy-in from the critical stakeholders.

9.3.4 Benefits of Keeping Stakeholders Involved

A successful EA Program & Governance depends on many things:
- o **People** (customers, EA team members, managers, executives, etc.)
- o **Resources** (financial resources, physical resources, schedules, products, supplies, vendors)
- o **Rewards** (benefits to be gained, savings to be achieved, new products to be built, new markets to be opened, new opportunities to be explored)
- o **Risks** (risk of remaining the same, risk of changing, outside factors, unknowns, mitigation of risks).

To make an EA Program & Governance successful means balancing many different aspects, constantly monitoring progress and status, and keeping stakeholders involved.

When stakeholdering is done successfully, those stakeholders take on some of the responsibility for making the program successful. They become the 'Champions' of their EA Program for their co-workers. They help train their co-workers, assist with changing internal procedures, provide early warning reports for things that might not work, help provide insights into other ways of approaching problems, and so much more.

When stakeholdering is not done successfully, those stakeholders become more problems to deal with, generate higher risks for the program and impede the successful flow of events because of their lack of awareness, lack of buy-in/agreement to the program's goals and resistance to the proposed changes.

9.4 *Accountability of EA Governance organisations*

When EA stakeholders have been identified, EA responsibilities and authorisations of different organisational levels become important. Different stakeholders on all kinds of organisation levels have different EA responsibilities and authorisations, tasks and roles. This paragraph provides best practices for EA responsibilities and authorisations on different organisational levels and the tasks and roles of the Enterprise Architecture Organisation.

EA responsibilities and authorisations on different organisational levels
On different organisational levels EA responsibilities and authorisations can be identified and distinguished. These organisational levels are corporate levels, division level, line of business level and unit level en is mentioned below.

Corporate Level

Enterprise Architecture

- Definition of responsibilities at Corporate Level
- Principles, guidelines and standards
- Enterprise Architecture for organisations all Common Facilities

Division Level

Enterprise Architecture

- Definition of responsibilities at Division Level
- Principles, guidelines and standards
- Enterprise Architecture for all Division Specific Facilities

Line of Business Level

Solution Architecture

- Definition of responsibilities at LoB Level
- Principles, guidelines and standards
- Solution Architecture at project level for LoB specific facilities

Unit Level

Solution Architecture

- Definition of responsibilities at Unit Level
- Principles, guidelines and standards
- Solution Architecture at project level

Roles, tasks and responsibilities of the Enterprise Architecture Organisation

Setting up the Enterprise Architecture organisation can require to have different teams with different assigned roles, tasks and responsibilities in the context of Enterprise Architecture, depending on the scope, the amount of people involved and the expected results. A suggested classification of dedicated EA teams which is derived from a Defence real life case is presented here.

Dedicated teams

1. EA Steering Group (EACS)
2. Enterprise Architects Team
3. EA Process Team
4. EA Communication & Support Team
5. EA Design / Maintain Team
6. EA Research Team

1. EA Steering Group
   o Programme Management of all activities
   o Decision Management

- o Enterprise Architecture Management / Process Management
- o Internal / External Representatives

2. Enterprise Architects coaching Team
   - o Expertise / Experience / Coaching by External Enterprise Architects using proven methods & approaches
   - o Training & Facilitation of Architects
   - o Responsible for bringing-in future Enterprise Architecture developments
   - o Quality Control and assessment of EA activities
   - o Support of the EA Process Team

3. EA Process Team
   - o Enterprise Architecture area design / development activities, with the focus at areas as:
     - o Business & Information Architecture
     - o Information-Systems & Technology Infrastructure Architecture
     - o Security and Governance
   - o Linking-pin Division Enterprise Architecture Groups
   - o Linking-pin Expert teams
   - o Process Co-ordination
   - o Training design / maintain team
   - o Mastering the details of Enterprise Architecture
   - o Supporting the design team
   - o Research and comparison of other enterprise architectures
   - o Facilitating the other teams

4. EA Communication and Support Team
   - o Responsible for all communication & PR activities
   - o Organising Events
   - o Developing Presentations / exposure documents
   - o Maintaining logistic activities
   - o Responsible for all exposure activities
   - o Supporting the whole enterprise architecture office & groups

5. EA Design / Maintain Team
   - o Production of (enterprise) architecture documents
   - o Organising enterprise architecture documents & standards
   - o Maintaining enterprise architecture documents & standards
   - o Responsible for the continuity of the core (enterprise) architecture activities
   - o Maintaining the enterprise architecture tools
   - o Support of Projects

6. EA Research Team
   - o Co-ordination of all experiments, proof of concepts or Pilots
   - o Planning of all tests and analysis
   - o Research / trend-watching on all technology topics

9.5   *Critical success factors for EA Governance*

Successful Enterprise Architecture Governance isn't simple. To make Enterprise Architecture Governance successful this paragraph provides some critical success factors for successful EA Governance.

- o   Enterprise Architecture's position in an organisation is not on top level and therefore EA doesn't receive top management attention and support
- o   Enterprise Architecture is being executed as a project, not as a continuous program, which leads to insufficient or no maintenance and management of the Enterprise Architecture and its deliverables
- o   The added value and economic benefits of Enterprise Architecture aren't clear enough for an organisation
- o   Lack of involvement and commitment of "the business" in creating and developing an Enterprise Architecture
- o   Insufficient or no communication about the role, place, responsibilities and results of the Enterprise Architecture function within an organisation, which leads to lack of commitment to the EA
- o   Insufficient knowledge and experience within an organisation to set up the EA organisation and function
- o   Insufficient or a lack of choices and agreements concerning EA methods, techniques, tools, frameworks and approaches

9.6   *Synopsis of best practices and future trends*

Some best practices and future trends on Enterprise Architecture Governance are presented here, to make EA Governance a success both now and in the future.

- o   Commitment to EA deliverables:
  - o   Make top management understand the role / place / function of EA
  - o   Gain sponsor at top level
  - o   Create simplicity and visibility
  - o   Organize the communication process both effective and efficient
  - o   Responsibilities and impact often unclear
  - o   Principles and guidelines are often not complied with
  - o   No means of power to enforce compliancy

- o   Limit Enterprise Architecture to common concern
  - o   Adjust depth of EA to goals and decision making
  - o   Provide and indicate scenarios and alternatives
  - o   Determine communality
  - o   Proper demarcation of the Enterprise Architecture

- o Enterprise Architecture results
    - o Visualizations are most effective
    - o Create visibility of AS-IS and TO-BE Enterprise Architecture on top level
    - o Don't create bulky reports, create visualizations which match and are tuned to the targeted audiences, preferably provided from a repository
    - o Make choices in modelling techniques for organization, processes, information, information systems and infrastructure
    - o Support data reproduction with tools

- o Influence of software suppliers on Enterprise Architecture
    - o Increasing influence of suppliers' architecture on Enterprise Architecture

- o Enterprise Architecture as an instrument for coordination and maintaining coherence
    - o Future Enterprise Architecture on transformation programs and the impact of change on business and technology
    - o Support Enterprise Architecture initiatives with financial foundations
    - o Manage and maintain the Enterprise Architecture

9.7 *Recommendations for successful Enterprise Architecture Governance*

Enterprise Architecture is becoming more and more important for organizations in terms of for example cost-reduction, efficiency, business/IT alignment, standardization and management of complexity. Successfully implementing and working with EA requires good governance of EA.

Different types of EA Governance Models exist – Centralized, Decentralized and Federal mode EA governance. The main conclusions and conditions for setting up successful EA Governance are:

- o Setting up and organizing the EA organization within the organization's internal governance structure;
- o Conditions, rules, principles, guidelines and standards;
- o Set up the EA Organization and identify stakeholders;
- o Assigning roles, responsibilities and authorizations to EA stakeholders on different organizational levels;
- o Commitment and support to Enterprise Architecture both on top-level as on operational level is necessary.

The ultimate operational goal of any organization is to optimize the alignment of their customer & partner needs, business strategy, organizational culture, business, people, processes and technology. This optimization, not only provides for efficient and cost effective performance, but also helps ensure proper execution of the defined organizational goals and objectives. So:

o   Make use of proven EA methods and techniques, preferably based on open standards
o   Measure an organization's EA maturity and set up the organization in accordance with its maturity
o   Respect an organization's own agreed upon selections, choices and concepts
o   Guarantee continuity by deploying organization-own Enterprise Architects for EA history and decision making, if necessary accompanied by external Enterprise Architects
o   Guarantee the transfer, sharing and management of knowledge by cooperation with an external organization and joining knowledge networks
o   Guarantee communication for both the EA process as the EA (intermediary) deliverables
o   Act both methodical as pragmatic
o   Future on commitment to the Enterprise Architecture process, then on EA deliverables, standardization, methodology and procedures
o   Stimulate cooperation between business and IT
o   Create visibility and recognition of the EA office

However, by itself, an Enterprise Architecture program & governance is not a panacea for success. It requires that:
o   The organizational goals and objectives are the right ones.
o   There are no inhibiting organizational, cultural, budgeting process, and people compensation issues.

These above items are beyond the scope of the Enterprise Architecture program & governance organization. Therefore, even a fully enabled Enterprise Architecture effort may only achieve incremental results, because the organizational issues presented above could limit the enterprise architecture's effectiveness.

10 Assessments of Enterprise Architectures

Today the area of (enterprise) architecture in the virtual digital world will become more and more full-grown. So the focus is changing to the quality of the work of enterprise architects. How can we review the results of the work of (enterprise) architects and how can we review their processes and activities. Can we define quality criteria to validate the products and results from other enterprise architects?

This chapter describes the main line of a methodology / approach in use by several organizations to review the activities and results of enterprise architects.

The effect of knowing that the results will be reviewed is that enterprise architects are taking more time and effort to implement and manage their enterprise architecture processes effectively as well as the take more attention to the quality of their results and decision-making.

10.1 *Proven approach for Enterprise Architecture assessments*

The approach developed by Jaap Schekkerman in 2001 is called the "Enterprise Architecture Score Card ™"

The attention for the quality of architecture work is growing, by the fact that the impact of enterprise architecture on organizations and technology is growing.

So how to measure that an enterprise architecture is 'good' given a certain situation and supporting well described goals and objectives.

So the question is when is an Enterprise Architecture Good Enough?

An Enterprise Architect knows he has achieved the perfect solution not when there is nothing left to add, but when there is, nothing left to take away. [Saint-Exupery][14]

'Good' in this context is a relative idea.

Before we can review an enterprise architecture, we have to define the Criteria how to review the enterprise architecture. These Criteria have a strong dependency of the goals and objectives of what has to be achieved with that enterprise architecture. So the first activity before starting an enterprise architecture study is to define these criteria.

---

[14] *From the Book, 'How to survive in the jungle of Enterprise Architecture Frameworks'; Publisher Trafford; ISBN 141201606-X; Author: J. Schekkerman; http://www.enterprise-architecture.info*

The term enterprise architecture results used in the context of this document means all results / deliverables produced by enterprise architects as a result of their activities, supporting the goals and objectives of that architecture study.

10.1.1 Goals and objectives of the Enterprise Architecture

To support an organizations goals and objectives, the EA program model can help us to understand the relations and elements that influence the decision-making about the adoption of enterprise architecture concepts in several ways.

10.1.2 Observing the Enterprise Architecture Program & Process

Enterprise Architecture provides a mechanism that enables communication about the essential elements and functioning of the enterprise.

It yields centralized, stable, and consistent information about the enterprise environment. In an insurance company, for example, an EA would help executives pinpoint the companies more lucrative markets, understand how well the company's current resources are meeting customer needs in those locations, and determine what kind of systems might be needed to improve services.
This EA program addresses at a holistic way the elements of strategy, frameworks, the overall EA process, methods & techniques, standards and tools.

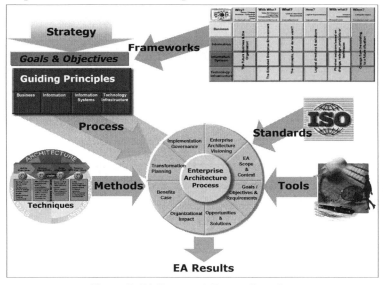

Figure 40. EA Program & Process Overview

This EA program model is focused on the goals & objectives and shows the influencing elements of an enterprise in such a way that the mission of an organization is the major driving force and the environment and the stakeholders are the influencing variables of the system. The enterprise architecture process shows the different elements compassing the process cycle.

There are tremendous rewards for organizations that are able to harness the vast array of available options into a holistic EA framework of flexible domains and supportive technology that meet the rapidly evolving needs of their stakeholder communities. Enterprise Architecture process and framework must effectively align business & IT resources and processes that they enable.

Defining a system based on the EA results is asking modelling methods that comply with the system development environment.

Supporting decision-making is asking other type of modelling methods and techniques.
So, besides the choices for an EA framework at the same time choices for supporting methods and techniques has to be made.
The decisions related to strategy, business goals, information needs, data mapping, selection of product- independent systems, and selection of specific hardware and software need to be guided by this framework to ensure maximal effectiveness and efficiency.

Unfortunately, while most Enterprise Architecture frameworks and processes are able to generate reasonably good descriptive enterprise architecture models, they do not create actionable, extended enterprise architectures that address today's rapidly evolving complex collaborative environments.

10.2   *The Enterprise Architecture Score Card™[15]*

The Enterprise Architecture Score Card is using a methodology related to the earlier in this guide mentioned enterprise architecture aspect areas and abstraction levels of E3A frameworks by the fact that during an enterprise architecture process most of these elements have to be addressed and described depending on the goals & objectives.

Based on these elements a methodology is developed to get insight and overview of de status of the addressed topics related to the quality of the enterprise architecture in scope.
Based on questionnaires per aspect area and abstraction level and over aspect areas, facts can be established to check the quality of the enterprise architecture efforts.

---

[15] *The Enterprise Architecture Score Card™ is a trademark of the Institute For Enterprise Architecture Developments.*

Institute For Enterprise Architecture Developments
Your - Return On Information ~

Enterprise Architecture Score Card ™

© Copyrights, 2001 - 2004, IFEAD

Clear = Well defined and documented
Partially Clear = partially addressed and documented
Unclear = NOT identified or addressed, NOT defined or NOT documented

ASC / Questions to the enterprise architecture result	Business (Status: Clear=2 Partially Clear=1 Unclear=0)	Information (Status: Clear=2 Partially Clear=1 Unclear=0)	Information Systems (Status: Clear=2 Partially Clear=1 Unclear=0)	Technology Infrastructure (Status: Clear=2 Partially Clear=1 Unclear=0)	Level of Alignment / Integration (Factor 0-2; 0=Insufficient 1=Average 2=Full)	Total Status 2	Total Status 1	Total Status 0
1 Are the Mission, Vision, Goals & Objectives of the enterprise architecture?	2	2	1	0	2	2	1	1
2 Is the Scope of the enterprise architecture program?	2	2	2	2	2	4	0	0
3 Is the Form & Function Level of deliverables?	2	2	2	2	1	4	0	0
4 Is the Business & IT Strategy?	1	1	0	0	1	0	2	0
6 Are the Guiding Principles & Drivers?	0	0	0	0	0	0	0	4
7 Are the Key Performance Indicators?	1	1	1	1	1	0	4	0
8 Are the Critical Success Factors?	2	2	1	1	1	2	2	0
9 Are the Critical Stakeholders?	1	1	1	1	0	0	4	0
Sub-Score Contextual Level	**11**	**11**	**8**	**7**				
10 Are the Collaborative Parties involved?	2	1	1	2	2	2	2	0
11 Are the Contractual Agreements?	2	0	0	1	1	1	1	2
12 Are the Interoperability Standards?	0	1	2	2	1	2	1	1
13 Are the related Law & Regulations?	1	1	0	0	0	0	2	2
14 Is the Ownership of Information?	1	1	0	2	1	1	2	1
Sub-Score Environmental Level	**6**	**4**	**3**	**7**				
11 Are the Functional Requirements?	1	1	2	2	1	2	1	0
12 Are the Non-Functional Requirements?	1	1	0	1	0	0	2	0
Are the Concepts in use?	2	1	1	2	1	2	2	0
13 Are the Security Requirements?	0	0	1	0	0	0	1	0
14 Are the Governance Requirements?	1	1	1	1	1	0	4	0
Sub-Score Conceptual Level	**5**	**4**	**5**	**6**				
15 Are the deliverables at logical level?	1	2	1	2	1	2	2	0
16 Are the critical logical design decisions?	1	1	2	2	0	2	2	0
17 Are the critical logical design decisions traceable?	0	0	1	1	1	0	2	2
18 Are the Logical Description Methods & Techniques?	2	1	1	0	1	1	2	0
19 Is at logical level the use of Modelling Tools?	1	1	1	0	1	0	3	1
20 Are the Logical Standards?	1	0	1	2	1	1	2	1
Sub-Score Logical Level	**6**	**5**	**7**	**7**				
21 Are the deliverables at physical level?	1	1	2	2	1	2	2	0
22 Are the critical physical design decisions?	1	2	2	2	1	3	1	0
23 Are the critical physical design decisions traceable?	1	2	2	2	0	3	1	0
24 Are the Physical Description Methods & Techniques?	2	1	1	0	1	1	2	1
25 Is at physical level the use of Modelling Tools?	0	1	1	0	1	0	2	2
26 Are the Physical Standards?	1	0	1	2	1	1	2	1
Sub-Score Physical Level	**6**	**7**	**9**	**8**				
27 Critical Design Decisions	0	0	1	1	0	0	2	0
28 Is the Organizational Impact?	1	1	2	2	1	2	1	0
29 Are the Costs Consequences?	0	0	0	0	2	0	0	4
30 Is the Security Impact?	0	0	0	0	1	0	0	4
31 Is the Governance Impact?	0	0	1	1	1	0	2	2
Sub-Score Transformational Level	**1**	**1**	**4**	**4**				
Total-Score All Level	**35**	**32**	**36**	**39**				

Figure 41. EA Score Card

10.2.1 Explanation of the used criteria & terminology

Using the Enterprise Architecture Score Card as a measurement instrument to check the quality of the EA efforts, can be done by answering the questions based on the assessed status with the goals and objectives of the enterprise architecture program in mind.

Every Question has to be assessed for the **Business, Information, Information-Systems** and **Technology Infrastructure** areas. A special item is focusing at the level of **Alignment / Integration** between these areas or *How* **Holistic** was the approach and *How* **Holistic** was this documented?

For each of these areas the result of each question can be assessed from 3 different situations.

Status 0 = Unknown and not documented (red);

Status 1 = Partly known and partly documented (yellow);

Status 2 = Fully known and well documented (green).

Besides these 3 values, the level of alignment / integrated for each question is assessed.

So the answer of each question encompasses the elements of **knowledge** and **documentation**.

Having the knowledge, but this knowledge is not documented, means maintenance cannot be done and the knowledge is not transferable to other people.

10.2.2 Explanation about the Calculations

Sub-totals and totals reflect the valuation for the quality of the assessed enterprise architecture results as well for the addressed completeness of the enterprise architecture process phases.

A more in-depth insight en overview of the quality of the enterprise architecture effort can be derived, based on this approach and steering can be done in areas with to less quality.

Questions with status 1 must be examined more in depth, to get more information about the availability, dependency, quality and level of documentation. Important is to get the **rationales of decisions** made during the enterprise architecture process.

10.2.3 Assessment of Maintainability

Besides the assessment of the quality, **maintainability** is even so a very important issue to address during the assessment process.

Are the enterprise architecture results in such a way documented that in a later stage other enterprise architects can easily understand and maintain that enterprise architecture? The topic of maintainability has to be explicitly addressed in the overall review report.
Enterprise Architecture Modelling & Documentation Tools can be very helpful in maintaining Enterprise Architectures.

Best practices within organizations will constantly update and refine this methodology. So if you have any experience with reviewing enterprise architecture projects and results, please share your experiences so that we can refine the Enterprise Architecture Score Card.

10.2.4 Benefits of the EA Score Card

Experiences within organizations show that enterprise architecture projects that will be reviewed, are better planned, better managed and better documented. So let your enterprise architecture team know up front that there processes and results will be reviewed. That will directly influence the overall quality of the enterprise architecture program.

11 How to define the Economic Value of Enterprise Architecture[16]

11.1 *Different Views, Different Values*

This section is a sub-set of the book, titled: 'The Economic Benefits of Enterprise Architecture'. Approaches are refined based on practical experiences of implementing EA Measurement Programs.

To remain competitive organisations must urgently address the growing dislocation between the business requirements and IT deliverables. This issue is directly impacting the enterprise's ability to make quick, accurate decisions and causing the slow implementation of the determined course of action. The gap between IT capability and business needs cannot be allowed to continue. Adoption of an end-to-end Enterprise Architecture approach will help to re-align IT developments with business objectives.

Senior management can no longer ignore Strategic Governance and compliance issues. The potential of hefty fines and the possibility of a jail sentence are usually guaranteed to gain everyone's attention. Additionally, many organisations are struggling to highlight the value that IT is delivering to the businesses. Enterprise Architecture provides a useful framework within which organisations can address their statutory and corporate governance requirements by better planning, ability to prove compliance, and providing a better understanding of the value of business & technology investments.

Many multi-national corporations struggle to get conformity across the local subsidiaries, and enterprises recently involved in mergers and acquisitions face similar assimilation problems across different separate entities. Again, Enterprise Architecture can offer a methodology that enables the use of common processes and unifies disparate companies into one cohesive organisation. The adoption of the same methods and procedures can also bring significant operational cost savings.

A number of issues have been outlined with which Enterprise Architecture can provide direct assistance, but the principal reward for adopting an enterprise architectural approach is at last to see the 'business' and 'IT' finding common ground, allowing them to relate with one another. IFEAD advocates the use of an organisation-wide enterprise architectural approach to change management and service delivery. Of course Enterprise Architecture is not without its challenges; however, these are surmountable given a corporate will to succeed.

---

[16] *See also the Book: 'The Economic Benefits of Enterprise Architecture'; Publisher Trafford Canada; ISBN: 141206729-4 or visit the website of the Institute For Enterprise Architecture Developments. http://www.enterprise-architecture.info*

11.1.1 Business View

The competitive and customer-focused landscape in which all organisations now operate means that change is an ongoing process, not a number of one-off events. There is a major concern with the sluggish reaction to both internal and external events within most organisations. Businesses must be able to carry out thoughtful analysis based on readily available, easily viewed and understood information. Another area of unease is the failure of many IT environments to deliver the anticipated business value and to meet the speed of change required by the business. Most of the IT department budget tends to be used on resources to stand still, rather than on the introduction of innovative new technologies and services.

Along with these increasing concerns there are growing regulatory pressures being brought to bear on organisations with US legislation such as Combined Code on Corporate Governance, Sarbanes-Oxley Act, Freedom of Information Act, and Data Protection Act and European legislations like Basel II and IFRS (International Financial Report Standards). Correspondingly, Strategic Governance will become progressively more pervasive, with technology being used to manage IT spending. To meet the demands of all these legislations the alignment of technology with business goals, risk management, portfolio management, and the deployment of an enterprise architectural approach will be required.

Enterprise Architecture frequently does not get beyond the end of the runway in many businesses, as it needs more than the odd evangelist within the organisation to ensure adoption throughout the whole enterprise. It is increasingly difficult, due to the economic climate, to justify any investment that does not have a good Return On Investment (ROI). Unfortunately, an enterprise architectural approach is also a huge change in culture of an organisation with the people aspects as important as the process, requiring commitment from the highest level of the company. Areas where Enterprise Architecture can bring significant financial savings include reduction in deployment times for enhancements and new services, more predictable project costs, economies of scale from standardisation, and the simplification of integration tasks.

It is imperative that business requirements drive the deployment of IT services, infrastructure, and technology. A new organisation wide enterprise architecture for Business & IT development that exploits existing IT investments and utilises a flexible IT environment is needed. A significant capability for an agile enterprise is the ability to quickly change and implement business processes. An enterprise architecture based approach can facilitate focus on business processes and information needs instead of the underlying technology and applications. Enterprise Architecture produces transparency to processes and information, promoting better understanding of the workings of the enterprise that, in turn, enables better decision-making and speedier deployment of changes.

To be effective, Enterprise Architecture must be more than models for business, information, and organisation. IFEAD recommends that the process encompass both services architecture and the deployment of a services platform. Only by embracing an end-to-end methodology and framework will organisations avoid analysis paralysis and separate islands of knowledge, maximizing the undeniable benefits and cost savings available from the use of Enterprise Architecture.

IFEAD believes that now is the time for organisations to start considering and deploying Enterprise Architecture based around a holistic business process and information view of operations. It is crucial that business and information requirements drive the creation of IT services. In many instances a rudderless IT department adopts a technology push approach due to the absence of any easily understood corporate direction and poorly articulated strategy.

11.1.2 Technology View

To provide maximum flexibility an IT strategy must be developed that is guided by Enterprise Architecture, and which is directed by a services model, uses Service Oriented Architecture (SOA) based around services standards, and has its foundation in a common services platform. This interlinked approach and use of a platform shields the inherent complexity of the IT environment from users, which as a consequence speeds up deployment, lowers the cost of integration, and exploits existing investment in IT applications and infrastructure.

There are many frameworks and tools existing to assist organisations deploying and maintaining Enterprise Architecture. Some are public sector-based while others originate from the commercial environment. Other frameworks concentrate on industry verticals, while others have strengths in architecture documentation, or the progression from present to future states. In his book, 'How to survive in the jungle of Enterprise Architecture Frameworks'[17] Jaap Schekkerman compares the most popular EA frameworks and helps the reader making the right choices. IFEAD believes that most of these frameworks are too technology and application focused, and need to be redesigned to take into account a holistic and more business and services-oriented approach. The Extended Enterprise Architecture Framework (E2AF) developed by IFEAD fulfils these needs.

The design of many current systems is made up of traditional 3-tier applications consisting of presentation, logic, and data layers, having developed from monolithic applications and 2-tier software. These applications tend to make use of their own user interfaces, databases, and security functionality. Point-to-point integration is usually employed between applications. These features have produced inflexible systems, which make upgrading applications time-consuming and expensive.

---

[17] *Book; 'How to survive in the jungle of Enterprise Architecture Frameworks'; Author: Jaap Schekkerman; Publisher Trafford, Canada; ISBN141201607-X*

There is an obvious need for better integration between applications to provide for business agility and the requirements of real-time business. This is leading to the deployment of SOA where composite applications can be created, modified, and removed dynamically, and software reused. SOA enables the building of functionality based on components and services, either abstracted from existing applications, provided by the platform, or from an external source. The move to a SOA can be achieved by the use of an Enterprise Services Bus (ESB) offering the opportunity to develop a process-driven view of application integration. It is also essential to be able to present a unified view of an organisation's data, and supply a common user interface.

There are a number of other important attributes that an enterprise architectural approach should embody throughout design, specification, and implementation. Security is a key issue with which all private and public sector organisations have to contend with. Security is a balance between usability and acceptable risk, which needs to be varied from service to service dependent on the context. The move to componentisation means that the granularity of security features has also to be finer. Security must not be left to the technicians. There are regulatory considerations to take into account and the requirements must be driven by a security policy including input from business needs, sensitivity of the information, and analysis of the risks.

IT solutions have to be adaptable, catering for the continual changes in the internal and external environments. Flexibility is important for the creation of robust IT services. Openness is crucial for protecting IT investments, both in the short and long term, and preventing supplier lock-in. The shift to componentisation relies heavily on standardisation, with openness also important for interoperability, enabling the quick deployment of new and innovative applications, and underpinning security and information protection. Some of these standards are still emerging. This should not preclude the adoption of relevant standards by the organisation.

Scalability must be part of the enterprise architecture design, with it being problematical to add as an after thought. The whole systems operation becomes more dependent on the performance of the weakest component. Scalability is no longer about matching a fixed system capacity, but the ability to supply resources to meet increases or decreases in demand, optimising the system resources to match the current needs in real-time. Additionally, the provision of services and resources highlights the need for end-to-end management with such features as policy-based management version control, full visibility, real-time monitoring, and Service Level Agreements (SLA's).

IFEAD believes that at the heart of an end-to-end enterprise architectural approach is an information services environment. The combination of standards-based integration, flexible business processes, unified information, composite applications, and real-time metrics into a services environment is an extremely strong proposition, enabling an evolutionary approach to linking business processes to enterprise databases, legacy systems, line-of-business applications, and external services.

11.1.3 Market View

The next big wave that the IT industry will ride is looking as though it could be Enterprise Architecture, driven in part by the need for compliance and a flexible Business & IT environment. The evolution of IT is at a crossroads. The dynamics of the IT market will be fundamentally altered, with the vendors having to adopt a services, rather than technology, focused approach, facilitated in no small part by SOA, the next step along the path to system modularization.

This componentisation and move to delivery of services will redraw the battle lines between the existing IT vendors in the market place, with the platform providers offering generic services, Independent Software Vendors (ISVs) offering generic and application-specific services, and System Integrators providing services orchestration. They will all need to quickly redefine their objectives and adopt a services perspective. The challenge of re-engineering monolithic applications into components and services could prove too much for many vendors.

The large services platform vendors are struggling to deliver all the components and services that go to make up Enterprise Architecture in its entirety. Most vendors focus on the technology aspects, providing platforms with strong horizontal integration with the many services on offer. However, there is little or no visible vertical integration with the higher business-focused layers of an enterprise architectural approach. Each vendor's services platform offering, not unsurprisingly, reflects the relative strengths being based on the origins of the platform. For example, a vendor with a strong database product will emphasize the importance of this service, whereas other vendors previously concentrating on development tools or on applications will seek to emphasize these aspects.

The dominant feature in services platform selection over the next years will be the ability to support service provision, thereby assisting the move to managed services for part or all of the organisation's Business & IT requirements. There is obvious appeal to IT management to support the deployment of a services platform that one vendor embodies. This is where the larger vendors that have adapted to a services rather than technology focus will have an advantage. Organisations will pay less attention to the technology and technical detail of the platform, but will instead focus on issues such as quality of service, cost of delivery, security, flexibility, and platform ecosystem.

11.1.4 Value View

According to a recent CFO survey, when the time comes to decide which Business & IT programs deserve funding, eight out of ten chief financial officers say improving customer value takes priority over cost-reduction.

There is a vital need to dig more deeply into CFO's investment goals and expectations surrounding business & technology that improves customer management. CFO's agree that their companies need to continue to invest in customer-centric value and technologies (e.g., CRM, call centre, sales force automation, personalization, e-self service, mobile technologies, data mining and business intelligence).

But many senior executives are no longer able or willing to make significant investments based merely on gut feel. They require a disciplined enterprise architecture approach and framework to determine and evaluate investment options and to measure these initiatives as they proceed.

11.2   *The role of EA Frameworks in defining Value*

Today's view of Enterprise Architecture takes a holistic and balanced look at the business and IT components within an organisation.

"Enterprise Architecture is a complete model of the enterprise; a master plan which acts as an integrating force between aspects of business planning such as goals, visions, strategies and governance principles; aspects of business operations such as business terms, organisation structures, processes and data; aspects of IT such as application systems and databases; and the enabling technological infrastructure of the business such as computers, operating systems and networks."

To support this enterprise-wide perspective, Enterprise Architecture frameworks have been created to provide communication and program structures for developing a comprehensive Enterprise Architecture. Several Enterprise Architecture Frameworks are developed overtime and in a recently published book[18] I have analyzed 15 well known Enterprise Architecture frameworks.

While today's Enterprise Architecture frameworks deliver a consistent overview and approach, they do also share a common concern for the various components of the enterprise that must be captured and analyzed. An Enterprise Architecture framework supports in a holistic way the integration between Business, Information, Information-Systems and Technology Infrastructures Architectures, while aligning support for the enterprise's strategy, principles and goals& objectives and taken into account the overall viewpoints about security, governance and privacy.

IFEAD's Extended Enterprise Architecture Framework populated diagram below illustrates the common components required in today's Enterprise Architecture solutions.

---

[18] Book, *'How to survive in the jungle of Enterprise Architecture frameworks'*; Author: *Jaap Schekkerman*; Publisher *Trafford - Canada; ISBN: 141201607-X*

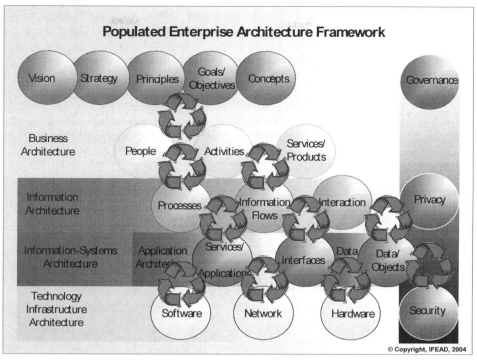

Figure 42. Populated EA Framework

A complete set of Enterprise Architecture models, objects, and artefacts will include the following components:

- o *Enterprise Architecture / Strategic Direction* – Creates a vision for the enterprise that will guide and control the development of each architecture area and its components.
- o *Business Architecture* – Describes the current and target business environments, focusing on the business activities and operations of the enterprise.
- o *Information Architecture* – Describes the current and target business environments, focusing on the business process, information flows and interactions of the enterprise.
- o *Information-System Architecture* – Defines what kinds of application systems are relevant to the enterprise and describes the applications as logical groups of capabilities that manage the information and support the business processes defined in the Business & Information Architecture.
- o *Technology Infrastructure Architecture* – Identifies technology principles and defines the technology platforms and the distribution of data and applications.

The comprehensive nature of Enterprise Architecture, though, is more than a collection of the constituent aspect architectures.

Enterprise Architecture frameworks and supporting tools must maintain the critical elements of each aspect architecture, as well as the interactions between the enterprise architecture components. It is through the analysis of the component relationships that the Enterprise Architecture becomes a valuable management tool.

11.3   Enterprise Architecture as a Management Tool

A documented Enterprise Architecture is a management tool that can be used to bring business and IT into closer alignment.

Paul Harmon executive editor/analyst for Business Process Trends says:

"An Enterprise Architecture program is a tool to help executives think about the organisation as a whole. An Enterprise Architecture captures a wide variety of information, establishes relationships among the various documents and diagrams and stores all of the information together in a single repository, so that managers can then see the relationships, ask questions, identify problems, or run simulations to help make decisions about changes they are considering."

11.4   The Enterprise Architecture Measurement Program & Framework_{sm}

Now we know what the areas are where we can focus on to measure the Economic Value of our organisation, we have to answer the following questions 'Why do we measure?' as a pre-requisite to the question 'What should be measured?' Even so it is extremely important to answer these questions before answering the questions 'How to measure?' the measuring method, 'With what to measure?' the measuring technique and 'When to measure?' the timing and measuring process cycle.

11.4.1   EA Measurement objectives

- o   Document the purposes for which EA measurement and analysis is done, use the GQM approach. (GQM= Goal-Question-Metric)
- o   Specify the kinds of actions that may be taken based on the results of the data analyses
- o   Continually ask the question – what value will this measurement be to those people who will be asked to supply the raw measurement data and who will receive the analyzed results
- o   Involve the end users of the measurement and analysis results in setting measurement objectives whenever possible
- o   Maintain traceability of the proposed EA measurement objectives to the information needs and business objectives

---

sm Enterprise Architecture Measurement Framework (EAMF) is a Service Mark of the Institute For Enterprise Architecture Developments, The Netherlands.

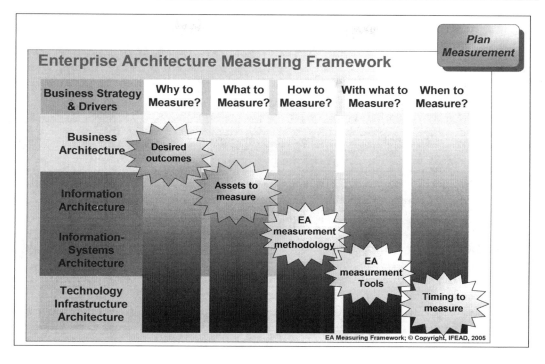

Figure 43. Enterprise Architecture Measuring Framework

In this way an explicit link is made between how to use the results of the EA measurements and the improved business effectiveness or improved technology efficiency that is sought during the EA transformation program.

To answer these questions in an efficient way the Enterprise Architecture Measurement Framework can be very helpful.

Supporting cross reference techniques can be used to lay down the rationales for these questions and the standards to measure against. In an initial situation a **zero** or **baseline** measurement can be the starting point and reference standard.

11.5　*Why to Measure?*

Traditional performance measurement focuses on financial performance, with the primary purpose of informing external stakeholders of the state of the business. When used for internal purposes, such techniques fail because they tend to control behaviour, rather than tracking the real results of effective use of knowledge. Being world class requires that an organisation's performance measurement system encourages behaviour that maximizes corporate results, both currently and in the future. To be effective, the system must be part of the strategic plan. Each measurement should be traceable and supportive of corporate purpose. The focus should be on performance measurement as information, not measurement as control. And the performance management system must constantly be re-evaluated.

11.6   What to Measure?

11.6.1   Costs & Benefits of the EA practice itself

First of all the costs and benefits of establishing an Enterprise Architecture practice itself in your organisation can be measured. A "generic" activity structure is given to provide insight into generic cost elements, activities, and cost content. This structure is intended to serve as a point of departure for discussion between cost analysts and enterprise architects in scoping an EA program as well as estimating its costs. A general equation for the cost of an enterprise architecture is:

EA Lifecycle Cost = EA Initiation/Definition Cost + EA Development Cost + EA Implementation Cost + EA Maintenance Cost

There are a number of costing challenges for an enterprise-wide capability, but EA's are important from a cost perspective because EA's should provide a more cost-effective use of limited resources (money, people, activities, and equipment) through economies of scale that offer ways of sharing services, elimination of duplicative, incompatible, or non critical capabilities, identification of new business initiatives or innovative IT solutions through gap analysis, and information for the Selection, Control, and Evaluation of decisions.

11.6.2   Effected Costs & Benefits of EA programs

Second and more important to the business is the performance measurement of costs and benefits related to the execution of Enterprise Architecture guided transformation programs.

The best performance and value measurement methods of the second area follow a performance budgeting approach.

A performance budget is an integrated annual performance plan and annual budget that shows the relationship between EA program funding levels and expected results. It indicates that a goal or a set of goals should be achieved at a given level of spending. An effective performance budget does more than act as an object class, program, or organisational budget with anticipated outcomes. It identifies the relationships between money and results, as well as explaining how those relationships are created. This explanation is key to managing the program effectively. As variances between plans and actuality occur, managers examine the resource inputs and how they relate to outcomes to determine program effectiveness and efficiency.

Costs to build an EA vary. Thus the resources, in terms of staffing, that each organisation commits to build the EA will vary. Determining the appropriate staffing level depends on many factors, including:

- o   Size and complexity of organization
- o   Objective of the enterprise architecture
- o   Specificity of recommendations to be made
- o   Extent of organization transformation
- o   Timeframe to be examined
- o   Number of communities involved
- o   Type of information required
- o   Fidelity of information required
- o   Volatility of information collected
- o   Risk willing to accept

Additionally, the cost analyst must consider the boundary of the estimate. In other words, the analyst must set ground rules that outline which costs are to be included and which costs extend beyond the scope of the analysis. Framework selection and product selection, including the level of detail projected for the program, will greatly influence EA costs.

11.6.3   Collecting Data

An EA program performance budget defines all activities, direct and indirect, required by an EA program for support, in addition to estimating activity costs. For example, if the measure for the "conduct criminal investigations" activity within a government agency is the number of completed investigations, then the next series of steps links the resources ultimately to outcomes. The following figure outlines this process. By tracking the cost and number of units for each activity, output, and outcome, unit cost information also may be generated.

Data have to be collected of all the sources, services and activities in scope of the EA measurement process. Managers must have accurate and timely cost and performance information to manage their resources most effectively. This applies to administrative support as well as program officials. In certain cases (e.g., computer services), managers require this information to establish unit prices. In other cases, managers simply want to ensure that every dollar supporting a program is spent wisely.

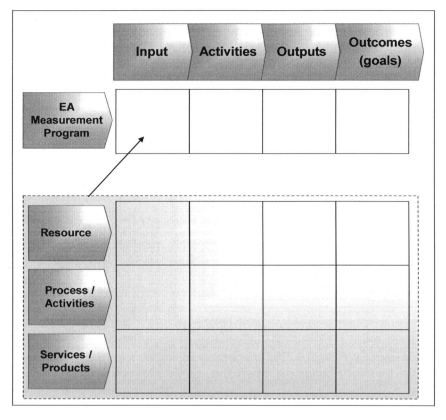

Figure 44. Collecting Data

11.6.4 Dealing with Risks & Uncertainty

As is evident, risk and uncertainty are closely linked. However, increasing uncertainty can actually reduce risks and vice versa. This phenomenon can be explained by the fact that uncertainty and complexity are closely linked and produce an undesirable side effect for decision makers, which is lack of precision.

Uncertainty and the value of flexibility in the face of uncertainty are at the core of both enterprise architecture development and finance. To reduce the risks in Enterprise Architecture programs, the Enterprise Architecture Scorecard© developed by IFEAD can be used to trace the quality of the EA process.

11.7 How to Measure in the Context of the Desired Outcome?

The EA measurement plan defines the conditions of an EA measurement program. Based on the mission and vision of the organization, the desired outcome has to be defined. Taken the desired outcome as the starting point the EA measurement program has to be set up based on a suitable methodology of EA measurement. Essential parts of the EA program are stable funds necessary for consistent support of the program; number, quality and productivity of people necessary to execute the program and sustain the organization and the right set of methodologies & tools that allow people to use techniques to efficiency run the program and organization.

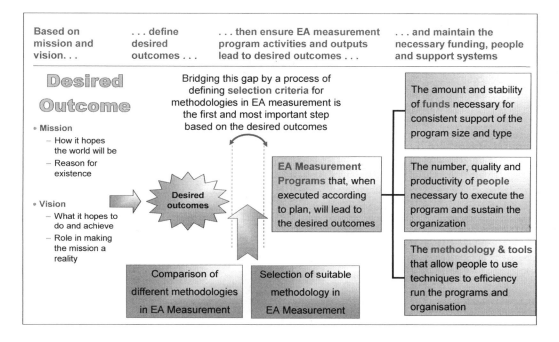

Figure 45. EA Measurement Plan

11.7.1   Criteria for EA Measurement

Criteria have to be:

o   **Relevant:** Truly important measurements whose outcome ultimately affects overarching goals (in terms of both efficiency and effectiveness)

o   **Valid:** Measures what it is supposed to (and thus promotes correct behaviour)

o   **Reliable:** Easy to measure, not susceptible to gross systematic errors

o   **Simple:** Easy to explain and understand

o   **Can be influenced/ permit accountability:** The relevant division, department, or individual exerts large degrees of influence over and can be held accountable for the measure

Perfection will never be possible. Create a set of guidelines for the organisation's work and be prepared to revise metrics, especially in the early stages of EA measurement

11.7.2   EA Measurement Process

Efficient EA Measurement Processes are required to ensure that Cost / Benefit Information is collected and reviewed.

- o   Assess EA measurement program in terms of inputs, activities, outputs and outcomes
- o   Focus on outcomes, but also measure key process / activity steps
- o   The term "outcome" does not apply as well these categories, but most will still be measured on outputs and outcomes (achievement of goals), and on crucial inputs and activities
- o   Do not measure assets in every layer – select only the key metrics that drive EA performance and achievement of goals

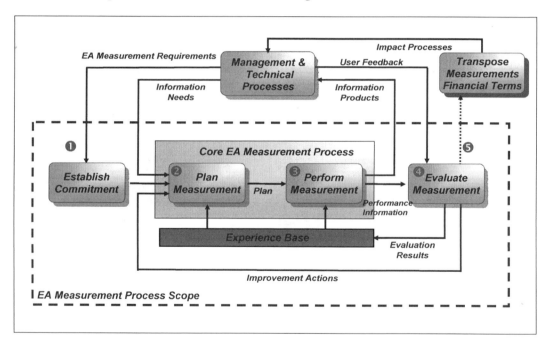

Figure 46. EA Measurement Process

An EA measurement initiative involves the following steps:

1.   Specifying the objectives of EA measurement and analysis such that they are aligned with established information needs and business objectives
2.   Defining the EA measures to be used, the data collection process, the storage mechanisms, the analysis processes, the reporting processes, and the feedback processes

3. Implementing the collection, storage, analysis, and presentation of the data
4. Collect & Analyze information about the measured assets
5. Providing objective results that can be used in making business judgments and taking appropriate corrective actions

11.7.3 Transpose EA Measurements in Financial terms

Most organisations today have already existing financial measurement techniques, the challenge is to stay at these existing measurement techniques and transpose them onto the EA domain so that existing measurement techniques can be used to measure EA related progress.

In some countries like the US, government is defining the performance measurement techniques for there agencies and states, defined in the US Government Performance and Results act and agencies have to comply with these regulations.

So in some areas you can use the existing (financial) measurement techniques and in other focus areas you have to introduce new (EA) comprehensive measurement techniques.

Discuss with your Chief Financial Offer or Controller how to measure the economic value so that the outcome is in line with the financial methods and techniques of your organisation.

11.7.4 Plan EA Measurement Program

Setting Up an effective EA Cost / Benefit measurement program is based on 4 major drivers. In the figure below these 4 major drivers are explained more in detail.

Figure 47. Major drivers of an EA Measurement Program

11.7.5 The Select, Control, Evaluate Approach

This structured method for EA investment management defines three phases of the investment management process. In the select phase, the costs and benefits of all available EA programs / projects are assessed and the optimal portfolio of EA programs / projects is selected.

During the control phase, the portfolio is monitored and corrective action is applied where needed. In the evaluate phase, executed EA programs / projects are reviewed to assure that they are producing the benefits expected and adjustments are made where appropriate.

Within an organisation, all phases may be underway at once as they are applied to EA programs/ projects at different stages of their lifecycle.

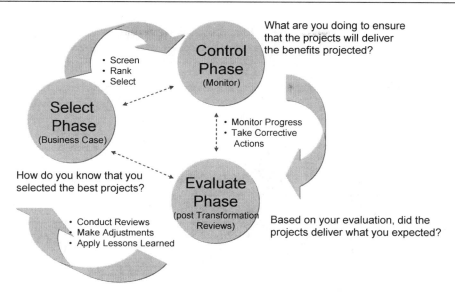

Figure 48. The Select, Control, Evaluate Approach

11.8   *Which What to Measure?*

The impact of enterprise architecture can be measured using several investment appraisal methods.

Costs are simply the accumulation of expenses, such as activities, services, people, labour, training, tools, verification and validation, and compliance or maturity assessment.

Benefits are the monetization of increased operational efficiency, reduced operational costs and personnel numbers, increased customer satisfaction, and consolidated information systems.

Costs and benefits are the basic inputs of most of the investment appraisal methods. Benefits are a little more challenging to identify and monetize.

11.8.1   EA investment methods & frameworks

Most of the investment appraisal methods mentioned in the next overview are described in short in the sections about investment appraisal methods.

Organisations need to select the appropriate EA investment appraisal method or techniques that best fits the organisations needs or law.

Institute For Enterprise Architecture Developments	**Enterprise Architecture Value Measurement Methods Framework**		
Traditional investment appraisal methods			
Costs	(Sum of Costs)	Total amount of money spent on Enterprise Architecture	$\sum_{i=1}^{n} Cost_i$
Benefits	(Sum of Benefits)	Total amount of money gained from Enterprise Architecture	$\sum_{i=1}^{n} Benefit$
NPV	(Net Present Value)	Deflated benefits of Enterprise Architecture (inflation)	$\frac{Benefits}{(1 + Inflation\ Rate)^{5\,Years}}$
B/CR	(Benefit to Cost Ratio)	Ratio of Enterprise Architecture benefits to costs	$\frac{NPV}{Costs}$
ROI	(Return On Investment)	Ratio of adjusted Enterprise Architecture benefits to costs	$\frac{NPV-Costs}{Costs} \times 100\%$
BEP	(Break Even Point)	Point when benefits exceed costs of Enterprise Architecture	$\frac{Costs}{NPV} \times 60Month.$
TCO	(Total Cost of Ownership)	TCO is a concept by which all costs associated with a capital purchase are accounted for in the value assessment	
Comprehensive investment appraisal methods			
AIE	(Applied Information Economics)	Hubbard Decision Research's Scientific and theoretically sound method for addressing the EA investment dilemmas	
EVM	(Earned Value Management)	Earned Value helps evaluate and control project risk by measuring project progress in monetary terms	$EV=\%PCxPB$
ABC	(Activity Based Costing)	ABC allows an organization to determine the actual cost associated with each product and service	
BC	(Business Case)	BC is a tool to determine and document the costs and benefits of functional process improvements	
EA focused Comprehensive investment appraisal methods			
ATAM	(Architecture Tradeoff Analysis Method)	ATAM provides software architects a framework for understanding technical tradeoffs by decision making	
CBAM	(Cost Benefit Analysis Method)	CBAM aids in the elicitation / documentation of the costs, benefits, and of a "portfolio" of architectural investments	$CBAM~ATAM$
EAAF	(EA Assessment Framework)	The USA-OMB EA Assessment Framework v1.5 is assessing agencies about their progress in EA	
EBV	(Economic Business View)	EBV is a set of B, F, I models required to evaluate and prioritize transition alternatives and modernization plans	$EBV=EBV1+2+3+4+5$
ITIM	(IT Investment Management)	ITIM framework is a maturity model that an organization can achieve in its IT investment management capabilities	

Figure 49. Overview of (EA) Investment Appraisal Methods & Frameworks

Any methodology proposed for investment management of EA development activities must synchronize with the overall EA initiative, as it is imperative to understand broadly the EA initiative in order to develop a reliable and acceptable investment management methodology for it.

11.8.2 Mapping methods & techniques to the EA Value Model

Back to the Enterprise Architecture Value Model, when the areas of cost reduction or value generation are identified in the current or future situation, the appropriate EA investment appraisal method can be chosen that best fits to the organisational financial methods. Best practices are showing that in one organisation different investment appraisal methods can be used, based on the performance measures as well as the goals and objectives of measurement and the areas of interest. Do us **to comply**, **to check** or **to challenge**.

The next figure is showing an example of mapping EA investment methods & techniques to the EA value model, showing the appropriate methods in a specific area.

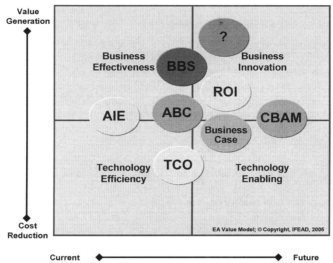

Figure 50. Mapping of EA investment methods to the EA Value Model

11.9   *Where & When to Measure?*

The US General Accounting Office has identified 5 categories of Costs & Benefits related to E-Gov and EA which can be measured.

(a)   **Financial improvement**; Financial improvements mean reducing the costs of organisations and enhancing revenue collection

(b)   **Constituent services**; Constituent services mean improved service to customers, suppliers, and key stakeholders

(c)   **Reduced redundancy**; Reduced redundancy means consolidating, reducing, or eliminating unneeded procedures, activities and legacy computer systems

(d)   **Economic development**; Economic development means to grow local, state, and federal economies

(e)   **Fostering democracy**; Fostering democracy may mean offering a consistent level of customer service to all stakeholders, regardless of political affiliation

These categories can be helpful in determining the focus areas of measuring the effects of EA programs.

Measuring everything continuously is not effective, so the timing of what to measure and when is crucial for the results of the measurement. Defining criteria for when to measure are helpful in comparing a baseline measurement with new measurements so that the circumstances of the measurement are comparable and representative for a given situation.

11.10 Some Golden Rules

1. Calculating the **COSTS & VALUE** of EA is hard to do, but……..
2. Costs & Value of EA can only be calculated if you collect **DATA** about it.
3. So, you have to define a **PROCESS** of collecting EA effected DATA.
4. Defining the PROCESS to collect the data, you are at least focusing on 2 **AREAS** of the EA value model of which you can calculate COSTS & VALUE.
5. Use (EA) **TOOLS** to store and explore the DATA
6. Check the DATA with the business owners and define the appropriate investment appraisal **METHODS.**

If we can't quantify the economic value of Enterprise Architecture programs at a time and we can't quantify the aimed added value of EA transformations, why should we put so much effort in it?

Not all the effects of EA programs can be easily translated in financial terms however we have to start with a mindset of trying to measure the effects of what we are doing. With real figures it is easier to discuss the aimed effects of change and it is easier to discuss about budgets, added value and costs.

In an open and mature society we need this type of information to manage organisations, to support decision making and to reflect to the dynamics of that society.

12   Compliancy & Enterprise Architecture

12.1   *What is Compliance?*

Having worked in the IT arena for quite some time, it's fun to see all the media focus on compliance, all the compliance-specific projects being implemented in organizations across the world (particularly in the United States), and the general buzz about compliance. A few years ago, we simply called it "following the rules."

12.2   *Defining Rules*

Until fairly recently, companies more or less were able to define the rules of IT conduct within their organizations. For example, they might decide that only members of the Human Resources (HR) department would have access to employee salary information, or they might write a policy stating that employees aren't allowed to test the company's internal security measures without written permission. Rules defined the answers to questions such as: Who was allowed to have keys to the filing cabinets? And Who was allowed to come into work late and who wasn't?

Those rules were the beginning of the more formal idea of compliance in application today, and they've been around since long before computers came on the business scene.

However, that is not to say that companies have been subject to only their own rules. For example, United States Department of Defence (DoD) contractors have always been subject to externally developed rules regarding the confidentiality of information, rules for performing background checks on potential employees, and so forth. By following these externally developed rules, the contractors helped ensure future business with the DoD. In other words, they were worried about *compliance* in order to maintain their businesses.

Today, several external organizations—primarily government legislators—have gotten into the act of writing business rules. These rules tend to target specific types of industries—such as healthcare, financial services, and so forth—and, rather than focusing on day-to-day business issues, these new sets of rules tend to concentrate on protecting the personal information that these businesses handle (for example, customer data, health care records, financial information, and so forth). These external rules are *no different* from the business rules that have been created and applied within organizations from the beginning. True, the new rules give organizations less control because the rules are externally developed rules and are enforced through legislation, but *complying* with those rules is the same activity that it always has been.

Compliance is simply the act or process of meeting rules. It doesn't matter from where those rules originate, and it doesn't really matter what *kind* of rules they are—business rules, legislation, security rules, and so forth—simply meeting them means that you're in compliance.

Thus, the first crucial idea that you should bear in mind throughout the rest of this section: *Compliance is simply the act or process of meeting rules, no matter who made the rules or what the rules apply to.* You'll find that compliance makes more sense, and is easier to plan for, if you think about *all* of your business rules in one big lump.

True, failing to comply with an externally developed rule might carry a heftier financial penalty than failing to comply with an internally developed rule. However, presumably your internally developed rules are just as important for other reasons, such as profitability, governance, and so forth. The second crucial idea to consider throughout this guide: *Meeting rules isn't sufficient.*

12.3   *Verifiable Compliance*

Organizations have often developed comprehensive policies for how their IT should work, and spent tens of thousands of dollars configuring the IT to meet those policies. But simply *doing* so doesn't tell you that you're compliant. And, while they had some great process flowcharts that described how various key processes would work, having those in place doesn't tell you that you're compliant either.

12.4   *Doing vs. Being*

In the compliance world, you're not compliant until someone looks at your environment and says that you are. Whatever processes or systems you've got in place don't matter; the rule of the road is that only an audit can determine whether your organization is compliant. Unfortunately, the general world of compliance, particularly when it comes to legislative compliance, doesn't understand anything beyond mere auditing. Look at it this way: Auditing serves the *letter* of the law, while enforcement serves, as I said earlier, its *spirit*.

A good auditor only checks the *end state* for compliance: The rule says no note-passing, so the auditor checks to see whether notes are being passed. The actual *means* of compliance aren't a concern because it doesn't matter how compliance is achieved, only that it is, in fact, achieved. In the IT industry, of course, testing the end state can be a complex, challenging, and technical task. For example, how do you test the end state for a policy that says that only HTTP traffic can be allowed into the network? You must conduct a test in which you try to get other forms of traffic in. Unfortunately, most auditors don't have the technical background necessary to conduct this type of end-state audit. Instead, they must rely on auditing your measures: They'll check the firewall configuration against a template, and if the configuration doesn't match their template, then there is a compliance issue.

The downside to auditing measures, as opposed to auditing end state, is that the technology for doing so is complex. Simply because some measures are in place to implement a policy doesn't mean that the policy is fully implemented. It's possible, for example, for a firewall's configuration to meet the requirements of the auditor's template while still allowing traffic that the firewall shouldn't. Had the auditor tested the end state rather than just looking at the firewall configuration, it would be obvious that something was letting illegal traffic into the network. It's the difference between *doing* and *being*: Implementing (and checking) your measures are the *doing*, but it doesn't guarantee compliance. *Being* compliant means testing for compliance to the rule, whatever it is, and not worrying about how the rule is being implemented.

12.5   Auditing vs. Enforcement

The difference between auditing and enforcement remains important. Because testing the end state of IT, especially network configurations, can be so complex, organizations are often forced to rely on configurations to ensure compliance. In other words, it's often impractical to test a firewall to make sure it's completely compliant with company policies, so you must rely on carefully crafted configurations to ensure that the firewall will behave as desired. Given this limitation, enforcement of the proper configuration, rather than simply conducting point-in-time audits, is absolutely critical. The smallest change to a firewall configuration can result in an out-of-compliance situation; because you're not able to readily test new configurations for end state compliance with policy, you instead need to catch those changes, even the smallest ones, and deal with them appropriately.

The crucial idea: Enforcement *compels* observance of your policies; it *imposes* your policies rather than simply prescribing them or monitoring them. Enforcement, then, is the key to compliance in the IT industry.

12.6   Compliance and Law & Legislations

As we explored, compliance has always been with us. Every time an employee is sent home to change into more appropriate workplace clothing, compliance is being maintained. Compliance is simply meeting a set of rules, whether those rules relate to dress code, business practices, or security practices. What has become so important in today's IT environment is compliance with legislation: External rules that literally carry the weight of law, and which, if not *enforced* within an organization, can also carry significant legal and financial consequences.

12.6.1   HIPAA

HIPAA is "summarized" in a 289 page tome available from the United States Department of Health and Human Services. Essentially, HIPAA boils down to two broad sets of rules governing how anyone involved in the health care industry must conduct business. The portability section of the act defines certain standards for health coverage to be moved between carriers; the accountability portions of the act, the ones that everyone's thinking about when they say "compliance" in most cases, define rules for the handling, storage, and disclosure of patient information. For example, HIPAA outlines strict guidelines for which personnel inside an organization can access patient information. The implications of HIPAA for an organization's network infrastructure are obvious: Your network provides access to much of this information. Ensuring that your network has been configured to support security will make HIPAA compliance and enforcement more practical.

Ensuring that your proper network configuration is being *enforced* will help prevent costly fines that result from accidental or even malicious reconfiguration.

12.6.2 The Sarbanes-Oxley Act

Although the Sarbanes-Oxley Act of 2002 imposes several new regulatory controls for financial services firms, primarily public accountants, the compliance issues surrounding this legislation pretty much boil down to accountability and recordkeeping. In other words, firms must maintain pretty tight security over their records, must be able to provide a report of who can and has accessed those records, and must maintain those records for specified periods of time. For example, Title VIII of the act defines the knowing destruction of documents to impede, obstruct, or influence a federal investigation as a felony. Does this legislation have any bearing on IT and, more specifically, network infrastructure?

Broadly speaking, the Sarbanes-Oxley Act requires the ability to audit and control the availability of information, and your network infrastructure is one of the most common means by which information will be made available. Section 404 of SOX contains guidelines about annual reports that state the responsibility of management for establishing and maintaining an adequate internal control structure and procedures for financial reporting, an assessment of those procedures' effectiveness, and so forth. In other words, you need to know how people are accessing your information, *prove* you know it, and issue a report evaluating your effectiveness.

Translating the Sarbanes-Oxley Act requirements into functional or compliance requirements as well as system requirements will help the enterprise architect in the determination where to implement relevant controls. Below are shown some extractions of these requirements.

Functional Requirements

o   Maintenance and regular evaluation of the effectiveness of disclosure controls and procedures and reporting of significant changes in such controls, including any corrective actions with regard to significant deficiencies and material weaknesses (Section 302), and issuance of a report on the effectiveness of internal control over financial reporting (Section 404), calling for:

  o   Documentation of business processes and process controls over all major activities.

  o   Assessment of control design and effectiveness.

- o Issue identification, remediation plan development, implementation and tracking.
- o Tracking changes in internal control over time.
- o Roll up ratings and sign-offs, aggregated in dashboard reports.

- o Disclosure by US-based SEC filers on a rapid and current basis, of additional information concerning material changes in the financial condition or operations (Section 409) relating to, requiring:
  - o Event identification and the flow of information for timely and adequate disclosures, considering key roles and responsibilities.
  - o Alignment of internal reporting mechanisms with external requirements for information on material changes in the financial condition or operations.
  - o Simulation of the effects of expected changes.
  - o Evaluation of the potential impact of change.
- o Whistleblower protection (Section 301) requiring:
  - o Confidential, anonymous submission by employees of the issuer of concerns regarding questionable accounting or auditing matters.
  - o Receipt, retention and treatment of complaints received by the issuer regarding accounting, internal accounting controls, or auditing matters.

System Requirements

- o Access and configuration controls to make for real-time, worldwide access to compliance data, accountability, and scalability to serve multiple objectives and involve business units as necessary.
- o Data management, particularly centralized storage of business process library, version control, point in time snapshots, and roll-forward of unresolved issues into the next period.
- o Communication platform, including a collaborative workspace for sharing of process and control best practices, and portal for anonymous submission of potential accounting issues or fraud.
- o Capturing of key attributes for analysis, e.g., scope and rationale as to why identified processes are relevant, process and control sequence and attributes for design analysis, linkage of financial statement assertions to specific controls, issue and action plan description and prioritization.
- o Facilitation of required compliance activities, e.g., process and control evaluation, triggering formulation, escalation, aggregation and tracking of issues, review and signoff.
- o Integration with underlying data and other systems (e.g., HR systems for organizational structure and names, financials for charter of accounts, operational modules for process controls, other document management tools such as policies and procedures repositories, attestation of conformance to code of ethics, director independence certifications, etc.).
- o Workflow support, including defined roles and shadow-roles, calendaring, thresholds and triggers.
- o Monitoring and reporting, including summary and exception reports with supporting details (drill-down) to provide visibility over compliance

activities and facilitate the signoff process, highlighting any issues (e.g., potential fraud) or changes in internal control, as may be necessary to report internally and externally.

The act doesn't lay down a lot of rules for exactly how you're supposed to accomplish compliance, but best practices have been developed in the industry: Rely on centralized control and management of all resources to the greatest degree possible. Enterprise Architecture is one of the helpful instruments to keep in control. If your company has 10 firewalls, managing them independently will result in inconsistent coverage and will make reporting on their effectiveness more difficult; centrally controlling them from one place makes reporting and configuration easy.

Another important consideration: Do you even *know* about all your network infrastructure devices? You're required to control them all, but companies almost always forget about a switch, hub, or router or two, especially in large networks. Enterprise Architecture landscapes as well as tools that can automatically discover devices as well as bring them into compliance (or at least alert you to out-of-compliance conditions) are valuable assistants in maintaining compliance with the Sarbanes-Oxley Act.

12.6.3 21 CFR Part 11

Targeting United States federal agencies (and in many cases their civilian contractors), 21 CFR creates criteria for electronic recordkeeping. 21 CFR is primarily focused on the pharmaceutical and other Food and Drug Administration (FDA)-controlled industries, outlining requirements for electronic records, electronic signatures, non-repudiation, authenticity, and other controls.

Doing the same translation for the 21 CFR part 11 requirements into functional or compliance requirements as well as system requirements will help the enterprise architect in the determination where to implement relevant controls. Below are shown some extractions of these requirements.

Compliance Requirements

o   Integrity of system operations and information:
  o   Validation;
  o   The ability to generate accurate and complete copies of records;
  o   Archival protection of records;
  o   Use of computer-generated, time-stamped audit trails;
  o   Use of appropriate controls over systems documentation; and
  o   A determination that persons who develop, maintain, or use electronic records and signature systems have the education, training, and experience to perform their assigned tasks.
o   System security:
  o   System access be limited to authorized individuals;

o   Operational system checks be used to enforce permitted sequencing of steps and events as appropriate;

o   Authority checks be used to ensure that only authorized individuals can use the system, electronically sign a record, access the operation or computer system input or output device, alter a record, or perform operations;

o   Device (e.g., terminal) checks be used to determine the validity of the source of data input or operation instruction; and

o   Written policies be established and adhered to holding individuals accountable and responsible for actions initiated under their electronic signatures, so as to deter record and signature falsification.

System Requirements

o   Identification of business process steps and systems used
o   Assessment of process and systems related risks
o   Document management
o   System security
o   Audit trail for changes to master data (e.g., material master, vendor, resource, recipe, and customer), central documents (e.g., standard operating procedures, task lists, inspection plans) and transaction documents (e.g., purchase orders, inspection lots).
o   Linkage and interface controls to ensure data migrates adequately from one system to another within the product lifecycle.
o   Controls testing and audit procedures

The effects on your IT infrastructure are obvious: Data must be transmitted securely and must not be modified in transit. Data must be protected. Quite simply, your network infrastructure, the basis for all electronic traffic and security, must be configured to facilitate data protection, and it must remain properly configured at all times. Again, *enforcement* becomes more important than mere auditing, because a momentary lapse in security, one an audit might not catch, can result in data modification or other actions that would result in non-compliance with this legislation.

12.6.4   Other Laws

In addition to HIPAA, the Sarbanes-Oxley Act, and 21 CFR, there are many other laws that might affect IT processes in your organization. The following list highlights some additional legislation to consider:

o   **The European Union (EU) Data Protection Directive and Electronic Signature Directive.** The Data Protection Directive in particular governs the use of personal information within the EU and requires both strict controls and comprehensive accountability.

o   **International Financial Reporting Standards (IFRS).** IFRS apply to the general purpose financial statements and other financial reporting by profit-oriented entities; those engaged in commercial, industrial, financial, and similar activities, regardless of their legal form.

o **Basel II** is the second of the Basel Accords, which are recommendations on banking laws and regulations issued by the Basel Committee on Banking Supervision. The purpose of Basel II, which initially was published in June 2004, is to create an international standard that banking regulators can use when creating regulations about how much capital banks need to put aside to guard against the types of financial and operational risks banks face.

o The United States' **Government Information Security Reform Act** (GISRA, which is part of the Defence Authorization Act of 2001); Requires agencies to implement electronic information security measures to assess their security management practices, and much more. Controlled by the Office of Management and Budget (OMB), this legislation has penalties for failing to comply such as total de-funding of all IT efforts within the noncompliant organization.

These pieces of legislation all have a common thread: They require your IT to be tightly configured and controlled. Your network infrastructure forms the basis for all IT security, protecting your network from unauthorized access and helping to protect information in transit between computers. *Enforcing* a secure infrastructure configuration is crucial to maintaining compliance with these pieces of legislation.

12.7 *Comparing of several functional and system requirements*

Comparing of several functional and system requirements related to different law and regulations.

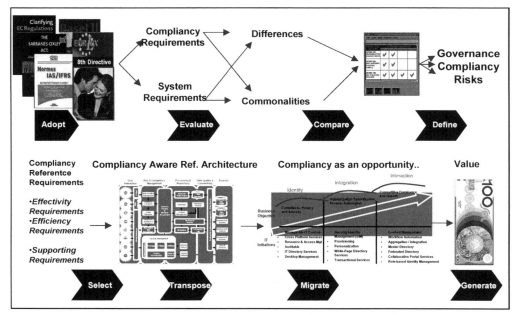

Figure 51. Compliancy Enterprise Architecture Approach

Comparing the functional and system requirements will deliver you an overview of common control object that can be implemented at once.

The next figure shows an example of common control objects related to common requirements.

Compare — Compliancy Requirements / Functional Requirements	Sarbanes Oxley	Basel II	IFRS
SOX Section 404			
Documentation of business processes and process controls over all major activities.	X		
Assessment of control design and effectiveness.	X		
Issue identification, remediation plan development, implementation and tracking.	X		
Tracking changes in internal control over time.	X		
Roll up ratings and sign-offs, aggregated in dashboard reports	X		
SOX Section 409			
Event identification and the flow of information for timely and adequate disclosures, considering key roles and	X		
requirements for information on material changes in the financial condition or operations.	X		
Simulation of the effects of expected changes.	X		
Evaluation of the potential impact of change.	X		
SOX Section 301			
Confidential, anonymous submission by employees of the issuer of concerns regarding questionable accounting or	X		
Receipt, retention and treatment of complaints received by the issuer regarding accounting, internal accounting controls, or	X		
Basel II			
Validation;		X	
The ability to generate accurate and complete copies of records;		X	
Archival protection of records;		X	
Use of computer-generated, time-stamped audit trails;		X	
Use of appropriate controls over systems documentation; and		X	
A determination that persons who develop, maintain, or use electronic records and signature systems have the education, training, and experience to perform their assigned tasks.		X	
System access be limited to authorized individuals;		X	

Compliancy Requirements / System Requirements	Sarbanes Oxley	Basel II	IFRS	FDA 21 CFR part 11	Clinger Cohen	GPRA
Access and configuration controls to make for real-time, worldwide access to compliance data, accountability, and scalability to serve multiple objectives and involve business units as necessary.	X	X	X	X		
Data management, particularly centralized storage of business process library, version control, point in time snapshots, and roll-forward of unresolved issues into the next period.	X		X			
Communication platform, including a collaborative workspace for sharing of process and control best practices, and portal for anonymous submission of potential accounting issues or fraud.	X		X			
Capturing of key attributes for analysis, e.g., scope and rationale as to why identified processes are relevant, process and control sequence and attributes for design analysis, linkage of financial statement assertions to specific controls, issue and act	X	X				
Facilitation of required compliance activities, e.g., process and control evaluation, triggering formulation, escalation, aggregation and tracking of issues, review and signoff.	X	X	X	X	X	X
Integration with underlying data and other systems (e.g., HR systems for organizational structure and names, financials for charter of accounts, operational modules for process controls, other document management tools such as policies and procedures repo	X	X		X		
Workflow support, including defined roles and shadow-roles, calendaring, thresholds and triggers.	X					
Monitoring and reporting, including summary and exception reports with supporting details (drill-down) to provide visibility over compliance activities and facilitate the signature highlighting any issues (e.g., potential fraud) or — Define inter	X	X	X			

Figure 52. Comparing Compliancy Requirements

These pieces of legislation all have a common thread and most of the time a common control object: They require your IT infrastructure to be tightly configured and controlled. Your Enterprise Architecture forms the basis for all of it. *Enforcing* a complete enterprise architecture is crucial to maintaining compliance with these pieces of legislation.

12.7.1 Planning for Compliance: Compliance Aware Reference Architecture

The first step will be to create a top-down compliance plan. By "top-down," means a business level plan that focuses on business-level goals. Don't focus simply on technology. In this regard, HIPAA is a great example of what you should do: Although HIPAA recognizes that most health care records these days are kept electronically, HIPAA doesn't place an undue emphasis on the medium in which patient information is stored. Instead, HIPAA defines standards and controls for patient information *regardless* of its medium, meaning HIPAA applies equally to both physical and electronic documents.

Thus, start planning by creating your policies at a high business level. From that point, you can begin creating more specific plans to implement those policies in a variety of ways. One way of doing that is by adopting the concept of a Compliance Aware Reference Architecture where you can locate the locations for specific controls related to the compliancy requirements.

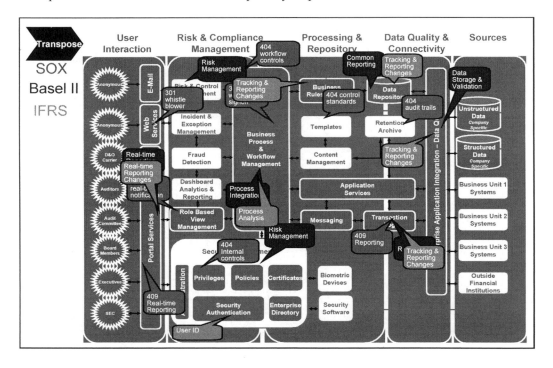

Figure 53. Compliancy Aware Reference Architecture

IFEAD's compliance reference architecture as an example shows Enterprise Architects that compliancy requirements must be part of the overall requirements set and can be implemented proactively in a coherent way.

Understanding compliancy requirements and translating them into control objects will help the enterprise architect in defining and designing the right places to implement such control objects.

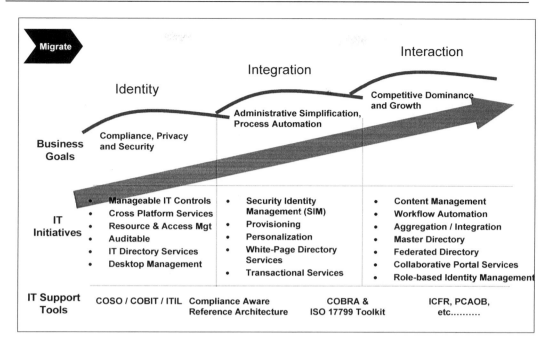

Figure 54. Migration path to competitive dominance & growth

It's useful to review all the types of compliance issues that commonly arise in an organization, particularly with regard to the IT environment. After all, the IT infrastructure itself isn't as simple or as straightforward as just setting up permissions, controls and auditing on a server system, making IT infrastructure compliance issues somewhat more of a gray area in many people's minds:

o **Permissions** — Typically, organizations are concerned about who has the ability to modify the IT infrastructure, specifically the configurations of routers, firewalls, and so forth. These components' configurations are your IT infrastructure and represent the basis for the IT's security.

o **Reliability** — Organizations are often concerned about disaster recovery and reliability: If a devices becomes miss-configured, how quickly can the miss-configuration be identified and the device reconfigured properly? One weakness implied by this question, of course, is that management is reactive. A better question is how can device miss-configuration be automatically prevented or how can the proper configuration be automatically enforced?

o **Auditing** — Even when authorized changes are made to a device, organizations typically need to understand who made the change and when they made it. Such is definitely the case for unauthorized or incorrect changes.

o **Standards** — As mentioned before, auditing the end-state of anything technological can be difficult, so organizations instead tend to rely on a set of configuration standards that implement a desired level of functionality and compliancy. Such being the case, a common compliance issue is ensuring that those standards are met. Organizations typically do so through sometimes-cumbersome manual reviews by peers and committees; in fact, this very review process is a part of most industry best practices, including the Information Technology Information Library (ITIL) standards.

These are four major categories that the IT infrastructure most often presents in terms of compliance. In addition to relating to the IT's stability and reliability, these issues all directly relate to compliancy of the IT in a fundamental sense.

12.8   Wrap up

We've covered a lot of good practices in this chapter, but this foundation of knowledge is important for setting the right steps in your own organization.

Compliance has been turned into a major issue, wrapped up with security and legislative controls, and has become unwieldy. By recognizing that compliance has always been around and that business policies are business policies no matter what they address, you can start to get a better handle on what companies and organizations are facing, and on how to deal with those challenges.

Consider compliance to be simply a matter of meeting your company policies and that your company policies incorporate *everything* you need to worry about: Internal rules, legislative controls, security requirements, and so on. In addition, make compliance a top-down effort, where you create standards that comply with your policies, and then simply enforce those standards on various business systems and processes. To address the weaknesses in traditional auditing as a means of ensuring compliance, consider both automated auditing and automated enforcement as more robust solutions.

13   All You need to know about EA & Services Orientation

"Things should be made as simple as possible, but not any simpler." – Albert Einstein

The terms Enterprise Architecture (**EA**), Services Oriented Enterprise (**SOE**), Service-Oriented Architecture (**SOA**) and Service Oriented Computing (**SOC**) are being exposed to an ever wider and more influential audience. Unfortunately, as with many "new concepts" there is a common misunderstanding about prior ideas and practices from which they are derived. Accordingly, these terms will be bandied about as buzzwords and/or marketing hyperbole assaults.

This section is a pre-emptory effort to provide both a basic and somewhat advanced understanding of these terms: why they are important to us, where they come from and what this means for business & information technology (IT). As with most innovative concepts that seemingly come into vogue in a sudden and haphazard manner, there is both a history leading up to its short sojourns in the spotlight of popular perception and a predictable fade unless popular uptake makes it a structuring paradigm of the Enterprise. With reference to EA, SOE, SOA and SOC, it is fairly certain that they will have their role in this paradigm shift.

tly asked questions that revolve around this topic include: What is SPA? SOE? What is SOA? And what is SOC and how are they interrelated? To his multi part question, let us first try to gain the proper perspective for e to see the overall Enterprise Architecture landscape.

e Architecture in the Context of Services Orientation

truly see the outlines and parameters of what is called EA, and from at perspective begin to understand how a SOE and SOA can enable an EA, we need to get up to sub orbital or low orbit viewpoint at least, and it could be argued that we need to get all the way out to the viewpoint of our moon to see the entire environment within which these concepts work. The fact is that the word enterprise is by no means restricted to a business, or even an industry, nor does it refer to a particular time in the life of an organization. The enterprise encompasses the entire life cycle of an organization or an organism.

After having achieved the desired scope of view, we can apply that perspective, the perspective of the economic or ecological lifecycle, to provide measures to ensure an extended life beyond the restrictions of the individual biological entity model we necessarily bring with us. Enterprises, like cultures, outlive individual members, and those life cycles require us to extend our vision further than our own lives. In many areas in our lives, such as in educational institutions, the familial clan or kinship networks, governments, etc., we take this viewpoint for granted, but in EA, we now need to be explicit and put in place the kinds of mechanisms that can conduct constant review and institute quality assurance as a matter of course and, in effect, institutionalize the cycle of build, use, learn, assess, build (adjust/rebuild), use, learn, etc., ad infinitum.

This presupposes, of course, that the "de facto" starting point for this process is where an enterprise or organization happens to be at that the point when it is decided to begin this process of building and deploying an EA. Some comprehensive review is not required to start. In effect, gaining the correct perspective should allow an enterprise to refocus on the immediate with that larger focus still in mind. Such reviews or foundational reports have their place, but, unless an enterprise is at its founding point, the larger picture can be developed while the more functional aspects of current operations and immediate planning based on immediate findings take precedence in simply getting the process moving.

13.2   Differences between hype, Hope and Reality

In the next diagram that is showing the management version of the Extended Enterprise Architecture Framework (**E2AF**) the concepts of SPA, SOE, SOA, SOC and STP are positioned on the framework to help the readers to understand the relative position of these concepts related to the E2AF. Around the E2AF, 4 Critical Success Factors (**CSF**) are positioned that are critical for the success of implementing Service Orientation in your organization and which makes the difference between Hype, Hope and Reality.

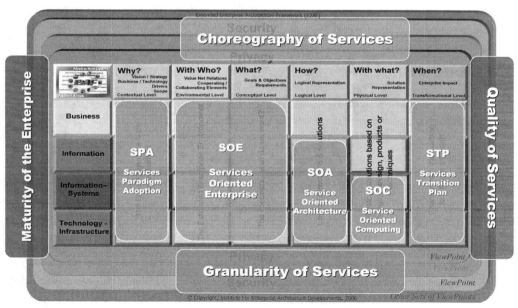

Figure 55. Enterprise Architecture Services Model

So let's have a look at the different concepts of Services Orientation, their relative position in the E2AF and the CSF's to adopt and implement the concepts of Services Orientation (**SO**).

13.3 *Services Paradigm Adoption (SPA)*

Services orientation presents an ideal vision of a world in which resources are cleanly partitioned and consistently represented in terms of services. Therefore the Services Paradigm has to be adopted by the Enterprise to structure the Enterprise in terms of Services. So the Enterprise aspect areas of Business, Information, Information-Systems and the Technology Infrastructure have to be decomposed in terms of functional Services. Doing that at a consistent and consequent matter will deliver loosely coupled functional services that can be outsourced or insourced or brought together in so called shared services centres.

Adopting the Services Paradigm by your Enterprise and implementing it in an appropriate way, will deliver the Enterprise more flexibility, adaptability and agility then organizations that don't want to adopt the Services Paradigm, however if you can't fulfil or implement the Critical Success Factors, Services Orientation can become a nightmare.

Services Orientation (SO) is an Architectural Style, NOT an Architecture itself.

So, Services Orientation as well as SOA is an architectural style whose goal is to achieve loose coupling among interacting services. A service is a unit of work done by a service provider to achieve desired end results for a service consumer. Both provider and consumer are roles played by organizational units as well as software agents on behalf of their owners.

Service Orientation (SO) is the architectural style that supports loosely coupled services to enable business flexibility in an interoperable, technology-agnostic manner. SO consists of a composite set of business-aligned services that support a flexible and dynamically re-configurable end-to-end business processes realization using interface-based service descriptions. The inherent, salient advantage of today's service descriptions is the decoupling of the SP and SC through open standards and protocols, and the deferment of implementation decisions from the SC to the SP. Moreover, individual or collections of services that enjoy various levels of granularity can be combined and choreographed to produce "new" composite services that not only introduce new levels of reuse but also allow the dynamic reconfiguration of business systems.

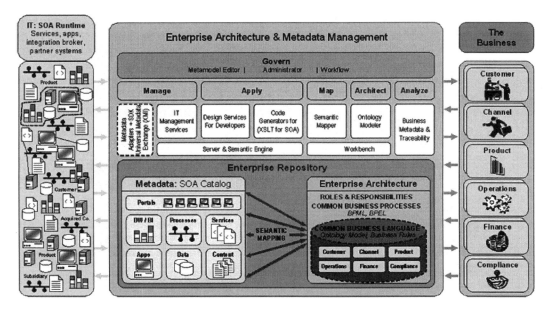

Figure 56. Concept of EA & Services Orientation

13.4   *Services Oriented Enterprise (SOE)*

A service-oriented enterprise is really connecting business processes in a much more horizontal fashion. It's having an Enterprise infrastructure that provides an enterprise architecture and security foundation to be able to run these services consistently across your enterprise.

While the concept of a service-oriented architecture has been considered a best practice by system architects for the past three decades, it is now being embraced by organizations everywhere as the key to business agility. But SOE and SOA don't come in a box, it's not a single technology and it doesn't render all problems solved. While SOE enables and even drives organizational change, it also requires executives, enterprise architects and program managers to think and act differently or simply find themselves in possession of new problems with few or no new benefits.

13.4.1   What is a Service?

A Service is an implementation of a well-defined business functionality that operates independent of the state of any other Service defined within the system. Services have a well- defined set of interfaces and operate through a pre-defined contract between the client of the Service and the Service itself.

13.4.2 Top-Down versus Bottom-Up Service Definition

In the ideal situation Services are defined and described Top-Down at Enterprise level in what is called the Service Oriented Enterprise (SOE). From a functional decomposition of well defined Business functionality we can identify the business function 'Financial Services'. This Business function can be decomposed in lower level services like Invoicing, Payments, Banking, etc.

In Service Oriented Architecture, the system operates as a collection of services. Each Service may interact with various other Services to accomplish a certain task. The operation of one Service might be a combination of several low level functions. In that case, these low level functions are NOT considered Services.

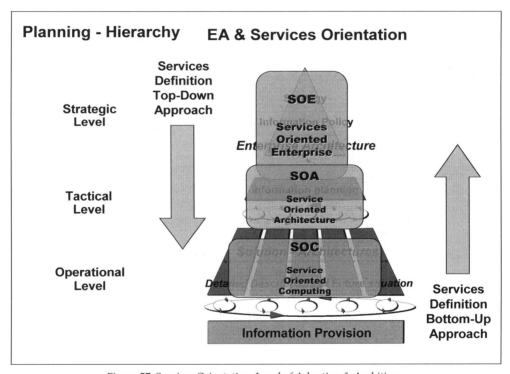

Figure 57. Services Orientation, Level of Adoption & Ambition

13.4.3 Top-Down — SPA / SOE / SOA

1. On Demand Business Transformation: Broad Business Transformation of existing business models or the deployment of new business models (SOE)
2. Enterprise-wide IT transformation: An enterprise architected implementation enabling integration across business functions throughout an enterprise (SOA/SOE)

13.4.4 Bottom-Up — SOC / SOA

1. Service-oriented integration of business functions Integrating services across multiple applications inside and outside the enterprise for a business objective (SOI/SOA)
2. Implementing individual Web services Creating services from tasks contained in new or existing applications (SOC/SOA)

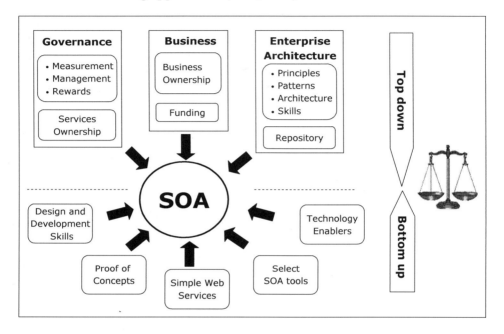

Figure 58. Services Orientation, Top down / Bottom up approach

Top-down domain decomposition (process modelling and decomposition, variation-oriented analysis, policy and business rules analysis, and domain specific behaviour modelling (using grammars and diagrams)) is conducted in parallel with a bottom-up analysis of existing legacy assets that are candidates for componentization (modularization) and service exposure. To catch the business intent behind the project and to align services with this business intent, goal-service modelling is conducted.

13.5 *Service Oriented Architecture (SOA)*

Service-orientation presents an ideal vision of a world in which resources are cleanly partitioned and consistently represented. When applied to IT architecture, service-orientation establishes a universal model in which automation logic and even business logic conform to this vision. This model applies equally to a task, a solution, an enterprise, a community, and beyond.

By adhering to this vision, past technical and philosophical disparities are blanketed by layers of abstraction that introduce a globally accepted standard for representing logic and information. This level of standardization offers an enormous benefit potential for organizations, as many of the traditional challenges faced by ever-changing IT environments can be directly addressed through the application of these standardized layers.

For example, by shaping automation logic through service-orientation, existing investments can be leveraged, business intelligence can be accurately expressed, and inherent automation agility can be achieved. When coupled with the Web services technology platform, SOA offers a significant and real potential for manifesting these benefits.

The service-orientation ideal has sparked a movement that has positioned SOA as the next phase in the evolution of business automation. In the same manner in which mainframe systems were succeeded by client-server applications, and client-server environments then evolved into distributed solutions based on Web technologies, the contemporary, Web services-driven SOA is succeeding traditional distributed architecture on a global scale.

All major software manufacturers and vendors are promoting support for SOA — some even through direct involvement in the development of open standards. As a result, every major development platform now officially supports the creation of service-oriented solutions.

Be forewarned, though, that SOA makes impositions. A change in mind set is required, as business logic now needs to be viewed within a service-oriented context. Applying this context also requires a change in automation logic, as solutions now need to be built in support of service-orientation. Finally, a technical architecture capable of hosting service-oriented automation logic further introduces new technology and infrastructure requirements.

13.6   *Services Oriented Computing (SOC)*

There has been an increase in interest recently within the service oriented community towards "Service Oriented" Computing. Services are often seen as a natural progression from component based software development, and as a means to integrate different component development frameworks. A service in this context may be defined as a behaviour that is provided by a component for use by any other component based on a network-addressable interface contract (generally identifying some capability provided by the service). A service stresses interoperability and may be dynamically discovered and used.

According to the "Open Grid Services Architecture" (OGSA) framework, the service abstraction may be used to specify access to computational resources, storage resources, and networks in a unified way. How the actual service is implemented is hidden from the user through the service interface. Hence, a compute service may be implemented on a single or multi-processor machine — however; these details may not be directly exposed in the service contract. The granularity of a service can vary — and a service can be hosted on a single machine, or it may be distributed.

13.6.1 Web Services

Web Services provide an important instantiation of the Services paradigm, and comprise infrastructure for specifying service properties (in XML — via the Web Services Description Language (WSDL) for instance), interaction between services (via SOAP), mechanisms for service invocation through a variety of protocols and messaging systems (via the Web Services Invocation Framework), support for a services registry (via UDDI), tunnelling through firewalls (via a Web Services Gateway), and scheduling (via the Web Services Choreography Language).

A variety of languages and support infrastructure for Web Services has appeared in recent months — although some of these are still specifications at this stage with no supporting implementation. Web Services play an important role in the Semantic Web vision, aiming to add machine-processable information to the largely human-language content currently on the Web. A list of publicly accessible Web Services (defined in WSDL) can be found at www.xmethods.net. By providing metadata to enable machine processing of information, the Semantic Web provides a useful mechanism to enable automatic interaction between software — thereby also providing a useful environment for agent systems to interact.

13.7 *Services Transition Plan (STP)*

The SOE, SOA and SOC is very much a work in progress, and your transition to Services Orientation will take place over a long period, in many phases. Consequently, transition management is one of the most critical concerns in the long ramp-up to Service Orientation everywhere.

Despite the magnitude of a migration to a services-oriented platform, the continuing uncertainty of critical WS-* standards, and the often thundering impact of large-scale SOA deployments, now is the time to start considering the move. The key to a successful transition is to find a spot of calm amidst the storm of activity surrounding SOA, and develop an intuitive plan that will guide your organization through a path of technical obstacles, organizational resistance, and ever-shifting industry trends.

13.7.1 Invest in an Impact Analysis before Developing the Transition Plan

In order to assess the feasibility of a transition to Services Orientation, you first need to estimate the real-world impact such a migration will have. Therefore, you should consider holding off any sort of planning until an initial impact analysis is complete. Using the impact analysis results as your primary guide, and factoring in budget constraints, related project requirements, and other external drivers (such as strategic business goals), you should be able to determine the scope of your planned transition. It is not uncommon for an SOA transition plan to apply only to a subset of an organization's technical environment. For instance, there may be several legacy areas of an enterprise that do not warrant any intrusion by service encapsulation. Perhaps your goal is to build a dedicated hosting environment intended only to support new service-oriented applications. More often than not, however, integration requirements drive SOA transitions, in which case the scope of your project could easily see the introduction of SOA affect a majority of your IT enterprise.

Service-oriented principles themselves are not complex; however, the application of these principles can result in relatively complex automation solutions. This is especially the case when services from different solutions are shared and composed to support new or modified business processes. If you're going to live in a service-oriented world, your project team will need to change the way it thinks about fundamental aspects of common architecture, such as componentization, integration, and process automation.

13.8   Governance of Services

Adopting and implementing a services oriented architectural style is one element, managing these services later on is another one. Without a well-defined plan to manage these services the continuity of the Enterprise is there.

13.8.1   Management of Services

Enterprise need to manage the delivery of business services (such as services direct to the citizen or to improve staff productivity), and delivery of technical services (such as support of IT infrastructure). Enterprises have to achieve common understanding between the customer and provider through managing service level expectations and service level delivery, and delivering and supporting desired results. Business services may be delivered direct to the customer or — in the case of e-government — to the general public on behalf of the customer.

Service management also looks at the dependence that businesses and organisations have on IS/IT services to acquire and process the elements which make up many of their services. Service quality monitoring demonstrates ongoing value for money and service improvement. You will also need to make arrangements for the management of infrastructure, which may be carried out on your behalf by service providers. You must have processes in place for business continuity, to ensure that the business can continue to deliver its objectives in the event of things going wrong. In addition, there must be support for the end-users in the form of training, help desk facilities and everything they need to make good use of the services.

The interaction between customer (that is, the business, its partners and end-users such as the citizen) and provider in managing services is managed by the 'informed partner' role, providing the interface to achieve the following goals:

o   gain a common understanding between customer and service provider(s) of service expectations and possible achievement;

o use service quality monitors as a basis for demonstrating on-going value for money and service improvements;
o manage ongoing change and the effect on relationships with partners and providers;
o assure consistency in the use of IT and conformance with standards and procedures, making the user community aware of how to exploit the facilities to best effect;
o preserve suitable flexibility in service arrangements, including contracts in order to proactively deal with unexpected changes and demands;
o establish suitable base-lines on which to track performance relating to service delivery and service improvement;
o understand and influence the factors which preserve and enhance relationships to achieve maximum business benefit;
o ensure that the benefits approach appraises the full investment in business change and not just individual components such as IT;
o ensure that Business Continuity plans are kept up-to-date to reflect changes and new service provision.

13.8.2 Requirements for Services Management

Services Management is the ability to manage both the deployed services and the elements of the services architecture as discrete resources regardless of their implementation. While services address many of the traditional problems of integrating disparate business processes and applications, deploying service-oriented applications introduces new complexities that must be managed. Some key requirements for Services Management are outlined briefly below:
o Discover the existence of all key elements of the Services architecture, including new service interfaces, and identifying their relationships to other services, the IT infrastructure, Business processes — whether or not these are defined using BPEL
o Monitor the services layer against Service Level Agreements. Performance and availability data collected can also be used to help define an SLA, as well as provide problem identification
o Respect and enforce management policies for the Services architectural elements
o Control the services through configuration and operations
o The Services architectural elements should surface notifications to the management application when states change or problems occur
o Service security
o Managing lifecycle of services in production, facilitating the graceful introduction and deprecation of services including versioning capabilities
o Root cause analysis and correcting problems based on errors at the services layer
o Transforming and/or routing messages based on message content and context, as well as policy (usually in support of SLA or version management)
o Tracking the business impact of services on the business processes that the Web Services support

> o   Managing the IT infrastructure that supports the services, and associating problems in the infrastructure with manifestation of the problems at the service layer

13.8.3   Testing of Services

Testing the security, compliance, and reliability of (web) services is paramount to successful Service Oriented implementations, particularly those that are externally facing and business critical. Enterprises need to be able to certify and approve services for business and IT standards and deployment readiness. Services need to scale for availability, reliability, integrity, reusability and overall quality. These requirements create the need for a new Service Oriented-specific testing paradigm and test tools that can test the complex layers of a (web) services transaction and guide the control and quality of an enterprise's SOE/SOA.

Services impose specialized testing challenges for Service Oriented implementations. Testing tools must be able to inject realistic usage scenarios onto the infrastructure and validate interoperability as well as transaction completeness for transactions spanning multiple services and involving multiple messaging protocols. Testing must address verification of a service's functionality as well as its performance, scalability and security. With the highly interactive and interdependent nature of SOA based applications even small changes can cause major disruptions. Reuse, service access and service availability are fundamental to achieving a robust service oriented architecture, promoting the additional need for automated regression testing as an integral element of the test process.

Traditional testing methods include some form of simple Unit Testing, often performed by developers. These tests are designed with a knowledge of the software internals, and are nearly always aimed at testing a very small and specific part of the product. These kinds of tests are well-suited to simple Web services which have little or no interaction with other code components.

Functional Verification is a testing process in which designers, who have limited knowledge of the product source code, identify the core functionality of a product or service. Tests are designed to prove this core function conforms to the specification. For example, does my online auction display the correct bid entered? Does my insurance broker system find the cheapest quote? If these tests fail, a fundamental problem with the product has usually been detected (and usually a problem that is straightforward to fix). Again these tests are suited to simple Web services, allowing you to check whether a service performs its individual function correctly.

System Test usually occurs after the functional verification stage is complete, which is after the core function has been verified. It is intended to find problems with the entire system as a whole — to see how Web services behave as part of a system and how they interact with each other. Since the system test phase occurs near the end of a development life cycle, there is often a lack of time allocated for its completion. Due to tight release schedules and slipping of development milestones, the stages of system test are often overlooked, and the unique bugs that each uncovers too often go undetected. Even if such bugs are found, it is often too late to determine their cause and attempt to fix them. It is therefore imperative that system test applications are designed to be as efficient as possible in finding code defects. System test usually comprises of three areas. These are:

- o   Performance: It involves the process of determining the relevant product statistics. For example: How many messages per second? How many simultaneous users of a service are acceptable?
- o   Scenario: It is the process of recreating an exact configuration that a customer requires. Any problems found in the scenario can therefore be detected before the customer uses the product.
- o   Stress (or workload balancing): It is different from the other two areas in that it is designed to strain the software by applying a large workload effort. If carried out effectively, by maintaining a highly strenuous usage of the product (but not beyond the limits determined by the performance statistics), stress testing often uncovers many obscure bugs that any of the other techniques mentioned above will not find (it is also often the case that they will be the most difficult to fix).

Arguably the most efficient of the three system test components, in terms of detecting code defects, is the area of stress testing. However, too often the process is confused with other elements of system or functional testing, and the methods involved in the process are not approached or implemented correctly.

13.9   *Critical Success Factors (CSF's) In SO, Adaptation & Implementation*

13.9.1   Services Oriented Maturity

Companies are at different levels of maturity in the adoption and incorporation of Services-Orientation (SO). Some are just beginning to explore the world of SO using its technology instantiation: Web services. They are wrapping legacy functionality and exposing it for invocation for third-parties, clients, and business partners. This gets them into the game: they ramp up the development team, start the process of changing the corporate culture to better support SO, and take the first steps in the exploration of new technologies and the business capabilities that may be impacted. The SOA road map is showing the different elements that have to be in place for successful SOA adoption.

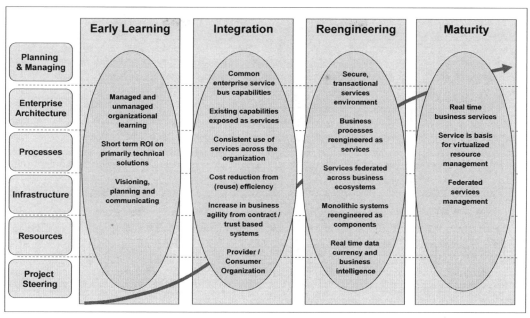

Figure 59. SOA Road Map

Another level of SO adoption is when the initial testing of Web services has been successfully overcome and now the organization is beginning to integrate systems and applications using services. As proprietary protocols, glue code, and point-to-point connections give way to more open, standards-based protocols and interaction based on service descriptions that each system externalizes, we step into the realm of Service-Oriented Integration (SOI). In this world, the enterprise service bus reigns supreme: a mechanism for mediation, routing, and transformation of service invocations irrespective of the target service provider. It helps overcome many of the shortcomings associated with point-to-point connections.

Service Oriented Maturity Model

This SOA Maturity Model provides a framework for discussion between IT and business users about the applicability and benefits of SOA in an organization across five levels of adoption maturity.

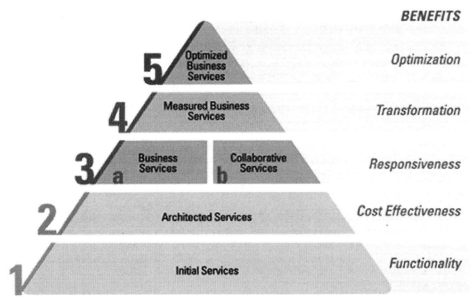

Figure 60. SOA Maturity Model

13.9.2 Choreography of Services

With the growing popularity of Service Oriented Architecture (SOA) and Web Services, these diverse assets can be made available as individual enterprise services. How do we build and expose them as such and how do we leverage them in building new service-based applications or business processes? This is the problem Business Process Choreography tries to solve.

Web Services Choreography Interface (WSCI) is an XML-based interface description language that describes the flow of messages exchanged by a Web Service participating in choreographed interactions with other services. WSCI describes the dynamic interface of the Web Service participating in a given message exchange by means of reusing the operations defined for a static interface. WSCI describes the observable behaviour of a Web Service. This is expressed in terms of temporal and logical dependencies among the exchanged messages, featuring sequencing rules, correlation, exception handling, and transactions. WSCI also describes the collective message exchange among interacting Web Services, thus providing a global, message-oriented view of the interactions.

13.9.3 Quality of Services

One important missing requirement often seen in the context of Services Orientation is the management of Quality of Service (QoS). Organizations operating in modern markets, such as e-commerce activities and distributed Web services interactions require QoS management. Appropriate control of quality leads to the creation of quality products and services; these, in turn, fulfil customer expectations and achieve customer satisfaction.

While QoS has been a major concern in the areas of networking, real-time applications and middleware, few research groups have concentrated their efforts on enhancing service oriented systems to support Quality of Service management. Most of the research carried out to extend the functionality of service oriented systems; QoS has only been done in the time dimension, which is only one of the dimensions under the QoS umbrella. Furthermore, the solutions and technologies presented are still preliminary and limited. The industry has a major interest on the QoS of service orientation and service oriented systems.

For organizations, being able to characterize Services, based on QoS, has four distinct advantages.

1. **QoS-based design**. It allows organizations to translate their vision into their business processes more efficiently, since services can be designed according to QoS metrics. For e-commerce processes it is important to know the QoS an application will exhibit before making the service available to its customers.

2. **QoS-based selection and execution**. It allows for the selection and execution of services based on their QoS, to better fulfil customer expectations. As service oriented systems carry out more complex and mission-critical applications, QoS analysis serves to ensure that each application meets user requirements.

3. **QoS monitoring**. It makes possible the monitoring of services based on QoS. Services must be rigorously and constantly monitored throughout their life cycles to assure compliance both with initial QoS requirements and targeted objectives. QoS monitoring allows adaptation strategies to be triggered when undesired metrics are identified or when threshold values are reached.

4. **QoS-based adaptation**. It allows for the evaluation of alternative strategies when service orientation adaptation becomes necessary. In order to complete a service according to initial QoS requirements, it is necessary to expect to adapt, replan, and reschedule a service in response to unexpected progress, delays, or technical conditions. When adaptation is necessary, a set of potential alternatives is generated, with the objective of changing a service as its QoS continues to meet initial requirements. For each alternative, prior to actually carrying out the adaptation in a running services environment, it is necessary to estimate its impact on the services QoS.

13.9.4 Granularity of Services

Stating that Services are the central part of both SOA and SOE will probably not offend anybody. But methods to identify Services are only slowly emerging. When talking about SOA the Services are often seen as a task that will require only a small effort – so small that we almost don't bother talking about it. The level of detail, in which this task is described, is usually focused on whether to approach this Top-Down or Bottom-up. In practice you will probably use a mix of both, but should have a strong emphasis on the Top-Down – this is necessary in order to control the coherence between the Services.

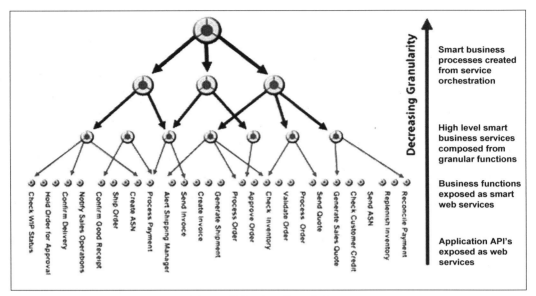

Figure 61. Services Granularity

But how do we actually identify our Services? This is now doubt a discipline normally mastered on the abstraction level of EA. In SOE we need a method to identify Services in a way that supports the paradigm of SOE and utilizes the experience of EA. The important notion here is that we don't start from scratch!

If you are experienced working with SOE, SOAA and EA you should however not expect any revolution – it is in fact a very simple method. But this is just where I see the strength of the method. The simple message is: when identifying your Services don't start developing your solution! Keep on track, and identify the Services one level of abstraction at a time.

14   Enterprise Portfolio Management & EA

14.1   *What is Enterprise Portfolio Management?*

This can best be answered by considering three epochs in the evolution of investment management procedures in both public and private-sector organizations. In the decades before 1990, organizations developed and implemented project-level investment selection and control methods and procedures. These procedures helped decision-makers select the individual projects and initiatives that were most closely linked with the strategic direction of the organization. Once selected, project management and control procedures were put in place to ensure that a funded project achieved its intended objectives within cost, schedule, technical, and performance baselines.

In the second epoch, which evolved in the 1990s, organizations recognized the need for a portfolio management approach to investment decision-making. Here, the focus was at a more aggregate level (rather than at the individual project level). A cornerstone of the portfolio management approach is the select-control-evaluate paradigm put forward by the GAO in 1997. This framework helps decision-makers achieve organizational goals and objectives by identifying, selecting, financing, and monitoring the most appropriate mix of projects and initiatives.

The third epoch-enterprise portfolio management-is now in the evolutionary stage. An enterprise involves an amalgamation of interdependent resources (people, processes, facilities, and technologies) organized to obtain a strategic advantage in support of mission or business objectives. Thus, by its very nature, enterprise investment management is larger in scope and more complex than either project management or portfolio management. This is because, at the enterprise level, decision-makers must not only consider the investment options under their control but also take into account how the alternatives they have analyzed affect, and are affected by, other components of the enterprise.[19]

IFEAD has conducted in 2005 a research project to address enterprise portfolio management and how it relates to the overall enterprise life cycle and the enterprise architecture of an organization. The emphasis is on developing and integrating value based methods, tools, and procedures. While today much of the focus in the public and private sector has been on business investments and IT cost reductions, the enterprise-level portfolio management process has applicability to other types of investment as well, such as human capital and non-IT assets, addressing all the elements of the Extended Enterprise Architecture Framework.

---

[19] *Definition by the Mitre Organization, USA*

14.2   Definition of (Extended) Enterprise Portfolio Management (E2PM)

Extended Enterprise Portfolio Management (E2PM) is an integrated strategic investment planning, portfolio risk analysis and operating system for scheduling, settlement and risk management that facilitates tight alignment of strategic objectives with operational actions, covering business and technology.

E2PM works by enabling separate organizational entities to use a common enterprise information management platform, common enterprise analytical methodologies and a common enterprise strategic business framework for optimal business & technology decisions, ensuring successful execution on the corporate enterprise strategy.

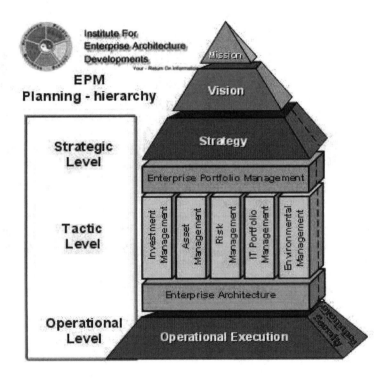

Figure 62. Relationship Extended Enterprise Portfolio Management & EA

14.3   The Building Blocks of E(2)PM, Triple-A

The three core values of E(2)PM that allows organizations to become more focused can be summarized as: **Alignment, Agility** and **Action**.

Alignment – Executives need to know if organizational units are following the corporate strategy or if they are doing their "own thing". EPM forces organizational units to use a common decision-making framework at the beginning of each decision-making process, thereby giving the CEO the ability to make sure that the organizational unit is on the same page with the corporate enterprise strategy. In addition, EPM provides the CEO with real-time information that will clearly indicate whether or not the organizational unit is on board with the implemented strategic objectives. The alignment of all organizational units has to be forced by the corporate development and maintenance of the overall Enterprise Architecture.

Agility – EPM is using information from a consistent enterprise-wide framework measured against the organization's risk and tolerance strategy, thus preventing executives from making critical financial decisions blindly. The corporate Enterprise Architecture can deliver the necessary information on the operational and technical risks. If a portfolio is underperforming because of for example, depressed prices, and cash flow is not enough to cover debt, CEO's need to know when that cash flow is going to turn around. EPM gives executives the information and tools to calculate what the cash flow risk is and to determine if their available options are consistent with their risk tolerance strategy.

Action – Once a strategy is in place, CEO's need to know if the organization can actually implement it on a day-to-day operational basis. The corporate Enterprise Architecture can deliver the necessary information on the operational and technical risks. The essence of EPM in the operational time horizon is the optimization of the tradeoffs between operational performance, financial performance, technical performance and load and contractual obligations in a fashion that is consistent with overall corporate enterprise strategy. Where are the risks in that portfolio? What day-ahead and real-time decisions have to be made to maximize the value of the generating assets? Has a facility or service gone down longer than originally scheduled? Because EPM links all of the pieces from separate organizational units together, information on each of them can be sent back to the CEO informing him in real-time as to how they are doing.

14.4   *Enterprise Architecture: Foundation for EPM*

As showed in the previous figure Enterprise Architecture will be the foundation for (Extended) Enterprise Portfolio Management. Using EA as a management tool it will deliver de input necessary for investment management, asset management, risk management, IT portfolio management and environment management.

Enterprise Portfolio Management (EPM) in this context is the strategic management of business and IT priorities, investments, and projects across the enterprise. The objective of EPM is to take full advantage of the synergies across your Enterprise Architecture, Investment & Asset management, IT portfolio management, and environment management like program management disciplines to get maximum strategic value and return on investments.

15   Planning for the Extended Enterprise

15.1   *Introduction to the connected economy*

Today, with the advent of the connected economy, we stand on the threshold of an economy where the fundamental processes of value exchange are being transformed. The sheer abundance of information has led to a surfeit of alternatives for consumers and reversed the signalling mechanisms that influence the very nature of supply and demand.

At the same time, transaction and coordination costs are about to vanish, forever reshaping the boundaries of the modern organization. Familiar economic entities such as large corporate hierarchies are becoming increasingly irrelevant as the connected economy, not the organization, becomes the most efficient means to conceive, create and exchange value.

The form and structure of economic entities is about to undergo rapid evolution. While not every segment of the economy will be pulled into this maelstrom immediately, we can now begin to see where the changes will occur. The challenge for each organization is to anticipate how those changes will affect our organizations, and how to use them to create lasting competitive advantage in the dawn of the connected economy.

15.2   *What is the Extended Enterprise?*

Extended Enterprise is the set of windows that describes the characteristics of a future proof organization anticipating to its environment and collaborating with its partners and customers by utilizing the technology possibilities.
Business has to be re-invented. Increasing complexity leads to entropy where too much energy is focused on internal issues. New competencies and roles have to be invented and innovative applications will be created.

Partnership management has since more than a decade been on the agenda of the CEO. After a decade of growing awareness how the new technologies like PC, Internet, mobile communication and broadband communication can be used, organizations undergo rapid evolution. The challenge is to anticipate how those changes will affect our organizations, and how to use them to create lasting competitive advantage in the dawn of the connected economy. In other words "How can they transform effectively towards those new rules of the game?" How can they become an 'Extended Enterprise' that matches these challenges?

15.3   *The windows of opportunity*

Each window represents a set of characteristics related to a specific theme.

Extended Strategy & Planning is one of the key themes of the Extended Enterprise Model. Other key themes are Extended IT, Extended Organization and Extended Lifestyle. All these themes together deliver the necessary extended behaviour for the Extended Enterprise.

The developing Extended Enterprise is dynamic and evolving rapidly. It demands parallel flexibility in all who take part, and therefore all Extended windows has to allow for this extreme flexibility, with changes accommodated in hours and days, to respond to the new electronic network based society rather than months and years as has been traditional.

There are three fundamental structures that govern the nature of all economic activity: supply; demand and the way in which value is exchanged between them. At its most rudimentary level, the entire economy can be viewed as a universe made up of just these three elements: **value producing**; **value consuming**: and **value exchanging** entities.

However, the ways in which each of these elements is constituted, and how each relates to the others, are not fixed. In fact, these entities change their boundaries and behaviours based on a number of different circumstances.

While most organizations would readily subscribe to the idea that supply influences demand, we're not nearly as comfortable with the idea that the way in which value is exchanged influences supply, or that the way in which transactions occur can influence demand. The connected economy, as a signalling, coordination and value-exchange mechanism, is reshaping the fundamental organization of economic activity along those very lines.

Economists have long debated the underlying principles that give rise to the overall structure of the economy. While there are many different models that attempt to explain the natural organization of economic activity, the Internet has brought three dominant economic organizational forms into prominent and stark relief: hierarchies, networks and collaborative value webs.
It's well understood that each of these forms becomes a preferred economic structure under certain conditions.

15.4 *Strategic Options multiply in an Extended Enterprise*

Not surprisingly, the extended enterprise benefits from more latitude than organizations that cannot cope with changing conditions. This latitude stems from focus, flexibility, and speed. From its technology-enhanced capabilities for "matching the environment," the enterprise gains extraordinary focus in a micro-context. This permits extreme attention to detail and subtle nuances in customer preference and behaviour, leading to larger profits. From its plug-and-play operating model, the enterprise derives flexibility that permits the organization to "morph" to fit the circumstances, thus reducing decision time and reducing costs. And finally, from its reserve of information and constant option specification, the enterprise can accelerate toward a conclusion or a change with decisive speed, when appropriate and not before, thus preserving the maximum set of options until it becomes necessary to commit.

15.5   *The Factors that will force Change Fastest*

Not every business model will be instantly altered by the changes wrought by the Internet. The longevity of today's business models is an indication of how well they've adapted to their economic environments.

However, the attributes that makes one business model successful for a given set of circumstances can jeopardize its future when those circumstances begin to change. The challenge for many organizations will be determining the sensitivity of existing business models to the rapidly evolving set of economic circumstances brought about by the adoption of the Internet.

15.6   *The Rate of Change*

The rate of change will often be dictated by how rapidly an industry's value-exchange mechanisms can evolve over networked environments. In some instances, the nature of how value is exchanged or how business is transacted will change very little. For instance, the sale of goods and services which require a high degree of customization will likely continue to be concluded on a case-by-case basis between a limited set of well known trading partners. While the network might facilitate the exchange of information between each of the parties involved, those kinds of bilateral transactions will remain unique and relatively complex in how they are negotiated and completed. In others cases, collaborative markets will become the dominant means of conveying value.

Other environmental factors will have an equally significant influence on the future of successful business models. Not least will be the issues noted above, including the certainty of demand, the degree of asset specialization, or the costs related to complete transactions. Changes in any one of these factors can influence how successful incumbent business models will be in a rapidly changing network environment.

One way to determine which existing business models will most likely be affected by changes to environmental factors would be to assess the degree of sensitivity of the current organization of economic activity for any given industry.

For instance, where asset specificity and transaction costs are relatively high, the chances are good that hierarchies will remain the preferred business model.

However, where goods and services are subject to high rates of demand uncertainty and consistently lower transaction costs, networks and collaborative value webs will emerge as the dominant business model. If your current business model isn't properly positioned against key environmental factors, chances are things are ripe for change.

15.7   Technology Enables Us to Reach a Higher Level of Extendibility

If we want to attain a higher level of adaptiveness, how do we go about it? Technology and creativity in its application together provide the answer as well as the behaviour of the people.

The culture and mindset of the people working in an Extended Enterprise must be open to new ideas, reacting fast on changing circumstances, creating new opportunities. So the people them selves have to be adaptive to react on events.

Today we can obviously measure events more precisely than ever, making it possible to act on such information more rapidly, completely, and *automatically*. This new granularity provided by technology — what we might call "micro-observation" — is a major enabler for enhanced pattern recognition and the generation of decision alternatives. With the cost of repeated or even continuous observation by "agent-based software" decreasing daily, we are entering a period when constant reading of variables will provide nearly on-line observe-react capability in customer relationship activities, supply chain management, and product development. Even more critical, however, is the power to act, to adjust, and to customize at low cost, creating a system that is so instantaneously reactive that it appears to shape its environment. The net result is an order of magnitude improvement in fit and far less "wasted profit" from missed opportunities or tardy corrections of problems.

15.8   Extended Technology

No one questions the fact that the Internet has revolutionized the computing experience for users, as well as for extended enterprises, the world over. But experts now see that the Internet has also triggered a revolution in the ways people use computing devices, and in the devices themselves.

In the past few years, a multitude of new application-specific and general-purpose devices has appeared, and many more are on the way. Also, thanks to continuing improvements in processing, memory and networking capabilities, this trend is likely to accelerate in the future. Many enterprises are now facing a challenge that may be orders of magnitude greater than the PC revolution in the 80's. Back then; IT management disregarded the fact that many line-of-business users were ordering personal computers for their offices. The result: near-chaos, as enterprise data, content and applications suddenly proliferate across thousands of user desktops.

Today, user devices are again proliferating. But today's challenges are even greater. Today's devices come in a wide range of shapes, sizes and capabilities, and they feature widely varying bandwidth-capacities, screen formats, browsers and other attributes. Many are wireless, but many are wired. For the Extended enterprise, the challenge is to accommodate these devices within an infrastructure that can both maintain order and still put each device to its best use.

Many enterprises have moved to create an e-business infrastructure that enables a wide array of users, whether they are customers, partners, or employees, and devices to access various enterprise application services and information. But now, the challenge becomes the increasing volumes of content and applications, as well as the diversity of user devices that are requesting access to the increasing amounts of content. Extended Enterprises that can anticipate and leverage these new Internet access device technologies and form factors, as well as the massive proliferation of content and applications, will stand to gain substantial and lasting competitive advantages.

Device differences in performance, footprint, screen format, bandwidth capacity and other factors must be accounted for by all relevant applications. A one-size fit all approach won't do the extended enterprise any good: user experiences will be disastrous. Also, if the enterprise attempts to serve content to all devices at maximum speed, intranet bandwidth will be wasted and compromised. Many devices have limited bandwidth capabilities, so by allocating extra cycles to them, the enterprise takes usable bandwidth away from other, higher-capacity resources.

Another challenge involves avoiding administrative complexity. By adding niche or one-time adaptive capabilities only, enterprises run the risk of adding a new layer of complexity to already overburdened software architectures, as well as adding new responsibilities to already overwhelmed in-house developers.

The best answer is to build an adaptive infrastructure, based on an adaptive enterprise architecture, one that can handle the device formats and bandwidth demands of today and tomorrow's personalized wireless and wired devices.

15.9   *Extended Enterprise Architecture: Criteria to Evaluate*

Once you understand the Extended Enterprise concept, management or enterprise architects can begin the Enterprise planning process.

Key to building an extended enterprise architecture & infrastructure that can scale to handle wide-ranging applications, device requirements and customization are these specific evaluation criteria:
  o   Per-device and per-bandwidth personalization — The Extended enterprise should be able to serve content in the form and by the performance mode that best suits the device.
  o   Content customization — Likewise, content should be customizable for each device or application. For instance, content-adaptation rules might be present that would add intelligence to the adaptation process, lowering the quality of content served to bandwidth-limited devices, and serving higher-quality content to higher-capacity devices.
  o   Functionality customization — Functionality to support users and customers should be customizable for each function, task or activity. Adaptable workflow functionality has to be present to serve the users in all their activities.

o   Bandwidth detection — Additional intelligence should be present that can detect the requesting device's bandwidth capabilities: a PDA communicating via a 128Kbps ADSL link would be served at a lower speed than, say, a laptop with a 10 Mbps wireless LAN link.

o   Image transformation — This would add the capability of adjusting graphic resolution according to the resolution capabilities, and the pre-set rules, of a given application and device.

o   Run-time, adaptive performance engine —The basic adaptation process involves converting one format, HTML, for instance, to another, say WML, by means of an intermediate step, that step involves moving the content through pre-written XSL (eXtensible Style sheet Language) templates. To avoid wasted, redundant conversions, the conversion should take place only as the content is requested, and it should happen at ultra-high speed, so that the conversion will be transparent to the requesting user.

o   Transparency – A uniform way the user is facilitated by the intelligent adaptive infrastructure in a logical and understandable manner, based on the functional personal workflow of the user, supported by a uniform user interface.

o   Distributed adaptation — This is an additional level of sophistication that permits content adaptation to take place at the network node closest to the content server. Since adaptation typically produces a slimmed-down version of the original content, the resulting file is smaller, and can travel more quickly to its destination.

o   Modularity — A modular architecture pays dividends in scalability, but it also means enterprises can start with a modest infrastructure installation, and then grow according to their ideal adaptive business model.

o   Scalability — An adaptive infrastructure must be capable of scaling quickly to take on more content, more applications, or more users. Often, these may happen at the same time, because the pervasive Internet, along with the many devices that populate it, forms a highly dynamic environment.

o   Extended Enterprise Architecture — An extended enterprise architecture delivers flexibility and adaptability in technology and business changes, but it also means business innovation can be facilitated very fast by technological possibilities.

o   Integration with industry-standard technologies — Finally, the infrastructure should fit within the existing enterprise infrastructure as cleanly as possible, tying into web servers and back-office applications easily. This way, the new infrastructure will maximize existing technology investments.

These evaluation criteria are very useful in the discussion with customers and others, to help to understand the real needs of the customer and to focus on quick wins in the context of the extended enterprise.

15.10 *Questions to Address when discussing the Extended Enterprise concept*

Management needs to ensure that their organizations executives are thinking about the implications of the Extended Enterprise. Here are five questions you can use as an enterprise architect to spur your management:

1. **Does the management team** have a shared vision of the long-term (five to ten years out) business implications of the collaborative market architecture?

2. **Do we have a transition plan** that balances the state of the enterprise architectures development with a clear understanding of the areas of highest business impact?

3. **Are we moving fast enough** today to build our expertise and exploit immediate opportunities for streamlining collaborative core tasks, outsourcing activities in which we don't have distinctive capabilities?

4. **Does the management have a clear understanding** of the obstacles within their organization that may hinder them from exploiting the full value of the new technological possibilities, and do we have initiatives under way to overcome these obstacles?

5. **Are we exerting sufficient leadership** in shaping both the functionality offered by providers of Internet services (defining, for example, the performance levels required for mission-critical applications) and the standards needed to collaborate with partners?

16   EA Good Practices Guide — Summary

This Enterprise Architecture Good Practices Guide offers a practical "how-to-manage" guide that will assist any organization in initiating, developing, and maintaining an EA in conjunction with other management processes. Through an illustrative set of "how-to" guidelines and directions, the EA process appears in the context of the enterprise Life Cycle Management process, which consists of such integrated processes as strategic planning, system develop/acquisition, Budget Planning and Investment Control, budgeting processes, human capital management, information security management, compliance management and data management. While intended primarily for organization architects, the guide is structured to meet the needs of all organization staff from the CEO and the CIO to the Chief Enterprise Architect, EA and line organization personnel.

The EA is, by definition, a model of the organization's "enterprise" and its future direction. Its value to the business operations should be more than simply IT investment decision management. The dynamic changes in technology and business practices impose greater pressure on an organization to respond more rapidly to these stimuli than ever before. The EA is the main tool to reduce the response time for impact assessment, trade-off analysis, strategic plan redirection, and tactical reaction.

Although EA's are required by legislative and regulatory in the USA, EA's are not yet required by European legislative and regulatory direction, they should be developed and used for other reasons, too. Along with their importance in the Budget planning and investment management arena, EA's provide a snapshot in time of the organization's business and technology assets. They are the blueprint to build upon–the roadmap to systems and business migration. They help mitigate risk factors in enterprise modernization, identify opportunities for innovative technology insertion, and aid executives and managers in key decision making at all levels of the organization. And these are but a few of the benefits of maintaining a thorough EA.

The EA process is a long-term, continuous effort. Once developed, the EA is a "living" entity with many parts, whether in the form of a document, database or repository, or web page. To remain current and of optimal value, this "living enterprise architecture" needs continual care and maintenance. This, in turn, demands an organizational commitment from top to bottom, since resources in time, money, and people should be dedicated to the enterprise architecture's maintenance for the long term.

As an organization begins its EA efforts, its enterprise architecture proponents should secure corporate commitment and buy-in from senior executives and all levels of the organization. Without engaging the entire organization from the top down, the enterprise architecture effort will face an uphill struggle during much of its existence. Thus, the initial stages of the enterprise architecture effort will need extensive work—obtaining commitment and backing, grounding the EA in an approved framework, and establishing a functioning enterprise architecture structure within the organization.

As one of the first steps, the organization's Chief Enterprise Architect should ground the enterprise architecture effort in an established framework, if at all possible, as discussed in Section 4 of this guide. The leading frameworks offer suitable examples, like the FEAF, E2AF, and DoDAF / C4ISR Architecture Framework discussed in this guide, for frameworks and methodologies. If these existing frameworks do not meet your organization's requirements, develop your own framework; however, consider well the resources and time needed to do so.

It must be emphasized again that you should tailor the contents of this guide to your own organization's needs: "one-size does not fit all" is the rule for EA development and maintenance. The guidance of this document can be used by industry as well as governmental organization regardless of size and resources, but this guidance should be tailored appropriately. This guide is not intended as the "one and only way" all organizations should accomplish EA development, but rather as a synopsis of the "best practices" currently employed in several Federal Organizations and private corporations. For example, in smaller organizations, multiple roles and responsibilities may have to be assumed by one individual, some of the committees and groups will have smaller memberships, and in general, participation will be on a more modest scale. The EA itself, the enterprise architecture results, and the associated data repository should be developed as appropriate for that individual organization.

Not all organizations will need the same level of detail, nor the same graphical representations. However, all organizations will need to ensure that they follow a top-down approach to defining their respective enterprise architectures and that at a minimum their respective the business views of their enterprise architectures provide an enterprise-wide understanding of operations.

Lastly, do not "suffer" alone! Take advantage of the enterprise architecture community's available resources. This guide and several of the other references discussed in this document can be found on the web site of the Institute For Enterprise Architecture Developments at http://www.enterprise-architecture.info. Many enterprise architecture frameworks are documented in an extensive body of literature and web sites. EA community working groups meet on a regular basis and there are numerous annual conferences and seminars on this topic.

Appendix A: EA Roles and Responsibilities

The following matrix summarizes the functional roles and responsibilities needed to support EA development, use, and maintenance.

Role	Members (If composite)	Responsibilities
CEO	N/A	Establishes EA as an organization-wide priority; charters an EA Executive Steering Committee (EAG); issues policy governing the development, implementation, and maintenance of the EA.
Capital / Budget Investment Counsel (BIC)	o Organization/Department heads and their Deputies o Division/Business Unit heads o Senior budget official o Senior procurement official o Legal counsel o CEA o CFO	Reviews the final proposed major information technology investments and makes the final funding decision. Selects projects, monitors progress, and evaluates results for investment decision making.
Chief Enterprise Architect	N/A	Selects the EA project team; works with CEA to develop EA Primer and enterprise architecture policy. Oversees EA product development, use, and refinement. Serves as owner of EA repository and is responsible for enterprise architecture transformation plan. Reports directly to the Head IDM. Engages and provides strategic direction to EA Executive Steering Committee (EAG); enhance the CEO's understanding and appreciation for EA; appoints a Chief Enterprise Architect; markets the benefits of an organization-wide EA to other organization executives and stakeholders via collaborative forums; obtains participatory commitment from senior executives; and introduces enforcement measures.
Configuration Control Board (CCB)	Chief Enterprise Architect, Domain Owners	Responsible for monitoring and controlling changes to the EA after initial development.
Configuration Manager	N/A	Responsible for maintenance and configuration control of all EA results.
Domain Owners	Business Unit Managers	Provides senior-level stakeholder and sponsor participation; works with

Role	Members (If composite)	Responsibilities
		enterprise architecture team on standards insertion and renewal, assigns business line resources [subject matter experts (SME's)] and oversees review of business enterprise architecture results.
Enterprise Architecture Executive Steering Committee (EASC)	Senior representatives from all organizations and operational missions within the organization; may include senior executives (e.g., CEA's) within the business community	Decides strategy, planning, and resource allocation related to the development and maintenance of the EA results; approves the initial EA; provides strategic direction and ensures corporate support; sponsors, reviews, and approves an overarching enterprise architecture management strategy; approves significant changes to the EA.
Enterprise Architecture Office(EAO)	Chief Enterprise Architect Core Enterprise architecture Team	Provides for management and control of EA activities as a formal program; creates and maintains the EA program plan and associated EA project plans; defines tasks, resources, and schedules; provides for program management, monitoring, and control of EA product development and maintenance.
Enterprise Architecture Core Team	o Chief Enterprise Architect o Business Architect o Systems Architect o Data Architect o Infrastructure Architect o Security Architect o Senior enterprise architecture consultants o Technical writer	Responsible for development and refinement of enterprise and application architectures and for populating the EA repository. Develops formal standards requirements and manages the enterprise architecture processes; provides guidance to other teams. Provides for administration of the EA processes; influences organization officials so that project resources are obtained/retained, objections are properly handled, progress is maintained, and a high-quality, usable enterprise architecture framework is established. Monitors and measures the enterprise architecture's effect on projects via process and product measurements.
Independent Validation and Verification (IV&V) Team	Neutral third party from the organization, external organization, or a contractor	Conducts enterprise architecture compliance evaluations; provides quality assurance checking on program information (cost, schedule, and performance data), as well as the proper implementation of the enterprise architecture methodology.

Role	Members (If composite)	Responsibilities
Quality Assurance Manager	N/A	Ensures quality of all enterprise architecture results; participates in enterprise architecture product working sessions and reviews. Reports directly to CEA.
Risk Manager	N/A	Identifies, monitors, controls, and takes action to mitigate EA program risks. Reports directly to CEA.
Subject Matter Expert (SME)	Domain experts from within the organization (one from each business unit); may be supplemented with outside consultants	Supports Chief Enterprise Architect and staff in documenting the defined mission or business requirements and related objectives; supports definition of policies that impact business goals; reviews EA repository results.
Technical Review Committee (TRC)	o Domain Owners o Senior Architectural consultants o Chief Enterprise Architect o Organization/Department Business and Technical representatives	Assesses business alignment, solution proposals, and technical compliance; evaluates enterprise architecture compliance; assesses waiver/exception requests; and conducts standards review.

Table 8. EA Roles & Responsibilities

Appendix B: Term & Definitions

Some of these definitions were obtained from government agencies such as the US Office of Management and Budget (OMB) and the US General Accounting Office (GAO); some were obtained from other authorities and John Mercer's website[20]. Links to sites that add more details can be found in the section Related Links.

Term	Source	Definition
Activity Based Costing	EAMF	A business practice in which costs are tagged and accounted in detailed activity categories, so that return on investment and improvement effectiveness can be evaluated. Implementing ABC requires proper data structures, and an adequate data reporting and collection system involving all employees in the activity.
Activity-Based Management	EAMF	The use of ABC data to ascertain the efficiency or profitability of business units, and the use of strategic initiatives and operational changes in an effort to optimize financial performance.
Agency	FEAF	In most US Federal Government legislation, an organization with a budget of at least $20 million per year.
Applied Information Economics (AIE)	EAMF	AIE is a practical application of scientific and mathematical methods to the Information Technology investment process. AIE uses statistical methods to maintain consistency in risk analysis and decision making with a specified level of uncertainty.
"As-Is" Enterprise architecture	E2AF	The current state of an enterprise's architecture (see current enterprise architecture).
"To-Be" or Future Enterprise architecture	E2AF	The future state of an enterprise's architecture (see future enterprise architecture).
Architectural Artefacts	*FEAF*	The relevant documentation, models, diagrams, depictions, and analyses, including a baseline repository and standards and security profiles.
Architecture Result	IEEE STD 610.12	The structure of components, their interrelationships, and the principles and guidelines governing their design and evolution over time.
Architecture	IEEE 1014-2000	A framework or structure that portrays relationships among all the elements of the subject force, system, or activity.
Architecture	John Zachman	A set of design artefacts, or descriptive representations, that are relevant for describing an object such that it can be produced to requirements (quality) as well as maintained over the period of its useful life (change).

---

[20]*John Mercer, the father of Performance Management, see his website at; http://www.john-mercer.com/*

Term	Source	Definition
Architecture (Enterprise) Repository	E2AF	An information system used to store and access architectural information, relationships among the information elements, and work results.
Artefact	E2AF	An abstract representation of some aspect of an existing or to-be-built system, component, or view. Examples of individual artefacts are a graphical model, structured model, tabular data, and structured or unstructured narrative. Individual artefacts may be aggregated.
Balanced Scorecard	EAMF	A measurement-based strategic management system, originated by Robert Kaplan and David Norton, which provides a method of aligning business activities to the strategy, and monitoring performance of strategic goals over time.
Baseline	FEAF	Data on the current process that provides the metrics against which to compare improvements and to use in benchmarking. [GAO]
Baseline or Current Enterprise architecture	E2AF	The set of results that portray the existing enterprise, the current business practices, and technical infrastructure. Commonly referred to as the "As-Is" enterprise architecture.
Baseline or Current Enterprise architecture	FEAF	Representation of the cumulative "as- built" or baseline of the existing enterprise architecture. The current enterprise architecture has two parts: o The current business architecture, which defines the current business needs being met by the current technology o The current design architecture, which defines the implemented data, applications, and technology used to support the current business needs.
Benchmarking	EAMF	The process of comparing one set of measurements of a process, product or service to those of another organization. The objective of benchmarking is to set appropriate reliability and quality metrics for your company based on metrics for similar processes in other companies.
Business Architecture	FEAF	A component of the current and future enterprise architectures and relates to the mission and goals. It contains the content of the business models and focuses on the business areas and processes responding to business drivers. The business architecture defines business processes, information flows, and information needed to perform business functions.
Business case	EAP	A structured proposal for business improvement that functions as a decision package for organizational decision-makers. A business case includes an analysis of business process performance and associated needs or problems, proposed alternative solutions, assumptions, constraints, and a risk-adjusted cost-benefit analysis. [GAO]

Term	Source	Definition
Business Process Improvement	EAP	A methodology for focused change in a business process achieved by analyzing the AS-IS process using flowcharts and other tools, then developing a streamlined TO-BE process in which automation may be added to result in a process that is better, faster, and cheaper. BPI aims at cost reductions of 10-40%, with moderate risk.
Business Process Reengineering	EAP	A methodology for radical, rapid change in business processes achieved by redesigning the process from scratch and then adding automation. Aimed at cost reductions of 70% or more when starting with antiquated processes, but with a significant risk of lower results.
Capability Maturity Model (CMM)	EAP	A scale for assessing the degree of built-in documentation and discipline in a process, in which the scale goes from Level 1, with no formal process, to Level 5, with a continuous, rigorous and self-improving process. Developed by the Software Engineering Institute of Carnegie Mellon University, and now being extended to a broader range of applications in management.
Capital Planning and Investment Control (CPIC) Process	OMB	A process to structure budget formulation and execution and to ensure that investments consistently support the strategic goals of the organization.
Compliance	EAP	Acting according to certain accepted standards; "their financial statements are in conformity with generally accepted accounting practices"
Concerns	EAP	Concerns are the key interests that are crucially important to the stakeholders in the enterprise, and determine the status and behaviour of the enterprise. Concerns may pertain to any generic or common aspect of the enterprise's functioning, organization, or operation, including considerations such corporate governance, security, privacy, risks, culture, laws & legislations, costs and benefits.
Core capability	EAP	A competitive advantage of an organization; e.g., specific organizational competencies such as intangible assets or resource deployments. These are built up over time and cannot be imitated easily. They are distinct from supplemental and enabling capabilities, neither of which is sufficiently superior to those of competitors to offer sustainable advantage. Technological capability is a term used to encompass a system of activities, tangible assets, skills, information bases, managerial systems, and values that together create a special advantage for an organization. [Dorothy Leonard-Barton]. Also called **core competency**.
Cost-benefit analysis	EAMF	A technique used to compare the various costs associated with an investment with the benefits that it proposes to return. Both tangible and intangible factors

Term	Source	Definition
		should be addressed and accounted for. [GAO]
Customers	EAP	In the private sector, those who pay for products or services. In government, customers consist of (a) the taxpayers; (b) taxpayer representatives in Congress; (c) the sponsors of the agency; (d) the managers of an agency program; (e) the recipients of the agency's products and services. There may be several more categories of 'customers'; they should be carefully identified for maximum strategic benefit.
Critical success factors	EAMF	See key success factors
Economic Value Added (EVA)	EAMF	Net operating profit after taxes minus (capital x cost of capital). EVA is a measure of the economic value of an investment or project.
Earned Value Management	EAMF	Earned value is a project management technique that relates resource planning to schedules and to technical cost and schedule requirements. All work is planned, budgeted, and scheduled in time-phased "planned value" increments constituting a cost and schedule measurement baseline. There are two major objectives of an earned value system: to encourage contractors to use effective internal cost and schedule management control systems; and to permit the customer to be able to rely on timely data produced by those systems for determining product-oriented contract status.
Effectiveness	EAMF	(a) Degree to which an activity or initiative is successful in achieving a specified goal; (b) degree to which activities of a unit achieve the unit's mission or goal.
Efficiency	EAMF	(a) Degree of capability or productivity of a process, such as the number of cases closed per year; (b) tasks accomplished per unit cost.
EFQM	EAMF	The European Foundation for Quality Management's Model of Excellence, which provides benchmarking and self-assessment in a framework similar to that of the Malcolm Baldrige criteria.
Elements	E2AF	A good definition of "elements" in this context are all the elements that enclose the areas of People, Processes, Business and Technology. In that sense, examples of elements are: strategies, business drivers, principles, stakeholders, units, locations, budgets, domains, functions, processes, services, information, communications, applications, systems, infrastructure, etc.
Enterprise	E2AF	A good definition of "enterprise" in this context is any collection of organizations that has a common set of goals/principles and/or single bottom line. In that sense, an enterprise can be a whole corporation, a division of a corporation, a government organization, a single department, or a network of geographically distant organizations linked together by common objectives.

Term	Source	Definition
Enterprise	FEAF	An organization supporting a defined business scope and mission. An enterprise is comprised of interdependent resources (people, organizations, and technology) that should coordinate their functions and share information in support of a common mission (or set of related missions).
Enterprise Architecture (EA)	FEAF/E2AF	A strategic information asset base, which defines the business, the information necessary to operate the business, the technologies necessary to support the business operations, and the transformational processes necessary for implementing new technologies in response to the changing business needs.
Enterprise Architecture	John Zachman	The set of primitive, descriptive artefacts that constitute the knowledge infrastructure of the enterprise.
Enterprise Architecture Description	E2AF	An enterprise architecture description is a collection of representations that document an enterprise architecture in such a way that it can be communicated to enterprise stakeholders.
Enterprise Architecture Policy	EAP	A statement governing the development, implementation, and maintenance of the Enterprise Architecture.
Enterprise Architecture Results or Deliverables	E2AF	The visualizations, graphics, models, and/or narrative that depict the enterprise environment and design.
Enterprise Engineering		A multidisciplinary approach to defining and developing a system design and architecture for the organization.
Enterprise Life Cycle	E2AF	The integration of management, business, and engineering life cycle processes that span the enterprise to align IT with the business.
Enterprise Stakeholders	EAP	Enterprise Stakeholders are groups of people who have key roles in, or concerns about, the enterprise: for example, shareholders, customers, partners or managers. Different enterprise stakeholders with different roles in the enterprise can have different concerns. Enterprise Stakeholders can be representative people, teams, or organizations.
Executive Information System	EAP	Generic term for a software application that provides high-level information to decision makers, usually to support resource allocation, strategy or priority decisions. This could include a balanced scorecard system, Enterprise Resource Planning (ERP) system, Decision Support System (DSS), etc. Technologies include databases, a data warehouse, and analytic applications such as OLAP (On-Line Analysis Protocol), and many mission-specific data reporting systems.
Extended	E2AF	In the context of extended enterprises are all the elements, relations and influences that are touching the boundaries of the enterprise.
Extended	E2AF	Extended Enterprise Architecture Viewpoints defines

Term	Source	Definition
Enterprise Architecture Viewpoints		the perspectives from which views are taken. From an extended enterprise perspective these viewpoints are addressing generic and common concerns covering the whole enterprise.
Extended Enterprise Architecture Views	E2AF	Extended Enterprise Architecture Views: are representations of the overall enterprise architecture that are meaningful to all stakeholders in and outside the organization. The enterprise architect chooses and develops a set of views that will enable the enterprise architecture to be communicated to, and understood by, all the stakeholders, and enable them to verify that the Enterprise Architecture will address the generic concerns.
Federal Enterprise Architecture Framework (FEAF)	FEAF	An organizing mechanism for managing development, maintenance, and facilitated decision making of an EA. The Framework provides a structure for organizing resources and for describing and managing EA activities.
Framework	FEAF	A logical structure for classifying and organizing complex information.
Functional Economic Analysis (FEA)	EAMF	An analytical technique for assessing the value added at various stages or functions in a process. Most relevant in manufacturing industries, where such increments in value can be readily measured.
Future or To-Be Enterprise architecture	FEAF	Representation of a desired future state or "to be built" for the enterprise within the context of the strategic direction. The future enterprise architecture is in two parts: o Future Business Architecture—defines the enterprise future business needs addressed through new or emerging technologies o Future Design Architecture—defines the future designs used to support future business needs.

Term	Source	Definition
Gap Analysis	EAP	Gap analysis naturally flows from benchmarking or other assessments. Once we understand what the general expectation of performance in industry is, we can then compare that with current capabilities, and this becomes the gap analysis.
Goal	EAP	A specific intended result of a strategy; used interchangeably with objective. See also Outcome Goal, Output Goal, Performance Goal, and Strategic Goal. [Note: the term "goal" is used in a wide variety of ways in planning; e.g. as a strategic result or outcome; an objective, a measure, a target, etc.]
Improvement	EAP	An activity undertaken based on strategic goals such as reduced cycle time, reduced cost, and customer satisfaction. All improvement efforts should be linked to the strategy. They are either improvements directly in mission activities (production, design, testing etc.) or in support activities for the mission. There may be some overlap in these; that is ok.
Indicator	EAP	A simple metric that is intended to be easy to measure. Its intent is to obtain general information about performance trends by means of surveys, telephone interviews, and the like.
Information technology (IT)	EAP	Includes all matters concerned with the furtherance of computer science and technology and with the design, development, installation, and implementation of information systems and applications [San Diego State University]. An information technology architecture is an integrated framework for acquiring and evolving IT to achieve strategic goals. It has both logical and technical components. Logical components include mission, functional and information requirements, system configurations, and information flows. Technical components include IT standards and rules that will be used to implement the logical enterprise architecture.
Intermediate Outcome	EAMF	An outcome from a business activity that can be identified and measured in the near term, which is practical when long-term outcomes are diffuse or otherwise difficult to measure. It is intermediate between outputs and outcomes.
IT investment management approach	EAP	An analytical framework for linking IT investment decisions to an organization's strategic objectives and business plans. The investment management approach consists of three phases — select, control and evaluate. Among other things, this management approach requires discipline, executive management involvement, accountability, and a focus on risks and returns using quantifiable measures. [GAO]
Key Performance Indicators	EAP	The three to five broad areas on which an organization must focus in order to achieve its vision. They may be major weaknesses that must be fixed before other goals

Term	Source	Definition
(KPI)		can be achieved. They are not as specific as strategies. Sometimes called critical success factors.
Knowledge Management	EAP	"Knowledge Management caters to the critical issues of organizational adaptation, survival and competence in face of increasingly discontinuous environmental change. Essentially, it embodies organisational processes that seek synergistic combination of data and information processing capacity of information technologies, and the creative and innovative capacity of human beings."
Legacy Systems	E2AF	Those systems in existence and either deployed or under development at the start of a modernization program. All legacy systems will be affected by modernization to a greater or lesser extent. Some systems will become transformation systems before they are retired. Other systems will simply be retired as their functions are assumed by modernization systems. Still others will be abandoned when they become obsolete.
Measurement	EAMF	An observation that reduces the amount of uncertainty about the value of a quantity. In the balanced scorecard, measurements are collected for feedback. The measurement system gathers information about all the significant activities of a company. Measurements are the data resulting from the measurement effort. Measurement also implies a methodology, analysis, and other activities involved with *how* particular measurements are collected and managed. There may be many ways of measuring the same thing.
Methodology	E2AF	A documented approach for performing activities in a coherent, consistent, accountable, and repeatable manner.

Term	Source	Definition
Metrics	EAMF	Often used interchangeably with measurements. However, it is helpful to separate these definitions. Metrics are the various parameters or ways of looking at a process that is to be measured. Metrics define *what* is to be measured. Some metrics are specialized, so they can't be directly benchmarked or interpreted outside a mission-specific business unit. Other measures will be generic, and they can be aggregated across business units, e.g. cycle time, customer satisfaction, and financial results.
Mission activities	EAP	Things that an organization does for its customers. For private companies, profit or value creation is an overarching mission. For non-profit organizations, the mission itself takes priority, although cost reduction is still usually a high priority activity.
Mission effectiveness	EAP	Degree to which mission activities achieve mission goals.
Mission value	EAP	(1) Mission outcome benefits per unit cost; a key metric for non-profit and governmental organizations. (2) For a collection of missions within an organization, the relative value contributed by each mission. (3) The combination of strategic significance and results produced by a mission.
Mixed system	EAP	An information system that supports both financial and non-financial functions. [GAO]
Model	EAP	A representation of a set of components of a process, system, or subject area, generally developed for understanding, analysis, improvement, and/or replacement of the process [GAO]. A representation of information, activities, relationships, and constraints [Treasury Enterprise Architecture Framework].
Net present value (NPV)	EAMF	The future stream of benefits and costs converted into equivalent values today. This is done by assigning monetary values to benefits and costs, discounting future benefits and costs using an appropriate discount rate, and subtracting the sum total of discounted costs from the sum total of discounted benefits. [GAO]

Term	Source	Definition
Non-value-added work	EAP	Work activities that add no value to the mission of the organisation. Such activities may or may not be necessary; necessary ones may include utilities, supplies, travel and maintenance; unnecessary ones may include searching for information, duplicating work, rework, time not working, etc.
Objective	EAP	An organisation internal aim or intended result of a strategy. See goal.
Organisation	EAP	The command, control and feedback relationships among employees in an agency, and their information. The data flow structure for the performance management system generally follows the organisational structure.
Outcome	EAMF / EAP	A description of the intended result, effect, or consequence that will occur from carrying out a program or activity. (OMB). A long-term, ultimate measure of success or strategic effectiveness.
Output	EAP	A description of the level of activity or effort that will be produced or provided over a period of time or by a specified date, including a description of the characteristics and attributes (e.g., timeliness) established as standards in the course of conducting the activity or effort. (OMB). A tactical or short-term quality or efficiency indicator for a business process.
Performance goal	EAP	A target level of performance expressed as a tangible, measurable objective, against which actual achievement can be compared, including a goal expressed as a quantitative standard, value, or rate. (OMB).
Performance indicator	EAP	A particular value or characteristic used to measure output or outcome.
Performance measurement (PM)	EAP	The process of developing measurable indicators that can be systematically tracked to assess progress made in achieving predetermined goals and using such indicators to assess progress in achieving these goals [GAO]. A performance gap is the gap between what customers and stakeholders expect and what each process and related sub processes produces in terms of quality, quantity, time, and cost of services and products [GAO].
Plan	EAP	A prescribed, written sequence of actions to achieve a goal, usually ordered in phases or steps with a schedule and measurable targets; defines who is responsible for achievement, who will do the work, and links to other related plans and goals. By law organizations must have strategic plans, business plans, and performance plans. They may also have implementation plans, program plans, project plans, management plans, office plans, personnel plans, operational plans, etc.

Term	Source	Definition
Profit	EAMF	Financial gain or revenues minus expenses. Profit is the overarching mission of private-sector companies. Non-profit or governmental organisations either operate at a loss or attempt to achieve a zero profit; for them the overarching mission is a charter for a service, or a goal to be achieved. Therefore, there is a basic distinction in measures of strategic success between profit and non-profit or governmental organisations.
Project management	EAP	A set of well-defined methods and techniques for managing a team of people to accomplish a series of work tasks within a well-defined schedule and budget. The techniques may include work breakdown structure, workflow, earned value management (EVM), total quality management (TQM), statistical process control (SPC), quality function deployment (QFD), design of experiments, concurrent engineering, Six Sigma etc. Tools include flowcharts, PERT charts, GANTT charts (e.g. Microsoft Project), control charts, cause-and-effect (tree or wishbone) diagrams, Pareto diagrams, etc. (Note that the balanced scorecard is a strategic management, *not* a project management technique).
Principle	E2AF	A statement of the preferred strategic direction. In terms of the Enterprise Architecture, the principles are statements that provide strategic direction to support the vision, guide design decisions, serve as a tie breaker in settling disputes, and provide a basis for dispersed, but integrated, decision making.
Principles	FEAF	A statement of preferred direction or practice. Principles constitute the rules, constraints, and behaviours that an organization will abide by in its daily activities over a long period of time.
Return on Investment (ROI)	EAMF	In the private sector, the annual financial benefit after an investment minus the cost of the investment. In the public sector, cost reduction or cost avoidance obtained after an improvement in processes or systems, minus the cost of the improvement.
Risk analysis	EAP	A technique to identify and assess factors that may jeopardize the success of a project or achieving a goal. This technique also helps define preventive measures to reduce the probability of these factors from occurring and identify countermeasures to successfully deal with these constraints when they develop. [GAO]
Repository	E2AF	An information system used to store and access architectural information, relationships among the information elements, and work results.
Sensitivity analysis	EAP	Analysis of how sensitive outcomes are to changes in the assumptions. The assumptions that deserve the most attention should depend largely on the dominant benefit and cost elements and the areas of greatest uncertainty of the program or process being analyzed.

Term	Source	Definition
		[GAO]
Stakeholder	EAP	An individual or group with an interest in the success of an organisation in delivering intended results and maintaining the viability of the organisation's products and services. Stakeholders influence programs, products, and services. Examples include congressional members and staff of relevant appropriations, authorizing, and oversight committees; representatives of central management and oversight entities such as OMB and GAO; and representatives of key interest groups, including those groups that represent the organisation's customers and interested members of the public. [GAO]
Standard	EAP	A set of criteria (some of which may be mandatory), voluntary guidelines, and best practices. Examples include application development, project management, vendor management, production operation, user support, asset management, technology evaluation, enterprise architecture governance, configuration management, problem resolution. [Federal Enterprise Architecture Framework]
Statistical Process Control (SPC)	EAP / EAMF	A mathematical procedure for measuring and tracking the variability in a manufacturing process; developed by Shewhart in the 1930's and applied by Deming in TQM.
Strategic goal or general goal	EAP	An elaboration of the mission statement, developing with greater specificity how an agency will carry out its mission. The goal may be of a programmatic, policy, or management nature, and is expressed in a manner which allows a future assessment to be made of whether the goal was or is being achieved. (OMB). The quantifiable aims of strategic activities, including outcome goals and output goals.
Strategic objective or general objective	EAP	Often synonymous with a general goal. In a strategic plan, an objective may complement a general goal whose achievement cannot be directly measured. The assessment is made on the objective rather than the general goal. Objectives may also be characterized as being particularly focused on the conduct of basic agency functions and operations that support the conduct of programs and activities. (OMB)
Strategic activities	EAP	Activities or initiatives that a company or agency does for itself, to achieve its overall strategic goals.
Strategic initiatives	EAP	Specific activities or actions undertaken to achieve a strategic goal, including the plans and milestones.
Strategic plan	EAP	A document used by an organisation to align its organisation and budget structure with organisational priorities, missions, and objectives. According to requirements of Government Performance and Results Act (1993), a strategic plan should include a mission statement, a description of the agency's long-term goals

Term	Source	Definition
		and objectives, and strategies or means the agency plans to use to achieve these general goals and objectives. The strategic plan may also identify external factors that could affect achievement of long-term goals. [GAO] Strategic planning is a systematic method used by an organisation to anticipate and adapt to expected changes. The IRM portion of strategic planning sets broad direction and goals for managing information and supporting delivery of services to customers and the public and identifies the major IRM activities to be undertaken to accomplish the desired agency mission and goals. [GAO]
Strategic targets	EAP	Numbers to achieve on each strategic metric by a specified time.
Strategic themes	EAP	The general strategy broken down into categories that focus on different perspectives of the company that can LEAD to overall success, such as customer satisfaction, reduced cost, employee growth, etc. Usually general and not quantified.
Strategy	EAP	(1) Hypotheses that propose the direction a company or agency should go to fulfil its vision and maximize the possibility of its future success. (2) Unique and sustainable ways by which organisations create value. (from Kaplan & Norton). Answers the question, "Are we doing the right things?"
Strategy Map	EAP	A 2-dimensional visual tool for designing strategies and identifying strategic goals. It usually shows the four perspectives of the balanced scorecard in four layers, with learning & growth at the bottom, followed by business processes, customer satisfaction, and financial results (or mission value in the case of nonprofits). Activities to achieve strategic goals are mapped as 'bubbles' linked by cause-effect arrows that are assumed to occur. Sometimes called "strategic map".
Support activities	EAP	Internal business activities that enable achievement of mission activities and strategic activities, but that are permanent and not directly linked to specific goals.
Spewak EA Planning Methodology	Enterprise Architecture Planning, S.H. Spewak	Formal methodology for defining architectures for the use of information in support of the business and the plan for implementing those architectures developed and published by Steven H. Spewak.
System	IEEE STD 610.12	A collection of components organized to accomplish a specific function or set of functions. [IEEE STD 610.12]
Systems Development Life Cycle (SDLC)	E2AF	Guidance, policies, and procedures for developing systems throughout their life cycle, including requirements, design, implementation, testing, deployment, operations, and maintenance.
Target	EAP	A quantitative measurement of a performance metric that is to be achieved by a given time. Both the metric and the schedule need to be specified for targets. A stretch target is the same thing, but its quantitative

Term	Source	Definition
		value is much higher, demanding breakthrough performance to achieve.
Total Quality Management (TQM	EAMF / EAP	A methodology for continuous monitoring and incremental improvement of a supply-line process by identifying causes of variation and reducing them. Originated by Deming in the 1950's, and widely applied in the Federal government, where it was sometimes called Total Quality Leadership (TQL).
Transformatio n Plan	EAP	A document that defines the strategy for changing the enterprise from the current baseline to the future enterprise architecture. It schedules multiple, concurrent, and interdependent activities and incremental builds that will evolve the enterprise.
Transformatio nal EA Components	E2AF	Representation of a desired state for all or part of the enterprise for an interim milestone between the current enterprise architecture and the future enterprise architecture. A time- sliced set of models that represent the increments in the sequence plan.
Unit	EAP	(1) A functional or business component of an agency, generally with a specified mission or support activity. (2) A standard basis for quantitative measurements.
Unit cost	EAMF	A financial metric in which cost is based on the unit of delivery or consumption of a product or service, such as number of requests processed per day.
Value	EAMF / EAP	Benefit per unit cost.
Value-added	EAMF / EAP	Those activities or steps that add to or change a product or service as it goes through a process; these are the activities or steps that customers view as important and necessary. [GAO]
Value chain	EAP	The sequential set of primary and support activities that an enterprise performs to turn inputs into value-added outputs for its external customers. An IT value chain is that subset of enterprise activities that pertain to IT operations, both to add value directly for external customers and to add indirect value by supporting other enterprise operations.
Value proposition	EAP	1. The unique added value an organisation offers customers through their operations. 2. The logical link between action and payoff that knowledge management must create to be effective; e.g., customer intimacy, product-to-market excellence, and operational excellence [Carla O'Dell & C. Jackson Grayson].
Values	EAP	General guiding principles that are to govern all activities.
View	EAP	A view is a representation of a whole system from the perspective of a related set of concerns.

Term	Source	Definition
Viewpoint	EAP	A viewpoint defines the perspective from which a view is taken. More specifically, a viewpoint defines: how to construct and use a view (by means of an appropriate schema or template); the information that should appear in the view; the modelling techniques for expressing and analyzing the information; and a rationale for these choices (e.g., by describing the purpose and intended audience of the view).
Vision	EAP	Long-term goal of strategy. Answers the question, 'How would the country be different if your mission were fully successful?'
Zachman Framework	John Zachman, 1987 *IBM Journal* Article	Classic work on the concepts of information systems architecture that defined the concept of a framework and provided a 6x6 matrix of architecture views and perspectives with products.

Table 9. Terms & Definitions

Appendix C: Acronyms & Abbreviations

ABC	Activity Based Costing
AWG	Architecture Working Group
BPR	Business Process Reengineering
BU	Business Unit
C4ISR	Command, Control, Communications, Computer, Intelligence, Surveillance and Reconnaissance Architecture Framework
CASE	Computer Aided Software Engineering
CBA	Cost-Benefit Analysis
CCB	Change Control Board and Configuration Control Board
CDM	Common Data Model
CD-ROM	Compact Disk-Read Only Memory
CEA	Chief Information Officer
CM	Configuration Management
CMM®	Capability Maturity Model®
COE	Common Operating Environment
CONOPS	Concept of Operations
CRUD	Create, Read, Update, Delete
DOT	Department of Transportation
EA	Enterprise Architecture
EAG	Enterprise Architecture Group
EAMF	Enterprise Architecture Measurement Framework
EAMP	Enterprise Architecture Measurement Program
EAO	Enterprise Architecture Office
EAP	Enterprise Architecture Program
EASC®	Enterprise Architecture Score Card®
EVM	Earned Value Management
E2AF®	Extended Enterprise Architecture Framework®
E2AMM®	Extended Enterprise Architecture Maturity Model®
FEAF	Federal Enterprise Architecture Framework
GAO	Government Accountability Office (USA)
HTML	Hypertext Markup Language
ICAM	Integrated Computer Aided Manufacturing
ICOM	Inputs, Controls, Outputs, and Mechanisms
ICTS	Information Communication Technology Services

IDEF	Integrated Computer Aided Manufacturing Definition Language
IDM	Information Data Management
IEM	Information Exchange Matrix
IER	Information Exchange Requirement
IT	Information Technology
KDP	Key Decision Point(s)
LOB	Line of Business
MC	Management Committee
MT	Management Team
MTAP	Medium Term Action Plan
NORA	Netherlands Government Reference Architecture
O&M	Operations and Maintenance
OC	Operating Committee
OMB	Office Of Management & Budget (USA)
ORC	Operating Risk Committee
PD	Project Delivery
PMP	Program Management Plan
PROMPT	Project Management Professional Tool
QA	Quality Assurance
QFD	Quality Function Deployment
RM	Risk Management
ROI	Return On Investment
ROI	Return On Information (IFEAD)
SBU	Strategic Business Unit
SDLC	System Development Life Cycle
SID	System Interface Description
SME	Subject Matter Expert(s)
SPC	Statistical process control
E2AF	Extended Enterprise Architecture Framework
TISAF	Extended Information Systems Architecture Framework
TOM	Target Operating Model
TQM	Total Quality Management
TRC	Technical Review Committee
TRM	Technical Reference Model
UML	Unified Modelling Language
WBS	Work Breakdown Structure

Table 10. Acronyms

Appendix D: Guiding Principles + Examples

Key definitions

Standards

In the international community we can identify several types of standards. Standards set by an international standardisation organisation; de-facto standards adopted as a standard by the users of the techniques or products (mostly known as a supplier standard) and standards set by an organisation themselves. A standard is an agreement on how things should be done, or, in other words, *a rule (or a set of rules) on which an agreement exists.*

These agreements can reach from a project scale (using a certain layout for the documentation of the project) to an inter-company or even international scale (like the famous IEEE, ISO-OSI standards). The use of standards enhances the ease with which interfaces (couplings) can be made. They allow computers to communicate, for example. Standards, in other words, enhance the connectivity. Another benefit of standards is that once a standard has been issued, and is supported widely, this will lead to economies of scale, decreasing prices and possibly enhancing the general quality of implementation.

Rules

In general, a rule is a prescription on how something has to be done. The aforementioned discussion suggests that a rule (in the narrow sense of the word) would be a prescription that has to be followed, but on which no agreement exists. Speaking of "in the narrow sense" doesn't clarify discussions. We think it will be clearer to speak of *prescriptions* for the broader sense of the word rule, and *rule* for the narrower sense.

Guidelines

Guidelines are less strict than rules or standards. The idea behind a guideline is, that it should be followed, because in many cases it will guide to (a route to) a good solution. Creativity or craftsmanship of the user of the guideline may lead him to deviate from it. A guideline can thus be simply formulated as being a *rule of thumb.*

Principles

Principles are definitely on a higher level of abstraction than the aforementioned prescriptions. A principle expresses an idea, a message (culture / behaviour) or value that comes from corporate vision, strategies, and business drivers, experience or from knowledge of a subject.

In dictionaries (e.g. Webster), the word principle has a few meanings. The first one mentioned is that of a *comprehensive and fundamental law, doctrine or assumption.* An important word in this definition is "fundamental"; other things (rules, prescriptions, and sometimes (-mathematical) laws) follow from principles. Another important element in this definition is the word "assumption"; apart from the fact that a principle can be an assumption the most fundamental parts of sciences often have to rely on assumptions.

D.1 Categories of Principles

A principle expresses an idea, a message (culture / behaviour) or value that comes from corporate vision, strategies, and business drivers, experience or from knowledge of a subject. Principles are used as general rules and guidelines, intended to be enduring and seldom amended, that inform and support the way in which an organization sets about fulfilling its mission.

In their turn, principles may be just one element in a structured set of ideas that collectively define and guide the organization, from values through to actions and results.

Depending on the organization, principles may be established at any or all of three levels:

o **Enterprise principles** provide a basis for decision making throughout an enterprise, and inform how the organization sets about fulfilling its mission. Such enterprise-level principles are commonly found in governmental and not-for-profit organizations, but are encountered in commercial organizations also, as a means of harmonizing decision making across a distributed organization. In particular, they are a key element in a successful strategy.

o **Enterprise Architecture principles** are a subset of business & IT Principles that relate to Enterprise Architecture work. They reflect a level of consensus across the enterprise, and embody the spirit and thinking the enterprise architecture. Enterprise Architecture principles can be further divided into:

   o **Principles that govern the enterprise architecture process**, affecting the development, maintenance, and use of the enterprise architecture; and

   o **Principles that govern the implementation of the enterprise architecture**, establishing the first tenets and related guidance for designing and developing information systems.

o **Information Technology (IT) principles** provide guidance on the use and deployment of all IT resources and assets across the enterprise. They are developed in order to make the information environment as productive and cost-effective as possible.

These sets of principles form a hierarchy, in that IT principles will be informed by, and elaborate on, the principles at the enterprise level; and enterprise architecture principles will likewise be informed by the principles at the two higher levels.

The remainder of this subsection deals exclusively with enterprise architecture principles.

D.2 *Characteristics of Enterprise Architecture Principles*

Enterprise Architecture principles define the underlying general rules and guidelines for the use and deployment of all Business & IT resources and assets across the enterprise. They reflect a level of consensus among the various elements of the enterprise, and form the basis for making future Business & IT decisions.

Each architecture principle should be clearly related back to the business objectives and key architecture drivers.

D.3 *Components of Enterprise Architecture Principles*

It is useful to have a standard way of defining principles. In addition to a definition statement, each principle should have associated rationale and implications statements, both to promote understanding and acceptance of the principles themselves, and to support the use of the principles in explaining and justifying why specific decisions are made.

A recommended template is given below.

Name	Should both represent the essence of the rule as well as be easy to remember. Specific technology platforms should not be mentioned in the name or statement of a principle. Avoid ambiguous words in the Name and in the Statement such as: "support," "open," "consider," and for lack of good measure the word "avoid," itself, be careful with "manage(ment)", and look for unnecessary adjectives and adverbs (fluff).
Statement	Should succinctly and unambiguously communicate the fundamental rule. For the most part, the principles statements for managing information are similar from one organization to the next. It is vital that the principles statement be unambiguous.
Rationale	Should highlight the business benefits of adhering to the principle, using business terminology. Point to the similarity of information and technology principles to the principles governing business operations. Also describe the relationship to other principles, and the intentions regarding a balanced interpretation. Describe situations where one principle would be given precedence or carry more weight than another for making a decision.
Implications	Should highlight the requirements, both for the business and IT, for carrying out the principle - in terms of resources, costs and activities/tasks. It will often be apparent that current systems, standards, or practices would be incongruent with the principle upon adoption. The impact to the business and consequences of adopting a principle should be clearly stated. The reader should readily discern the answer to "How does this affect me?" It is important not to oversimplify, trivialize, or judge the merit of the impact. Some of the implications will be identified as potential impacts only, and may be speculative rather than fully analyzed.

Table 11. Recommended Format for Defining Principles

D.4 *Developing Enterprise Architecture Principles*

Enterprise Architecture principles are typically developed by the Chief Enterprise Architect, in conjunction with the enterprise CIO, Enterprise Architecture Board, and other key business stakeholders.

Appropriate policies and procedures must be developed to support the implementation of the principles.

Enterprise Architecture principles will be informed by overall Business & IT principles and principles at the enterprise level, if they exist. They are chosen so as to ensure alignment of Business strategies with IT strategies and visions. Specifically, the development of enterprise architecture principles is typically influenced by the following:

o   Organization Mission and Plans: The mission, plans, and organizational infrastructure of the enterprise
o   Organization Strategic Initiatives: The characteristics of the enterprise - its strengths, weaknesses, opportunities, and threats - and its current enterprise-wide initiatives (such as Process Improvement, Quality Management)
o   External Constraints: Market factors (time-to-market imperatives, customer expectations, etc.); existing and potential legislation
o   Current Systems and Technology: The set of information resources deployed within the enterprise, including systems documentation, equipment inventories, network configuration diagrams, policies, and procedures
o   Computer Industry Trends: Predictions about the usage, availability, and cost of computer and communication technologies, referenced from credible sources along with associated best practices presently in use.

D.5 *Qualities of Principles*

Merely having a written statement that is called a principle does not mean that the principle is good, even if everyone agrees with it.

A good set of principles will be founded in the beliefs and values of the organisation and expressed in language that the business understands and uses. Principles should be few in number, future oriented, and endorsed and championed by senior management. They provide a firm foundation for making architecture and planning decisions, framing policies, procedures, and standards, and supporting resolution of contradictory situations. A poor set of principles will quickly become disused, and the resultant architectures, policies, and standards will appear arbitrary or self-serving, and thus lack credibility. Essentially, principles drive behaviour.

There are five criteria that distinguish a good set of principles:

- o **Understandable:** The underlying tenets can be quickly grasped and understood by individuals throughout the organization. The intention of the principle is clear and unambiguous, so that violations, whether intentional or not, are minimized.
- o **Robust:** Enable good quality decisions about architectures and plans to be made, and enforceable policies and standards to be created. Each principle should be sufficiently definitive and precise to support consistent decision making in complex, potentially controversial, situations.
- o **Complete:** Every potentially important principle governing the management of information and technology for the organization is defined. The principles cover every situation perceived.
- o **Consistent:** Strict adherence to one principle may require a loose interpretation of another principle. The set of principles must be expressed in a way that allows a balance of interpretations. Principles should not be contradictory to the point where adhering to one principle would violate the spirit of another. Every word in a principle statement should be carefully chosen to allow consistent yet flexible interpretation.
- o **Stable:** Principles should be enduring, yet able to accommodate changes. An amendment process should be established for adding, removing, or altering principles after they are ratified initially.

D.6 Applying Enterprise Architecture Principles

Architecture principles are used to capture the fundamental truths about how the enterprise will use and deploy information technology resources and assets. The principles are used in a number of different ways:

1. To provide a framework within which the enterprise can start to make conscious decisions about IT
2. As a guide to establishing relevant evaluation criteria, thus exerting strong influence on the selection of products or product architectures in the later stages of managing compliance to the IT Architecture.
3. As drivers for defining the functional requirements of the architecture.
4. As an input to assessing both existing IS/IT systems and the future strategic portfolio, for compliance with the defined architectures. These assessments will provide valuable insights into the transition activities needed to implement an architecture, in support of business goals and priorities.
5. The Rationale statements (see below) highlight the value of the architecture to the enterprise, and therefore provide a basis for justifying architecture activities.
6. The Implications statements (see below) provide an outline of the key tasks, resources and potential costs to the enterprise of following the principle. They also provide valuable inputs to future transition initiative and planning activities.
7. Support the architectural governance activities in terms of:
   - o Providing a 'back-stop' for the standard compliance assessments where some interpretation is allowed or required

- o Supporting the decision to initiate a dispensation request where the implications of a particular architecture amendment cannot be resolved within local operating procedure

Principles are interrelated, and need to be applied as a set.

Principles will sometimes compete: for example, the principles of "accessibility" and "security" tend towards conflicting decisions. Each principle must be considered in the context of "all other things being equal".

At times a decision will be required as to which information principle will take precedence on a particular issue. The rationale for such decisions should always be documented.

A common reaction on first reading of a principle is "this is motherhood", but the fact that a principle seems self-evident does not mean that the principle is actually observed in an organization, even when there are verbal acknowledgements of the principle.

Although specific penalties are not prescribed in a declaration of principles, violations of principles generally cause operational problems and inhibit the ability of the organization to fulfil its mission.

D.7 Enterprise Architecture Principles

Too many principles can reduce the flexibility of the enterprise architecture. Many organizations prefer to define only high level principles, and to limit the number to between 10 and 20.

D.8 Business Principles

1. Principle: **Primacy of Principles**

Statement: These principles of information management apply to all departments within an organization.

Rationale: The only way we can provide a consistent and measurable level of quality information to decision makers is if all (S) BU's abide by the principles.

Implications:

- o Without this principle, exclusions, favouritism, and inconsistency would rapidly undermine the management of information.
- o Information management initiatives will not begin until they are examined for compliance with the principles.
- o A conflict with a principle will be resolved by changing the framework of the initiative.

2. Principle: **Maximize Benefit to the Enterprise**

Statement: Business & IT decisions are made to provide maximum benefit to the Enterprise as a whole.

Rationale: This principle embodies "Service above self." Decisions made from an Enterprise-wide perspective have greater long term value than decisions made from any particular organizational perspective. Maximum return on investment requires information management decisions to adhere to Enterprise-wide drivers and priorities. No minority group will detract from the benefit of the whole. However, this principle will not preclude any minority group from getting its job done.

Implications:

o   Achieving maximum   Enterprise-wide benefit will require changes in the way we plan and manage information. Technology alone will not bring about this change.

o   Some organizations may have to concede their own preferences for the greater benefit of the entire Enterprise.

o   Application development priorities must be established by the entire Enterprise for the entire Enterprise.

o   Applications components should be shared across organizational boundaries.

o   Information management initiatives should be conducted in accordance with the Enterprise plan. Individual organizations should pursue information management initiatives which conform to the blueprints and priorities established by the Enterprise. We will change the plan as we need to.

o   As needs arise, priorities must be adjusted. A forum with comprehensive Enterprise representation should make these decisions.

3. Principle: **Information Management is Everybody's Business**

Statement: All organizations in the Enterprise participate in information management decisions needed to accomplish business objectives.

Rationale: Information users are the key stakeholders, or customers, in the application of technology to address a business need. In order to ensure information management is aligned with the business, all organizations in the Enterprise must be involved in all aspects of the information environment. The business experts from across the Enterprise and the technical staff responsible for developing and sustaining the information environment need to come together as a team to jointly define the goals and objectives of information technology.

Implications:

o   To operate as a team, every stakeholder, or customer, will need to accept responsibility for developing the information environment.

o   Commitment of resources will be required to implement this principle.

4. Principle: **Business Continuity**

Statement: Enterprise operations are maintained in spite of system interruptions.

Rationale: As system operations become more pervasive, we become more dependent on them; therefore, we must consider the reliability of such systems throughout their design and use. Business premises throughout the Enterprise must be provided the capability to continue their business functions regardless of external events. Hardware failure, natural disasters, and data corruption should not be allowed to disrupt or stop Enterprise activities. The Enterprise business functions must be capable of operating on alternative information delivery mechanisms.

Implications:

o   Dependency on shared system applications mandates that the risks of business interruption must be established in advance and managed. Management includes but is not limited to periodic reviews, testing for vulnerability and exposure, or designing mission-critical services to assure business function continuity through redundant or alternative capabilities.

o   Recoverability, redundancy and maintainability should be addressed at the time of design.

o   Applications must be assessed for criticality and impact on the Enterprise mission, in order to determine what level of continuity is required and what corresponding recovery plan is necessary.

5. Principle: **Common Use Applications**

Statement: Development of applications used across the Enterprise is preferred over the development of similar or duplicative applications which are only provided to a particular organization.

Rationale: Duplicative capability is expensive and proliferates conflicting data.

Implications:

o   Organizations which depend on a capability which does not serve the entire Enterprise must change over to the replacement Enterprise-wide capability. This will require establishment of and adherence to a policy requiring this.

o   Organizations will not be allowed to develop capabilities for their own use which are similar/duplicative of Enterprise-wide capabilities. In this way, expenditures of scarce resources to develop essentially the same capability in marginally different ways will be reduced.

o Data and information used to support Enterprise decision making will be standardized to a much greater extent than previously. This is because the smaller, organizational capabilities which produced different data (which was not shared among other organizations) will be replaced by Enterprise-wide capabilities. The impetus for adding to the set of Enterprise-wide capabilities may well come from an organization making a convincing case for the value of the data/information previously produced by its organizational capability, but the resulting capability will become part of the Enterprise-wide system, and the data it produces will be shared across the Enterprise.

6. Principle: **Compliance with Law**

Statement: Enterprise information management processes comply with all relevant laws, policies, and regulations

Rationale: Enterprise policy is to abide by laws, policies, and regulations. This will not preclude business process improvements that lead to changes in policies and regulations.

Implications:

o The Enterprise must be mindful to comply with laws, regulations, and external policies regarding the collection, retention, and management of data.

o Education and access to the rules. Efficiency, need and common sense are not the only drivers. Changes in the law and changes in regulations may drive changes in our processes or applications.

7. Principle: **IT Responsibility**

Statement: The IT organization is responsible for owning and implementing IT processes and infrastructure that enable solutions to meet user defined requirements for functionality, service levels, cost, and delivery timing.

Rationale: Effectively align expectations with capabilities and costs so that all projects are cost effective. Efficient and effective solutions have reasonable costs and clear benefits.

Implications:

o A process must be created to prioritize projects
o The IT function must define processes to manage business unit expectations
o Data, application, and technology models must be created to enable integrated quality solutions and to maximize results.

8. Principle: **Protection of Intellectual Property**

Statement: The enterprise's IP must be protected. This protection must be reflected in the IT Architecture, Implementation, and Governance processes.

Rationale: A major part of an enterprise's Intellectual Property is hosted in the IT domain.

Implications:

- o While protection of IP assets is everybody's business, much of the actual protection is implemented in the IT domain. Even trust in non-IT processes can be managed by IT processes (email, mandatory notes, etc.).
- o A Security Policy, governing human and IT actors, will be required that can substantially improve protection of IP. This must be capable of both avoiding compromises and reducing liabilities.

D.9 *Data Principles*

9. Principle: **Data is an Asset**

Statement: Data is an asset that has value to the Enterprise and is managed accordingly.

Rationale: Data is a valuable corporate resource; it has real, measurable value. In simple terms, the purpose of data is to aid decision making. Accurate, timely data is critical to accurate, timely decisions. Most corporate assets are carefully managed, and data is no exception. Data is the foundation of our decision making, so we must also carefully manage data to assure that we know where it is, can rely upon its accuracy, and can obtain it when and where we need it.

Implications:

- o This is one of three closely related principles regarding data: **data is an asset; data is shared;** and **data is easily accessible**. The implication is that there is an education task to ensure that all organizations within the Enterprise understand the relationship between value of data, sharing of data, and accessibility to data.
- o Stewards must have the authority and means to manage the data for which they are accountable.
- o We must make the cultural transition from "data-ownership" thinking to "data-stewardship" thinking.
- o The role of data steward is critical because obsolete, incorrect, or inconsistent data could be passed to Enterprise personnel and adversely affect decisions across the Enterprise.

o   Part of the role of data steward, who manages the data, is to ensure data quality. Procedures must be developed and used to prevent and correct errors in the information and to improve those processes that produce flawed information. Data quality will need to be measured and steps taken to improve data quality -- it is probable that policy and procedures will need to be developed for this as well.

o   A forum with comprehensive Enterprise-wide representation should decide on process changes suggested by the steward.

o   Since data is an asset of value to the entire Enterprise, data stewards accountable for properly managing the data must be assigned at the Enterprise level.

10. Principle: **Data is Shared**

Statement: Users have access to the data necessary to perform their duties; therefore, data is shared across Enterprise functions and organizations.

Rationale: Timely access to accurate data is essential to improving the quality and efficiency of Enterprise decision making. It is less costly to maintain timely, accurate data in a single application, and then share it, than it is to maintain duplicative data in multiple applications. The Enterprise holds a wealth of data, but it is stored in hundreds of incompatible stovepipe databases. The speed of data collection, creation, transfer, and assimilation is driven by the ability of the organization to efficiently share these islands of data across the organization.

Shared data will result in improved decisions since we will rely on fewer (ultimately one virtual) sources of more accurate and timely managed data for our entire decision making. Electronically shared data will result in increased efficiency when existing data entities can be used, without re-keying, to create new entities.

Implications:

o   This is one of three closely related principles regarding data: **data is an asset; data is shared;** and **data is easily accessible.** The implication is that there is an education task to ensure that all organizations within the Enterprise understand the relationship between value of data, sharing of data, and accessibility to data.

o   To enable data sharing we must develop and abide by a common set of policies, procedures and standards governing data management and access for both the short and the long term.

o   For the short term, to preserve our significant investment in legacy systems, we must invest in software capable of migrating legacy system data into a shared data environment.

o   We will also need to develop standard data models, data elements, and other metadata that defines this shared environment and develop a repository system for storing this metadata to make it accessible.

o   For the long term, as legacy systems are replaced, we must adopt and enforce common data access policies and guidelines for new application developers to ensure that data in new applications remains available to the shared environment and that data in the shared environment can continue to be used by the new applications.

o   For both the short tern and the long term we must adopt common methods and tools for creating, maintaining and accessing the data shared across the Enterprise.

o   Data sharing will require a significant cultural change.

o   This principle of data sharing will continually "bump up against" the principle of data security. Under no circumstances will the data sharing principle cause confidential data to be compromised.

o   Data made available for sharing will have to be relied upon by all users to execute their respective tasks. This will ensure that only the most accurate and timely data is relied upon for decision making. Shared data will become the Enterprise-wide "virtual single source" of data.

11. Principle: **Data is Accessible**

Statement: Data is accessible for users to perform their functions

Rationale: Wide access to data leads to efficiency and effectiveness in decision-making, and affords timely response to information requests and service delivery. Using information must be considered from an Enterprise perspective to allow access by a wide variety of users. Staff time is saved and consistency of data is improved.

Implications:

o   This is one of three closely related principles regarding data: **data is an asset; data is shared;** and **data is easily accessible**. The implication is that there is an education task to ensure that all organizations within the Enterprise understand the relationship between value of data, sharing of data, and accessibility to data.

o   Accessibility involves the ease with which users obtain information.

o   The way information is accessed and displayed must be sufficiently adaptable to meet a wide range of Enterprise users and their corresponding methods of access.

o   Access to data does not constitute understanding of the data. Personnel should take caution not to misinterpret information.

o   Access to data does not necessarily grant the user access rights to modify or disclose the data. This will require an education process and a change in the organizational culture, which currently supports a belief in "ownership" of data by functional units.

12. Principle: **Data Trustee**

Statement: Each data element has a trustee accountable for data quality.

Rationale: One of the benefits of an architected environment is the ability to share data (e.g., text, video, sound, etc.) across the Enterprise. As the degree of data sharing grows and business units rely upon common information, it becomes essential that only the data trustee make decisions about the content of data. Since data can lose its integrity when it is entered multiple times, the data trustee will have sole responsibility for data entry which eliminates redundant human effort and data storage resources. (Note that a trustee is different than steward - trustee is responsible for accuracy and currency of the data while responsibilities of a steward may be broader and include data standardization and definition tasks.)

Implications:

o   Real trusteeship dissolves the data "ownership" issues and allows the data to be available to meet all users' needs. This implies that a cultural change from data "ownership" to data "trusteeship" may be required.

o   The data trustee will be responsible for meeting quality requirements levied upon the data for which the trustee is accountable.

o   It is essential that the trustee has the ability to provide user confidence in the data based upon attributes such as 'data source.'

o   It is essential to identify the true source of the data in order that the data authority can be assigned this trustee responsibility. This does not mean that classified sources will be revealed nor does it mean the source will be the trustee.

o   Information should be captured electronically once and immediately validated as close to the source as possible. Quality control measures must be implemented to ensure the integrity of the data.

o   As a result of sharing data across the Enterprise, the trustee is accountable and responsible for the accuracy and currency of their designated data element(s) and subsequently, must then recognize the importance of this trusteeship responsibility.

13. Principle: **Common Vocabulary and Data Definitions**

Statement: Data is defined consistently throughout the Enterprise, and the definitions are understandable and available to all users.

Rationale: The data that will be used in the development of applications must have a common definition throughout the Headquarters to enable sharing of data. A common vocabulary will facilitate communications and enable dialogue to be effective. In addition, it is required to interface systems and exchange data.

Implications:

o   We are lulled into thinking that this issue is adequately addressed because there are people with "data administration" job titles and forums with charters implying responsibility. Significant additional energy and resources must be committed to this task. It is a key to the success of efforts to improve the information environment. This is separate from but related to the issue of data element definition, which is addressed by a broad community - this is more like a common vocabulary and definition.

o   The Enterprise must establish the initial common vocabulary for the business. The definitions will be used uniformly throughout the Enterprise.

o   Whenever a new data definition is required, the definition effort will be co-ordinated and reconciled with the corporate "glossary" of data descriptions. The Enterprise Data Administrator will provide this co-ordination.

o   Ambiguities resulting from multiple parochial definitions of data must give way to accepted Enterprise wide definitions and understanding.

o   Multiple data standardization initiatives need to be co-ordinated.

o   Functional data administration responsibilities must be assigned.

14. Principle: **Data Security**

Statement: Data is protected from unauthorized use and disclosure. In addition to the traditional aspects of national security classification, this includes, but is not limited to, protection of pre-decisional, sensitive, source selection sensitive and proprietary information.

Rationale: Open sharing of information and the release of information via relevant legislation must be balanced against the need to restrict the availability of classified, proprietary, and sensitive information.

Existing laws and regulations require the safeguarding of national security and the privacy of data, while permitting free and open access. Pre-decisional (work-in-progress, not yet authorized for release) information must be protected to avoid unwarranted speculation, misinterpretation, and inappropriate use.

Implications:

o   Aggregation of data both classified and not, will create a large target requiring review and declassification procedures to maintain appropriate control. Data owners and/or functional users must determine if the aggregation results in an increased classification level. We will need appropriate policy and procedures to handle this review and declassification. Access to information based on a need-to-know policy will force regular reviews of the body of information.

o   The current practice of having separate systems to contain different classifications needs to be rethought. Is there a software solution to separating classified and unclassified data? The current hardware solution is unwieldy, inefficient, and costly. It is more expensive to manage unclassified data on a classified system. Currently, the only way to combine the two is to place the unclassified data on the classified system, where it must remain.

o   In order to adequately provide access to open information while maintaining secure information, security needs must be identified and developed at the data level, not the application level.

o   Data security safeguards can be put in place to restrict access to "view only", or "never see". Sensitivity labelling for access to pre-decisional, decisional, classified, sensitive, or proprietary information must be determined.

o   Security must be designed into data elements from the beginning; it cannot be added later. Systems, data, and technologies must be protected from unauthorized access and manipulation. Headquarters information must be safeguarded against inadvertent or unauthorized alteration, sabotage, disaster, or disclosure.

o   Need new policies on managing duration of protection for pre-decisional information and other works-in-progress-- in consideration of content freshness.

D.10 *Application Principles*

15. Principle: **Technology Independence**

Statement: Applications are independent of specific technology choices and therefore can operate on a variety of technology platforms.

Rationale: Independence of applications from the underlying technology allows applications to be developed, upgraded, and operated in the most cost-effective and timely way. Otherwise technology, which is subject to continual obsolescence and vendor dependence, becomes the driver rather than the user requirements themselves.

Realizing that every decision made respect to information technology makes us dependent on that technology, the intent of this principle is to ensure that applications software is not dependent on specific hardware and operating systems software.

Implications:

o   This principle will require standards which support portability.

o   For COTS and GOTS applications, there may be limited current choices, as many of these applications are technology and platform dependent.

o   Application Programming Interfaces (APIs) will need to be developed to enable legacy applications to interoperate with applications and operating environments developed under the Enterprise architecture.

o   Middleware should be used to decouple applications from specific software solutions.

- o   As an example, this principle could lead to use of JAVA, and future JAVA-like protocols, which give a high degree of priority to platform independence.

16. Principle: **Ease of Use**

Statement: Applications are easy to use. The underlying technology is transparent to users, so they can concentrate on tasks at hand.

Rationale: The more a user has to understand the underlying technology the less productive that user is. Ease of use is a positive incentive for use of applications. It encourages users to work within the integrated information environment instead of developing isolated systems to accomplish the task outside of the Enterprise's integrated information environment. Most of the knowledge required to operate one system will be similar to others. Training is kept to a minimum, and the risk of using a system improperly is low.

Using an application should be as intuitive as driving a different car.

Implications:

- o   Applications will be required to have a common "look and feel" and support ergonomic requirements. Hence, the common look and feel standard must be designed and usability test criteria must be developed.
- o   Guidelines for user interfaces should not be constrained by narrow assumptions about user location, language, systems training, or physical capability. Factors such as linguistics, customer physical infirmities (visual acuity, ability to use keyboard/mouse) and proficiency in the use of technology have broad ramifications in determining the ease of use of an application.

D.11 *Technical Principles*

17. Principle: **Requirements-Based Change**

Statement: Only in response to business needs are changes to applications and technology made.

Rationale: This principle will foster an atmosphere where the information environment changes in response to the needs of the business, rather than having the business change in response to information technology changes. This is to ensure that the purpose of the information support -- the transaction of business -- is the basis for any proposed change. Unintended effects on business due to information technology changes will be minimized. A change in technology may provide an opportunity to improve the business process and hence, change business needs.

Implications:

o   Changes in implementation will follow full examination of the proposed changes using the Enterprise architecture.
o   We don't fund a technical improvement or system development unless a documented business need exists.
o   Change management processes conforming to this principle will be developed and implemented.
o   This principle may bump up against the responsive change principle. We must ensure the requirements documentation process does not hinder responsive change to meet legitimate business needs. Purpose of this principle is to keep us focused on business, not technology, needs-- responsive change is also a business need.

18. Principle: **Responsive Change Management**

Statement: Changes to the Enterprise information environment are implemented in a timely manner.

Rationale: If people are to be expected to work within the Enterprise information environment, that information environment must be responsive to their needs.

Implications:

o   We have to develop processes for managing and implementing change that do not create delays.
o   A user who feels a need for change will need to connect with a "business expert" to facilitate explanation and implementation of that need.
o   If we are going to make changes, we must keep the architectures updated.
o   Adopting this principle might require additional resources.
o   This will conflict with other principles (e.g., Maximum Enterprise-wide benefits, Enterprise-wide Applications, etc.).

19. Principle: **Control Technical Diversity**

Statement: Technological diversity is controlled to minimize the non-trivial cost of maintaining expertise in and connectivity between multiple processing environments.

Rationale: There is a real, non-trivial cost of infrastructure required to support alternative technologies for processing environments. There are further infrastructure costs incurred to keep multiple processor constructs interconnected and maintained.

Limiting the number of supported components will simplify maintainability and reduce costs.

The business advantages of minimum technical diversity include: standard packaging of components; predictable implementation impact; predictable valuations and returns; redefined testing; utility status; and increased flexibility to accommodate technological advancements. Common technology across the Enterprise brings the benefits of economies of scale to the Enterprise. Technical administration and support costs are better controlled when limited resources can focus on this shared set of technology.

Implications:

- o   Policies, standards, and procedures that govern acquisition of technology must be tied directly to this principle.
- o   Technology choices will be constrained by the choices available within the technology blueprint. Procedures for augmenting the acceptable technology set to meet evolving requirements will have to be developed and emplaced.
- o   We are not freezing our technology baseline. We welcome technology advances and will change the technology blueprint when compatibility with the current infrastructure, improvement in operational efficiency, or a required capability has been demonstrated.

20. Principle: **Interoperability**

Statement: Software and hardware should conform to defined standards that promote interoperability for data, applications and technology.

Rationale: Standards help ensure consistency, thus improving the ability to manage systems and improve user satisfaction, and protect existing IT investments, thus maximizing return on investment and reducing costs. Standards for interoperability additionally help ensure support from multiple vendors for their products, and facilitate supply chain integration.

Implications:

- o   Interoperability standards and industry standards will be followed unless there is a compelling business reason to implement a non-standard solution.
- o   A process for setting standards, reviewing and revising them periodically, and granting exceptions must be established.
- o   The existing IT platforms must be identified and documented.

D.12 *Enterprise Architecture Principles*

1.   Enterprise Architectures must be appropriately scoped, planned, and defined based on the intended use of the architecture.

Rationale: The enterprise architecture development effort needs direction and guidance to meet expectations for specific uses of the enterprise architecture end results.   Detailed models may not be needed for high-level decision making; similarly, simple, descriptive enterprise architectures may not provide enough information to support engineering choices.

Implications: The enterprise architecture must be generated with a specific purpose and for a specific audience to ensure it meets the expectations of its intended stakeholders.

2.   Enterprise Architectures must be compliant with the law as expressed in legislative mandates, executive orders, regulations, and other guidelines.

Rationale: Organization's must abide by laws, policies, and regulations. However, this does not preclude business process improvements that lead to changes in policies and regulations.

Implications: Organization's should be aware of laws, regulations, and external policies regarding the development of architectures and the collection, retention, management, and security of data.   Changes in the US law (Clinger-Cohen Act) and changes in policy (OMB Circular A–130) may drive changes in architectural processes or applications.

3.   Enterprise Architectures facilitate change.

Rationale: In the rapidly changing Business & IT environment, organizations need tools to manage and control their business and technical growth and change. As the technical development life cycle shortens, with new technologies replacing older systems every 18 months, organizations require an overarching enterprise architecture to capture their systems design and operating environment.

Implications: The systems developer and the Chief Enterprise Architect should ensure the coordination between technology investments and business practices. Enterprise Architectures must be used in the evaluation function of the Capital Planning and Investment Control process.

4.   Enterprise architectures must reflect the organization's strategic plan.

Rationale: The target enterprise architecture has maximum value when it is most closely aligned with the organization's strategic plan and other corporate-level direction, concepts, and planning.

Implications: The target enterprise architecture must be developed in concert with strategic planners as well as the operational staff. As the strategic plan changes, so do the future environment and the target architecture.

5.   Enterprise Architectures continuously change and require transition.

Rationale: The organization is constantly evolving towards its future. As today's enterprise architecture transitions to the target enterprise architecture, the target becomes the organization's baseline enterprise architecture at some point in the future. The baseline enterprise architecture continuously moves and transitions toward the target enterprise architecture.

Implications: The target enterprise architecture is a rolling set of products, continually portraying the out-year environment. As a component of strategic planning and change management, the target enterprise architecture captures the future environment including data requirements and systems transitions. The transition plan is the organization's roadmap to systems migration.

6.   Target enterprise architectures should project no more than 3 to 5 years into the future.

Rationale: Business & Technology life cycles currently are in the neighbourhood of 18 months, and new Business & IT products appear on the market every 18 months. Organization's acquisition practices are aligning to these rapid changes, which mean that an organization's future information needs and technical infrastructure requirements are changing just as rapidly. Consequently, no one can accurately predict what business practices will prevail 10 to 20 years into the future and what type of IT capabilities and resources will be available.

Implications: Target enterprise architectures will need to be revised and updated regularly. The transition plan, illustrating intermediate points in time, may become more valuable than the target enterprise architectures.

7.   Enterprise Architectures provide standardized business processes and common operating environments (COEs).

Rationale: Commonality improves interoperability, cost avoidance, and convergence. For example, the integration of enterprise architectural Activity Models and Operational Sequence Diagrams (on the business side) and the Technical Reference Model and technology forecasts (on the technical side) helps establish a COE within the organization's logical and physical infrastructures.

Implications: The systems architect and the Chief Enterprise Architect must ensure the coordination between technology investments and business practices. A COE grounded on standard business practices yields improved data structures.

8.   Enterprise Architecture results are only as good as the data collected from subject matter experts and domain owners.

Rationale: The enterprise architect is not vested with the organizational information. It is incumbent upon the enterprise architect to collect the needed enterprise architectural information from the members of the organization who possess the knowledge of the business processes and associated information. These subject matter experts tend to be operational staff, field representatives, systems developers, software designers, etc.   The domain owners are the responsible managers of specific business areas.

Implications: The development of the enterprise architecture can be a slow process, dependent on the enterprise architect's access to subject matter experts and domain owners. The validity of the enterprise architecture can be limited by the accuracy of the collected data. Development of the enterprise architecture is an iterative process of data gathering and interviewing to obtain verification and validity checks of the architectural products.

9.   Enterprise Architectures minimize the burden of data collection, streamline data storage, and enhance data access.

Rationale: Data, as a corporate asset, is key to an organization's vision, mission, goals, and daily work routine. The more efficiently an organization gathers data, stores and retrieves that data, and uses the data, the more productive the organization. Information is power.

Implications: Business processes are best improved by streamlining the flow and use of data and information. The development of architectural Node Connectivity Descriptions, Information Exchange Matrices, and other information models will aid in the design of improved data management systems.

10. Target enterprise architectures should be used to control the growth of Business & Technical diversity.

Rationale: The rapid adoption of new and innovative Business & IT products can easily lead to introducing a diverse set of IT products that may not always be fully compatible within the existing enterprise infrastructure.   This necessitates the selection and implementation of proven market technologies.

Implications: The target enterprise architecture must be used in conjunction with the organization's investment review process and technology insertion plans. Relying on the enterprise architecture as an integral component of IT decision making helps control the introduction of incompatible products.

Appendix E: Views & Viewpoints in Extended Enterprise Architecture

E.1   Introduction

What are Extended Enterprise Architecture Viewpoints and Views? Before answering that question let's have a look what Webster's New Collegiate Dictionary is saying about viewpoints and views.

- **VIEWPOINT: POINT OF VIEW, STANDPOINT.**

    - POINT OF VIEW: a position from which something is considered or evaluated.
    - STANDPOINT: a position from which objects or principles are viewed and according to which they are compared and judged.

Viewpoint and views are representing specific stakeholder concerns and are describing the enterprise from a specific perspective.
In IEEE 1471-2000 (Architectural Descriptions), viewpoints and views are introduced to describe stakeholder concerns when describing **systems** architectures. This section is adopting the basic concepts from IEEE 1471-2000 and is transforming them to the **Enterprise** Architecture domain.
To understand the basic concepts of IEEE 1471-2000 a short summary of these concepts are taking down in this section to show the differences between viewpoints and views in systems architecture and in enterprise architecture.

Based on these definitions, viewpoint and views are meaningful things in describing Extended Enterprise Architectures from specific perspectives. So they are playing an important role in the communication with stakeholders.
From the concept of architecture viewpoints another, relatively new view on enterprise architecture **sets of viewpoints** is given, to reflect extended enterprise stakeholders' responsibilities and involvement in organizations and societies.

E.2   Basic Concepts from IEEE 1471-2000

The following concepts are central to the topic of views. These concepts have been adapted from more formal definitions contained in ANSI/IEEE Std 1471-2000; *Recommended Practice for Architectural Description of Software-Intensive Systems*. A system is a collection of components organized to accomplish a specific function or set of functions.

- The architecture of a system is the system's fundamental organization, embodied in its components, their relationships to each other and to the environment, and the principles guiding its design and evolution.

o An architecture description is a collection of artefacts that document an architecture.
o Stakeholders are people who have key roles in, or concerns about, the system: for example, as users, developers, or managers. Different stakeholders with different roles in the system will have different concerns. Stakeholders can be individuals, teams, or organizations (or classes thereof).
o Concerns are the key interests that are crucially important to the stakeholders in the system, and determine the acceptability of the system. Concerns may pertain to any aspect of the system's functioning, development, or operation, including considerations such as performance, reliability, security, distribution, and evolvability.
o A view is a representation of a whole system from the perspective of a related set of concerns.

In capturing or representing the design of a solution architecture, the architect will typically create one or more architecture **models**, possibly using different tools. A view will comprise selected parts of one or more models, chosen so as to demonstrate to a particular stakeholder or group of stakeholders that their concerns are being adequately addressed in the design of the system architecture.

A **viewpoint** defines the perspective from which a view is taken. More specifically, a viewpoint defines: how to construct and use a view (by means of an appropriate schema or template); the information that should appear in the view; the modelling techniques for expressing and analyzing the information; and a rationale for these choices (e.g., by describing the purpose and intended audience of the view).

A **view** is what you see. A **viewpoint** is where you are looking from - the vantage point or perspective that determines what you see.
Viewpoints are generic, and can be stored in libraries for reuse. A view is always specific to the architecture for which it is created.

Every view has an associated viewpoint that describes it, at least implicitly.
ANSI/IEEE Std 1471-2000 encourages architects to define viewpoints explicitly. Making this distinction between the content and schema of a view may seem at first to be an unnecessary overhead, but it provides a mechanism for reusing viewpoints across different architectures.

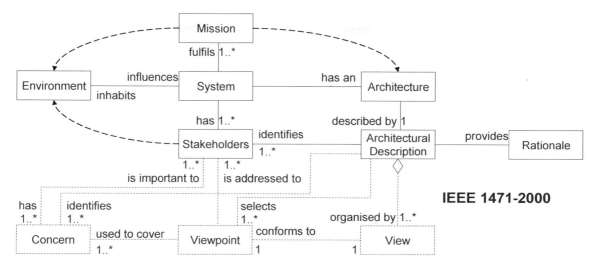

Figure 63. IEEE 1471-2000

In summary, then, architecture views are representations of the overall architecture in terms meaningful to stakeholders. They enable the architecture to be communicated to and understood by the stakeholders, so they can verify that the system will address their concerns.

E.3   *Extended Enterprise Architecture Viewpoints and Views*

Translating the IEEE 1471-2000 definitions to the Extended Enterprise Architecture domain is resulting in a redefinition of these concepts and terms. Below you will find a set of concepts and terms related to enterprise architecture.

- o **Extended** in this context are all the elements, relations and influences that are touching the boundaries of the enterprise.
- o **Enterprise Architecture** is about understanding all of the different elements that go to make up the enterprise and how those elements inter-relate.
- o An **Enterprise** in this context is any collection of organizations that has a common set of goals/principles and/or single bottom line. In that sense, an enterprise can be a whole corporation, a division of a corporation, a government organization, a single department, or a network of geographically distant organizations linked together by common objectives.
- o **Elements** in this context are all the elements that enclose the areas of People, Processes, Business and Technology. In that sense, examples of elements are: strategies, business drivers, principles, stakeholders, units, locations, budgets, domains, functions, processes, services, information, communications, applications, systems, infrastructure, etc.
- o An **enterprise architecture description** is a collection of representations that document an enterprise architecture in such a way that it can be communicated to enterprise stakeholders.

o **Enterprise Stakeholders** are groups of people who have key roles in, or concerns about, the enterprise: for example, shareholders, customers, partners or managers. Different enterprise stakeholders with different roles in the enterprise can have different concerns. Enterprise Stakeholders can be representative people, teams, or organizations.

o **Concerns** are the key interests that are crucially important to the stakeholders in the enterprise, and determine the status and behaviour of the enterprise. Concerns may pertain to any generic or common aspect of the enterprise's functioning, organization, or operation, including considerations such corporate governance, security, privacy, risks, culture, laws & legislations, costs and benefits.

o **Extended Enterprise Architecture Viewpoints** defines the perspectives from which views are taken. From an extended enterprise perspective these viewpoints are addressing generic and common concerns covering the whole enterprise.

Here is an important differentiator between the IEEE 1471-2000 definition that is addressing viewpoints from a stockholder's perspective, where in extended enterprise architecture the viewpoints are representing generic, common business and technology concerns derived from enterprise stakeholders groups or dictated by the extended environment (e.g. law & regulations).

o **Extended Enterprise Architecture Views** are representations of the overall enterprise architecture that are meaningful to all stakeholders in and outside the organization. The enterprise architect chooses and develops a set of views that will enable the enterprise architecture to be communicated to, and understood by, all the stakeholders, and enable them to verify that the Enterprise Architecture will address the generic concerns.

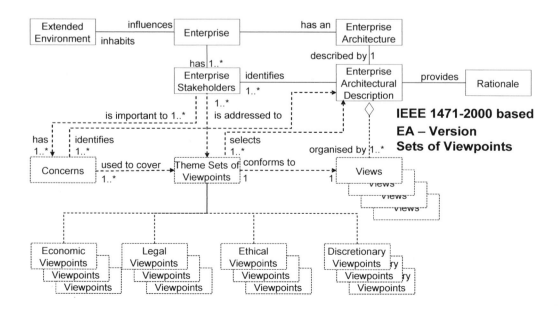

Figure 64. IEEE 1471-2000 EA Version

Extended enterprise architecture is usually represented by means of a set of enterprise architecture representations that together provide a coherent description of the extended enterprise. A single, comprehensive representation is often too complex to be understood and communicated in its most detailed form, showing all the relationships between the various business and technology elements. As with zoning planning, it is normally necessary to develop multiple **views** of the architecture of an enterprise, to enable the enterprise architecture to be communicated to, and understood by **all** stakeholders of the enterprise.

Appendix F: Extended Enterprise Architecture Framework (E2AF) Essentials

F.1   Introduction

This appendix describes the background and philosophy of IFEAD's Extended Enterprise Architecture Framework (E2AF).

This appendix describes the Extended Enterprise Architecture Framework (E2AF) style and foundation. E2AF by itself is a **Communication Framework** describing the topics and relations that can be addressed during an enterprise architecture program. The purpose of E2AF is to communicate with all the stakeholders involved in the program.

E2AF at a whole and the identified aspect areas are subject of IFEAD's – research & development and address the relevant topics and process steps to deliver an overall result related to the goals and objectives to achieve in a certain situation.

The **Extended Enterprise Architecture Essentials Guide** is the foundation of E2AF. It describes in generic terms the context, drivers, principles and rules related to the philosophy behind E2AF. Based on the style elements of this guides, IFEAD has developed several methods, approaches to address specific EA topics.

These **Methods & Approaches** describe the content to address in a specific aspect area and guides the enterprise architect in doing the appropriate activities.

Enterprise Architecture in the context of this essentials guide addresses aspects and issues for the 'enterprise' architecture of organizations & technology as envisioned by IFEAD's Enterprise Architecture style.
This document explains in general terms the rules and principles (style) that are used as the foundation for the way IFEAD thinks about enterprise architecture.

It explains the Extended Enterprise Architecture Framework and relates the methods & approaches to the framework. The approaches themselves are described in separate documents like the Enterprise Architecture Score Card and accompanied articles, white papers and books.

F.1.1   Intended audience

This document is intended for (potential) 'enterprise' architects, using IFEAD 's Extended Enterprise Architecture Framework, who: Are working in the field of 'Enterprise' Architectural Design; Want to understand the role of the E2AF; Are looking for a context description of IFEAD's Architecture approach.

F.2   'Enterprise Architecture'

IFEAD has developed architectural design methods, which **prescribe** a coherent design and realization of new business and the supporting IT systems. This guarantees the full integration between the *business & human* perspective of an organization and the *technology* functionality of supporting IT systems.

IFEAD describes architecture as a set of principles, rules, standards and guidelines reflecting the organizational culture and behaviour that prescribe architects, program / program mangers and developers how to deal with the transformation of both the business and IT systems.

See the **Appendix D** *for an explanation of the terms: principles, rules, standards and guidelines.*

F.2.1   The definition of enterprise architecture

IFEAD uses the following definition for enterprise architecture: *Enterprise Architecture is about understanding all of the different elements that go to make up the Enterprise and how those elements inter-relate.*

Enterprise Architecture embodies a set of principles, rules, standards and guidelines, expressing and visualizing the vision, culture & behaviour of an organization while implementing certain concepts that serves as prescription for the design and construction of a certain object type. It contains a combination of style, engineering and construction principles, guaranteeing the uniformity and quality of the resulting object.

IFEAD has developed such an architectural approach for the design and realization of both the business & Information areas of an organization as well as for the supporting IT systems. This approach is applicable for different organizations, in different situations and at different contemplation levels.

The enterprise architecture style reflects the philosophy and mindset behind the framework and approaches and delivers a certain commonality in execution with respect to organizations unique situation.

F.2.2   The role of Enterprise architecture

In the development of a house, building or any object we can always identify the following main steps:

- o A discovery process to identify the needs and requirements in the context of a certain situation;
- o A design process which leads to a design of the object in the form of drawings and/or models;
- o A transformation process to plan the realisation of the object in its environment;

o   A construction process that regards the realisation of the actual object based on the design and realisation plan.

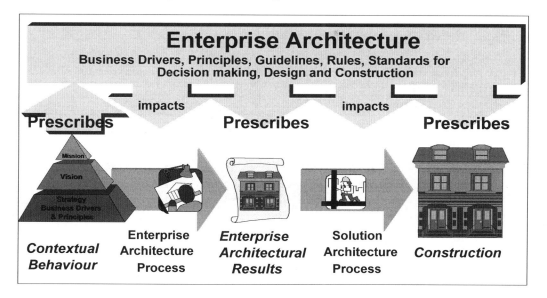

Figure 65. Enterprise Architecture Prescribes

The principles, guidelines and rules identified in the discovery phase are used in the decision making, design, transformation and construction process. As such, the enterprise architecture *impacts* all processes.

The enterprise architecture constraints the freedom of the designer and constructor of the object and guides them towards a structure that complies with the business vision and concepts of the enterprise architecture. The enterprise architecture serves as a *prescription* for the design, transformation and construction of the object. As a result the object will be recognised as being 'designed and constructed under enterprise architecture'.

The object will inherit the added value of the enterprise architecture and will support the **(cultural) values**, **goals** and **objectives** of the organisation.

The described role of architecture originates from the building industry. In prescribing the structure, function and style of a *building* the architecture defines principles, guidelines and rules for:
o   The type of components of which the building may be composed;
o   How these components must fit together;
o   What assemblies of the components are allowed;
o   What functions (usage, living, and working) do the components and component assemblies support;
o   And how the style represents the values of the owner.

The prescription concerns the overall architecture as well as the design models and the actual construction of the building.

IFEAD uses the same approach by defining the architectural steps for architecting business / organisations and IT systems.

In prescribing the structure of *an organisation and its related business* or an *IT system* the architecture defines principles, guidelines and rules for:
o   The type of components of which the business or system may be composed;
o   How these components must fit together;
o   How the components communicate and co-operate;
o   What assemblies of the components are allowed;
o   What functions (communication, control, security, and information) the components and component assemblies support;
o   And how the style expresses the (cultural) values of the stakeholders of that organisation.

The prescription concerns the overall enterprise architecture, the design models and the actual construction of the business and the IT system.
A special point of interest in IFEAD's approach is the attention for the dynamics of organizations and systems. This approach is developed not only for IT applications but also for the other aspect areas of the Extended Enterprise Architecture framework. The enterprise architecture must describe what criteria are useful to discern components, what functionality should be put in one component and when should functionality be split over more components. Especially the criteria for the design of frameworks are important.

Frameworks are special components that act as base for the structuring and assembly of components in more complex constructions.

The use of enterprise architecture will not only has consequences for the design and constructions content but will also impact the design and construction *process*.

The most important consequences are that:
o   An architect prepares a design that provides a clear picture of the style, construction and the structure of the resulting business and IT system.
o   The organization reviews the design for reflecting the style elements, usability and functionality and the developers assess the feasibility of the design and also the risks and costs of realisation. This may cause changes in the design.
o   The organization accepts the final design, which meets their expectations regarding style, usability, functionality and costs of realisation.
o   The architect defines the impact of change and realisation in a transformation plan.
o   The developers realise the change in conformance to the final design.

The use of components and frameworks both in the design and construction of business and IT system will considerably reduce the effort of designing and building new business and IT systems.

F.3   Enterprise Architecture Prescriptions

F.3.1   Enterprise architecture Drivers, Guiding Principles and Rules

This chapter describes the most important business drivers, guiding principles and rules, related to the philosophy of IFEAD's Extended Enterprise Architecture Framework and the Architecture approaches.

These drivers and principles are the rule of the game for the enterprise architects them selves, preserving them for mistakes or uncertain conditions.

Enterprise Architecture Rules and Principles are the fundamental elements of IFEAD's architectural philosophy.

This is the remember icon that depicts the most fundamental guiding principles and rules

Principles and rules can be translated into visualisations, expressing the style, rules and principles of IFEAD enterprise architecture approach.

The Enterprise architecture Rules will be described by first explaining what the rule stands for and then why it is necessary.

There are principles and rules related to the context of enterprise architecture and there are principles and rules related to the methods & approaches. The approaches describe the enterprise architecture process roadmap.

F.3.2   Enterprise Architecture Context Principles and Rules

Enterprise Architecture is a means not a goal

Every object from it selves has an architecture, it can be an explicit or be an implicit architecture.

By creating architecture explicitly, the architecture can be used to express harmony, style and construction of a certain situation.

Enterprise architecture is a means, not a goal in itself. The general expectation is that having and using an architectural design in the development of IT systems will have added value. But what is that added value and why do we need it?

Every architectural design study should start with the question why? (Contextual level) What are the goals and objectives of the architectural design study? Most of the time we will find that the goal is to enforce a certain change and/or to create or pertain a particular structure in the business, information, information systems or infrastructure area. The enterprise architecture should be chosen and applied in such a way that it will support or enable that goal. The goal and objectives have to be clearly defined to enable the right approach to the architectural design process and results.

Strategies set the direction of the enterprise architecture

Strategies set the direction the organisation wants to go. The business strategy is the most important one and is leading. Derived from the business strategy, the Information, IT, Security and Governance strategies have to be extracted.

In most situations an architectural design describes the to-be picture of future changes, based on the existing or a Greenfield situation.

An architectural design gives guidelines and prescriptions to support the development of the business enablers, so they support the strategy, to reach the organisation's business goals.

No strategy, no enterprise architecture

If there is no strategy, an enterprise architecture study cannot be started.
A business strategy describes the direction the business wants to go it shows the goals to achieve and explains the most important environmental variables.

Development policy is Input

A part of the IT strategy is the development policy. The development policy expresses the development direction, based on development techniques, tools or products, etc. from the viewpoint of the client. These development statements are input for an enterprise architecture study and verify the usability related to the business principles.

No Scope - No enterprise architecture

Before we can start a program, it is necessary to know the boundaries of the program, the level of detail required the purpose of the program, the timelines, the roles and responsibilities, etc.

The program scope has to be clear before the enterprise architecture study can start, otherwise architects don't know what to describe or to design.

The Scope and the Goals & Objectives sets the level of abstraction of the enterprise architecture

The program scope, goals & objectives define the level of contemplation to start with.

An enterprise wide program requires a different level of detail than a program that is scoped at unit level or information systems level. The enterprise level encloses the overall view and is the foundation for a program level approach.

Organisation not in the right "maturity phase" for enterprise architecture

The enterprise architecture maturity model shows the enterprise architecture maturity level an organisation is in, regard to enterprise architecture usage. The organisation's maturity phase determines if the organisation is ready to use an architectural approach at all.

Organisations, which are not in the right phase, must be facilitated to get enough value out of using enterprise architecture.

Enterprise Architecture teams

A combined, organization – enterprise architects team; will execute an enterprise architectural design study.

The team must be mandated to make decisions regarding enterprise architectural issues for the whole scope of the program.

The organization provides business specific input and makes decisions regarding the business direction during the enterprise architecture study as well as its architect's carries the enterprise architecture result.

(Certified) Enterprise Architects bring in practical experience, knowledge of the methods, business and IT content and will facilitate the organization's enterprise architecture process fulfilling the program goal and objectives.

Only enterprise architects can facilitate enterprise architectural design studies

(Certified) Enterprise Architects are trained in enterprise architectural approaches and have the knowledge and understanding of the impact of the business drivers and guiding principles for the enterprise architecture process. They have the experience to facilitate enterprise architectural design studies and to improve the methods based on scientific background and practical experience.

Toolbox ➔ flexibility

Enterprise Architectural design studies have to be flexible to adapt to the organization's requirements. The approaches are like a toolbox, not a cookbook. Many decisions that have to be made during an enterprise architectural design study have to be discussed with the organization and have to be relatively weighed in relation to other topics. Most of the time during an ea design study; the enterprise architect uses the approach as a guideline to check the completeness of his activities, not to do the entire task and activities in every situation. Methods & approaches are used as process tools for the architect to plan and check the necessary steps in a certain organization situation.

Business Drivers, Goals & Objectives are leading

Business drivers, Goals & Objectives are the most fundamental elements of the contextual level describing the ambition of the organisation and supported by strategic elements, they explain the motivators of the organisation to achieve a certain goal.

During decision-making in the enterprise architecture process, different possible solutions are presented in terms of business benefits (often translated to costs or benefits).

This is the one of the most important enterprise architecture rules.

Business related choices

All major choices made in the enterprise architecture process will be related and validated to business issues (drivers / requirements / principles).

An enterprise architectural design in the context of Business change or IT System support delivers a coherent and integrated set of visualisations of the future situation related to its environment.

Our opinion is that IT systems have to support the business; therefore the choices made during an enterprise architecture study have to be translated to added value to the business.

Business centric thinking instead of technology centric thinking

The business activities to be performed are key in the way of setting up the enterprise architecture process.

Technology can enable and support the business in a certain way; however the benefits for the business must be the driver to use these technologies.

There must be a balance between the business perspective from the business architecture and the human perspective from the information architecture to deliver these benefits.

Business principles are mandatory

Business principles are a subset of all guiding principles and mandatory in guiding and evaluating choices. All the decisions during an enterprise architecture process will be guided by these principles.

Therefore the business principles are the discriminators during the enterprise architecture process.

Business Concepts thinking

Different business situations, can be fulfilled by different business approaches, therefore different scenarios can be identified up front to achieve the goals &

objectives. These scenarios are called concepts; so different business concepts have to be discussed at contextual level and the preferred concept will be used to start the enterprise architecture study.

Different enterprise architecture areas fulfil different goals.

Enterprise Architecture in the context of this guide addresses the aspect areas required to design an Extended Enterprise Architecture of organisations and IT systems. Therefore the following main enterprise architecture areas are identified as mandatory for an Extended Enterprise Architecture.

- o Business or Organisation; starting point and expressing all business elements and structures in scope.
- o Information; extracted from the business an explicit expression of information needs, flows and relations is necessary to identify the functions that can be automated.
- o Information - Systems; the automated support of specific functions.
- o Technology - Infrastructure; the supporting environment for the information systems.

All these areas have to be related to each other in such a way that a coherent set of relations can be identified.
Integration of these aspect areas is a necessity for an Integrated Architectural design.

These four aspect areas are internationally accepted as the basis areas for enterprise architecture.

Technology Infrastructure is more than hardware and networks

The status and position of specific enterprise architecture items can change in time. For example software developed for a specific situation can become so common, that it is used throughout the whole organisation in such a way that it actually is part of the technology infrastructure. Physical examples are the 'Office Suite' packages with common business functionality used by the whole organisation. In our terms this type of common functionality (realised in products) has become part of the technology infrastructure.

Enterprise Architectural Viewpoints

Enterprise Architectural Viewpoint: a perspective from which to view an architecture (IEEE 1471-2000).
Besides the aspect areas of enterprise architecture, specific views can be created, based on specific viewpoints of themes.
Viewpoints deliver added value to the aspect areas by addressing and focusing on specific themes, covering all aspect areas.

The results of viewpoints should be incorporated in the Extended Enterprise Architecture. This is necessary, because the results of these viewpoints influences at all levels.

Governance is an important Viewpoint

Governance is one of the viewpoints taken into account when creating an enterprise architecture. Especially the organisational governance structure, responsibilities and service level agreements are influencing architectural decisions.

Security is an important Viewpoint

Security is one of the other important Viewpoints supporting the organisation and IT in a consistent way.

Working on an Extended Enterprise Architecture or dealing within a specific aspect area, security has to be taken into account all the time. Always balancing between maximum security and maximum usability.

F.3.3 Separation of Concerns

'Separation of concerns' allow us to deal with conflict of interest between these concerns. We distinguish six main levels of concern within enterprise architecture studies often called levels of abstraction and related to specific questions:

1. The Contextual level, describing the context of the organization and the scope of the enterprise architecture study; the Why question.
2. The Environmental level, addressing the (extended) key stakeholders involved; the With-Who question.
3. The Conceptual level, addressing the requirements; the What question.
4. The Logical level, addressing the ideal logical solutions; the How question.
5. The Physical level, addressing the physical solution of products & techniques; the With-What question.
6. The transformational level, describing the impact for the organization of the proposed solutions; the When question.

Separate the context from the environment

The clear distinction between the context and the environment is necessary to identify all aspects and elements that can influence the progress of the enterprise architecture trajectory. The contextual level is key for the success of the overall result, by identifying the Business Mission, Vision, Strategies, Business Drivers, Guiding Principles and all stakeholders involved. Market conditions are identified as well as the Governance and Security policies of the organisation. At contextual level all influencing factors have to be identified.

Separate the environment from the requirements

It is necessary for the success of Enterprise Architecture trajectories to identify all key stakeholders including the extended stakeholder groups. Their impact will influence the requirements as well as the overall EA results. Cultural elements have to be taken into account by reflecting the organisation values. The maturity level of the organisation reflects the feasibility of the possible solutions. The relative position in the extended value net will even so influence the EA environment.

Separate requirements from logical solutions

The clear distinction between requirements (conceptual level) and logical solutions (logical level) helps to separate business drivers, principles and requirements from logical solutions. Visualising and modelling the requirements helps understanding the needs of the organization to support his business.

At logical level, the logical solution can be developed based on a clear understanding of the drivers, principles and requirements.

This 'separation of concerns' between requirements and solutions allow us to deal with the conflict of interest between business requirements versus functional / quality solution constraints.

Separate logical solutions from physical solutions

The clear distinction between logical solutions and physical solutions helps to design the best-fit solution and create the boundaries for a migration path toward that solution.

Logical solutions are implementation independent, physical solutions are related to specific products, frameworks and technology.

By focussing on logical solutions only, we can compare multiple architectural designs without being disturbed by physical issues. We can then make a clean choice for a particular design and pursue the 'ideal' solution to fulfil the organization requirements.

At physical level we focus on the techniques and products available to implement a preferred solution. By focussing on techniques only, we can compare multiple products in order to find the best possible support for the selected solution.

This 'separation of concerns' between logical solutions and physical solutions allow us to deal with the conflict of interest between implementation independent solutions and implementation dependent solutions.

[Example:] In the discussion of data placement we can choose the solution to have a single central database solution. This is a decision on a logical level that will impact the structure of e.g. the information system and the concerning solutions for transaction management and data locking. Due to technical constraints of the available technology we could however choose to implement the 'central' database on multiple locations using a replication mechanism. This mechanism can be provided by e.g. the DBMS. By using this mechanism we can comply with required performance or availability service levels without compromising the 'nature' or structure of the information systems itself.

Separate physical solutions from the transformation path

The timeframe to implement a physical solution can be differ in time, priority and scope based on technological or organisational constraints.
So for each aspect area the impact of the transformation has to be defined and the dependencies have to be clear.

Enterprise Architectural exist at different abstraction levels (following the rules above)

There are six levels of abstraction we are dealing with, a contextual level (context of the enterprise), environmental level (position in the value net and the influence of stakeholder groups), conceptual level (the principles & requirements), a logical level (the logical solutions), a physical level (the physical solutions) and the transformation level (impact for the organisation).

A level of abstraction deals with specific issues and topics of the content and addresses a specific question within the architectural process.

Adoption of international standards

International standards are used where necessary or possible, to align the way of working with the international community.
International standards are widely accepted and adopted and will therefore be used as anchor points to the international community.
This is done to improve communication of the architectural design results.

Common source of information

Common information that is used in different enterprise architecture areas should have the same sources.
An architectural design reflecting the best result of all the identified enterprise architecture areas requires that all enterprise architecture areas start with the same source of information and the same starting-points (the results from the contextual level).

Single entrance point of input

All information necessary for the enterprise architecture study in all aspect areas is collected at the contextual level or at least identified at the conceptual level. This is done to validate all information and to prevent unexpected manipulations in the enterprise architecture process. Iterations to the contextual level can be fulfilled to collect new input information.

AS-IS situation is input

The AS-IS situation will be most of the time, the start situation for the Enterprise architecture study.

This is done because only a few enterprise architecture studies are starting from a Greenfield situation.

F.3.4 Enterprise Architectural design principles and rules

Enterprise Architectural design principles and rules also deal with the methods and approaches, i.e. how to do an enterprise architecture study. All the architectural design methods have the same foundation and therefore encompass all enterprise architectural process rules. Characteristic for all the architectural design approaches is the presence of a process roadmap and an enterprise architecture framework.

The process roadmap describes the process steps in general –which phases to address during an architectural study- in a certain situation; the enterprise architecture framework identifies the topics to address.

Process roadmap is your guide

The process roadmap will be established after a clear opinion of the goals & objectives and the supporting deliverables. It will guide the team to deliver appropriate results.

The Process Roadmap distinguishes the following phases: start-up, discovery, design and transform.

The process roadmap (start-up, discovery, design, transform) is universal for all enterprise architecture approaches. TOGAF's ADM process is also a well known and open standard with clear process steps.

Deliverables drives the appropriate process

The goals and objectives of the enterprise architecture study define the set of deliverables that will support these goals and objectives. Related to the deliverables, a process will be defined that at the end delivers the results in such a way that the goals and objectives can be achieved.

This means the process is unique to the organization's situation for every enterprise architecture study.

Besides the developing results, creation of buy-in for the results is one of the most important things to do.

Program Management Rules

Every enterprise architecture study has to be set up as a normal program, with a program plan, resource plan, communication plan, time plan, risk analysis and validation milestones with the organization.

Communication to all stakeholders

The process roadmap describes the tasks and activities to derive the appropriate results, the results can be architectural design models or free format visualisations. Using tuned visualisation techniques these architectural results can be used for communication purposes to all stakeholders.

Visualisation of results

All major results are at least visually presented.
This is done to show the structure and to show the impact of the decisions made during the enterprise architectural design study. It makes the abstract effects of a decision on the enterprise architectural design visual, which supports communication, between enterprise architects and all stakeholders.

F.4 *Translation of EA Principles and Rules into a Framework*

F.4.1 Enterprise Architecture Environment Principles and Rules

IFEAD has created an Extended Enterprise Architecture framework by translating the most important enterprise architecture environment rules & principles into a coherent framework. This framework is the foundation of IFEAD's enterprise architecture world of thought.

The following paragraphs depict the elements of the framework and the principles and rule that have been used to create it.

F.4.2 Definition of the major enterprise architecture aspect areas

Principles and rules used to define this part of the model are:
  o *Business Benefits are leading*
  o *Business based choices*
  o *Business centric thinking instead of technology centric thinking*
  o *Business Principles are mandatory*
  o *Business Scenario thinking*
  o *Technology enabling by business benefits (Or Technology rationalised by business benefits)*

The Structuring of the enterprise architecture areas is from business to IT.

Starting from a business point of view, a structuring in aspect areas from business to IT is a way to address the right areas.

All these areas have to be related to each other in such a way that the business will and can be supported by IT. Integration of these aspect areas is a necessity for Enterprise Architecture.

Enterprise architecture in the context of this document is addressing topics to design the enterprise architecture of organisations and IT systems.

F.4.3 Separation of levels of abstraction

The 'separation of concerns' between levels allow us to deal with the conflict of interest between these levels.

- o *Separate the strategy from the environment*
- o *Separate the environment from requirements*
- o *Separate requirements from solutions*
- o *Separate solutions from implementations*
- o *Separate implementations from transformations*

Enterprise Architectures exist at different abstraction levels (Following the rules above)

There are six levels of abstraction we are dealing with, the context, the environment, a conceptual level, a logical level, a physical level and the transformation level. A level of abstraction deals with content and addresses a specific question as part of the enterprise architectural process activities.

F.4.4 Combining aspect areas with abstraction levels

Combining the structuring from business to IT and the identified abstraction levels, delivers the first skeleton of the framework.

F.4.5 Adding Viewpoints to the framework

Certain specific viewpoints of the enterprise architecture are not by default incorporated in the overall result. These viewpoints are difficult to implement after implementation, so they should be taken into account during every phase of the enterprise architecture process. These enterprise architecture viewpoints are covering all cells of the framework.

- o *Governance incorporation from start over all the main areas*
- o *Security incorporation from start over all the main areas*
- o *Privacy incorporation from start over all the main areas*

When an organisation is in the "maturity phase" of using Enterprise architecture for its Business and IT, the importance of security of business & information becomes a vital issue. So by taking security into account in the Enterprise architecture the business can decide on the importance of security on specific services.

During the enterprise architecture study, the architects have to establish the impact of these viewpoints for every aspect area. Examples of enterprise architecture viewpoints are Security and Governance.

F.4.6   Integrating all these elements into a Framework

The combination of the aspect areas and the abstraction levels together with the enterprise architecture viewpoints delivers an Extended Enterprise Architecture framework.

This framework represents the most important enterprise architecture rules and principles of IFEAD's enterprise architecture philosophy and mindset.

F.5   *Extended Enterprise Architecture Framework (E2AF)*

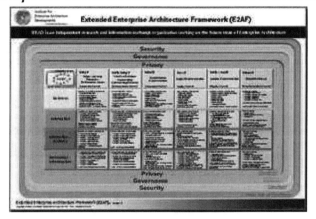

Figure 66. E2AF

IFEAD's Extended Enterprise Architecture Framework (E2AF) positions the way IFEAD communicates about enterprise architecture with all stakeholders, based on the philosophy and mindset behind the framework.

So these principles and rules guide the architect by approaching enterprise architectures and reflect IFEAD's Enterprise architecture Style.

F.5.1   Visualization of E2AF

Based on the basic model of E2AF described in the former chapters, IFEAD has created a simpler framework, with fewer details, which can be easily used to explain E2AF.

This chapter explains why IFEAD believes that enterprise architecture needs to be created in an integrated approach, what E2AF is, how E2AF is used and which methods, tools and techniques are available to conduct an Extended Enterprise Architecture Study.

F.5.2   Why E2AF

Every complex thing that has to operate as a whole has to be designed as a whole. This to guarantee integration and coherency of all its components and to ensure the whole will operate the way required when it is created.

The Extended Enterprise Architecture Framework forces enterprise architects to ensure that the organisation fully benefits from the alignment of business and IT by integrating all enterprise architecture aspect areas into one overall result, i.e. The enterprise architectural design has to consist of interlinked business, information, information systems, infrastructure, security and governance aspects.

The risk taken when not creating an **Extended Enterprise Architecture** is that time and money are thrown away due to inefficiencies and insufficient insight in the complexity of the overall structure.

F.5.3   How to use E2AF

Enterprise Architecture isn't a panacea for all problems in the world of business and information & communication technology. It serves its own specific objectives and has to be used when appropriate.

The framework is a communication vehicle for all stakeholders involved in an enterprise architecture study to explain en show relations, dependencies, influences and complexity of the situation of study.
- o   Enterprise Architecture results as well as E2AF itself can be used as an Atlas for management to navigate to all relevant topics.
- o   From E2AF, roadmaps can be defined to identify the necessary tasks and activities.
- o   E2AF can show the complexity of elements to be addressed.
- o   E2AF can show the people to be involved in the process.
- o   E2AF shows the relations and dependencies.
- o   E2AF is your Guide in all Architectural Activities.

F.5.4   E2AF Full Blown [21]

Figure 67. E2AF Full Blown – Next Page

---

[21] *Download the Full-blown A0 format picture of E2AF from the website: http://www.enterprise-architecture.info*

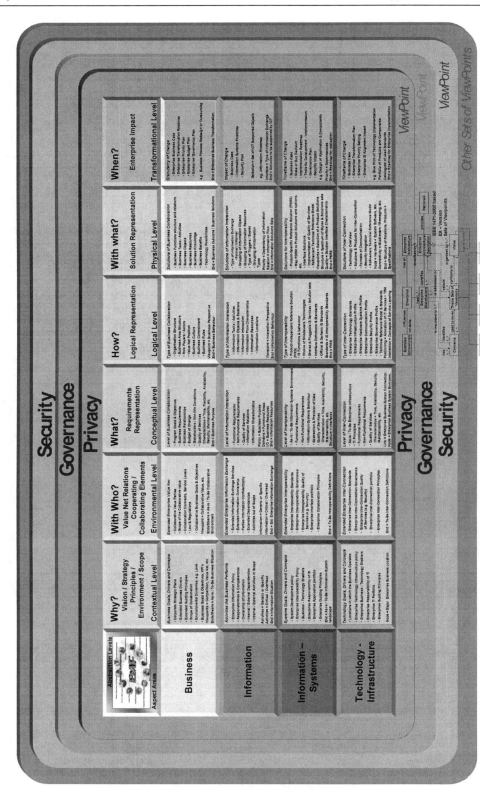

Extended Enterprise Architecture Framework (E2AF) SM Version 1.4

Appendix G: Enterprise Architecture Tool Selection Guidelines

G.1   Introduction

Enterprise Architectures are an emerging approach for capturing complex knowledge about organizations and technology. Enterprise Architectural approaches range from broad, enterprise focused approaches, through to approaches aimed at specific domains.

The focus of enterprise architecture efforts is now shifting to become more holistic, thereby necessitating the use of comprehensive modelling tools to analyze and optimize the portfolio of business strategies, organizational structures, risks, compliancy issues, business processes / tasks and activities, information flows, applications, and technology infrastructure.

Important to adoption of an enterprise architectural approach is the availability of tools to support the development, storage, presentation and enhancement of enterprise architecture representations. As with enterprise architecture methodologies, enterprise architecture tools to support the architectural development process are still emerging.

High value is derived from consolidating this portfolio of business artefacts into a single repository in a standardized manner to support enterprise analysis and optimization.

G.2   EA Landscape Mindset

Before selecting and evaluating EA tools, be aware about the original goals & objectives to achieve with your EA results. When the focus is on the creation of a well defined and artistic visualisation of the Business & IT landscape, most repository based tools can't deliver that by that fact that these tools first collect data, relate date to other data and then draw a picture of that relationship.

These kinds of repository based EA tools have their strength in the presence of meta-models, their support of modelling languages and the traceability along these items. Their weakness is that the visualisation is a result of data storage in the repository.

G.2.1 Good Practice in EA Landscape Visualisations

Most management and decision making people like it to see visualisations that are in line with the image and culture of the company, therefore more artistic visualisations in multi layer techniques are most of the time more efficient then the repository based drawings. For creating landscapes of the enterprise, a good starting point is to visualise the business function model first for example in Visio, then transpose that model to the background and visualize the IT landscape over the business function model. Using transparent colours will deliver you a 2 layer visualisation. By the fact that Visio has limited artistic capabilities, transpose the 2 layered Visio image to PowerPoint where you can bring in a third transparent layer, most of the time expressing one of the Viewpoints. The end result is a 3 layered visualisation placed in a company window with company logo and company related style. These kinds of visualisations are mostly appreciated by CxO's and top management. The counter side of these kinds of visualisations is that there is no control for consistency and related data is stored in separate documents. However for decision-making purposes this is most of the time not a problem.

So decide up front what you want to achieve with selecting an EA toolset and what you expect from the tool, then you can decide which kind of toolset fits the best in your situation. The EA Tool Review Framework will help you in this process.

G.3 *EA Tools Review Framework*

To consistently review enterprise architecture tools, a review framework is defined. The review framework consists of two dimensions: the basic functionality of the tool, and the utility of the tool to different professionals.

When reviewing an EA tool's basic functionality, the reviewer has to describe how well the tool performed the different functions needed for the enterprise to support their activities. The tools basic functionality was examined in the following areas:

- o   **Methodologies and Models;**
- o   **Model Development Interface;**
- o   **Tool Automation;**
- o   **Extendibility and Customization;**
- o   **Analysis and Manipulation;**
- o   **Repository;**
- o   **Deployment Architecture;**
- o   **Costs and Vendor Support.**

The second dimension, the tool's utility to different professionals, captures the fitness for purpose of the tool, and describes how useful the tool would be to particular professionals. The types of professionals considered were:

- o   **Enterprise Architects;**
- o   **Strategic Planners;**
- o   **Enterprise Program Managers.**

G.4 *Functionality Dimension*

This dimension of the EA Tools review framework attempts to capture how well the tool performs the core functions needed to support the enterprise architecture development activity. This dimension breaks the functionality of an enterprise architecture tool into eight key areas.

G.4.1 Methodologies and Models

The most important feature of an enterprise architecture tool the methodologies and modelling the approaches it supports. The approaches the tool supports dictate the types of enterprise architectures the tool is capable of supporting, and to an extent, the type of analysis and manipulation functions the tool is capable of performing. As well as reviewing the methodologies and modelling approaches, this functional area also reviews how well, or how completely, the tool implements the methodologies and modelling approaches it claims to support.

For tools that are capable of supporting multiple methodologies and modelling approaches, this functional area also examines how well the different approaches are integrated. For example, when complementary methodologies and modelling approaches (for example process modelling and data modelling) are used, how well can the different approaches are used together in an overall enterprise architectural approach?

When a tool supports competing approaches (for example two approaches to data modelling) how well can the data being modelled are moved between the different perspectives offered by the competing approaches?

G.4.2 Model Development Interface

The model development interface is the most obvious part of an enterprise architecture development tool. It is the interface used to design, build, maintain and often manipulate, the models that make up the enterprise architecture. Generally, models are built and maintained graphically, by manipulating icons and the connections between them. The tool's model development interface may also use textual interfaces to allow additional information to be appended to the graphical models.

The overall quality of the model development interface is an important characteristic of any enterprise architecture development tool. The interface must support the modelling activity well, for example by automating some of the drawing functions, by automatically laying out models, or by providing pick lists of alternative values at the appropriate places during the modelling activity. The model development interface must also be intelligently structured, make good use of limited screen space, be logical and consistent to use and navigate. The tool should ideally follow the graphical user interface conventions and guidelines that apply to its host operating system.

G.4.3 Tool Automation

Developing and populating enterprise architecture models is often the most time consuming part of the enterprise architecture development activity. By providing support for automating parts of the enterprise architecture development processes, a tool can help speed up the overall development activity.

A tool may support the creation of macros or scripts, to automate common functions or actions, or to group several functions together into one action. These may be used to automate parts of the model development activity. This feature is closely related to the tool's ability to be customized, which is described in the next section.

The tool may also provide the ability to automatically generate enterprise architecture models based on data held within the tool's repository, or have the ability to generate enterprise architecture models as a result of data manipulation functions.

G.4.4 Extendibility and Customization

This functional group captures how well an enterprise architecture tool can be modified to meet the unique enterprise architectural requirements of a unique organization. Enterprise Architecture tools may support customization by allowing users to add new modelling approaches or to modify the modelling approaches already supported by the tool. A tool may also support modification by providing a programming interface, allowing the functions of the tool to be modified, or allowing the tool to be integrated with other software products. Most enterprise architecture tools that support high levels of customization allow the underlying meta-models of the tool to be modified, and new meta-models added. Meta-models are literally models about models. They describe what entities can exist within particular models, the legal relationships between the different entities, and their properties. By modifying the existing meta-models, or adding completely new meta-models, a tool can be customized to support new modelling approaches. The ability to modify the tool via a programming interface allows the functionality and behaviour of the tool to be customized to meet the unique requirements of the organization.

Programming customization may be achieved though the use of an application scripting language, for example Visual Basics for Applications (VBA), or through support for adding external components, for example, Active X/DCOM components.

Enterprise Architecture tools may be extended by integrating them with other software products. This may be achieved via direct integration through XML or an exposed API within the tool, or via a middleware layer, for example ActiveX/DCOM, CORBA, and so on. Integration may also be supported via importing and exporting data into and out of the tool via standard file types; for example, XML, character delimited or fixed width delimited text files, HTML, or SYLK files and so on.

G.4.5 Analysis and Manipulation

As well as supporting the development of enterprise architecture models, an enterprise architecture tool may also provide support for analysis and manipulation of the developed models. The type of analysis and manipulation support provided by the tool is often tied to the particular modelling approaches supported by the tool. For example, Flow Analysis is often tied to process/workflow modelling.

Analysis support provided by a tool may simply examine how correct or complete the model is, relative to a particular modelling approach used. More sophisticated analysis support may allow the model to be interrogated in some way, or be subjected to particular analysis methods. Analysis support may include the ability to compare different versions of models, allowing current and to-be enterprise architectures to be compared. Manipulation functions capture a tool's ability to change the way the models are represented and viewed. This may include the ability to view models from particular perspectives, for example showing only particular classes of entities, or the ability to amalgamate separate models into a single model.

G.4.6 Repository

Most of the tools on the market make use of some kind of data repository to hold the developed models. The functions provided by the tool's repository have a significant impact on the overall functionality, scalability and extendibility of an enterprise architecture tool.

Some tools make use of commercial relational database management systems, or commercial Object Orientated or Object/Relational database systems, while others use proprietary repository systems.

A tool's repository often dictates the way users can collaborate. A repository may provide support for collaboration by supporting multiple, concurrent, users on the one repository, or by providing the ability to combine models developed by different modellers into one model.

The repository may also provide many different data management functions, including the ability to support model versioning, the ability to roll back to previous versions, the ability to lock parts of the model against change, and the ability to control access to part or the entire model.

G.4.7 Deployment Architecture

A tool's deployment architecture describes the tool's software structure and software implementation. Generally, enterprise architecture tools tend to adopt one of two deployment architectures: either a single user/single client structure, or a simple two-tier client/server structure.

Single user/single client structured tools are designed to operate on one workstation, and can generally only be used by one user at a time. Tools that implement this style of deployment architecture generally have a very tight coupling between the tool and its repository. In this type of deployment architecture, only one modeller can have access to the repository at any one time.

The second common deployment architecture found within the enterprise architecture tool domain is a simple two tier client/server structure. Tools that implement this style of deployment architecture generally have looser coupling between the tool and the repository. Generally, the repository is stored on a network server, and can often be accessed by multiple concurrent users. This deployment architecture allows multiple modellers to work on the same models concurrently.

G.4.8 Costs and Vendor Support

The final functional group considered is the cost of the tool and after sales support provided by the vendor. The cost of enterprise architecture tool licenses can range anywhere from € 1,500 to € 7,000 per license, and optional extras are often available for an additional cost. Given the high costs of this type of tool, the types of licensing agreements offered by the vendor, and how they may lower the overall cost, is important. For example, does the vendor support floating licenses, allowing expensive licenses to be shared among a large group of users? Does the vendor offer discounts for bulk purchases, or site licenses? Does the vendor offer discounts to government or non-profit organizations?

Also important in the overall cost of adopting an enterprise architecture tool, are the cost and type of maintenance and/or after sales support contracts offered by the vendor. Is the vendor able to offer comprehensive, in-house training? If the vendor is a foreign company, do they have an Australian representative available to provide training? Does the vendor offer free technical support? Is the vendor able to offer free or heavily discounted upgrades? How does the vendor address software faults discovered by the user? What is the yearly maintenance costs associated with the tool?

G.5 *Different Professionals Dimension*

The evaluation of the tools considered their suitability for use by different professionals. The needs of other groups, such as software architects, are not considered in this EA tools selection framework.

G.5.1 Enterprise Architects

Enterprise Architects investigate all aspects of enterprise architectural approaches and methodologies. This can involve researching different representations and enterprise architectural structures, including the development and investigation of alternative modelling approaches. As such, the requirements for a tool to support enterprise architectural research are quite challenging. The over-arching requirement is flexibility in defining and adapting modelling approaches. However, a robust tool is also required to develop large-scale demonstrators to investigate, and promote these alternative approaches.

G.5.2 Strategic Planners

Strategic planners, including executive management and innovating staff, use the enterprise architectures results for strategic decision making. They need to be assembled and modified quickly, and should be based on current (or planned) future capability.

Strategic planners need a tool that is easy to use. It is highly desirable that local support is available when required. The tool should have strong drawing and reuse facilities including support for multiple, related, configurations within a single architecture. Quick, automated, analysis and consistency checking is highly desirable. Integration with existing data sources is essential, particularly when implementing planning facilities.

G.5.3 Enterprise Program Managers

Enterprise Program Managers as well as domain program managers and often project managers supports the enterprise architecture program in order to support the implementation and transformation phase. The enterprise architecture tools should be able to capture current and future resources (such as platforms, assets and components), organizations, people, information exchanges, tasks or activities, and processes and their relationships as well as program planning facilities.

Enterprise Program managers need a tool that is easy to use, with support available when required. Local support is desirable, but probably not essential providing it is very responsive. The tool should have a strong planning and analysis capability and allow reuse between enterprise architectures for different activities undertaken at different times.

G.6 *Candidate Tool Requirements Checklist*

First and foremost, objectives for acquiring and using a comprehensive modelling tool must be articulated and agreed to by all stakeholders.

Since this tool is to support enterprise architecture, enterprise-level objectives must be included. Once that is accomplished, the objectives must be translated into requirements for both vendor presence and performance.

Also, architectural principles both high-level conceptual and domain-level detailed must be included as screening criteria. Principles can either be converted into requirements or left as-is, requiring vendors to demonstrate their support of such principles.

The functional requirements of a tool must be understood prior to embarking on a selection. Only the functionality that is currently required of the tool or that which will be realistically necessary in the future should be selected.

The next list is a candidate listing of requirements and specifications. **Enhance this list for your own specific situation.**

Only the functionality that is currently required of the EA tool, or that which will be realistically necessary in the future, should be selected.

G.6.1 Candidate list of EA Tool Requirements & Specifications

Table 12. List of EA Tool Requirements & Specifications

1	Operational & Technical Fit
1.1	**Platform Environment**
1.1.1	Can the client software be installed on MS Windows XP?
1.1.2	Can the client software be installed on MS Windows Vista?
1.1.3	Can the client software be installed on Linux?
1.1.4	Can the server component be set up on MS Windows 2003 Server?
1.1.5	Can the server component be set up on Sun Solaris?
1.1.6	Can the server component be set up on Linux Servers?
1.1.7	Can the server component be set up on Unix Servers?
1.1.8	Can the repository be set up using the latest versions of Oracle DB? Which Versions?
1.1.9	Can the repository be set up for SQL Server? Which Versions?
1.1.10	Can the web client be set up for MS Internet Explorer? Which Versions?
1.1.11	Are there specific requirements or specifications to setup the repository? Which?
1.2	**Performance & Availability**
1.2.1	Can additional licenses be added dynamically without the need to affect users PC's?
1.2.2	Can the tool still operate for a period of time if the server holding the licenses fail, e.g. crashes?
1.2.3	Does the tool handle extreme amounts of data e.g. millions of records?
1.2.4	Does the tool operate at the same performance if there are 100 users accessing the same repository?
1.2.5	Offers the tool facilities to monitor its performance?
1.2.6	Is remote access feasible and practical (e.g. via GPRS/notebook)?
1.2.7	Can the tool perform several tasks at the same time? (E.g. run a report in the background)?
1.2.8	Does the tool have a simultaneous update of open views without user interaction?
1.3	**Security (User Admin)**
1.3.1	Is the user required to log on every time he uses the tool?
1.3.2	Is it possible to authorize the user at the level of objects?
1.3.3	Is it possible to authorize the user at the level of class properties?
1.3.4	Does the tool support role based user management?
1.3.5	Does the tool support check-in/check-out items of repository?
1.3.6	Does the tool support read only access?
1.3.7	Does the tool support management of user groups?
1.3.8	Does the tool support more than 100 simultaneously logged on users?
1.3.9	Assuming there are licenses, can any number of users access the repository at the same time?
1.3.10	Are there at least four different user profiles which can have hierarchical relationships to each other?
1.3.11	Does the tool record the full history of changes to objects?
1.3.12	Does the tool run reports on utilization of its licenses?
1.3.13	Does the tool support external Accountancy Audits?
1.3.14	Does the tool stamp all changes done to objects with a time-user stamp?
1.3.15	Is it possible to define own user profiles?
1.3.16	Is it possible to (explicitly) lock models or parts of models?
1.4	**Software Distribution**
1.4.1	Is a central shared installation possible, which allows users to access the tool without local installation procedures?
1.4.2	Does the tool support shared installation of upgrades?
1.4.3	Are upgrades possible without a system (esp. server) shutdown?

1.4.4	Does the tool support a shared initial installation? (I.e. can the tool be site-installed and the installation shared by users)?
1.4.5	Are bug fixes distributed in the form of patches?
1.4.6	Are patches freely available?
1.4.7	Can patches be downloaded from the Internet?
1.4.8	Do you have less than three releases a year with well before published release plans?

1.5   Release Management

1.5.1	Does the tool support rollback?
1.5.2	Does the tool support replication/synchronization mechanisms?
1.5.3	Is it possible to replicate parts of the repository to local repositories?

1.6   Tool Architecture

1.6.1	Does the tool have a client / server architecture?
1.6.2	Does the tool provide a thin client?
1.6.3	Does the tool provide a thick client?
1.6.4	Does the tool provide standalone usage?

1.7   Technical and Operational Requirements

1.7.1	Does the tool have below or average requirements on operational memory? Please define.
1.7.2	Does the tool have below or average requirements on CPU? Please define.
1.7.3	Does the tool have below or average requirements on external memory (disks)? Please define.
1.7.4	Does the tool use a standard RDBMS? Please define.

2   Vendor Support

2.1   Help Desk Support

2.1.1	Can help desk support be offered in English or other languages?
2.1.2	Can you offer time to repair guarantee?
2.1.3	Do you provide standard escalation procedures for problem resolution?
2.1.4	Is a log of all known bugs, including date of first occurrence, status and date of closure, available on-line for at least the last 6 months?
2.1.5	Can these resources be contacted by phone and e-mail?
2.1.6	Does the help desk have a list of all customizations/work carried out by consultants on the clients site?
2.1.7	Can the tool be installed without training?
2.1.8	Does the tool provide interactive help?
2.1.9	Is the interactive help comprehensive and easy to navigate?
2.1.10	Does the tool have an online tutorial?
2.1.11	Does the tool have tutorial/help on features?
2.1.12	Does the tool have online documentation?
2.1.13	Do you run a global bulletin board for raising bug enquiries?

2.2   Training

2.2.1	Do you have dedicated in-house product trainers?
2.2.2	Do you provide training specifically for Enterprise Modellers?
2.2.3	Can the training be conducted in other languages then English? Which languages?
2.2.4	Do you publish regular training schedules?
2.2.5	Do you provide formal training of the product?
2.2.6	Is courseware available for purchase?
2.2.7	Do you provide web based training /e-learning?
2.2.8	Do you offer on-site trainings all over the world?

2.3   Professional Services (Migration)

2.3.1	Do you provide consulting services?
2.3.2	Do you offer tools for (assistance with) a one-off conversion of documents from Excel, Visio, Word or other format to your tool?

2.4   Documentation

2.4.1	Will you provide us with a full comprehensive set of documentation covering all

	aspects of the tool?
2.4.2	Are changes made available on the Web?
2.4.3	Are all documents made available in both hard and soft format?
2.4.4	Is the documentation available other languages than English? Define
2.4.6	Is there additional documentation available for purchase?

2.5 **Local Support**
2.5.1 Do you offer local support world-wide or in only some regions? Please explain.
2.5.2 Do you offer guaranteed reaction times?

2.6 **Newsgroups**
2.6.1 Is there a user group for your product?
2.6.2 Do they meet regularly?
2.6.3 Do they have a website?
2.6.4 Do you run a global newsgroup for discussion?

3   Functional Fit (Specific)

3.1 **Support Analysis**
3.1.1 Does the tool search enterprise architecture design patterns in order to suggest a possible solution?
3.1.2 Does the tool support the process of enterprise architecture requirement analysis and the process of generating architecture design?
3.1.3 Does the tool offer consistency checking and quality checks for designed architectures in accordance to architecture principles and rules?
3.1.4 Does the tool support impact analysis at all levels?
3.1.5 Does the tool support delta analysis at all levels?
3.1.6 Are there syntax checks through the given data?
3.1.7 Are there semantic checks through the given data?
3.1.8 Can new consistency checks be defined at any time?
3.1.9 Does the tool support bottleneck analysis?
3.1.10 Does the tool offer a common meta-model?
3.1.11 Does the tool offer mean to force mandatory inputs?
3.1.12 Does the tool support the structured access to stored objects and attributes (trees, hierarchy)?

3.2 **Support of Enterprise Architecture Frameworks**
3.2.1 Delivers the tool Support for Zachman Framework?
3.2.2 Delivers the tool Support for FEAF (Federal Enterprise Architecture Framework)?
3.2.3 Delivers the tool Support for E2AF (Extended Enterprise Architecture Framework)?
3.2.4 Delivers the tool Support for DoDAF (C4ISR)?
3.2.5 Delivers the tool Support for TOGAF v8x EA Framework?
3.2.6 Delivers the tool Support for a custom or proprietary enterprise architecture framework?
3.2.7 Can the tool handle references to an external custom enterprise architectural framework?
3.2.8 Does the tool aid user with navigation in a custom enterprise architecture framework?

3.3 **Support of Enterprise Architecture Program (Time)**
3.3.1 Does the tool have a timeline marking of objects (e.g. objects valid from..to..)?
3.3.2 Does the tool handle different stages of existence of objects (e.g. under discussion, valid, in operation, discarded)?
3.3.3 Can the tool produce time-related output? (E.g. to show the enterprise architectural landscape at a specific date (to any freely chosen date)?

3.4 **Simulation**
3.4.1 Does the tool support simulation of alternative enterprise architecture scenarios?
3.4.2 Can the tool generate landscapes of (selected) objects of one or more classes?
3.4.3 Can the tool generate a landscape of objects which existed on a certain date or over a certain period if time in the past?
3.4.4 Is it possible to generate a to-be landscape of objects planned for certain dates?

3.4.5   Does the tool simulate impact of changes in a scenario?
3.4.6   Does the tool support hierarchy?
3.4.7   Has the tool the ability to support discrete simulation?
3.4.8   Has the tool the ability to perform Monte Carlo simulation?
3.4.9   Have the tool facilities to graphical simulation of processes to demonstrate bottlenecks?

3.5   *Repository management*

3.5.1   Does the tool support Enterprise Architecture Diagrams?
3.5.2   Does the tool have Domain Architecture Diagrams?
3.5.3   Does the tool have Application Architecture Diagrams?
3.5.4   Does the tool have Information Architecture Diagrams?
3.5.5   Does the tool have IT Architecture Diagrams?
3.5.6   Does the tool fully support Custom Type Diagrams (e. g. Management Dashboard View)?
3.5.7   Does the tool support workflow?
3.5.8   Does the tool have process modelling functionality i.e. process decomposition and process charts?
3.5.9   Does the tool support enterprise architecture design diagrams as standard or can be customized to support this, with the ability to reuse applications and system interfaces from the application architecture diagrams?
3.5.10 Does the tool support logical models?
3.5.11 Does the tool support physical models (system level)?
3.5.12 Does the tool support data flow diagrams?
3.5.13 Can the user reuse all objects/definitions (metadata items)?
3.5.14 Can the user define and reuse applications within the tool?
3.5.15 Can the user define and reuse system interfaces?
3.5.16 Can the user define and reuse data flows?
3.5.17 Can the user define and reuse functions?
3.5.18 Can the user define and reuse services in de context of SOA?
3.5.19 Can the user define and reuse technology?
3.5.20 Can the user define and reuse requirements?
3.5.21 Can the user define and reuse business processes?
3.5.22 Can the user define and reuse goals?
3.5.23 Is the user able to view the architecture through a function view?
3.5.24 Is the user able to view the architecture through an information view?
3.5.25 Is the user able to view the architecture through an integration view?
3.5.26 Is the user able to view the architecture through a distribution view?
3.5.27 Can the user define and reuse location?
3.5.28 Can the user define and reuse roles?
3.5.29 Does the tool support organization models?
3.5.30 Can the user have an is-a relationship between a class of objects and its objects within the tool?
3.5.31 Can the user have a belong to relationship between some defined object class?
3.5.32 Does the tool support extensibility of repository?
3.5.33 Does the tool support different abstraction levels (level of detail)?
3.5.34 Can the tool generate diagrams using objects, their properties and relationships out of the repository?
3.5.35 Has the tool the ability to create / design network & hardware systems diagrams / models?
3.5.36 Has the tool the ability to create / design communication diagrams / models?
3.5.37 Has the tool the ability to scan networks and build network systems topology?
3.5.38 Has the tool the ability to create an enterprise meta data dictionary?
3.5.39 Does the tool support the incorporation of service level agreements?
3.5.40 Has the tool the ability to support Business & IT strategy definitions?
3.5.41 Has the tool the ability to store Enterprise principles and trace them to decisions?

3.5.42	Has the tool the ability to support / trace risk & compliancy issues?

3.6   *Validation of Models*

3.6.1	Does the tool support a goal model, showing business goals?
3.6.2	Does the tool support hierarchy and linking of goals?
3.6.3	Does the tool support linking of goals to other categories of objects?
3.6.4	Does the tool support polymorphism?
3.6.5	Does the tool support inheritance?
3.6.6	Does the tool support encapsulation?
3.6.7	Does the tool have automatic parsing of requirements? (E.g. by keywords Note: Requirement means anything to comply with, e.g. business rules, IT Strategy etc.)
3.6.8	Does the tool have a text and graphical interface to follow the links?
3.6.9	Does the tool support versioning of requirements, history of requirement changes, log of modifications etc?
3.6.10	Does the tool ensure compliance to defined meta model at all levels?
3.6.11	Does the tool ensure that involved responsible users for certain objects (e. g. systems) must agree when changes to interfaces between objects will be done? (workflow)
3.6.12	Has the tool the ability to do impact analysis?
3.6.13	Has the tool the ability to trace inconsistencies over models?
3.6.14	Has the tool the ability to trace incompleteness?

3.7   *Support of Standard modelling languages, methods and techniques*

3.7.1	Does the tool support UML?
3.7.2	Delivers the tool Support for MDA (i.e.., Model Driven Architecture, OMG)?
3.7.3	Delivers the tool Support for BPML (i.e., Business Process Modelling Language)?
3.7.4	Delivers the tool Support for BPEL 2.0 (i.e.., Business Process Execution language)?
3.7.5	Delivers the tool Support for BPMN (i.e., Business Process Modelling Notation)?
3.7.6	Delivers the tool Support for ADML (i.e., Architecture Description Markup Language, Open Group)?
3.7.7	Does the tool support the Yourdon methodology?
3.7.8	Does the tool support the Archimate Modelling language?
3.7.9	Does the tool support SSADM (i.e., Structured Systems Analysis & Design Methodology)?
3.7.10	Does the tool support modelling processes with a swim-lane diagramming approach?
3.7.11	Has the tool the ability to develop IDEF0 diagrams?
3.7.12	Has the tool the ability to develop IDEF1 diagrams?
3.7.13	Has the tool the ability to perform IDEF 1X data modelling?
3.7.14	Has the tool the ability to develop IDEF 3 diagrams?
3.7.15	Does the tool support for IDL (IDEF Interchange Definition Language)?
3.7.16	Does the tool support a Six Sigma approach?
3.7.17	Does the tool support ISO 900x methodology?
3.7.18	Has the tool the ability to develop ANSI standard flowcharts?
3.7.19	Does the tool Support for ABC (i.e., activity based costing)?
3.7.20	Hast the tool the ability to create UML v 2.0 diagrams (e.q., use cases, state diagrams sequence diagrams, etc)?
3.7.21	Has the tool the ability to create IE entity relationship (ER) diagrams?
3.7.22	Does the tool support for cardinal notation to create up to fifth normal form ER diagrams?
3.7.23	Has the tool the ability to associate multiple attributes per entity (e.q.., >25)?
3.7.24	Has the tool the ability to generate physical data models (e.q.., DDL)?
3.7.25	Has the tool the ability to create DFDs (i.e., data flow diagrams)?
3.7.26	Does the tool support for Jackson use cases?

3.8   *Support for Enterprise Architecture Review Management*

3.8.1	Does the tool support identification of components where counter steering is required?
3.8.2	Does the tool provide information objects to store, access review reports and results in a structured manner?

4	Functional Fit (General)

4.1   *User Interface*

4.1.1   Can the user decide on what level to navigate through the tool?

4.1.2   Does the tool navigate through a browser?

4.1.3   Does the tool support drill down/drill up between levels of detail?

4.1.4   Does the tool support undo/redo functionality?

4.1.5   Can any number, without a limit, of levels of diagrams be attached to a top level diagram?

4.1.6   Does the tool support navigation between the graphical tool and the database in both directions?

4.1.7   Does the tool have a search engine for structured and unstructured information?

4.1.8   Does the tool have a database of patterns?

4.1.9   Does the tool have a database of customizable examples / solutions?

4.1.10   Does the tool have a framework of orientation within the whole projects?

4.1.11   Is there a common look and feel across all products?

4.1.12   Do all elements of your product employ similar usability functions?

4.1.13   Can the system use graphical and non-graphical user interfaces?

4.1.14   Is the use of either interchangeable?

4.1.15   Can drag & drop be used in the graphical user interface?

4.1.16   Does the tool support the definition of specific views for defined objects through all levels?

4.1.17   Does the tool model connection between objects as own objects with attributes?

4.1.18   Can attributes of connections be displayed automatically?

4.1.19   Can the visualization of connections be changed manually/automatically?

4.1.20   Has the tool the ability to mine for patterns within multiple models?

4.2   *Customization*

4.2.1   Can the user create new diagram types?

4.2.2   Can the user create new definitions?

4.2.3   Can the user create custom visualizations (symbols) for objects?

4.2.4   Can the user create new matrices (relations)?

4.2.5   Can the user create new properties for existing definitions?

4.2.6   Is possible to create custom queries/filters?

4.2.7   Is there no limit to the amount of diagrams, definitions, objects and matrices that can be created?

4.2.8   Are the reports easy configurable (i.e. with little coding or very little with the help of examples and tutorials)?

4.2.9   Can the user define custom views?

4.2.10   Does the tool support aggregation of information in order to create one big picture (Overview)?

4.2.11   Has the tool the ability to spell-check?

4.2.12   Has the tool the ability to find and replace?

4.3   *Import/Integration*

4.3.1   Are there interfaces to other DB programs like: OracleX, MS SQL Server, MS Access, DB2, other?

4.3.2   Does the tool import/export using XML?

4.3.3   Does the tool integrate with BEA Workshop?

4.3.4   Does the tool integrate with Oracle Designer?

4.3.5   Does the tool integrate with Rational Rose?

4.3.6   Has the tool the ability to support/export to a certain ERP solution?

4.3.7   Has the tool the ability to support/export to certain CRM solution?

4.3.8   Has the tool the ability to support/export to a certain SCM solution?

4.3.9   Has the tool the ability to generate WFSL?

4.3.10   Has the tool the ability to import models and diagrams from other tools (e.q., Visio, etc)?

4.3.11	Has the tool the ability to import from CSV (i.e., comma delimited ASCII)?
4.3.12	Has the tool the ability to import from XML files)?
4.3.13	Has the tool the ability to publish models in Microsoft Word
4.3.14	Has the tool the ability to maintain model relationships in HTML via hyperlinks
4.3.15	Has the tool the ability to export to Microsoft Project?

4.4   *Reporting*

4.4.1	Is it possible to generate, to save and to export user defined reports and graphics?
4.4.2	Is it possible to generate HTML output, including diagrams?
4.4.3	Is it possible to export to MS WinWord?
4.4.4	Is it possible to export to MS Excel?
4.4.5	Can the tool produce a summary in MS WinWord to give a summary of the architecture landscape?
4.4.6	Can the tool produce a summary in MS WinWord or Excel to give a picture of the mappings and how it fits together?
4.4.7	Can the MS WinWord templates/reports be changed through GUI?
4.4.8	Does the tool support drill down reporting?
4.4.9	Does the tool support summary reporting?
4.4.10	Does the tool support queries?
4.4.11	Is it possible to export to MS Visio?
4.4.12	Is it possible to import from MS Visio?
4.4.13	Is it possible to export to MS PowerPoint?
4.4.14	Is it possible to print all generated reports, graphics to standard output formats (DIN A0-A4), PDF?
4.4.15	Is it possible to publish defined information automatically based on predefined states, events or time?

4.5   *Version Management*

4.5.1	Is there a version mechanism within the tool?
4.5.2	Can the tool provide several versions of one metadata object?
4.5.3	Is it possible to compare models within a repository?
4.5.4	Can the tool handle conflicts on import and merge commands?
4.5.5	Does the tool allow multiple versions of an object?
4.5.6	Does the tool support comparisons between versions of objects?
4.5.7	Does the tool support migration of individual objects/components through development phases?
4.5.8	Does the tool support resolution of migration conflicts during the migration of multiple releases?

4.6   *Documentation Management*

4.6.1	Does the tool produce documents in industry standard formats (ISO, IEEE …)?
4.6.2	Does the tool support generating of presentations?
4.6.3	Does the tool support WYSWIG preview of output documents and presentations?
4.6.4	Does the tool support concurrent review, markup and comment of documents, designs, etc?

4.7   *Help and Tutorials*

4.7.1	Installation: Can the tool be installed without vendor's assistance?
4.7.2	Installation: Can the tool be installed without training?
4.7.3	Can the tool be configured without vendor's assistance?
4.7.4	Can the tool be configured without training?
4.7.5	Does the tool have interactive help?
4.7.6	Is the interactive help comprehensive and easy to navigate?
4.7.7	Does the tool have an online tutorial?
4.7.8	Is the online tutorial comprehensive and easy to navigate?
4.7.9	Does the tool have a tutorial/help on features?
4.7.10	Does the tool have online documentation?

4.8   *Libraries, as in Customization*

4.8.1	Can the user extend the supplied graphical library?
4.8.2	Can the user extend the supplied graphical library with inheritance?
4.8.3	Does the tool have a branch / market specific library?

4.9   *Code Generation*

4.9.1	Has the tool the ability to generate code in Java, J2EE?
4.9.2	Has the tool the ability to generate code in C++?
4.9.3	Has the tool the ability to generate code in C#?
4.9.4	Has the tool the ability to generate other codes? Which?

5   **Commercial & Credibility**

5.1   *Financial Status of Vendors*

5.1.1	Do you have sufficient cash reserves to fund operations for the next financial year?
5.1.2	Do you have any joint ventures or do you plan any?
5.1.3	Can you confirm that you are not aware of any attempts to acquire your company?
5.1.4	Has your company been in the business for longer than 10 years?
5.1.5	Has your company been in the business for longer than 5 years?
5.1.6	Is your company making profit?

5.2   *Experiences (within Branches / Markets)*

5.2.1	Have you previously delivered solutions to specific branches / markets? Which?
5.2.2	Have you previously delivered solutions to system integrators & consultancy firms? Which?
5.2.3	Which markets perform a significant portion of your revenue stream?
5.2.4	Are you building branch specific functionality?
5.2.5	Can you provide references in specific branch / market environments?
5.2.6	Are these references available in Europe?
5.2.7	Are these references available in the USA?
5.2.8	Can you provide contacts of references?
5.2.9	Do you have a list of the number of licenses that are active?
5.2.10	Do you sell and support your products globally?
5.2.11	Do you sell your products via resellers?
5.2.12	Do you have an aligned vision of the tool developments?
5.2.13	Is the products commercial release 3 or higher?
5.2.14	Do you have more than 1000 licensed customer sites
5.2.15	Do you have more between 500-1000 licensed customer sites?
5.2.16	Do you have more than 10000 product licenses active?
5.2.17	Do you have between 5000-9999 licenses active?

5.3   *Sharing Risks and Revenues*

5.3.1	Are you willing to negotiate fixed prices for any customization/integration work?
5.3.2	Are you prepared to undertake the proof of concept free of charge?
5.3.3	Are you willing to incur missed target penalties?
5.3.4	Has your product been on the market for how many years?
5.3.5	Is enterprise architecture a core competency of your product portfolio?
5.3.6	Do you support old versions for at least two years?
5.3.7	Are any significant changes to your product portfolio planned?
5.3.8	Are you willing to allow customers to influence your product roadmap?
5.3.9	Do you actively participate in forums for defining industry standards?
5.3.10	Do you conduct research for long term requirements?
5.3.11	Are new releases backward compatible?
5.3.12	Can you offer a warranty?

5.4   *Strategic Partnership*

5.4.1	Do you have any strategic alliances with other companies? Which?

5.5   *Capital Expenditure*

5.5.1	Is the software priced on an enterprise basis?
5.5.2	Is the software priced on a registered user pricing model?
5.5.3	Is the software priced on a concurrent user pricing model?

5.5.4   Can you provide a standard price list?
5.5.5   Can you provide a detailed cost breakdown?
5.6   ***Operational Expenditure***
5.6.1   Do you have support packages available?
5.6.2   Do you charge runtime fees?
5.6.3   Are licenses based on user rather than on installation? (I.e. can I access from my PC or my notebook on one license?)
5.6.4   Do you charge maintenance costs based on purchase price?
5.6.5   Are there additional costs related to the use of your product (DB licenses...)?
5.6.6   Would you support potential customers to calculate a detailed TCO scenario?

These requirements should be weighted in importance relative to one another. This will enable the selection of the tool with the best functional fit. However, all modelling efforts within the enterprise and their functional requirements should be considered. A desired outcome is to minimize the number of modelling tools and repositories.

Each of the aforementioned criteria under presence and performance must be decomposed into related sub criteria and weighted or ranked. In addition, the content for the enterprise technical architecture must be included in the decision criteria.

Selecting a comprehensive modelling tool that violates the enterprise technical architecture of the enterprise erodes the credibility of the tool and the EA team.

G.6.2 The purpose of adopting an EA Tool?

Supporting decision making of management requires another level of detail in models and diagrams then supporting application development. One of the common mistakes in using EA tools is to spend too much time at details that or not relevant for decision making. While supporting application development requires enough details in the models and diagrams for developers to continue their work. So decide up front what kind of activities must be supported and check which tools support your requirements.

Appendix H: EA Quality of Services (Space Ufo Method[22])

The Space Ufo (System Product Advanced Certification and Evaluation - User Focus) method is developed under the auspices of the European Union as part of the European Commission ESPRIT Information Technologies RTD Fourth Framework Programme.

H.1   Introduction

Until recent years, the Information Technology society has focused its attention on the software development process and software process improvement. However, improvement of the software process does not guarantee the "fitness-for-use" of products, as experienced by the actual user. Recent European projects and standardisation efforts have addressed software product quality, but primarily from a "technical" point of view. Other projects aimed at user related software quality, but only partly covering the software quality spectre as described by ISO 9126.

Users now feel an increasing need to be able to assess the "fitness-for-use" software quality. Manufacturers wish to be able to prove this quality by means of generally accepted standards. They intend to reduce the "time-to-market" and the number of software changes of release by taking the user needs into account effectively, in an early development stage. User oriented software quality principles will not only improve the effectiveness of the evaluation of software products in final development stages, but will also improve the specification of software, as the basis for software design and evaluation of intermediate products.

The main objective of the project is the development of the SPACE-UFO methodology for specification and evaluation of software product quality requirements with an emphatic user focus.

A second main objective is the acceptance of the methodology by the IT market so that it becomes a widely recognized de-jure or defacto standard which may be considered as a best practice. Derived objectives are the development of techniques and tools which support the application of the methodology and the dissemination of results.

Application of the SPACE-UFO methodology, techniques, tools and training material will enable users to assess the quality of software. This will result in better "fitness for purpose" and lower costs and risks. Benefits for software developers will be that user needs can be taken into account for software quality specification and evaluation and that software can be evaluated with respect to user needs. This will lead to reduction of the number of releases and of the time-

---

[22] *http://www.cse.dcu.ie/essiscope/sm2/atwork/spaceufo.html*

to-market. Evaluators will be able to evaluate the software quality in a deterministic and widely accepted way. The methodology, methods and techniques are expected to affect existing and newly developed standards and methods, including software process improvement.

H.2   *Enterprise Architecture SPACE-UFO Methodology*

The Institute For Enterprise Architecture Developments (IFEAD) had enhanced the Space Ufo method for use in the Enterprise Architecture Domain. By adopting the concepts of the method, IFEAD has added new techniques to the process and to visualize results as well as to prioritize the quality categories.

As a basis for the SPACE-UFO methodology a reference model has been defined. The concept of the SPACE-UFO reference model is displayed in the figure below. The picture consists of two levels:
- o   the high level
- o   the conceptual level

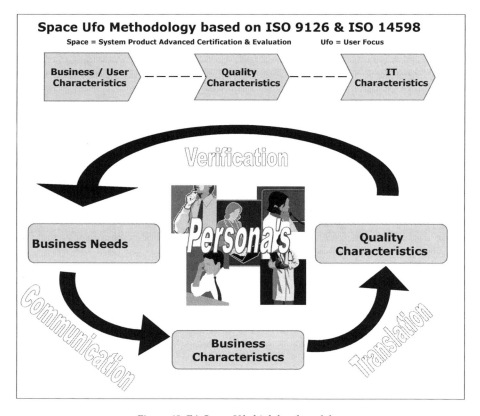

Figure 68. EA Space Ufo high level model

H.2.1   The high level

Business processes to be supported by IT products and user needs (or expectations) to be fulfilled require a certain business & IT quality objective. This quality objective is expressed by one or several quality characteristics. These characteristics have to meet certain requirements that are set, so as to ensure that the user needs are fulfilled. The quality characteristics can be met by the more technical characteristics of the system and its components itself.

For instance, the business process "production to order" requires easy adaptation of programs, the computer infrastructure and the database. This implies that the aspect of maintenance is important and that certain requirements have to be set with regard to this aspect. This requirement can, again as an example, be met by a certain number of source code comment lines or the structure complexity which are system characteristics.

H.2.2   The conceptual level

The conceptual level gives a more detailed description of the high level.
The business & IT quality specification and assessment process starts with a description of the business processes that have to be supported by IT, the needs (or expectations) of the user/customer and the IT product (type) itself (e.g. wireless network, office automation or not). Related to the product are issues such as applicable laws, standards and conditions necessary for use of certain hardware, software or technologies (e.g. operating system).

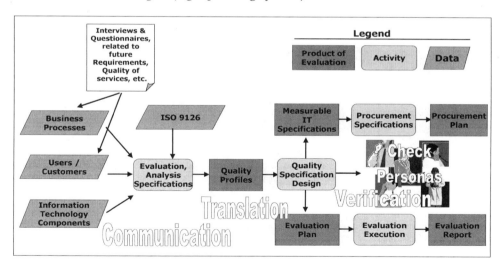

Figure 69. EA Space Ufo Reference model

This diagram is called the EA Space Ufo reference model. Processes are drawn as squares with rounded corners and real entities are drawn as simple squares.
The business & IT product quality level is described by means of a quality profile based on the ISO 9126 model. A quality specification and an evaluation plan are developed from this.

They describe:

- o which quality specifications will be set for the business and /or IT to be developed;
- o which standards, methods, techniques and tools will be used to develop or to evaluate the business and / or IT with respect to the aspects that were described in the quality profile?

The quality specification is a description of the quality characteristics that have to be fulfilled by business and /or IT being acquired. This specification is input to the business and /or IT obtaining process.

The evaluation plan is the formal description of the way the business and /or IT will actually be evaluated. The end result of the evaluation is the evaluation report. The equivalent of the evaluation plan regarding development is the business and /or IT architecture and technical plan.

H.2.3　ISO / IEC / NEN 9126 Quality Model

The objective of this standard originally is to provide a framework for the evaluation of software quality. However the framework is even so suitable for evaluation of business & IT quality as part of Enterprise Architecture efforts.

ISO/IEC 9126 does not provide requirements, but it defines a quality model which is applicable to every kind of situation. It defines six product quality characteristics and in an annex provides a suggestion of quality sub-characteristics.

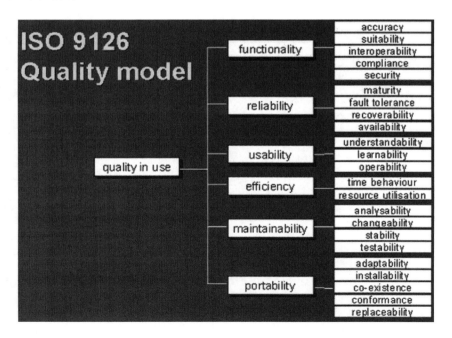

Figure 70. ISO 9126 Quality Model

Functionality - the capability of systems to provide functions which meet stated and implied needs when the system is used under specified conditions.

o   **Accuracy** - the capability of the business and /or IT to provide right or agreed results or effects.

o   **Suitability** - the capability of the business and /or IT to provide an appropriate set of functions for specified tasks and user objectives.

o   **Interoperability** - the capability of the business and /or IT to interact with one or more specified systems.

o   **Compliance** – the capability of the business and /or IT to be in line with rules & regulations.

o   **Security** - the capability of the business and /or IT to prevent unintended access and resist deliberate attacks intended to gain unauthorised access to confidential information, or to make unauthorised modifications to information or to the program so as to provide the attacker with some advantage or so as to deny service to legitimate users.

Reliability - the capability of the business and /or IT to maintain the level of performance of the IT when used under specified conditions.

o   **Maturity** - the capability of the business and /or IT to avoid failure as a result of faults in the business and /or IT.

o   **Fault tolerance** - the capability of the business and /or IT to maintain a specified level of performance in cases of faults or of infringement of its specified interface.

o   **Recoverability** - the capability of the business and /or IT to re-establish its level of performance and recover the data directly affected in the case of a failure.

o   **Availability** – the level of availability of the business and /or IT to continue the operations.

Usability - the capability of the business and /or IT to be understood, learned, used and liked by the user, when used under specified conditions.

o   **Understandability** - the capability of the business and /or IT to enable the user to understand whether the IT is suitable, and how it can be used for particular tasks and conditions of use.

o   **Learnability** - the capability of the business and /or IT to enable the user to learn its application.

o   **Operability** - the capability of the business and /or IT to enable the user to operate and control it.

o   **Attractiveness** - the capability of the business and /or IT to be liked by the user.

Efficiency - the capability of the business and /or IT to provide the required performance, relative to the amount of resources used, under stated conditions.

o   **Time behaviour** - the capability of the business and /or IT to provide appropriate response and processing times and throughput rates when performing its function, under stated conditions.

- o **Resource utilisation** - the capability of the business and /or IT to use appropriate resources in an appropriate time when the system performs its function under stated conditions.

Maintainability - the capability of the business and /or IT to be modified.
- o **Analysability** - the capability of the business and /or IT to be diagnosed for deficiencies or causes of failures, or for the parts to be modified to be identified.
- o **Changeability** - the capability of the business and /or IT to enable a specified modification to be implemented.
- o **Stability** - the capability of the business and /or IT to minimise unexpected effects from modifications.
- o **Testability** - the capability of the business and /or IT to enable modified IT to be validated.

Portability - the capability of business and /or IT to be transferred from one environment to another.
- o **Adaptability** -the capability of the business and /or IT to be modified for different specified environments without applying actions or means other than those provided for this purpose for the system considered.
- o **Installability** - the capability of the IT to be installed in a specified environment.
- o **Co-existence** - the capability of the IT to co-exist with other independent system in a common environment sharing common resources.
- o **Conformance** – the capability of the business and /or IT to be in line with current or future standards.
- o **Replaceability** - the capability of the IT to be used in place of other specified system in the environment of that system.

H.2.4 The instrumental and technical level

The instrumental and technical level addresses the operational aspects of the methodology and comprises the methods, techniques and tools (based on the concepts of the conceptual level) to carry out the processes and describe the entities mentioned at the conceptual level. It can be ISO standards, questionnaires, checklists, decision matrices, description methods, guidelines, etc.

The quality profile can be described by means of a number of ISO 9126 characteristics (e.g. 'functionality', 'maintainability',) and a level indication of each characteristic.

By collecting all the quality elements, statements, principles and attributes derived from interviews and documents of the business as well as the IT systems in for example a spreadsheet and categorizing them in line with the ISO 9126 Quality categories delivers Quality Profiles for each relevant business item and IT system.

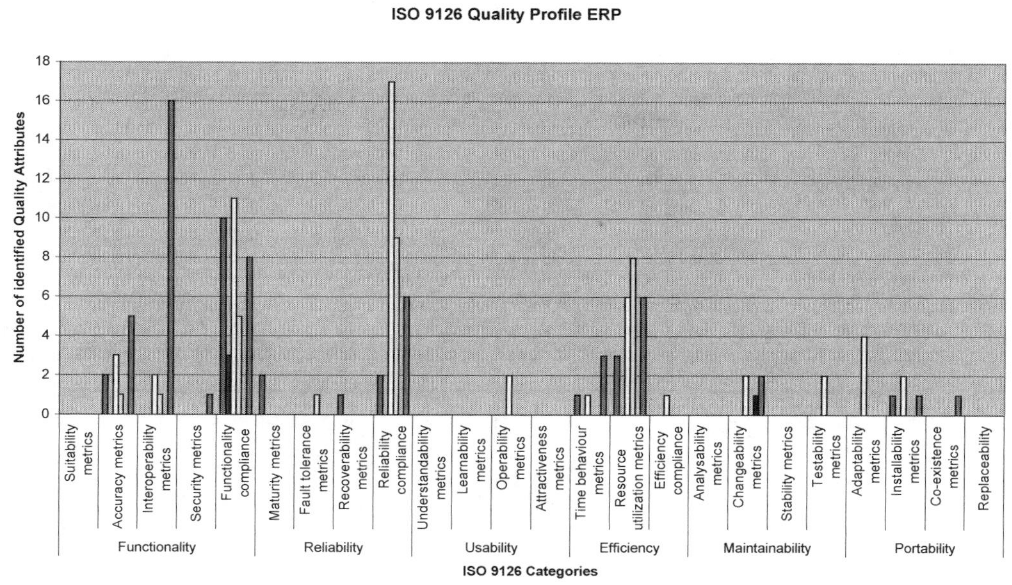

ISO 9126 Quality Profile ERP

Figure 71. ISO 9126 Quality Profile

H.2.5 The Weighted Criteria Method for Quality Categories

The method of weighted criteria is a tool to prioritize criteria in such a way that it is easily to clarify how the weighting of criteria is assigned.

If there is long list of quality criteria it is hard to define the right weighting factors intuitively. The weighted criteria method makes this process more easily by comparing two by two the criteria and defining each time the most important criteria relative to the other. Doing this process in a consequent way will deliver you automatically a relative ranking of the most important criteria.

The method will be explained by using an example. The following list of ISO 9126 categories of quality criteria for ERP must be ranked by using the weighted criteria method.

1. Functionality
2. Reliability
3. Usability
4. Efficiency
5. Maintainability
6. Portability

We define a matrix with in the rows as well as the columns all categories of criteria. Then we check for every cell if the category of criteria for the row is more or less important then the category of criteria for the column. If the row is more important, mark the cell with 1, is the column is more important mark the cell with 0. The total score per row is added in a sum column. By doing that consequently an overall ranking of categories of criteria will be pop up. The highest score is the most important category of criteria; the lowest score the less important category of criteria.

Weighted Criteria Method for ERP		Functionality	Reliability	Usability	Efficiency	Mantainability	Portability	Sum
		1	2	3	4	5	6	
Functionality	1		0	1	1	1	1	4
Reliability	2	1		1	1	1	1	5
Usability	3	0	0		0	0	0	0
Efficiency	4	0	0	1		1	1	3
Maintainability	5	0	0	1	0		0	1
Portability	6	0	0	1	0	1		2

Ranking weighted criteria ERP		
2	Realiability	5
1	Functionality	4
4	Efficiency	3
6	Portability	2
5	Maintainability	1
3	Usability	0

Figure 72. Weighted Criteria Method

H.2.6 Quality Profiles

Adopting the official Weighted Criteria Method as an approach to define the relevant weighting factors for each ISO 9126 Quality Category, will deliver a relative ranking for each category as a Quality Profile (QP). As an example in the next figure the current and future needs of Quality Categories for ERP are showed.

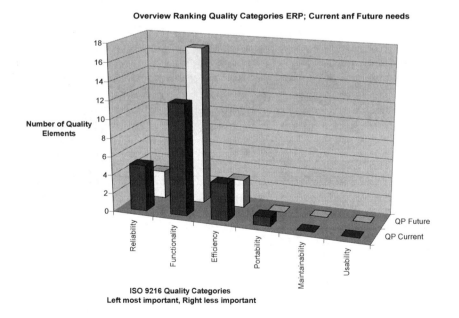

Figure 73. Overview Ranking Quality Profile ERP; Current and Future needs

The main objective of this process is to produce the quality profile of the business / IT item or product from the user needs. A quality profile is intended to be a list of prioritised quality characteristics (and sub-characteristics, as defined by ISO 9126), and of a set of requirements associated to these quality characteristics.

The activities proposed in this process are the following:
o To introduce the approach to all persons which will be involved in the process;
o To collect data (by questionnaire, checklists...) related to the system product in its contexts of use (technical characteristics, context and conditions of use, features of users...);
o To analyse data collected and combine to provide an unformal, accessible and reusable data basis, to identify the potential inconsistencies between the different participants' points of view, to determine potential quality levels (A possible support are predefined requirements/quality levels decision tables, i.e. data base which suggests relationship between a set of common contexts of use and their corresponding quality levels);
o To consolidate the combined results by obtaining feedback (inconsistencies resolved, modifications/adjustments to the quality levels initially proposed...);
o To elaborate the Quality Profile with the explanations and additional information to support a correct interpretation of the quality profile established, to translate the quality levels into evaluation levels.

For the transformation process between quality profile and evaluation plan a selection has to be made from a number of standards, methods, techniques and tools such as ISO 9241, ISO 14598, QSEAL, SUMI, checklists, guidelines, etc. This selection depends on the characteristics to be evaluated.

Translating the Quality Profiles in Quality Specifications for each quality category will help the organization in setting the quality standards for that specific item / product or organization entity.

These Quality Specifications can be used in a procurement process, a sourcing process or to enhance the Quality Awareness of the organization.

Appendix I: TOGAF - Architecture Development Method (ADM)

I.1   Introduction

I.1.1   History

Developed by the Open Group in 1995, this architectural framework was based on the TAFIM, developed by the DoD.

TOGAF Version 8.1.x is a superset of the well-established framework represented by TOGAF Version 7. Version 8.x uses the same underlying method for developing IT architectures that was evolved, with a particular focus on Technical Architectures, in the Versions of TOGAF up to and including Version 7.

However, Version 8.1.x applies that architecture development method to the other domains of an overall Enterprise Architecture - the Business Architecture, Data Architecture, and Application Architecture, as well as the Technical Architecture.

I.1.2   Purpose

[TOGAF] intends to provide a practical, freely available, industry standard method of designing an EA, leveraging all relevant assets in the process. TOGAF is supported by a number of different architecture consultants, and it is sufficient for an organisation to use "as-is" or to adapt as an EA development method for use with other deliverables-focused frameworks.

TOGAF focuses on mission-critical business applications that will use open systems building blocks. The framework embodies the concept of the Enterprise Architecture Continuum (described in Part III of the definition), to reflect different levels of abstraction in an architecture development process. It provides a context for the use of multiple frameworks, models, and architecture assets in conjunction with the TOGAF Architecture Development Method.

I.2   TOGAF Enterprise Architecture

I.2.1   Scope

The scope of application for TOGAF includes any organisation whose:
- o   Products and services are in the business and industry domains;
- o   Technical infrastructure is based on open systems building blocks;
- o   Definition of EA includes:
- o   Business Process architecture
- o   Applications Architecture
- o   Data Architecture
- o   Technology Architecture

I.2.2   Principles

Rather than providing a set of architecture principles, TOGAF explains the rules for developing good principles. Principles may be defined at three levels:

- o Enterprise principles to support business decision making across the entire Enterprise;
- o IT principles guide use of IT resources across the enterprise;
- o Architecture principles govern the architecture development process and the architecture implementation.

Example of TOGAF Principle.

Principle: Maximize Benefit to the Enterprise
Statement: Information management decisions are made to provide maximum benefit to the Enterprise as a whole.

Rationale: This principle embodies "Service above self." Decisions made from an Enterprise-wide perspective have greater long-term value than decisions made from any particular organisational perspective. Maximum return on investment requires information management decisions to adhere to Enterprise-wide drivers and priorities. No minority group will detract from the benefit of the whole. However, this principle will not preclude any minority group from getting its job done.

Implications: Achieving maximum Enterprise-wide benefit will require changes in the way we plan and manage information. Technology alone will not bring about this change. Some organisations may have to concede their own preferences for the greater benefit of the entire Enterprise.
Application development priorities must be established by the entire Enterprise for the entire Enterprise. Applications components should be shared across organisational boundaries

TOGAF recommends a standard way for defining principles. In addition to a definition statement, each principle should have associated rationale and implications statements, both to promote understanding and acceptance of the principles themselves and to support their use in explaining and justifying why specific decisions are made. A standard definition should include a name; a statement of the rule; the rationale with accompanying benefits; and implications of required cost, resources, and activities. See the example from the TOGAF documentation.

Architecture principles are influenced by enterprise mission and plans, strategic initiatives, external constraints such as market factors, the current set of systems and technology deployed throughout the enterprise, and industry trends.

A good set of principles can be recognised through five quality criteria:
- o **Understandability.** The intention of the principle is clear and unambiguous to all so that violations are minimized
- o **Robustness.** Consistent decisions can be made about complex, potentially controversial situations, and enforceable policies and standards can be created.
- o **Completeness.** Every possible situation that can be imagined regarding the government of IT is covered.
- o **Consistency.** Strict adherence to one principle should not compromise the adherence to another.
- o **Stability.** Principles should be long lasting, but an amendment process should be set up after initial ratification.

I.2.3 Structure

TOGAF consists of three main parts:

TOGAF Architecture Development Method *[ADM]*, which explains how to derive an organisation-specific enterprise architecture that addresses business requirements. The ADM provides:
- o A reliable, proven way of developing the architecture;
- o Architecture views, which enable the architect to communicate concepts;
- o Linkages to practical case studies;
- o Guidelines on tools for architecture development.

The Enterprise Architecture Continuum, which is a taxonomy for all the architecture assets, both within the enterprise and in the IT industry at large, that the enterprise may consider when developing architectures. At relevant places throughout the TOGAF ADM, there are reminders to consider which architecture assets from the Enterprise Continuum might be appropriate for reuse. TOGAF provides two reference models that may be the start of an organisation's Enterprise Continuum:

The TOGAF Foundation Architecture, an architecture of generic services and functions that provides a foundation on which specific architectures and architectural building blocks can be built. This Foundation Architecture in turn includes:
- o TOGAF Technical Reference Model [TRM], which provides a model and taxonomy of generic platform services;
- o TOGAF Standards Information Base [SIB], which is a database of open industry standards that can be used to define the particular services and other components of an enterprise-specific architecture;
- o The Integrated Information Infrastructure Reference Model, which is based on the TOGAF Foundation Architecture and is meant to help design architectures that enable and support the vision of "Boundaryless Information Flow."

TOGAF Resource Base, which is a set of resources including guidelines, templates, and background information to help the architect in the use of the ADM.

I.2.4 Guidance

The ADM is iterative, over the whole process, between phases, and within phases. For each iteration of the ADM, a fresh decision must be made as to:

1. Breadth of coverage of the enterprise to be defined;
2. Level of detail to be defined;
3. Extent of the time horizon aimed at, including the number and extent of any intermediate time horizons
4. Architectural assets to be leveraged in the organisation's Enterprise Continuum, including:
    o Assets created in previous iterations of the ADM cycle within the enterprise
    o Assets available elsewhere in the industry (e.g., other frameworks, systems models, or vertical industry models)

These decisions need to be made on the basis of a practical assessment of resource and competence availability and the value that can realistically be expected to accrue to the enterprise from the chosen scope of the architecture work. As a generic method, the ADM is developed to be used by enterprises in a wide variety of different geographies and applied in different vertical sectors/industry types. As such, it may be, but does not necessarily have to be, tailored to specific needs.

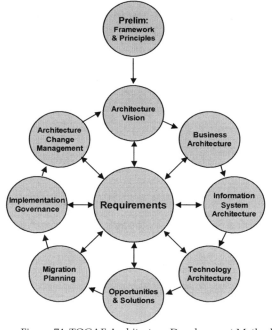

Figure 74. TOGAF Architecture Development Method (ADM)

I.3   *Enterprise Continuum*

TOGAF recognises the need for multiple architectures within the enterprise. These architectures represent progressions from logical to physical, horizontal to vertical, generalized to specific, and an overall taxonomy. The continuum has several benefits:

o   The Enterprise Continuum aids communication and understanding, within enterprises, between enterprises, and with vendor organisations. Individuals sometimes talk at cross-purposes when discussing architecture because they are referencing different points in the architecture continuum at the same time without realizing it. The continuum helps to prevent these misunderstandings;

o   Architectures are context-specific; for example, there are architectures that are specific to individual customers, industries, subsystems, products, and services. Architects need a consistent language to communicate the differences between architectures effectively. Such a language is particularly important when engineering systems using COTS products. The continuum provides that consistent language;

o   The continuum represents a taxonomy for classifying architecture assets, an aid to organising reusable solution assets.

The continuum comprises two parts: the Architecture Continuum and the Solutions Continuum.

The Architecture Continuum provides a consistent way to define and understand the generic rules, representations, and relationships in an information system. The Architecture Continuum classifies reusable architecture assets and is directly supported by the Solutions Continuum. This is illustrated in the figure, which shows how different architectures stretch across a continuum, ranging from foundational architectures such as TOGAF's, through common systems architectures and industry-specific architectures, to an enterprise's own individual architectures.

The arrows in the next figure represent the bi-directional relationship between different architectures. The arrows pointing left focus on meeting enterprise needs and business requirements, while the arrows going right focus on leveraging architectural components and building blocks. An architect often will look to the left of the continuum to find reusable architectural elements. When elements are not found, new requirements for these elements are passed to the left of the continuum for implementation. The Architecture Continuum is a useful tool to discover commonality and eliminate unnecessary redundancy.

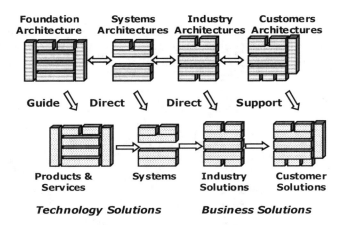

Figure 75. TOGAF Architecture Continuum

The Solutions Continuum provides a consistent way to describe and understand the implementation of the Architecture Continuum. The Solutions Continuum defines what is available in the organisational environment as reusable building blocks and addresses the commonalties and differences among the products, systems, and services of implemented systems. The Solutions Continuum is illustrated in the next figure.

The Solutions Continuum represents a reuse repository for the implementations of architectures at the corresponding levels of the Architecture Continuum. At each level, the Solutions Continuum is populated with reference building blocks; either purchased products or built components. A populated Solutions Continuum can add significant value to the task of managing and implementing improvements to the IT environment.

The arrows pointing right in the previous figure represent providing solutions value. Products and Services provide value for creating Systems Solutions, which in turn are used to create Industry Solutions. Industry Solutions are used to create Customer Solutions. The arrows pointing left focus on addressing enterprise needs.

I.3.1   TOGAF Resource Base

The Resource Base contains the example templates and sample procedures that provide a specific head start to architectural development. The collection of materials includes:

- o   Guidelines for establishing and operating an Enterprise Architecture Board;
- o   Guidelines for ensuring project compliance to architecture;
- o   Guidelines for defining and using architecture contracts;
- o   Guidelines for using architectural patterns;
- o   Principles for the use and deployment of IT resources across the enterprise;

- o   Guidelines for viewpoints and views in architecture models;
- o   A fictional example illustrating building blocks in architecture;
- o   A set of function views aligned with the business process structure of the enterprise;
- o   A method for deriving business requirements for architecture and the implied technical requirements;
- o   Real-life examples of TOGAF in use;
- o   Definitions of key terms;
- o   Arrangements for effective control of IT by enterprise management;
- o   Other architecture frameworks and their relationship to TOGAF;
- o   Strategies to ensure architecture is linked to requirements;
- o   Tools and techniques helpful in using TOGAF;
- o   Mapping the TOGAF ADM to the Zachman Framework.

The Open Group's Standards Information Base *[SIB]* is a database of facts and guidance about information systems standards. The standards to which it refers come from many sources: formal standards bodies such as ISO or IEEE; authoritative standards makers such as the Internet Society; and other consortia, like the W3C and the OMG.

I.3.2   The SIB has three main uses:

- o   **Architecture development.** For an organisation that is creating an architecture for its information systems, the SIB is a valuable source of information about standards that may be used to populate the architecture.

- o   **Acquisition/Procurement.** An organisation that is planning a procurement can use t he SIB to help ensure that the procurement gives a clear statement of technical requirements, with an assurance of conformance.

- o   **General information.** The SIB can be a source of information about relevant IT standards, for use by anyone at any time. The standards listed in the various tables are all Open Group standards, standards endorsed by The Open Group as appropriate for architecture specification and procurement.

The entries in the SIB are linked to other Open Group databases and resources, in particular those relating to Product Standards and Registered Products. Where relevant, the SIB also may be linked to the Websites of other de facto standards organisations. In this way, the SIB provides the architect with a gateway to a uniquely powerful set of tools for defining the standards that an architecture is to mandate and for checking the availability in the marketplace of products guaranteed to conform to those standards.

I.3.3   TOGAF Support

The Open Group has introduced certification programs for the following offerings:

- o **Architecture tools**, which support TOGAF, to ensure that the meaning of a claim of conformance with TOGAF is clear and that TOGAF ADM is supported consistently in different architecture tools.
- o **Training courses**, which instruct in TOGAF, to ensure that the course syllabus includes coverage of the necessary elements of TOGAF and its ADM.
- o **Architects** trained in the use of TOGAF, to ensure that a common core of knowledge and understanding is transmitted in such courses and that architects who have completed the necessary training course and have up-to-date knowledge about TOGAF deliver professional services offered in support of TOGAF.
- o **Professional services** offered in support of TOGAF, to ensure that organisations that offer such services abide by an approved code of practice and use only properly trained architects for such services.

Appendix J: Examples of Enterprise Architecture Results / Deliverables

J.1 EA Standard Deliverables Overview

Depending on the scope, principles and goals + objectives to achieve during an EA trajectory, different EA results or deliverables can be the output of this EA trajectory.

To help organizations in defining their EA results a non limitative list of results or deliverables is developed based on the experiences within IFEAD, the US Department of Defence and the usage of the E2AF, DoDAF & FEAF.
These experiences and deliverables are the basis for this set of results however experiences and practices outside the Government & Defence world have enhanced this list with additional results.

Use this list as a set of reference results and select and enhance this list to your own situation depending on the goals and objectives to achieve.

Define and select your own visualization / modelling techniques to visualise the context, landscape models and diagrams to meet your stakeholder's demands. Our experience is that visualizing the EA results in the format of large photographic / picturized posters that are coloured in line with the organizations house style is very effective. Figure 76 is showing an overview of EA results & relations. Customize the results in such a way that it will support the overall goals & objectives.

J.2 EA Deliverables List (non limitative)

EA Results / Deliverables	Results	Description
Overview and Summary Information	EA-1	Description, purpose, scope, time frame and mission; optional external graphic
Mission & Vision Statements	EA-2	Description of the organizations mission and vision
Information Dictionary	EA-3	Enterprise Architecture Description Document (EAD), Report / Repository
Enterprise Architecture Principle Overview	EA-4	Overall table representing the weighted EA principles guiding the EA activities
Enterprise Architecture sets of Viewpoints	EA-5	Definition and description of relevant sets of viewpoints
Business Activity – Information Exchange Diagram	EA-6	Diagram representing Business processes and related information exchange items

Business Activity / Information Exchange – Systems Mapping	EA-7	Diagram representing Business processes / related information exchange items and related information systems
Information Systems –Mappings & Views	EA-8	Diagram representing the Information Systems and related Relational Database usage & positioning
Information Systems – Technical Infrastructure Mapping	EA-9	Diagram representing the Information Systems and related Technical Infrastructure
High-Level Business Concept Graphic	BA-1	Identified in repository as an External Graphic. Viewable in EA tool and incorporated in EA reports.
Business Node Connectivity Description	BA-2	Geographic diagram for Business Connections displaying the Business Nodes decomposition with Business Information exchanged and the Exchange Characteristics connecting internal and external nodes.
Organization Relationships Chart	BA-3	Hierarchy Diagram showing governance and coordination relationships of the Organization
Business Process & Activity Models	BA-4	Archimate, UML, BPMN, EFFBD, FFBD or IDEF0 representing behaviour models including control, input/output, sequencing and decomposition of Business Activities and relations. (processes)
Business Activity Sequence and Timing Descriptions	BA-5	Complete business activity model as Archimate, BPMN or IDEF0 including all relations. Optional output includes rules, a captured timeline file or an external event trace file.
Business Information Exchange Matrix	IA-1	A summary or full information exchange matrix listing Business Information exchanged and the Exchange Characteristics
Business Information Exchange Diagram	IA-2	A summary or full information exchange diagram listing Business Information exchanged and the Exchange Characteristics
Logical Information / Data Model	IA-3	Business Information characterization table
Information Systems Interface Description	ISA-1	Physical Diagram showing systems interface descriptions and standards; (external file

		that augments the system interface choice)
Information Systems Communications Description	ISA-2	Physical Diagram for communication components descriptions or an external file that augments the components
Information Systems Functionality Description	ISA-3	BPMN, EFFBD, FFBD, N2 or IDEF0 representing behaviour models including control, input/output, sequencing and decomposition of Functions
Business Activity to Systems Function Traceability Matrix	ISA-4	Matrix tracing between the Business Activities and Functions with an option to show the Component performing each Function.
Information System Evolution Description	ISA-5	An External File (text or graphic).
Information System Technology Forecast	ISA-6	Table containing technology forecast information for Components and their associated Interfaces, Links, Functions and Items.
Information System Activity Sequence and Timing Descriptions	ISA-7	Complete functional model as UML or EFFBDs diagrams. Optional output includes rules, a captured timeline file or an external event trace file.
Information Systems Physical Data Schema	ISA-8	Item characterization table / diagram and/or an External File.
Technical Standards Profile	TA-1	Table listing Standards governing the Components and their associated Interfaces, Links, Functions, and Items.)
Technical Reference Model (TRM)	TA-2	Diagram showing Technical Services Categories governing the Components and their associated Interfaces, Links, Functions, and Items.)

J.3　All View: EA-1 - Overview and Summary

J.3.1　Project Identification

MPS tracking system enterprise architecture developed by the MPS EA group.

J.3.2　Scope

Context, Business and Technology reflections & views developed to describe the to-be-developed parcel tracking system.

J.3.3　Purpose

Provide guidance to management & developers. Enterprise Architecture results developed supporting the business owner and Enterprise Architect perspectives.

J.3.4　Context

The tracking system provides in-transit-visibility to both MPS staff and MPS customers.

Figure 76. EA Results Overview & Relations

J.4   EA-2 Mission & Vision Statements

The Mission Statement describes the charter of the enterprise and the scope of work the enterprise needs to perform. The Vision Statement describes critical success factors for achieving the enterprise's mission, including the resolution of key issues involving current performance of the mission. Vision Statements cover both business process aspects of the enterprise and IT aspects.

A sample outline for this work product includes:

o   Organizational Mission Statement

o   Customer Needs

o   Business Goals and Objectives

o   Business Vision

o   Critical Business Issues

o   Critical Success Factors

o   High-level Operational Concept Description (text and graphics).

The graphics for the High-level Operational Concept Description are informal, presentation-style (MS PowerPoint) graphics, and are not part of a formal model.

J.5   EA-3 Information Dictionary & Common Data Model

Many of the enterprise architectural results have a graphical representation. However, there is textual information in the form of definitions and metadata (i.e., data about an item) associated with these graphical representations.   The Information Dictionary provides a central source for all definitions and metadata, including those that may be provided for convenience within another product as well.   Each labelled graphical item (e.g., icon, box, or connecting line) in the graphical representation of an architectural product should have a corresponding entry in the Information Dictionary.   The type of metadata included in the Information Dictionary for each type of item will depend on the type of architectural product from which the item is taken.

At a minimum, the Information Dictionary is a glossary with definitions of terms used in the given architecture description. The Information Dictionary consists of the attribute table information for all the other work products. The Information Dictionary makes the set of architecture products stand-alone so that it may be read and understood as a standalone document without reference to other documents.

Each labelled graphical item (e.g., icon, box, or connecting line) in the graphical representation of an architectural product should have a corresponding entry in the Information Dictionary. The type of metadata included in the Information Dictionary for each type of item will depend on the type of architectural product from which the item is taken.

J.6   *EA-4 Enterprise Architecture Principle Overview*

The foundation of Enterprise Architecture is related to the guiding principles of the organization. Guiding principles can be categorised in Enterprise, business, Information, Application, Technical Infrastructure, Security and Governance principles.

Principles have to be prioritized and will guiding the design and evolution of the Enterprise Architecture overtime. Principles have to be described by their Rationale and Implications.

Examples of enterprise principles can be found in Appendix D.

J.7   *EA-5 Enterprise Architecture sets of viewpoints*

Viewpoint and views are representing specific stakeholder concerns and are describing the enterprise from a specific perspective.

In IEEE 1471-2000 (Architectural Descriptions), viewpoints and views are introduced to describe stakeholder concerns when describing architectures.

Based on the IEEE definitions, viewpoint and views are meaningful things in describing Extended Enterprise Architectures from specific perspectives. So they are playing an important role in the communication with stakeholders.

From the concept of architecture viewpoints another, relatively new view on enterprise architecture **sets of viewpoints** is given, to reflect extended enterprise stakeholders' responsibilities and involvement in organizations and societies.

A **viewpoint** defines the perspective from which a view is taken. More specifically, a viewpoint defines: how to construct and use a view (by means of an appropriate schema or template); the information that should appear in the view; the modelling techniques for expressing and analyzing the information; and a rationale for these choices (e.g., by describing the purpose and intended audience of the view).

A **view** is what you see. A **viewpoint** is where you are looking from - the vantage point or perspective that determines what you see.
Viewpoints are generic, and can be stored in libraries for reuse. A view is always specific to the enterprise architecture for which it is created.

Every view has an associated viewpoint that describes it, at least implicitly.

See Appendix E for more information about Views and Viewpoints.

J.8   EA-6 Business Activity – Information Exchange Diagram

Figure 77 captures the operational concept of modern Defence organisations for information exchange of its operational missions. The figure shows the layers of information exchange via sea, air, and ground nodes. The graphic portrays the movement of different sensor and shooter systems. The Business Activity – Information Exchange Diagram shows the flow of information from sensor to shooter over bread spread areas.

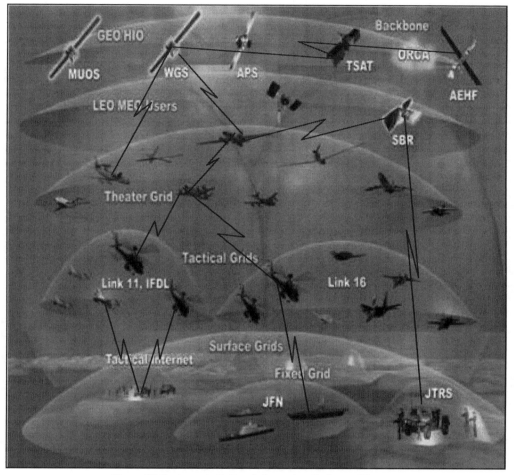

Figure 77. Business Activity – Information Exchange Diagram

J.8.1   Comments

- o   The EA-4 Business Activity – Information Exchange Diagram is an overall high-level graphic representation of the Business Activities (Processes), the relations and the Information Flows between the Business Activities

- o   Top decision-makers comprise its audience.

- o   There is no particular required content or format, but it should be accompanied by explanatory text.

J.9 EA-7 Business Activity / Information Exchange – Systems Mapping

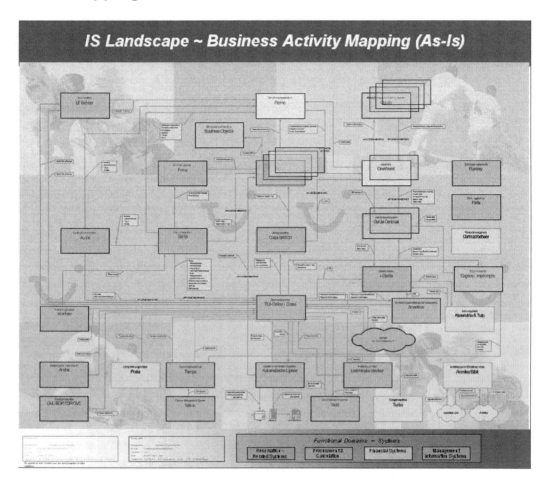

Figure 78. Business Activity – Information Systems Mapping

J.9.1 Comments

- o The EA-5 Business Activity – Information Systems Diagram is an overall high-level graphic representation of the Information Systems landscape and the related Business Activities (Processes), the relations and the Information Flows between the Business Activities

- o Top decision-makers comprise its audience.

- o There is no particular required content or format, but it should be accompanied by explanatory text.

J.10 EA-8 Information Systems –Mappings & Views

At an Enterprise Level most organizations are interested to see the overall relationship between an information-systems (IS) landscape and the mapping of processes, information, ownership, etc. A series of IS related landscapes delivers the overview and insight of complexity, supporting decision making of management.

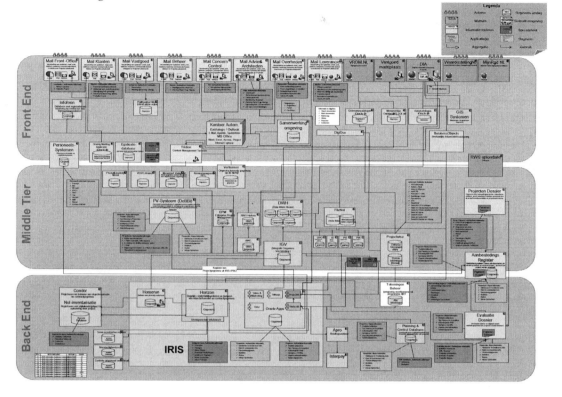

Figure 79. Information Systems Landscape - RDBMS Mapping 1

The next figure is another representation of an Information Systems landscape with the RDBMS Mapping.

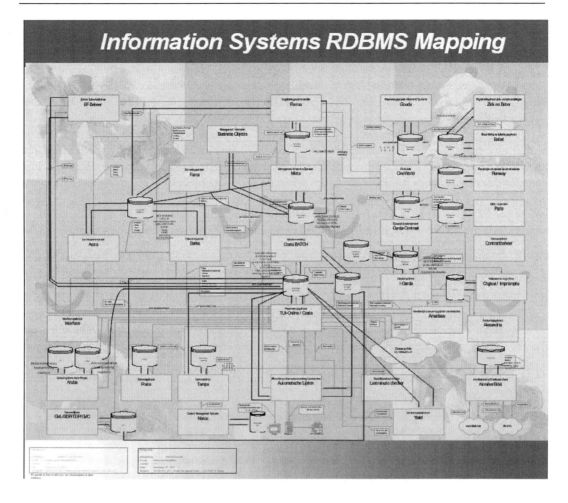

Figure 80. Information Systems Landscape - RDBMS Mapping 2

J.10.1 Viewpoints & Views

Information Systems Landscape – Functional Owners View

All the visualisations are modelled in an **A0 Poster format**, so that these posters can be put on the wall for better communication and explanation about the results. All the visualisations are created by using a combination of MS Visio modelling using Archimate shapes in 2 layers and then bringing over the results to MS PowerPoint to add a third layer representing the Viewpoint result.

Enterprise Application Landscape – Functional Owner View

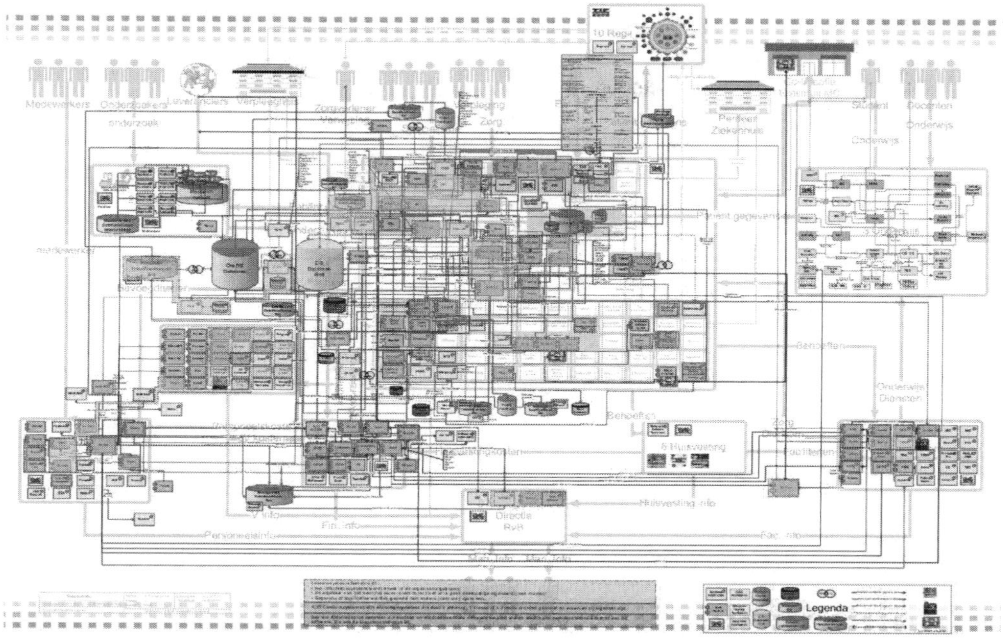

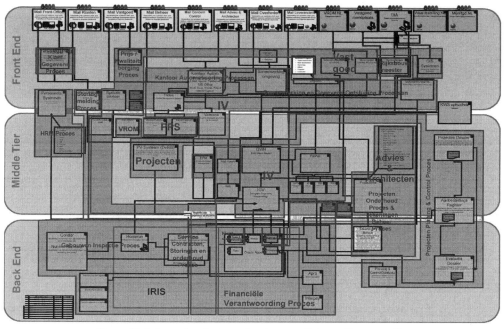

Figure 81. Information Systems Landscape – Functional Owner View

Information Systems Landscape – Primary Processes View

Figure 82. Information Systems Landscape – Primary Processes View

Information Systems Landscape – Governance View

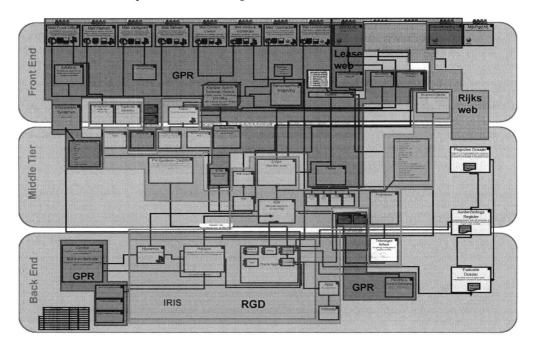

Figure 83. Information Systems Landscape – Governance View

Information Systems Landscape – Life Cycle View

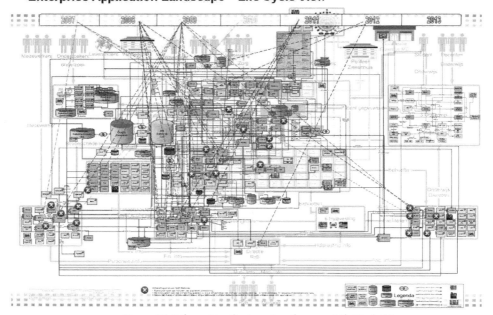

Figure 84. Information Systems Landscape – Life Cycle View

Information Systems Landscape – DataWareHouse / BI View

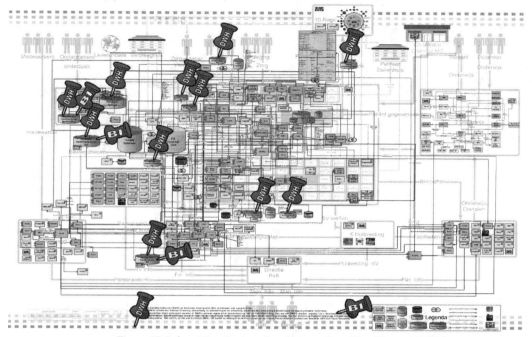

Enterprise Application Landscape – DataWareHouse / BI View

Figure 85. Information Systems Landscape – DataWareHouse / BI View

J.10.2 Comments

- o The EA-8 is an overall high-level graphic depiction of the Information Systems Landscape with the mapping and or views to different viewpoints.
- o Top decision-makers comprise its audience.
- o There is no particular required content or format, but it should be accompanied by explanatory text.

J.11 EA-9 Information Systems – Technical Infrastructure Mapping

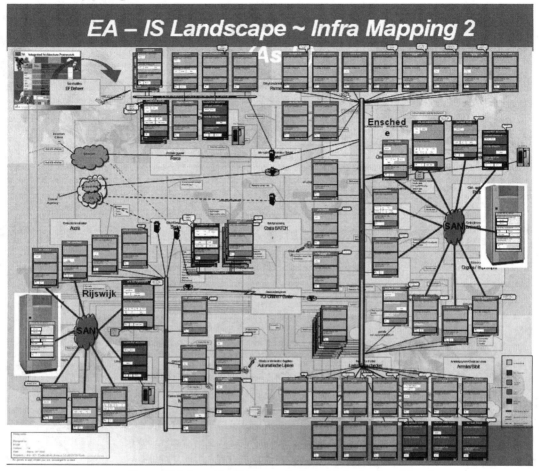

Figure 86. Information Systems – Technical Infrastructure Mapping

J.11.1 Comments

- o The EA-9 is an overall high-level graphic depiction of the Information Systems Landscape with the mapping of the Technical Infrastructure including internal and external interactions.

- o Top decision-makers comprise its audience.

- o There is no particular required content or format, but it should be accompanied by explanatory text.

J.12   BA-1 Business Concept Diagram

The high-level Business Concept Diagram sometimes called the Concept of Operations (CONOPS) Graphic is the most general of the enterprise architecture results and the most flexible in format. It is intended to portray the business activities of the organization (the enterprise) in a single graphic. This work product graphic provides a concise illustration of the business of the enterprise.

The CONOPS Graphic shows the transition of activities and illustrates the flow of information. The graphic can also portray the geographic distribution of enterprise architectural elements.

The next figure illustrates the multi-dimensional view of the modern travel industry and the various elements of channels, internet access, tour operator, product comparison and the environment.

Figure 87. Business Concept Diagram

J.12.1 Comments

- o   The BA-1 is a high-level graphic depiction of the mission context including internal and external interactions,
- o   Top decision-makers comprise its audience.
- o   There is no particular required content or format, but it should be accompanied by explanatory text.

J.13   BA-2 Business Function Model

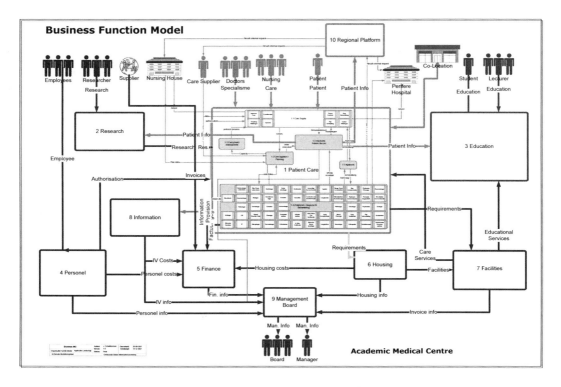

Figure 88. Business Function Model

J.13.1 Comments

- o   The BA-2 helps to define the key functional areas and the functional relationships.

- o   It relates functional areas to each other through information exchanges where:

    - o   Functional area = information source or sink e.g., a role (manager), a logical/functional group (distribution centre), or an organization (Corporate HQ).

    - o   Line = the major information connection between functional areas that denotes one or more information exchanges.

- o   One method of representation is the Block Diagram in which block represent functional areas and arrows represent lines.

- o   Another method is the Functional Collaboration Diagram in which actors represent users or entities of functional areas and / or external information sources while information exchange represents the lines.

J.14   BA-3 Business Node Connectivity

The Node Connectivity Diagram illustrates and describes the business locations (nodes), the *needlines* between them, and the characteristics of the information exchanged.

The Node Connectivity Description can be produced at three levels:

- o   Conceptual Node Connectivity Description—an essential work product that describes the prominent, high-level nodes

- o   Logical Node Connectivity Description—a supporting work product that describes the design that details all categories and classes of nodes, but does not describe the physical implementation or locations of nodes

- o   Physical Node Connectivity Description—a supporting work product that describes the physical implementation and locations of nodes.

Each needline is represented by an arrow (indicating the direction of information flow), which is annotated to describe the characteristics of the data or information. Examples of characteristics include its substantive content;, media (voice, imagery, text and message format, etc.); volume requirements; security or classification level; timeliness; and requirements for information system interoperability. Information exchange characteristics are shown selectively, or in summarized form, on this diagram and more comprehensively in the Information Exchange Matrix.

It is important to note that the arrows on the diagram represent needlines only. Each arrow indicates that there is a need for some kind of information transfer between the two connected nodes. There is a one-to-many relationship between needlines and information exchanges; that is, a single needline arrow on the Node Connectivity Description is a rollup of multiple individual information exchanges. The individual information exchanges are shown on the Information Exchange Matrix.

The diagram should illustrate connectivity with external nodes, i.e., nodes that are not strictly within the scope of the architecture but that act as important sources of information needed by nodes within the architecture or important destinations for information produced by nodes within the architecture. These external needlines should be labelled to show the external source or destination, as well as the information exchanged.

Functional/Operational views are not required to name real physical facilities as nodes. Functional/Operational views can instead focus on "virtual" nodes, which could be based on business "roles." These "virtual" nodes will not always be capable of directly integrationable with real (physical) nodes from other architectures, but they could provide insight concerning which physical nodes might be able to assume the roles portrayed.

A node can represent a role (e.g., a Bureau Chief Information Officer); an organization (e.g., U.S. Secret Service); a business facility (e.g., a specific IRS Service Centre); and so on. The notion of "node" will also vary depending on the level of detail addressed by the architecture effort.

Organizations may choose to represent some nodes in physical terms (i.e., geographic location) if these nodes are intended to remain "constant" in the architecture analysis, e.g., an effort to determine the most cost-effective communications options between two facilities. On the other hand, organizations may choose to represent nodes much more generically, or notionally, if the entire business practice is being analyzed without constraints imposed by the existing architecture.

To emphasize the focus of the analysis and to ensure comparability and integration across efforts, it is important that each organization carefully document its use of the "node" concept.

The activities associated with a given information exchange should be noted in some way to provide linkages between each node and the activities performed, and to link the Node Connectivity Diagram with the Activity Model. When more than one Node Connectivity Description is included in an EA description, the architecture team should perform the appropriate mapping of conceptual to logical and/or logical to physical levels.

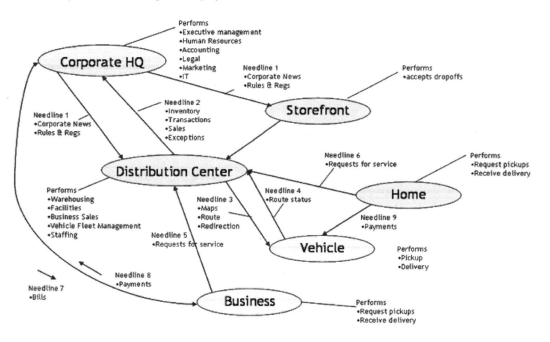

Figure 89. Business Connectivity Diagram

The Node Connectivity Diagram depicted in figure 90 illustrates high-level information exchanges between major operational nodes in the concept of Network Centric Warfare (NCW). At this level of detail, only the minimum essential, mission connectivity's are illustrated. This graphic is layered to show the connectivity required for the various mission areas. These layers are presented as a legend in the left and right margin of the chart.

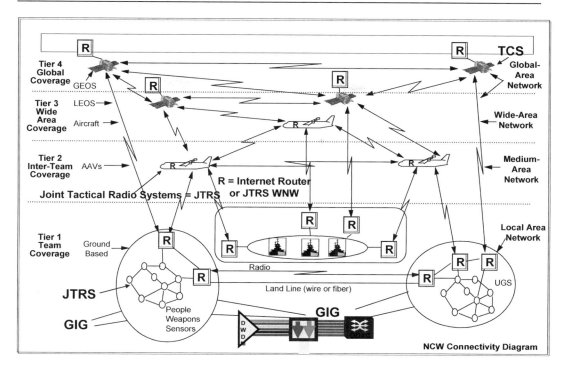

Figure 90. NCW Connectivity Diagram

J.14.1 Information Exchange Matrix

The Information Exchange Matrix documents the Information Exchange Requirements (IERs) for an EA. IERs express the relationships across three basic entities (activities, business nodes and their elements, and information flow) and focus on characteristics of the information exchange, such as performance and security. IERs identify *who* exchanges *what* information with *whom, why* the information is necessary, and in *what manner*. IERs identify the elements of information exchanged between nodes in support of a particular activity. Relevant attributes of the exchange are noted. The specific attributes included are dependent on the objectives of the specific architecture effort, but may include the type of information media (e.g., data, voice, and video), quality (e.g., frequency, timeliness, and security), and quantity (e.g., volume and speed).

The IEM can be produced at three levels:

o Conceptual Information Exchange Matrix—an essential work product that describes the prominent, high-level information exchanges between prominent nodes

o Logical Information Exchange Matrix—a supporting work product that describes the design that details all categories and classes of information exchanges, but does not describe the physical implementation of them

o Physical Information Exchange Matrix— a supporting work product that describes the physical characteristics of the implementation of information exchanges.

Particular capabilities such as security level of communications may also be captured for each exchange. This work product emphasizes the logical and operational characteristics of the information, namely, what information is needed by whom, from whom, and when. Figure 91 illustrates an example of an entry in the Logical IEM of the US Customs Service EA. In the table, AIS is the automated information system at the source and destination that sends and receives the information exchange and LISI is the Level of Information System Interoperability. LISI is scaled from zero for a totally manual interface to five for a fully electronic connection.

No.	Source	Destination	Information	Associated Activity	Source AIS	Destination AIS	Media	LISI	Event Trigger	Frequency of Transmission	Interoperability Issues
208a	Customs	DOT (NHTSA)	Vehicle Declaration (Form HS-7)	Cargo Release Processing	ACS	MVII	electronic	3	Import of Vehicle	Daily	Two data fields missing from transmission
208b	DOT (NHTSA)	Customs	Tariff Data Data Updates	Maintain Systems Information	MVII	ACS	electronic	3	Data Update Required	As needed	None

Figure 91. Logical Information Exchange Matrix

The IEM is not intended to be an exhaustive listing of all the details contained in every IER of every node associated with the architecture. That would be too much detail for an enterprise architecture description. Rather, this work product is intended to capture the most important aspects of selected information exchanges. Selecting the important details of the information exchanges depends on the purpose of the enterprise architecture description.

The number of information exchanges associated with an enterprise architecture may be quite large, even though the matrix may not contain all details about all IERs. To aid in understanding the nature of the information exchanges, developers and users of the enterprise architecture may want to view the IER data sorted in multiple ways, such as by task, by node, or by attribute. Consequently, using a matrix to present that information is limiting and frequently not practical. A spreadsheet or relational database is well suited to the highly structured format of the IEM. In practice, hardcopy versions of this product should be limited to high-level summaries or highlighted subsets of particular interest.

J.14.2 Comments

o The BA-3 helps to define key operational groupings and information exchange needs.

o It relates operational nodes to each other through information exchanges where:

o Operational Node = information source or sink e.g., a role (manager), a logical/functional group (distribution centre), or an organization (Corporate HQ).

o Needline = an information connection between operational nodes that denotes one or more information exchanges.

- o One method of representation is the Block Diagram in which block represent nodes and arrows represent needlines.
- o Another method is the Collaboration Diagram in which actors represent operational nodes and external information sources while messages represent the needlines.

J.15   BA-3 Organization Relationship Diagram

The Organization Chart illustrates the relationships among organizations or resources. These relationships can include oversight, coordination relationships (influences and connectivity), and many others, depending on the purpose of the architecture. It is important to show these fundamental roles and management relationships in an architecture. For example, oversight relationships may differ under various circumstances, which will affect the activities that may be performed differently or by different organizations. Different coordination relationships may mean that connectivity requirements are changed. Figure 92 shows a generic example of an Organization Chart.

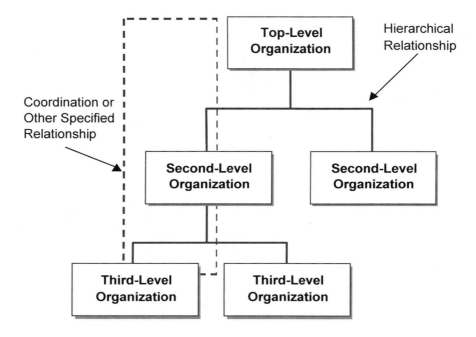

Figure 92. Organization Relationship Diagram

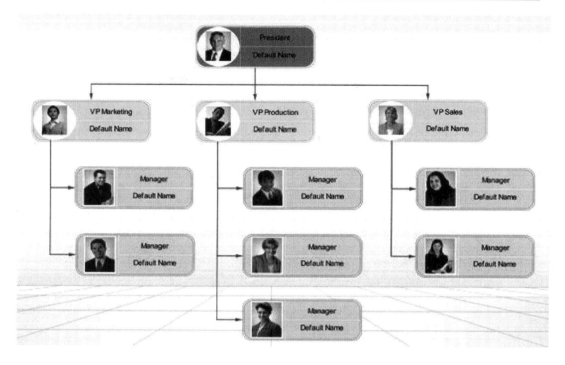

Example: Organization Relationship Diagram

J.15.1 Comments

- o The BA-3 illustrates organizational or command structure separately from operational information flows.
- o It can be represented with a traditional organization chart or with a UML Class Diagram.

J.16 BA-4 Business Process or Activity Models

The BPM or Activity Model (also called a Business Process Model) describes the applicable functions associated with organization's business activities, the data and/or information exchanged between activities (internal exchanges), and the data and/or information exchanged with other activities that are outside the scope of the model (external exchanges). Activity Models are hierarchical in nature. They begin with a single box that represents the overall activity and proceed successively to decompose the activity to the level required for the architecture.

The Activity Model captures the activities performed in a business process or mission and the inputs, controls, outputs, and mechanisms (ICOMs) of those activities. Mechanisms are the resources that are involved in the performance of an activity. Controls, such as legislation or a business rule, represent constraints on an activity. The ICOMS are called activity constraints because each in some way constrains the business processes being modelled. The Activity Model can be annotated with explicit statements of business rules, which represent relationships among the ICOMs. For example, a business rule can specify who can do what under specified conditions, the combination of inputs and controls needed, and the resulting outputs.

J.16.1 Business Process Model Archimate

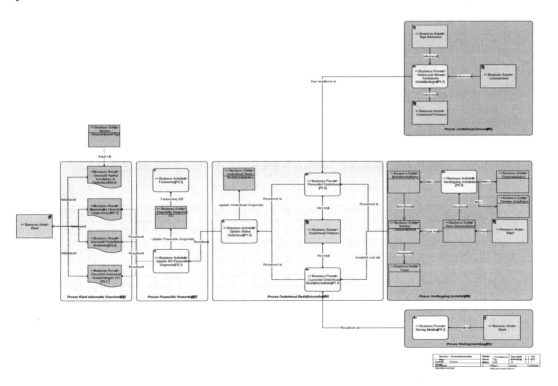

Figure 93. Archimate Business Process Model

The Activity Model identifies the mission domain of the model and the viewpoint reflected by the model. Textual descriptions of activity definitions and business flows should be provided, as needed. Annotations to the model may identify the nodes (business locations) where the activities take place or the costs (actual or estimated) associated with performing each activity.

J.16.2　Business Process Model IDEF

Certain Activity Models are created using the IDEF (Integrated Computer Aided Manufacturing (ICAM) Definition) modelling technique. In this technique, activities are chronologically related as information flows through the process. Inputs are shown entering the activity from the left, while outputs or results of the activity are shown exiting on the right.

Figure 94 provides an example of an IDEF Activity Model. The mechanisms (who or what performs the activity) are shown as arrows into the bottom of the activity. These can be people, roles, systems, computer programs, etc. The arrows entering from the top of the activity boxes are controls. Controls are the parameters that direct the activity, such as guidance or regulations from superior organizations, and physical, time, or other resource limitations.

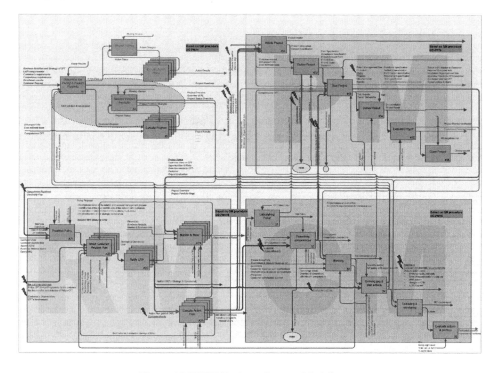

Figure 94. IDEF0 Business Process Model

J.16.3 Activity Tree

An Activity Model may also be represented in a tree format. As shown in Figure 95, the highest level activity is represented as the first node in the tree. The lowest level activities called *leaves* are activities that are not further decomposed.

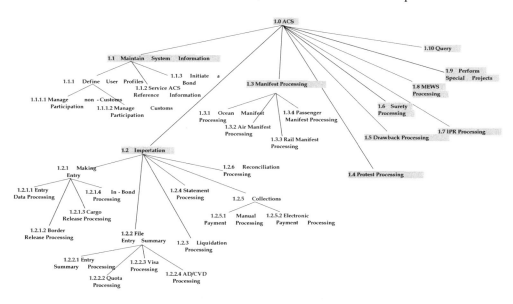

Figure 95. Activity Tree, U.S. Customs Service Automated Commercial System Activity Tree

The Activity Model can be annotated with explicit statements of business rules, which represent relationships among the ICOMs. For example, a business rule can specify who can do what under specified conditions, the combination of inputs and controls needed, and the resulting outputs.

Activity Models can be represented in Unified Modelling Language (UML), a standard modelling language adopted by the Object Management Group to support object-oriented analysis, design, and development. Figure 95 depicts an activity diagram represented in UML.

J.16.4　Business Activity Model UML

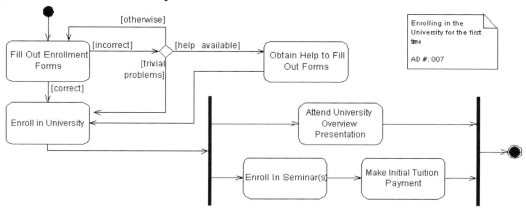

Figure 96. Business Activity Model UML

J.16.5　Workflow Model ECOMOD

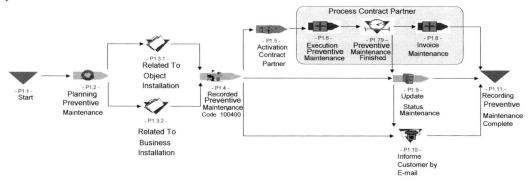

Figure 97. Workflow Model ECOMOD

A Workflow Model shows the relationships between automated and non-automated functions and shows the activities to perform a certain activity. Workflow models are particularity helpful in defining elements that are candidates for services orientation. Figure 97 is modelled with the E-Commerce Modelling Techniques (ECOMOD).

J.16.6　Services Model

A Services Model shows the decomposition from a business activity model into composables (reusable) services that supporting a well defined part of functionality including the related data.

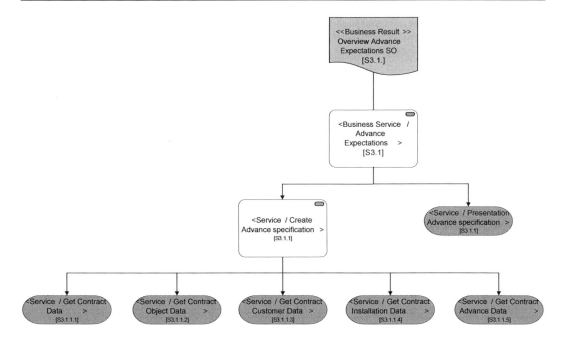

Figure 98. Services Model Archimate

J.16.7 Business Use Case Models

A Use Case Model can describe either business processes or systems functions depending on the focus of the modelling effort. A Business Use Case Model describes the business processes of an enterprise in terms of business use cases and business actors corresponding to business processes and organizational participants (people, organizations, etc.). The Business Use Case Model is described in Use Case Diagrams and Use Case Specifications. In addition to representing business participation and process, the Use Case Diagram can also depict interrelationships among use cases such as Includes and Extends Relationships. An Includes Relationship represents inclusion or containment of use cases. An Extends Relationship depicts variations or alternative sequences or paths beyond the normal course of action.

The following figures show Use Case Diagrams and Specifications for Customs Trade Compliance Processing. Figure 99 and Figure 100 depict UML Use Case Diagrams and Figure 101 shows a Use Case Specification.

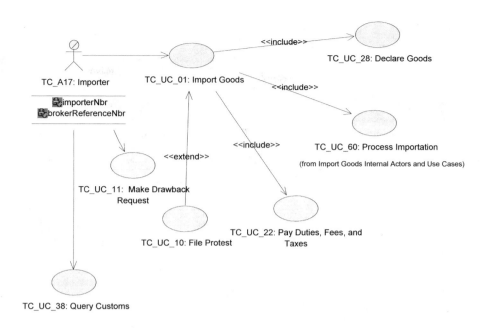

Figure 99. UML Business Use Case Diagram, Trade Compliance Business Process — External

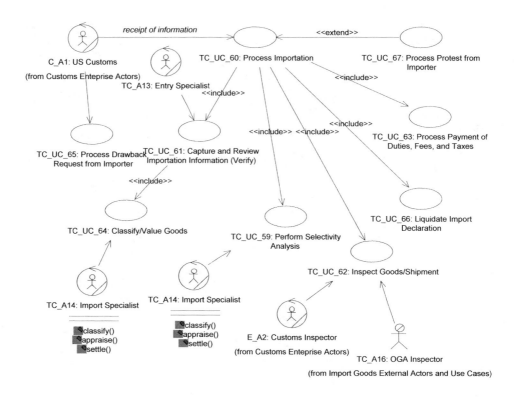

Figure 100. UML Business Use Case Diagram, Trade Compliance Business Process – Internal

TC_A_1.0 Declar Good
:   e   s

1   Overvie :
.   The Importer of Record provides information about an intended importation to Customs. Customs will process the information and respond with notices that determines what the Importer of Record will do next. The Importer of Record corrects or completes the transaction until it is known that the items will or will not be released.

2.   Characteristic Information

Use Case Name:	Declare Goods
Owner:	Mary Lou Collins
Version Creation Date:	December 13, 2000
Date Last Updated:	December 19, 2000
Scope:	Trade compliance
Level:	Strategic
Primary Actor:	Importer of Record
Secondary Actors:	Customs
Focus Classes:	Goods, Entry, Entry docs, License, Permit, Visa, Release Notification
Trigger Event:	The Importer of Record decides to import goods.
Goal:	Receive notification that the goods have been released.

3.   Pre-conditions:

1	Importer of Record has made transportation arrangements for the items.
2	Importer of Record is in good standing with Customs, e.g., registered, licensed, bonded

4.   Main Scenario (Normative Path)

Step	**Action Description**
1	Compile the information required for an entry (CF 3461 or 7501)
2	Collect documentation required by Customs to accompany the entry.

5.   Post-conditions:

1	Customs records entry information
2	Importer of Record's payment due or 10-day clock for payment tarts.
3	Goods available for carrier to move them into the U.S.

6.   Scenario Exceptions / Variations

Step	**Variable**	**Possible Variations**
1	Information needed	Query Customs for tariffs, currency rates, AD/CVD case numbers, etc.
4	Method of filing	Broad range of manual to highly automated alternatives

7.   Related Information

Priority:	
Performance Target:	
Frequency:	Once for each set of items that can be released at one time – determined by the Importer or Record
Super Use Case:	
Sub Use Case(s):	
Dependent Use Cases:	Process Entry

8.   Target Architecture Differences

Baseline Architecture	**Target Architecture**
Declaration is for a single import transaction	Declarations will be associated with an account for payment of duties, fees, and taxes.

9.   Open Issues

Issue ID	**Issue Description**

Figure 101. Use Case Specification, Declare Goods

J.16.8 Class Model

A Class Model is similar to a logical data model. It describes static information and relationships between information. A Class Model also describes informational behaviours. Like many of the other models, it also can be used to model various levels of granularity. Depending on the intent of the model, a Class Model can represent business domain entities or systems implementation classes. A business domain model represents key business information (domain classes), their characteristics (attributes), their behaviours (methods or operations), and relationships (often referred to as multiplicity, describing how many classes typically participate in the relationship), and cardinality (describes required or optional participation in the relationship). Each class, attribute, and relationship appearing in the Class Diagram is specified or defined in a class, attribute, or relationship specification. In the case of a relationship, the specification describes how each class participates in the relationship. Specifications further elaborate and detail information that cannot be represented in the class diagram. Figure 102 illustrates a Customs UML Business Class Diagram.

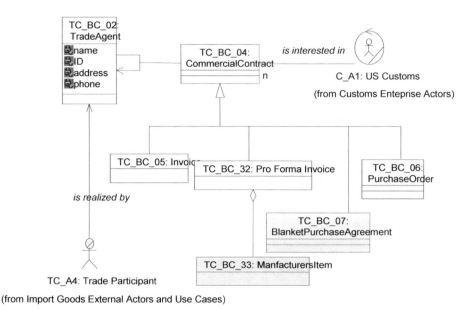

Figure 102. UML Business Class Diagram, Trade Class Model (Commercial View)

J.16.9 State Model

State Models are useful in understanding and representing complicated business or system behaviours over time. A State Model can be used to describe the behaviour of a specific business process, systems function, business class, or system class. State modelling is not a good technique to describe interactions among business processes or classes. Other techniques such as activity modelling or interaction modelling should be used for this purpose.

A UML State Model begins with a start state represented as a solid dot. Middle states are represented as ovals. The ending state is represented as a solid dot within a circle. State transitions are represented as arrows between states. Figure 103 presents a sample Customs UML State Diagram.

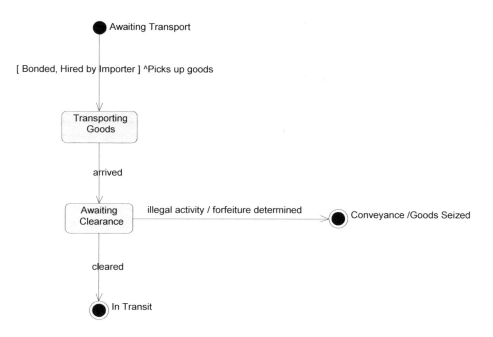

Figure 103. UML State Diagram, Carrier Transition

J.16.10 Comments

o   The BA-4 documents Business Process Models, Business Activity Models, Workflow Models, Services Models, State Models, and Class Models, i.e., what is done.

o   It depicts activities and information exchanges (both internal and external).

o   It is represented as a hierarchy of activities using process flow nomenclatures such as Archimate, IDEF0, ECOMOD or UML Use Cases and Activity Diagrams.

J.17 BA-5 Business Activity Descriptions

J.17.1 BA-5A Business Rules

- o Parcel status will be available online within 15 minutes of any change in status.
- o Receivers must be identified and recorded (receivers need not be addresses)
- o Parcels can be left on doorsteps if permission is given by sender.
- o Parcels can be insured for replacement value.
- o No hazardous materials.
- o Business customers may have accounts with MPS that enable them to be billed for usage.
- o Business customers may have accounts with MPS that they can review online.
- o Customers without accounts pay drivers or storefront operators with cash, checks, or credit cards.

J.17.2 Comments

- o The BA-5A provides precise definitions of what should happen or be enforced.
- o It's most frequent use is to describe constraints on business actions such as:
  - o Mission, e.g., guidance, doctrine
  - o Operation, e.g., behaviour under specific conditions
  - o Business rules expressed by the cardinality and ordinality of relationships among entities.
- o Business rules are typically expressed as plain English statements or in a formal language such as Object Constraint Language can be used.

J.18   Operational Event Trace Descriptions

J.18.1   BA-5B Event Trace for Pickup Use Case

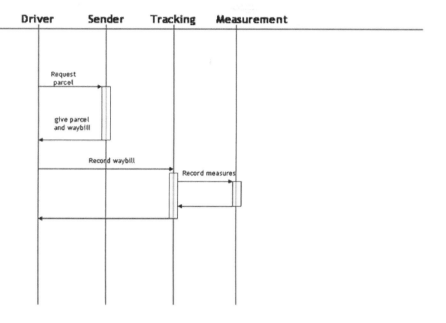

Figure 104. Event Diagram 1

J.19　BA-5C Event Trace for Deliver Use Case

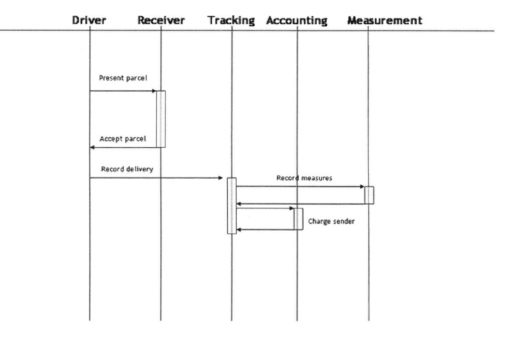

Figure 105. Event Diagram 2

J.19.1　Comments

- o　The BA-5c helps to define node interfaces and ensure that information will be available when and where it's needed.
- o　These descriptions show a time-ordered view of information exchanges per scenario.
- o　UML Sequence Diagrams are the tool of choice.

J.20 IA-3 Logical Information / Data Model

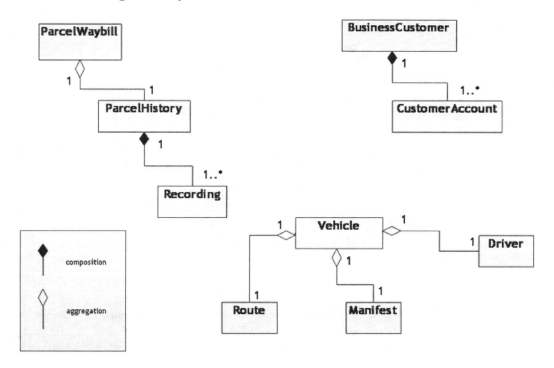

Figure 106. Logical Information Model

J.20.1 Comments

o   The IA-3 describes the data of interest to the planner and the owner.

o   It transmits the data requirements and any structural constraints on that data.

o   It is represented using data modelling techniques such as UML Class Diagrams or IDEF1.

J.21   Traceability among Results in the EA's Business View

- o   The Business View is about real-world activities.

- o   The Business Concept Diagram (BA-1) summarizes the common operations in a picture, showing key actors and locations.

- o   The Business Node Connectivity (BA-2) shows logical aggregates of activities.

- o   The Information Exchange Matrix (IA-1) identifies in tabular form what information moves, who produces and consumes it, why, and how.

- o   The Organizational Relationships Chart (BA-3) depicts organizational or command structure separately from operational information flows.

- o   The Activity Model (BA-4) identifies who does what in some detail using process flow techniques such as IDEF0 or UML Use Cases and Activity Diagrams.

- o   The BA-5 a-c product series helps you to identify constraints on activities, sequencing of events, and states.

- o   The logical data model (IA-3) illustrates the essential information for the Operational View.

J.22 ISA-1 Information Systems Interface Description & Connectivity Diagram

The System Interface Description (SID) depicts the assignments of systems and their interfaces to the nodes and needlines described in the Node Connectivity Diagram. The Node Connectivity Description for a given architecture shows nodes (not always defined in physical terms), while the SID depicts the systems corresponding to the system nodes.

The SID identifies the interfaces between nodes, between systems, and between the components of a system, depending on the needs of a particular architecture. A system interface is a simplified or generalized representation of a communications pathway or network, usually depicted graphically as a straight line, with a descriptive label. Pairs of connected systems or system components often have multiple interfaces between them. The SID depicts all interfaces between systems and/or system components that are of interest to the architect.

The graphic descriptions and/or supporting text for the SID should provide details concerning the capabilities of each system. For example, descriptions of information systems should include details concerning the applications present within the system, the infrastructure services that support the applications, and the means by which the system processes, manipulates, stores, and exchanges data. Figure 107 depicts a sample SID Connectivity Diagram.

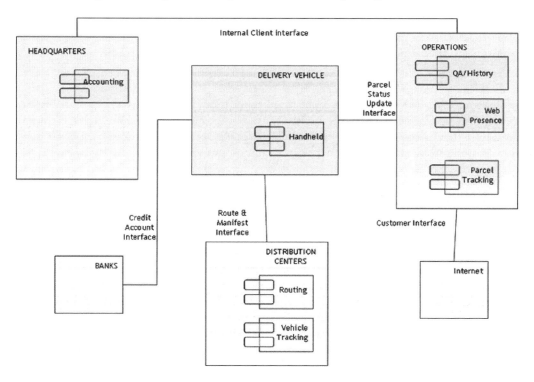

Figure 107. Interface Description Diagram

J.22.1 Comments

- o The ISA-1 identifies system nodes and key interfaces.
- o Details about connections and data traffic are documented elsewhere.
- o System nodes (e.g., platforms, units, facilities, locations) house operational nodes (e.g., organizations, roles).
- o Interfaces can connect node-to-node or system-to-system.
- o "Key" interfaces cross organizational boundaries, is mission critical, complex, or has other issues that need attention.
- o A common method of representation is the UML Deployment Diagram.

J.23　ISA-2 Information Systems Communications

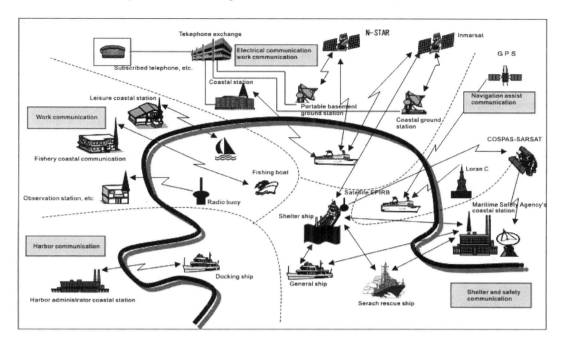

Figure 108. Information Systems Communication Diagram

J.23.1　Comments

- o　The ISA-2 provides the designer's view of systems and interconnects.
- o　It is a picture of communications systems, links, services connecting systems and implementing interfaces.
- o　It provides details of communications, e.g., radio frequencies, bandwidth, encryption methods, protocols, standards references.
- o　This product is frequently produced as a free-form graphic with annotation.

J.24   ISA-3 Information Systems Functionality Description

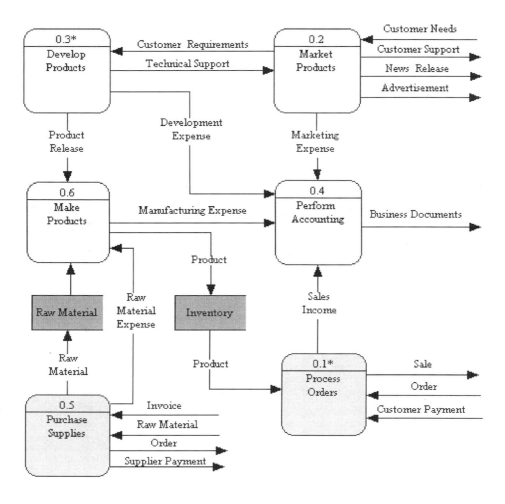

Figure 109. Information Systems Functionality Diagram

J.24.1 Comments

o The ISAV-3 provides a detailed definition of data input and output from systems and ensures completeness of inputs-to-outputs transformations.

o It is a decomposition of system functions and data flow.

o Its scope can be enterprise-wide or system-specific.

o It is traceable to operational activities, but the mapping is not necessarily 1-to-1.

o It can be represented in several ways: Data Flow Diagrams, Functional Hierarchy, UML Use Cases + Class Diagrams + Sequence or Collaboration Diagrams.

J.25   ISA4 - Business Activity to Information Systems Function Traceability

	Pickup	Deliver	Transfer	Locate	Charge account
Arrive location	X	X			
Scan waybill	X	X	X		
Authorize account	X				
Charge account		X			X
Add parcel (manifest)	X				
Remove parcel		X			

Figure 110. Business Activity - Systems Functionality Matrix

J.25.1 Comments

o   The ISA-4 maps operational activities and/or capabilities onto system functions.

o   It illustrates the "how" for planners/owners as well as designers.

o   It is represented as matrix mapping the operational activities to the system functions. Text annotations can be used to indicate the degree to which each capability is covered by existing functionality (e.g., planned but not yet built; partial; not fielded; or built and fielded).

J.26   ISA-5 – Information Systems Life Cycle / Evolution Description

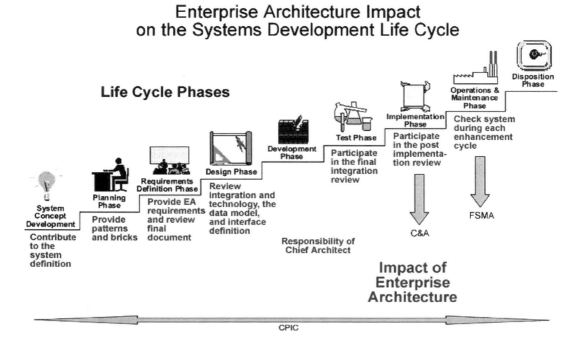

Figure 111. Systems Life Cycle Overview

J.26.1 Comments

o   The ISA-5 describes how the system (or the underlying architecture) will evolve over a period of time.

o   When linked with other products related to evolution such as the ISA-10 (Technology Forecast) and the TA-2 (Standards Forecast), the ISA-9 provides a definition of how the architecture and its systems will evolve over time.

o   An ISA-9 can be used as either an architecture evolution plan or a transition plan.

o   There is not formal technique for representing this product - a combination of graphics and text can be used, but it is important to depict milestones.

J.27 ISA-6 – Information Systems Technology Forecast

TECHNOLOGY AREA	TECHNOLOGY FORECASTS		
	SHORT TERM	MEDIUM TERM	LONG TERM
APPLICATION SOFTWARE			
OFFICE APPLICATIONS	MICROSOFT OFFICE 2000	MICROSOFT OFFICE 2005 (DISTRIBUTED)	MICROSOFT DISTRIBUTED OFFICE APPS
BUSINESS APPLICATIONS	INDIVIDUAL APPS - BATES, QP24	BISA'S	INTEGRATED BISA SUITE
APPLICATION PLATFORM			
DATA MANAGEMENT	ORACLE 9	ORACLE 10	
OPERATING SYSTEM	WINDOWS 2000	NEXT WINDOWS OS	OPEN SOURCE OS
EXTERNAL ENVIRONMENT			
USER INTERFACE		THIN TOUCH SCREEN	BIOMETRIC INTERFACE
STORAGE	HDD	SOLID STATE MEMORY CHIPS	ORGANIC STORAGE
COMMS	BOWMAN	BOWMAN+VOIP	ALL IP COMMS

Figure 112. Systems Technology Forecast

J.27.1 Comments

- The ISA-6 uses three ranges to forecast technologies, Short Term, Medium Term and Long Term.
- The ISA-6 focuses on forecasts of different technology areas and technical solutions.
- The Technical Standards Forecast (TA-2) that is part of the Technical View focuses on forecasts of standards.

J.28   ISA-7 – Information Systems Functionality Sequence and Timing Descriptions (generic examples)

J.28.1   ISA-7A Information Systems Rules Model

If field A *in* FORM-X *is set to* value T,
　Then field B *in* FORM-Y *must be set to* value T
　And field C *in* FORM-Z *must be set to* value T
End If

J.28.2   ISA-7B Information Systems State Transition Description

Figure 113. Systems State Transition Diagram

J.28.3　ISA-7C Information Systems Event Trace Description

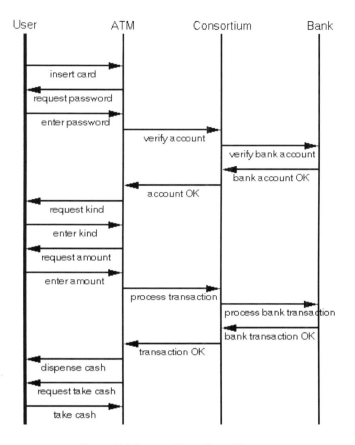

Figure 114. Systems Event Trace Diagram

J.28.4　Comments

o　The ISA-7 series (ISA-7a, b, and c) define and describe the System View's dynamic behaviour and performance characteristics.

o　When an event occurs, the action taken by the system in response might be subject to rules specified in ISA-7a.

o　ISA-7b and ISA-7c can be used separately or in tandem to describe timing and sequencing behaviour.

o　Both ISA-7b and ISA-71c describe system responses to sequences of events (i.e., inputs, transactions, or triggers).

o　ISA-7a can be represented as plain text, but more formal methods might be used if the rules to be described are complex. For example, guard conditions on the state charts of ISA-7b and pre- and post-conditions on classes and use cases in ISA-5 can be included.

o　UML State chart Diagrams are an effective means to represent ISA-7b.

o　UML Sequence Diagrams are the preferred method of representing ISA-7c.

J.29 ISA-8 – Information Systems Logical Data Schema

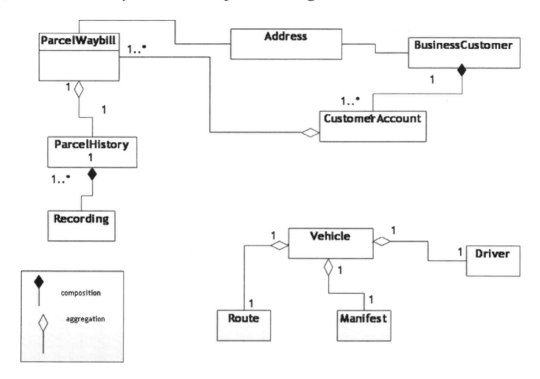

Figure 115. Systems Logical Data Schema

J.29.1 Comments

o   The ISA-8:

  o   provides system data structures for use in system design, and

  o   provides as much detail as possible about on the data elements exchanged between systems in order to reduce the risk of interoperability errors.

o   The ISA-8 is an implementation-oriented data model that describes how the information requirements contained in the Logical Data Model (IA-3) are implemented.

o   There should be a mapping between an IA-3 and its counterpart ISA-8.

o   Entities in the data model represent:

  o   System data flows from ISA-5

  o   System data elements from ISA-7

  o   Triggering events in ISA-7b and/or

  o   Events in ISA-7c.

o   The ISA-8 can be represented as a UML Class Diagram or any other product used to depict data models.

J.30   TA-1 Standards Profile

An enterprise architecture Standards Profile is the set of rules that governs information systems implementation and operation. In most cases, especially in describing architectures with less than a department-wide scope, building a Standards Profile will consist of identifying the applicable portions of existing standards guidance documentation, tailoring those portions in accordance within the latitude allowed, and filling in any gaps.

This architecture product references the technical standards that apply to the architecture and how they need to be, or have been, implemented. The profile is time-phased to facilitate a structured, disciplined process of system development and evolution. Time phasing also promotes the consideration of emerging technologies and the likelihood of current technologies and standards becoming obsolete.

A Standards Profile documents the usage of the following items within an enterprise:

o   Industry standards or technologies

o   Organization, department, or bureau standards or technologies

o   Commercial products

o   Organization, department, or bureau products.

J.30.1   Comments

o   The following table is an illustrative subset of possible standards that govern systems implementation and operation of the enterprise architecture.

o   Construction of a TA-1 will typically start with a companion reference model or collection of standards.

o   Standards are divided into at least two categories: mandatory and emerging.

J.30.2   Mandated Standards

Technology Service Area: Human Computer Interface Services

Service	Standards	Description
User Interface Style Guide	ISO 13407 (E)	Human-centred design processes for interactive systems, June 1999.
X Windows Interface	T251	For UNIX-based systems: T251: CDE 2.1 and MOTIF 2.1 Documentation - Full Set, Open Group Publication Set, October 1997.

Figure 116. Mandated Standards: TSA - HCI Services

Technology Service Area: Information Processing

Service	Standards	Description
Data Markup Language	Extensible Hyper text Markup Language	XHTML 1 or HTML 4.01.

	(XHTML)	
	Extensible Markup Language (XML)	Extensible Markup Language (XML) 1.0 (Second Edition) W3C Recommendation, 6 October 2000 . An extensible meta markup language partially derived from SGML.
	Extensible Stylesheet Language (XSL)	W3C. Extensible Stylesheet Language (also known coloquially as XSL - Formatting Objects (FO)) transforms XML represented data into formatted objects.
		2.3.2.1- Document Interchange, http://www.w3.org/TR/xsl/, http://www.xml.com/pub/a/2002/03/20/xsl-fo.html
	XSLT	W3C. This specification defines the syntax and semantics of XSLT, which is a language for transforming XML documents into other XML documents. XSLT is designed for use as part of XSL, which is a stylesheet language for XML. In addition to XSLT, XSL includes an XML vocabulary for specifying formatting. XSL specifies the styling of an XML document by using XSLT to describe how the document is transformed into another XML document that uses the formatting vocabulary.
Database Language	SQL - ISO/IEC 9075:1992	For any system required to use a Relational Database Management System: ISO/IEC 9075:1992 Information Technology - Database Language - SQL as modified by FIPS Pub 127-2:1993, Database Language for relational DBMSs.
	SQL - ISO/IEC 9075-3:1995	For both database application clients and database servers using CLI: ISO/IEC 9075-3:1995 Information Technology - Database Languages - SQL - Part 3: Call Level Interface (SQL/CLI) ODBC (3.0) or JDBC are permitted.
Distributed Computing Services	OMG 99-10-07 V2.3.1	OMG document formal/99-10-07, Common Object Request Broker: Architecture and Specification, Version 2.3.1, October 1999. The JTA does not mandate a single middleware technology. However, the JTA does mandate a requirement for interworking with the Object Management Group (OMG) Object Management Architecture (OMA). The OMA is composed of the Common Object Request Broker Architecture (CORBA), CORBA services, and CORBA facilities.
	OMG document formal/2000-06-15	Event Notification Service, 7 December 1993 , contained in CORBA services: Common Object Services Specification, OMG document formal/ 24 February 1997 .
	OMG document formal/2000-06-19	Naming Service Specification, Version 1.0, Provides a mapping or white pages directory of services
	OMG document formal/2000-06-28,	Object Transaction Service, 6 December 1994 , contained in CORBA services: Common Object Services Specification, OMG document formal/ 24 February 1997 . The OTS provides a mechanism for distributed CORBA Objects to participate in a distributed transaction through a two phase commit protocol.
Document Interchange	Extensible Markup Language (XML) 1.0	The Extensible Markup Language (XML) is a meta-language, based on SGML, for describing languages based on name-attribute tuples.
	HTML 4.01	HTML 4.01 format, .htm W3C, Compound Document.
	Adobe PDF 1.3	Adobe Acrobat 4.0 format, .pdf, Adobe PDF 1.3, Compound Document.
Graphics Data Interchange	GIF, Version 89a	For the lossless interchange of raster images that have no geospatial context and where none of the above cases apply:
		Graphics Interchange Format (GIF), Version 89a, 31 July 1990 , CompuServe Incorporated.
	IETF RFC 2083	For the interchange of other single raster images that have no geospatial context and where lossy compression is not acceptable, the mandated

standard is:

		IETF RFC 2083, Portable Network Graphics (PNG) Specification, Version 1.0, January 1997.
JPEG Interchange Format, Version 1.02	File	For the interchange of very large still-raster images that have no geospatial context and where lossy decompression is acceptable, the mandated standard is:
		JPEG File Interchange Format, Version 1.02, C-Cubed Microsystems, 1 September 1992 .
Operating System Services	Win32 API	Win32 APIs, as specified in the Microsoft Platform SDK. For operating systems running (or intended to run) Win32 applications:
Distributed Computing Services	OMG document orbos/97-09-07	COM/CORBA Part A Revision, 19 November 1997 . Specify support for two-way communication between CORBA objects and COM objects.

Figure 117. Mandated Standards: TSA - Information Processing

Technology Service Area: Information Security

Service	Standards	Description
Authentication Security Standards	IETF RFC-1510	If Open Group Distributed Computing Environment (DCE) Version 1.1 is used: IETF RFC-1510, The Kerberos Network Authentication Service, V.5, 10 September 1993 .
Security Protocols	IETF RFC-1828	IETF RFC-1828, IP Authorization Using Keyed MD5, August 1995.
	IETF RFC 2311, S/MIME version 2, Message Specification, March 1998	IETF RFC 2311, S/MIME version 2, Message Specification, March 1998T is mandated for individual messages that use digital certificates issued by the DoD PKI to protect sensitive but unclassified individual messaging (e-mail).
Web Security Standards	SSL Protocol Version 3.0	The Secure Sockets Layer (SSL) protocol allows client/server applications to communicate in a way designed to prevent eavesdropping, tampering, or message forgery. It is currently the de facto standard used by most browsers and popular e-mail packages that are associated with the browser: Secure Sockets Layer (SSL) Protocol Version 3.0, 18 November 1996

Figure 118. Mandated Standards: TSA - Information Security

Technology Service Area: Information Transfer

Service	Standards	Description
Domain Name System (DNS)	IETF RFC-1034	IETF Standard 13/IETF RFC-1034/IETF RFC-1035, Domain Name System, November 1987.
	IETF RFC-1035	IETF Standard 13/IETF RFC-1034/IETF RFC-1035, Domain Name System, November 1987.
	IETF RFC-2136	IETF RFC-2136, Dynamic Updates in the Domain Name System, April 1997.
Dynamic Host Configuration Protocol (DHCP)	IETF RFC-2131	JTA v4.0. IETF RFC-2131, Dynamic Host Configuration Protocol, March 1997.
Electronic Mail	IETF RFCs 2045-2049	For SMTP: IETF RFCs 2045-2049, Multipurpose Internet Mail Extensions (MIME) Parts 1-5, November 1996.
	IETF Standard	For SMTP: IETF Standard 10/IETF RFC-821/IETF RFC-1869/IETF RFC-

	10/IETF RFC- 821/IETF RFC- 1869/IETF RFC- 1870	1870, Simple Mail Transfer Protocol (SMTP) Service Extensions, November 1995.	
Ethernet	ISO/IEC 8802- 3:1996	For the minimum LAN requirements: ISO/IEC 8802-3:1996, Carrier Sense Multiple Access with Collision Detection (CSMA/CD) Access Method and Physical Layer Specifications, 10BASE-T Medium-Access Unit (MAU). Local Area Network (LAN)/MAN CSMA/CD Access Method Standards Package, which includes 10Base-5 (Thick Coaxial), 10Base-2 (Thin Coaxial), 10Base-T (Unshielded Twisted Pair), 10Base-F (Fiber-Optic Cable), 100Base-T, and 100Base-F.	
	IETF Standard 9/IETF RFC-959	IETF Standard 9/IETF RFC-959, File Transfer Protocol, October 1985, with the following FTP commands mandated for reception: Store unique (STOU) and Abort (ABOR).	
Internet Protocol (IP)	IETF Standard 37/RFC 826	IETF Standard 37/RFC 826, An Ethernet Address Resolution Protocol, November 1982.	
Internet Protocol (IP)	IETF Standard 41/RFC 894	IETF Standard 41/RFC 894, Standard for the Transmission of IP Datagrams Over Ethernet Networks, April 1984.	
Lightweight Directory Access Protocol (LDAP)	IETF RFC-1514	To standardize the management scope and view of end systems and networks: IETF RFC-1514, Host Resources MIB, September 1993.	

Figure 119. Mandated Standards: TSA - Information Transfer

J.30.3 Emerging Standards

Technology Service Area: Information Modelling, Metadata and Information Exchange

Service	Standards	Description
Information Modelling	Unified Modelling Language (UML)	Object Modelling The Unified Modelling Language™ (UML) is the industry-standard language for specifying, visualizing, constructing, and documenting the artefacts of software systems. It simplifies the complex process of software design, making a blueprint for construction.

Figure 120. Emerging Standards: TSA - Information Modelling

Technology Service Area: Information Processing

Service	Standards	Description
Application Servers	Java Servlet	Server applications that execute within a J2EE Application server or within a simple Servlet Runner. Servlets support a synchronous request/reply workflow similar to CGI over HTTP. Servlets provide a simple, convenient way to extend basic Web functionality.
	Enterprise Java Beans (EJB)	Software, mostly server-side, components that are reusable and provide portability across all Java application servers. Reference: http://java.sun.com/products/ejb/
Asset Management	Radio Frequency Identification (RFID)	Radio frequency identification (RFID) first appeared in tracking and access applications during the 1980s. These wireless AIDC systems allow for non-contact reading and are effective in manufacturing and other hostile environments where bar code labels could not survive. RFID has established itself in a wide range of markets including livestock identification and automated vehicle identification (AVI) systems because of its ability to track moving objects. - reference: http://www.google.com/search?hl=en&lr=&ie=UTF-8&oe=UTF-8&q=Radio+Frequency+Identification&btnG=Google+Search
Data Markup Language	Open Management Interface (OMI)	Defines a standards-based (XML/SOAP/HTTP) management interface for an integration platform. Recently developed by webMethods & HP. Endorsed by Tivoli , BMC, and CA.

	XML Datatypes	Schema W3C Recommendation, XML Schema Part 2: Datatypes, 2 May 2001.
	XML Structures	Schema W3C Recommendation, XML Schema Part 1: Structures, 2 May 2001.
	XML-Namespaces	W3c XML namespaces provide a simple method for qualifying element and attribute names used in Extensible Markup Language documents by associating them with namespaces identified by URI references
ebXML	Electronic Business Using Extensible Markup Language (ebXML)	ebXML (Electronic Business using eXtensible Markup Language), sponsored by UN/CEFACT and OASIS, is a modular suite of specifications that enables enterprises of any size and in any geographical location to conduct business over the Internet. Using ebXML, companies now have a standard method to exchange business messages, conduct trading relationships, communicate data in common terms and define and register business processes.
Software Development	Java 2 Platform, Enterprise Edition (J2EE)	http://java.sun.com/j2ee/ A component-based software standard for building Java-based applications. J2EE has historically been the most successful distributed application component standard.
	Java 2 Platform, Standard Edition (J2SE)	http://java.sun.com/j2se/ Includes the 'standard' JDK libraries (non-J2EE), platform-specific JVM, and developer tools.
	ANSI/ISO/IEC 14882-1998	C++ is a general purpose programming language based on the C programming language as described in ISO/IEC 9899:1990 Programming languages - C (also adopted by the U.S. in 1992). In addition to the facilities provided by C, C++ provides additional data types, classes, templates, exceptions, namespaces, inline functions, operator overloading, function name overloading, references, free store management operators, and additional library facilities. http://www.iso.org/iso/en/CatalogueDetailPage.CatalogueDetail?CSNUMBER=258 45&ICS1=35&ICS2=60&ICS3= When programming in C++: ANSI/ISO/IEC 14882-1998, Information Technology - Programming Languages - C++. An offspring of C. C++ introduced object-oriented concepts such as the class and virtual functions to C. C++ is a general purpose, relatively low-level, high-performance (compared to its OOP brethern) computer language. http://www.iso.org/iso/en/CatalogueDetailPage.CatalogueDetail?ICS1=0&ICS2=0& ICS3=0&CSNUMBER=25845
	C#	http://msdn.microsoft.com/vstudio/techinfo/articles/upgrade/Csharpintro.asp Essentially a Microsoft version of Java with additional features and complexities pulled from C++. http://msdn.microsoft.com/vstudio/techinfo/articles/upgrade/Csharpintro.asp
	Remote Method Invocation / Internet Inter-ORB Protocol (RMI/IIOP)	http://java.sun.com/marketing/collateral/rmi_ds.html With RMI, creates remote interfaces for Java-to-Java application communication; the RMI/IIOP extension uses the CORBA-standard IIOP for communication.
Web Services	Simple Object Access Protocol (SOAP)	http://xml.coverpages.org/soap.html Industry standard for enveloping XML messages. SOAP is an XML/HTTP-based protocol for accessing services, objects and servers in a platform-independent manner.
	Web Services Description Language (WSDL)	Defines a service interface (like Interface Definition Language, or DNL) for a web service implemented with SOAP.
	Business Process Execution Language for Web Services (BPEL4WS)	A language for describing business processes that include multiple Web services and standardizing message exchanges internally and between partners. The Business Process Execution Language for Web Services (BPEL4WS) is an XML-based process definition language, which supersedes existing IBM (Web Services Flow Language, WSFL) and Microsoft specifications (Xlang). http://www.webservices.org/index.php/article/articleview/633/1/24/
	Business Process Modelling Language (BPML)	A meta-language for modelling business processes. BPML was developed to support the modelling of end-to-end processes including private implementations and public interfaces for transactional and collaborative business processes. http://www.webservices.org/index.php/article/articleview/633/1/24/ Created and maintained by BMPI.org
	Business Transaction Protocol (BTP)	The Business Transaction Protocol, or BTP, provides a common understanding and a way to communicate guarantees and limits on guarantees between organizations. Ref: http://www.oasis-open.org and http://www.oasis-open.org/committees/business-transactions/documents/primer/Primerhtml/BTP%20Primer%20D1%2020020602.ht

ml

JavaServer Pages (JSP) A way to extend Web server functionality and create dynamic Web content; JSP technology enables rapid development of Web applications that are server and platform independent while still developing components which are J2EE compliant.

Figure 121. Emerging Standards: TSA - Information Processing

Technology Service Area: Information Security

Service	Standards	Description
Authentication Security Standards	IETF RFC 2058	Remote Authentication Dial In User Service (RADIUS) RFC 2058 is a protocol for carrying authentication, authorization, and configuration information between a Network Access Server which desires to authenticate its links and a shared Authentication Server.
Network Security Standards	Draft-IETF-secsh-architecture-05.txt	Secure Shell (SSH) Protocol Architecture, May 2000. SSH is a protocol for secure remote login and other secure network services over an insecure network.

Figure 122. Emerging Standards: TSA - Information Security

Technology Service Area: Information Transfer

Service	Standards	Description
Directory Services	Universal Description, Discovery and Integration (UDDI)	Registry interface definition for publishing and accessing Web services. An initiative whereby companies are maintaining global registries for listing web services.
	Java Naming and Directory Interface (JNDI)	Provides access to naming and directory services, such as domain name service (DNS), Lightweight Directory Access Protocol (LDAP), Novell Directory Services and CORBA COSNaming.
Wireless LAN	IEEE 802.11a-1999	For non-sensitive operations: IEEE 802.11 Supplement to Information Technology - Telecommunications and Information Exchange Between Systems - Local and metropolitan area networks - Specifications requirements - Part 11: Wireless LAN Medium Access Control (MAC) and Physical Layer (PHY) Specifications: Higher Speed Physical Layer (PHY) Extension in the 2.4 GHz.
	IEEE 802.11b-1999	For non-sensitive operations: IEEE 802.11b-1999 Supplement to Information Technology - Telecommunications and Information Exchange Between Systems - Local and metropolitan area networks - Specifications requirements - Part 11: Wireless LAN Medium Access Control (MAC) and Physical Layer (PHY) Specifications: Higher Speed Physical Layer (PHY) Extension in the 2.4 GHz.
	IP v6 Protocol IETF RFC	Next Generation IP - IPv6 is the next generation protocol designed by the IETF to replace the current version Internet Protocol, IP Version 4 (IPv4). http://www.ipv6.org/
Lightweight Directory Access Protocol (LDAP)	Directory Enabled Network Protocol LDAPv3 -	IETF Draft - Initiative designed to provide the building blocks for intelligent management by mapping concepts such as systems, services and policies to a directory. http://www.dmtf.org/standards/standard_den.php

Figure 123. Emerging Standards: TSA - Information Transfer

J.31 TA-2 Technical Reference Model

A Technical Reference Model (TRM) is a taxonomy that provides:

o   A consistent set of service areas, interface categories, and relationships used to address interoperability and open-system issues

o   Conceptual entities that establish a common vocabulary to better describe, compare, and contrast systems and components

o   A basis (an aid) for the identification, comparison, and selection of existing and emerging standards and their relationships.

The TRM organizes the Standards Profile and any standards or technology forecast documents. It can also organize technology infrastructure documentation. Frequently, some combination of the documents organized using the TRM are presented in a single document. Figure 124 depicts the service areas of the U.S. Customs Service TRM.

Technology domains and sub-domains are defined along with key roles and points of contacts. A Technical Architecture Strategy is established for each sub-domain, with specifications and selection criteria, outlining how the products and technologies are going to be utilized. Figure 125 illustrates the domain and sub-domain definition being used in the planning strategy and as building blocks to aid project planning. Components are constructed to represent a set of sub-domains that are used together to build a functional component of the architecture.

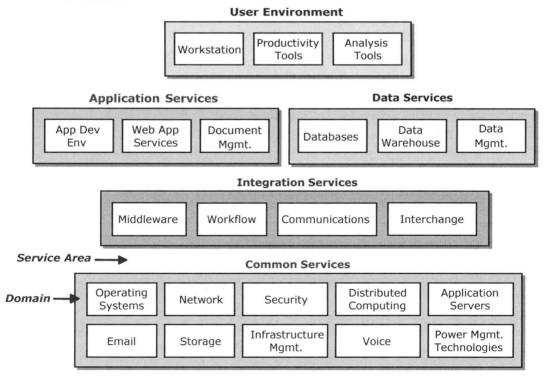

Figure 124. Technical Reference Model, Example

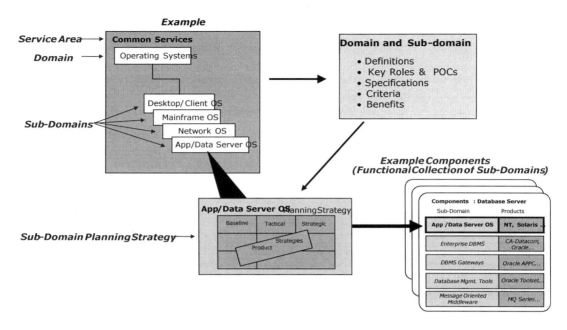

Figure 125. TRM Domain and Sub-domain Definitions and Components

Appendix K: Enterprise Architecture Modelling

K.1 *Introduction*

A coherent description of enterprise architectures provides insight, enables communication among different stakeholders and guides complicated (business and IT) change processes.

Unfortunately, so far no enterprise architecture description language exists that fully enables integrated enterprise modelling. In this chapter the focus is on the requirements and design of such a language. This language defines generic, organization-independent concepts that can be specialized or composed to obtain more specific concepts to be used within a particular organization. It is not the intention to re-invent the wheel for each enterprise architectural domain: wherever possible there will be a conformation to existing languages or standards such as UML. Then these standards will be complemented with missing concepts, for example focusing on concepts to model the relationships among enterprise architectural domains. The concepts should also make it possible to define links between models in other languages. The relationship between enterprise architecture descriptions at the business layer and at the application layer (business-IT alignment) plays a central role.

Changes in an organizations strategy and business goals have significant consequences for the organization structure, processes, software systems, data management and technical infrastructures. Organizations have to adjust processes to their environment, open up internal systems and make them transparent to both internal and external parties. Enterprise architectures are a way to chart the complexity involved. Many enterprises have recognized the value of architectures and to some extent make use of them during system evolution and development. Depending on the type of enterprise or maturity of the architecture practice, in most cases a number of separate enterprise architectural domains are distinguished such as business, information, application and technology infrastructure domain. For each enterprise architectural domain architects have their own concepts, modelling techniques, tool support, visualization techniques and so on. Clearly, this way of working does not necessarily lead to a coherent view on the enterprise.
Enterprises want to have insight into complex change processes.

The development of coherent views of an enterprise and a disciplined enterprise architectural working practice significantly contribute to the solution of this complex puzzle. Coherent views provide insight and overview, enable communication among different stakeholders and guide complicated change processes. Unfortunately there is a downside to this euphoria. So far no enterprise architecture description language exists that fully enables integrated enterprise modelling. There is a need for an enterprise architecture language that enables coherent enterprise modelling. Enterprise architects need proper instruments to constructs architectures in a uniform way. The next figure illustrates the scope of such an integrated set of enterprise architecture results.

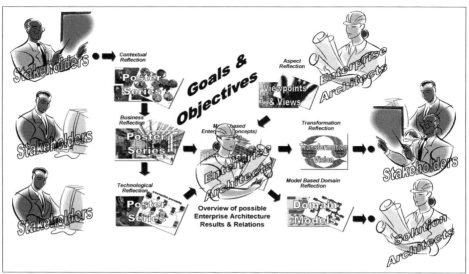

Figure 126. Scope of Enterprise Architecture Results

Important elements of such an approach include:
- o The development of a coherent enterprise modelling language.
- o Development of specialized views and visualization techniques in order to provide insight for different stakeholders.
- o Development of analysis techniques that aid in understanding the complex models.

By using a uniform modelling language enterprise architects can avoid a Babel-like confusion. At the same time an architectural modelling language should allow the development of specialized visualization techniques for different stakeholders, such as business managers, end-users, project managers, system developers, etc. After all, enterprise architectures are the means by which enterprise architects communicate with the different stakeholders, and this communication works best if it is tailored towards the specific concerns and information needs that they have. Additionally, analysis techniques, for example, impact-of- change analysis, provide ways to study the properties of an integrated model in more detail. In this way enterprise architecture provides the desired insight and overview, which allows a well-organized change process.

K.2   *The ArchiMate Modelling Language*[23]

By realizing that multiple languages and dialects will always exist, striving for one unique language would be like chasing windmills. Therefore, the flexibility to use other languages is recognized, and is addressed by means of a specialization and generalization requirement of the language itself. In the view of the ArchiMate project a well-defined enterprise architecture language forms the core of such an architecture approach. In this chapter the focus is on the requirements and a first design of such a language. It is not the intention to re-invent the wheel for each architecture domain. When possible standards will be followed, such as UML, as closely as possible. The focus is on the identification of specific relationship concepts and the definition of cross-domain relations. In order to arrive at a coherent architectural description, several architectural domains and layers as well as their relations must be modelled. This chapter describes the first steps towards a language to support this. The relations between the business and application layer, which play a central role in this version of the language, are a first contribution to the solution of the business-ICT alignment problem that ArchiMate try to tackle.

For the state of the art in enterprise modelling, languages have to consider for organisation and process modelling and languages for application and technology modelling.
Although there is a trend towards considering the relationship between the organisational processes and the information systems and applications that support them (often referred to as "business-IT alignment), modelling techniques to really express this relationship hardly exist yet.

A wide variety of organisation and process modelling languages are currently in use: there is no single standard for models in this domain. The conceptual domains that are covered differ from language to language. In many languages, the relations between domains are not clearly defined. Also, most languages are not really suitable to describe *architectures*: they provide concepts to model, e.g., detailed business processes, but not the high-level relationship.
Some of the most popular languages are proprietary to specific software tools.
Relevant languages in this category include:

   o   The Business Process Modelling Language BPML of the Business Process Management Initiative is an XML-based language for modelling business processes that has roots in the workflow management world. It can be used to describe the inner workings of, e.g., ebXML business processes.
   o   IDEF originating from the US Ministry of Defence is a collection of 16 (unrelated) diagramming techniques, three of which are widely used:

---

[23] *The ArchiMate project (http://archimate.telin.nl), a research initiative that aims to provide concepts and techniques to support architects in the visualisation, communication and analysis of integrated architectures. The ArchiMate consortium consists of ABN AMRO, Stichting Pensioenfonds ABP, the Dutch Tax and Customs Administration, Ordina, Telematica Instituut, Centrum voor Wiskunde en Informatica, Katholieke Universiteit Nijmegen, and the Leiden Institute of Advanced Computer Science.*

IDEF0 (function modelling), IDEF1/IDEF1x (information and data modelling) and IDEF3 (process description).

o   ARIS is part of the widely used ARIS Toolset. Although ARIS also covers other conceptual domains, there is a clear focus on business process modelling and organization modelling.

Architecture description languages (ADLs) define high-level concepts for architecture description, such as components and connectors. A large number of ADLs have been proposed, some for specific application areas, some more generally applicable, but mostly with a focus on software architecture. In the basics of ADLs are described and the most important ADLs are compared with each other. Most have an academic background, and their application in practice is limited. However, they have a sound formal foundation, which makes them suitable for unambiguous specifications and amenable to different types of analysis.

The *Architecture Description Markup Language* (ADML) was originally developed as an XML encoding of ACME. The Open Group promotes ADML as a standard for enterprise architectures. The Reference Model for Open Distributed Processing (RM-ODP) is a joint ISO/ITU-T standard for the specification open distributed systems. It defines five viewpoints on an ODP system that each has their own specification language. Although the above overview shows that there is a fairly complete language coverage of the separate architectural domains, the integration between the languages for the different domains is weak.

K.3   *The ArchiMate Background*

Organisations need to adapt increasingly quickly and anticipate changing customer requirements and business goals. This need influences the entire chain of activities of a business, from the organisational structure to the network infrastructure. How can you control the impact of these changes? Architecture may be the answer. The ArchiMate project will develop an integrated architectural approach that describes and visualises the different business domains and their relations. Using these integrated architectures aids stakeholders in assessing the impact of design choices and changes.

Enterprise Architecture is a consistent whole of principles, methods and models that are used in the design and realisation of organisational structure, business processes, information systems, and infrastructure. However, these domains often are not approached in an integrated way, which makes it difficult to judge the effects of proposed changes. Every domain speaks its own language, draws its own models, and uses its own techniques and tools. Communication and decision making across domains is seriously impaired.

The goal of the ArchiMate project is to provide this integration. By developing an architecture language and visualisation techniques that picture these domains and their relations, ArchiMate will provide the architect with instruments that support and improve the architecture process. Existing and emerging standards will be used or integrated whenever possible. ArchiMate will actively participate in national and international fora and standardisation organisations, to promote the dissemination of project results. The project will deliver a number of results. First of all, ArchiMate will provide a visual design language with adequate concepts for specifying interrelated architectures, and specific viewpoints for selected stakeholders. This will be accompanied by a collection of best practices and guidelines. Furthermore, ArchiMate will develop techniques that support architects in visualisation and analysis of architectures. Finally, project results will be validated in real-life cases within the participating organisations.

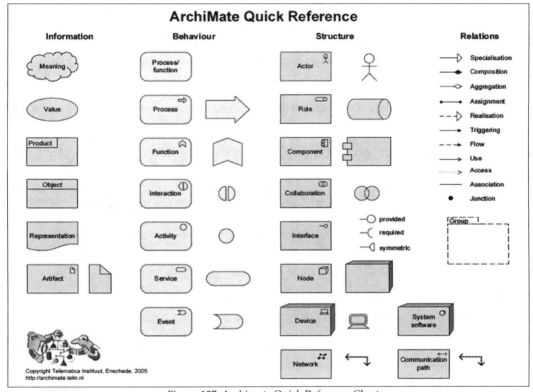

Figure 127. Archimate Quick Reference Chart

To have a real impact on the state of the art in enterprise architecture, the ArchiMate project consists of a broad consortium from industry and academia. ArchiMate's business partners are ABN AMRO, Stichting Pensioenfonds ABP, and the Dutch Tax and Customs Administration (Belastingdienst); its knowledge partners are Telematica Instituut, Ordina, Centrum voor Wiskunde en Informatica (CWI), the Leiden Institute for Advanced Computer Science (LIACS), and Katholieke Universiteit Nijmegen (KUN).

K.4   *Layered Viewpoints*

ArchiMate is based on layered viewpoints in line with the IEEE 1471-2000 standard. The layered viewpoint shows multiple layers and multiple aspects in one diagram. The main purpose of this viewpoint is to provide an overview of a part of business architecture in a single picture. Furthermore, it can be used for impact-of-change or performance analysis and for extending the business with new services.

Typical stakeholders of the layered viewpoints are (enterprise) architects, but also operational managers that are responsible for business processes, application or IT services.

There are two categories of layers, namely dedicated layers and service layers. The layers are the result of the use of the "grouping" relation for a partitioning of the entire set of objects and relations that belong to a model. The infrastructure, the application, the (application and business) function, the process and the actors/roles layers belong to the first category. The structural principle behind a fully layered view is that each dedicated layer exposes, by means of the "realisation" relation a layer of services, which are further on "used by" the next dedicated layer. So we can easily separate the internal structure and organisation of a dedicated layer from its externally observable behaviour expressed as the service layer that the dedicated layer realises. The order, number, or nature of these layers are not fixed, but in general a (more or less) complete and natural layering of an ArchiMate model will contain the succession of layers depicted in figure 127. With respect to the dedicated layers, the ArchiMate concepts are clustered according to the business, application, and technology layers of an EA framework. The service layers in between contain the corresponding business, application, resp. technology services.

This layered view on ArchiMate models has the following immediate consequences:

o   Any model is a hierarchy, which in terms of graph theory can be described as an acyclic directed graph, having one or more sources, typically lying in the infrastructure layer and one or more sinks, typically lying in the External business actors/roles layer. A source is an object, in which no incoming arcs enter. A sink is an object from which no outgoing arcs leave.

o   Any relation between different layers is either "used by" or "realises" or sometimes "assigned to".

o   Any connector having the ends in two consecutive layers is the depiction of either a "realises" relation or a "used by" relation.

o   In general, each vertical path, for instance from a source to a sink, consists of an alternating sequence of "realise" and "used by" arcs.

The example given in the next figure covers a number of layers from business to infrastructure. The example is centred on a single business process, the Handle Claim process.

Alternatively, a layered view could, for example, focus on a single application and all related infrastructure, business processes, etc., or on a single business service and all layers contributing to the realisation of that service.

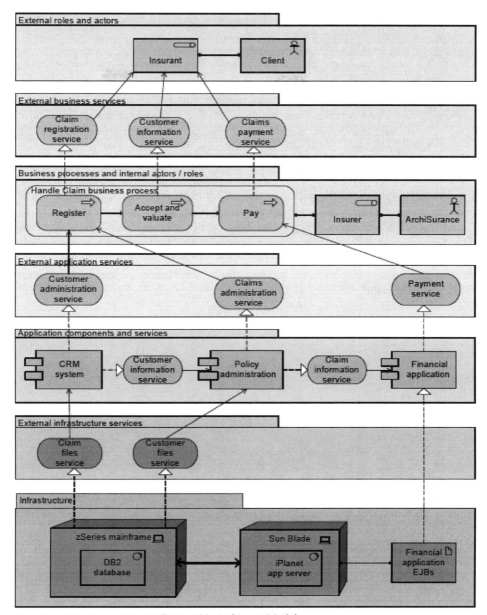

Figure 128. Archimate Model

The layered view of ArchiMate models is a very powerful instrument, which provides the user with more than just a viewpoint. It is easy to see that the usage of layering is beneficial at least for the following reasons:

- o It gives a clear structure to models.
- o It reduces the complexity of diagrams.
- o It creates a style of architecting and designing.
- o Although structured, it offers a certain degree of flexibility, since the number, and nature of the layers is not fixed. One can abstract from those layers that are not relevant for the problem under investigation. The order

of the dedicated layers in a layered view, however, has to be compliant with the meta-model of the ArchiMate language. More precisely, the order in which two dedicated layers occur is dependant on the existence in the meta-model of a directed path between the types of concepts that are typically used in the two layers. For example the application layer cannot be placed on top of the process layer because no directed path, for instance, from a process to an application component can be found in the meta-model of the ArchiMate language. The reverse order is, obviously, possible.

o   It is an excellent approach when an overview of complex structures is needed.

o   Nevertheless, it allows the designer to create models at any level of detail, since each layer can be as complex as necessary.

o   The layered view can be fully or partially used.

For more information about the Archimate modelling language as well as the Archimate meta-models visit the website of the Archimate forum. (*http://archimate.telin.nl*)

Appendix L: Other EA Books in this series

How to Survive in the Jungle of Enterprise Architecture Frameworks: Creating or Choosing an Enterprise Architecture Framework

By Jaap Schekkerman

266 pages; Third Edition 2006; Quality trade paperback (softcover); catalogue #03-1984; ISBN 1-4120-1607-X; Publisher Trafford, Canada.

How to survive in the jungle of Enterprise Architecture Frameworks is describing the dilemma of creating or choosing an Enterprise Architecture Framework. Several popular EA frameworks are described with their specific characteristics and an overview of the supporting EA Tools is given.

http://www.trafford.com/robots/03-1984.html

The Economic Benefits of Enterprise Architecture: How to Quantify and Manage the Economic Value of EA

By Jaap Schekkerman

295 pages; First Edition 2005; Quality trade paperback (softcover); catalogue #05-1640; ISBN 1-4120-6729-4; Publisher Trafford, Canada.

This book is giving a holistic overview of the areas of Economic Benefits of Enterprise Architecture as well as the role, position and purpose of Enterprise Architecture measurement programs in organizations as the foundation for change in Business and IT. Cost / benefit figures from public sources are added to this book to show the effects of economic measurement. For the in-depth details of the described Enterprise Architecture economic approaches and methods, several references to the original sources of information are added.

http://www.trafford.com/05-1640

17   References & Bibliography

1. Antoine de Saint-Exupery ;
    http://www.thinkexist.com/English/Author/x/Author_1147_3.htm
2. 'A Standard for Business Architecture description'; McDavid D.W.; published in IBM Systems Journal 1999.
3. Asundi, Jayatirtha; Kazman, Rick; & Klein, Mark. Using Economic Considerations to Choose Among Architecture Design Alternatives (CMU/SEI-2001-TR-035).
4. Beckner, S. G., & Norman, S. T. Air Force Architecture Development Guide. MITRE Technical Report 98B0000074. Colorado Springs, CO, 1998.
5. Boar, B. H. Constructing Blueprints for Enterprise IT Architectures. Wiley Computer Press. New York, NY, 1999.
6. Brundage, George. "Federal Enterprise Architecture Framework Presentation." Washington, D.C.: Department of the Treasury, July 2001
7. Capital Programming Guide, version 1.0, U.S. Office of Management and Budget, (July 1997).
8. Capital Programming Guide Supplement to Part 7 of Circular No. A-11 (U.S. Office of Management and Budget Circular No. A-11, July 2003).
9. Clinger-Cohen Act of 1996 [formerly, Information Technology Management Reform Act (ITMRA)], Public Law 104-106. 10 Feb 1996.
10. Cook, M. A. Building Enterprise Information Architectures: Reengineering Information Systems. Prentice Hall. Upper Saddle River, NJ, 1996.
11. Dello Russo, Francis M., Garvey, Paul R., and Woodward, Beverly S.; "How do You Cost an Enterprise Architecture?", MITRE Institute Training Program, January 27, 2003.
12. Department of Defence, C4ISR Architecture Working Group, DoD C4ISR Architecture Framework,. Version 2.0, 18 December 1997.
13. Department of the Extended, Chief Information Officer Council, Extended Enterprise Architecture Framework (E2AF), Version 1.0, 3 July 2000.
14. Department of the Extended, Extended Information Systems Architecture Framework (TISAF), Office of the Deputy Assistant Secretary for Information Systems and Chief Information Officer, 3 January 1997.
15. Department of Defence Architecture Framework Working Group. "DoD Architecture Framework Ver. 1.0." Washington, D.C.: Department of Defence, Oct. 2001; *http://aitc.aitcnet.org/dodfw*
16. Enterprise Architecture Survey 2004; IFEAD; *http://www.enterprise-architecture.info*
17. Executive Guide: Measuring Performance and Demonstrating Results of IT Investments. GAO/AIMD-98-89. March 1998.
18. Extended Enterprise Architecture Maturity Model (SM), E2AMM(sm); Institute For Enterprise Architecture Developments; 2004.
19. Evaluating Information Technology Investments; A Practical Guide, U.S. Executive Office of the President, Office of Management and Budget, November 1995.

20. Federal Chief Information Officer (CIO) Council, Federal Architecture Working Group, Architecture Alignment and Assessment Guide, October 2000.
21. Federal Chief Information Officer (CIO) Council, Federal Enterprise Architecture Framework (FEAF). Version 1.1, September 1999.
22. Federal Chief Information Officer (CIO) Council, Capital Planning and IT Management Committee, Smart Practices in Capital Planning, October 2000.
23. Freedom of Information Act (FOIA). 5 U.S.C. §552, as amended by Public Law 104-231, 110 Stat. 3048 (1996).
24. Gartner Inc.; http://www3.gartner.com
25. GAO and OMB IT investment guidance (see GAO/AIMD-10.1.13; AIMD-99-32; AIMD-98-89; AIMD-94-115 and OMB A- 130; A-11, M-97-12; M-97-02).
26. Government Paperwork Elimination Act (GPEA) of 1998. Public Law 105-277, Title XVII. 21 Oct 1998.
27. Government Paperwork Reduction Act (PRA) of 1980, amended 1996. Public Law 104-13, 44 USC Chapter 35.
28. Government Performance Results Act (GPRA) of 1993. Public Law 103-58. 16 June 1993.
29. IEEE 1058 Standard for Software Project Management Plans for an example of additional guidance on creating a project management plan.
30. *Institute For Enterprise Architecture Developments, IFEAD; The Netherlands; http://www.enterprise-architecture.info*
31. Information Strategies Group, OMB Circular A-94: New Complexity in Present-Value Discounting, IDC Government Publication Number W1625, 1993.
32. Information Technology Investment Evaluation Guide: Assessing Risks and Returns. A Guide for Evaluating Federal Agencies' IT Investment Decision-making. GAO/AIMD-10.1.13. February 1997.
33. Information Technology Investment Management: A Framework for Assessing and Improving Maturity. GAO/AIMD-10.1.23. Exposure Draft.
34. IT Assessment Guide (AIMD-10.1.13), 52-55, (CCA, PRA, FASA, EO 13011, OMB A-11, Part 3); Information Technology Investment (AIMD-96-64), 65; IT Assessment Guide (AIMD-10.1.13), 61- 62, (CCA, GPRA, CFO, OMB A-127, OMB A-123). U.S. Office of Management and Budget.
35. Kaplan, Robert S., and David P. Norton. Translating Strategy into Action: The Balanced Scorecard. Cambridge: Harvard Business School Press, Sept. 1996.
36. Kaplan, Robert S., and David P. Norton. Translating Strategy into Action: The Balanced Scorecard. Cambridge: Harvard Business School Press, Sept. 1996.
37. Kazman, Rick; Asundi, Jai; & Klein, Mark. Making Architecture Design Decisions: An Economic Approach (CMU/SEI-2002-TR-035).
38. Kazman Rick; Presentation Assessing the Economic Impacts of Architectural Decisions.
39. Kazman, Rick; Asundi, Jai; & Klein, Mark. Quantifying the Costs and Benefits of Architectural Decisions, Proceedings of the 23rd International Conference on Software Engineering (ICSE 23), (Toronto, Canada), May 2001, 297-306.
40. Kazman Rick, Jai Asundi, Mark Klein; Making Architecture Design Decisions: An Economic Approach; September 2002, TECHNICAL REPORT CMU/SEI-2002-TR-035; ESC-TR-2002-035

41. Keen, Peter G.W., Shaping The Future, Business Design through Information Technology, Harvard Business School Press, 1991.
42. Koskinen, John A., Evaluating Information Technology Investments, A Practical Guide, Version 1.0, Information Policy and Technology Branch, Office of Information and Regulatory Affairs, Office of Management and Budget, Executive Office of the President, November 1995.
43. King, 1995: "Creating a strategic capabilities architecture." *Information Systems Management*, Vol. 12, No. 1, pp. 67-69, 1995, William R. King, Professor University of Pittsburgh, USA.
44. Meskell, D. (2003). High payoff in electronic government: Measuring the return on e-government investment. Washington, DC: U.S. General Services Administration (GSA).
45. Moore, M.; Kazman, R.; Klein, M.; & Asundi, J. "Quantifying the Value of Architecture Design Decisions: Lessons from the Field", *Proceedings of the 25th International Conference on Software Engineering (ICSE 25)*, Portland, Oregon, May 2003, to appear.
46. Nolan & Mulryan: Richard L. Nolan and Dennis W. Mulryan, "Undertaking an Architecture Program," Stage by Stage, Vol. 7, Number 2 (March-April, 1987).
47. OMB Circular A–11. Preparation and Submission of Budget Estimates. 19 July 2000.
48. OMB Circular A–130. Management of Federal Information Resources. 30 November 2000.
49. Porter; Book, 'Competitive Strategy'; Porter, Michael E. 1980.
50. Rechtin, E., & Maier, M. W. The Art of Systems Architecting. CRC Press. New York, NY, 1997.
51. Robi D.B.; Enterprise DoD Architecture Framework and the Motivational View; CROSSTALK The Journal of Defence Software Engineering; April 2004.
52. Rico, David F.; A Framework for Measuring the ROI of Enterprise Architecture; http://davidfrico.com/free-f.htm
53. Saarinen, 1956; Eero Saarinen, President of the Cranbrook Academy of Art.
54. Saint-Exupery; 'The Little Prince', Antoine de Saint-Exupery, 1900 – 1944.
55. Schekkerman, Rijsenbrij, Hendrick; Book 'Architectuur, besturingssysteem voor adaptieve organisaties'; Publisher Lemma, 2002.
56. Schekkerman Jaap; 'Extended Enterprise Architecture Maturity Model'; E2AMM;, Published IFEAD, 2004.
57. Schekkerman, J. The Extended Enterprise Architecture Framework (E2AF). IFEAD Publication, The Netherlands, November 2002.
58. Solution Sets; White Paper, Interoperability Clearing House, USA, 2002.
59. Sowa, J. F., & Zachman, J. A. Extending and Formalizing the Framework for Information Systems Architecture. IBM Publication G321-5488. IBM Journal, Vol. 31(3). 1992.
60. Sowell, P. Kathie. "The C4ISR Architecture Framework: History, Status, and Plans for Evolution." McLean, Va.: The MITRE Corporation, 1999 *www.mitre.org/work/tech_papers/tech_papers_00/sowell_evolution/sowell_evolution. pdf.*

61. Spewak, Steve H. with Steven C. Hill. Enterprise Architecture Planning: Developing a Blueprint for Data, Applications, and Technology. New York: John Wiley & Sons, Sept. 1993.

62. The Open Group; *http://www.opengroup.org/*

63. The Open Group; TOGAF, Version 8.0.

64. Thomas, R, II, Beamer, R. A., & Sowell, P. K. Civilian Application of the DoD C4ISR Architecture Framework: A Extended Department Case Study. Proceedings of 5th International Command and Control Research and Technology Symposium, Canberra, Australia. October 2000.

65. U.S. General Accounting Office, Executive Guide: Measuring Performance and Demonstrating Results of Information Technology Investments, GAO/AIMD-98-89 (Washington D.C.: March 1998.

66. USA General Accounting Office, ITIM Framework GAO/AIMD-10.1.23, May 2000.

67. U.S. General Accounting Office; A Framework for Assessing and Improving Process Maturity; GAO-04-394G.

68. U.S. General Accounting Office, *Information Technology: A Framework for Assessing and Improving Enterprise Architecture Management* (Version 1.1), GAO-03-584G (Washington, D.C.: April 2003).

69. U.S. E-Government Act of 2002, Public Law 107-347 (Dec. 17, 2002).

70. U.S. General Accounting Office; Assessing Risks and Returns: A Guide for Evaluating Federal Agencies' IT Investment Decision-making GAO/AIMD-10.1.13 (Washington D.C.; February 1997);

71. U.S. General Accounting Office; Executive Guide: Improving Mission Performance Through Strategic Information Management and Technology (GAO/AIMD-94-115, May 1994);

72. Villiers de, D. J. 2001; Using the Zachman Framework to Assess the Rational Unified Process, The Rational Edge 2001.

73. Wagner, G. Martin, An Analytical Framework for Capital Planning and Investment Control for Information Technology, Associate Administrator, Policy, Planning and Evaluation (M), United States Government.

74. Zachman, J. A. and J. F. Sowa 1992: Extending and Formalizing the Framework for Information Systems Architecture, *IBM Systems Journal.* (31) 3: 590-616 (1992).

75. Zachman, J. A.; The Zachman Institute For Framework Advancements.

76. Zachman, John A. "A Framework for Information Systems Architecture." IBM Systems Journal 26.3 (1987) *www.research.ibm.com/journal/sj/382/zachman.pdf.*

18   Related Links

- o   Benchmarking: *http://www.benchnet.com/*

- o   Cost Benefit Analysis; *http://www.rff.org/rff/Cost-BenefitAnalysis.cfm*

- o   Capability Maturity Model CMM; Software Engineering Institute of Carnegie Mellon University, USA; *http://www.sei.cmu.edu/cmm/*

- o   Clinger-Cohen Act; *http://www.defenselink.mil/cio-nii/docs/ciodesrefvolone.pdf*

- o   Creating a strategic capabilities architecture. William R. King, Professor University of Pittsburgh, USA; *http://www.business.pitt.edu/katz/*

- o   Department of Defence Enterprise Architecture Technical Reference Model, Version 0.04, August, 2005; *http://www.defenselink.mil/cio-nii/docs/DOD_TRM_V0.4_10Aug.pdf*

- o   Earned Value Management; *http://www.balancedscorecard.org/Definitions/tabid/145/Default.aspx*

- o   EA Assessment Framework (USA-OMB); *http://www.whitehouse.gov/omb/egov/a-2-EAAssessment.html*

- o   Extended Enterprise Architecture (E2A) Framework, the Institute For Enterprise Architecture Developments; *http://www.enterprise-architecture.info*

- o   EFQM: The European Foundation for Quality Management's; *http://www.efqm.org/*

- o   Federal Enterprise Architecture Framework, and the CIO Council Web page for information on FEAF; *http://www.cio.gov/Documents/fedarch1.pdf*

- o   Federal Chief Information Officer Council; *www.cio.gov*

- o   Framework for Measuring the ROI of Enterprise Architecture; *http://davidfrico.com/free-f.htm*

- o   General Accounting Office, Assessing Risks and Returns: A Guide for Evaluating Federal Agencies' IT Investment Decision-making; *www.gao.gov*

- o   Hubbard Research; Applied Information Economics (AIE); *http://www.hubbardresearch.com*

- o Institute For Enterprise Architecture Developments; *www.enterprise-architecture.info*

- o John Mercer, the father of Performance Management; *http://www.john-mercer.com*

- o Knowledge Management Definition; *http://www.brint.com/*

- o Object Management Group; *www.omg.org*

- o ROI ; *http://www.valuebasedmanagement.net/methods_roi.html*

- o Software Engineering Institute (SEI) Architecture Technology Page *http://www.sei.cmu.edu/architecture/arche.html*

- o Work on the web of Steven Spewak; *http://www.eapontheweb.com/*

- o Stanford University, Enterprise Architecture Home Page *http://www.stanford.edu/dept/archdesign/*

- o Six Sigma; *http://www.qualityamerica.com/six_sigma.html*

- o The Open Group; *http://www.opengroup.org/*

- o The US General Accounting Office; *http://www.gao.gov/*

- o The USA Office of Management & Budget; *http://www.whitehouse.gov/omb/*

- o TOGAF Version 8.1.x: Enterprise Edition, the Open Group's official Web version of TOGAF; *http://www.opengroup.org/architecture/togaf*

- o USA General Accounting Office, ITIM Framework (GAO/ AIMD-10.1.23, May 2000); *http://www.gao.gov/special.pubs/10_1_23.pdf.*

- o UML – Unified Modelling Language; *http://www.uml.org/*

- o Zachman Institute for Framework Advancement; *www.zifa.com*

19   About the Author

 **Jaap Schekkerman, B.Sc.** (1953) is an international recognised Thought Leader in the areas of Business Technology Strategy & Enterprise Architecture and the Founder and President of the 'Institute For Enterprise Architecture Developments' (IFEAD) the Netherlands (2001). *http://www.enterprise-architecture.info*

This institute is today one of the most important sources of information related to Enterprise Architecture and working close together with other research organisations, institutes and universities all over the world to create an independent platform for Enterprise Architecture research, developments and knowledge exchange.

Mr. Schekkerman is managing IFEAD besides his Management Consulting and Enterprise Architecture Thought Leader activities for Logica a world-class Business & IT services organization.

Mr. Schekkerman has a broad history in the Defence world as the former chief enterprise architect responsible for the Royal Netherlands Army's (RNLA) C3I architecture program, as well as in the Healthcare environment as the former CIO of the Red Cross Hospital in the Netherlands.

Mr. Schekkerman is working for more than 30 years in the Business, IT & Consultants world and has more than 25 years experience in managing complex and large enterprise architecture programs in the Defence World, the Governmental area, Healthcare, Travel Industry and High Tech Industry.

Mr. Schekkerman is giving lectures on Information Management, Enterprise Architecture and Service Orientation at different Universities and Institutes for Higher Professional Education.

Mr. Schekkerman has published more than 45 articles and several books on topics related to Enterprise Architecture. He is a frequently invited and highly appreciated speaker on national and international congresses and symposia.

For more information about his publications, visit the web site of the Institute For Enterprise Architecture Developments. *http://www.enterprise-architecture.info*

Contact Mr. J. Schekkerman; E-mail: *jschekkerman@enterprise-architecture.info*

ISBN 142515687-8

Edwards Brothers Malloy
Oxnard, CA USA
July 17, 2014